INDO-PORTUGUESE TRADE AND THE FUGGERS OF GERMANY

INDO-PORTUGUESE TRADE AND THE FUGGERS OF GERMANY

SIXTEENTH CENTURY

K.S. MATHEW

MANOHAR
2020

First published 1997
Reprinted 1999
POD reprint 2020

ISBN 978-81-7304-137-2

Published by
Ajay Kumar Jain *for*
Manohar Publishers & Distributors
4753/23 Ansari Road, Daryaganj,
New Delhi 110 002

Printed at
Replika Press Pvt. Ltd.

CONTENTS

PREFACE

The idea of writing in detail about the connection of the Fuggers with Portuguese India dawned on me some eighteen years ago while I was doing research on Portuguese trade with India in the sixteenth century in archives and libraries in Portugal. My contact with the late Professor Hermann Kellenbenz convinced me that I would be able to find relevant documents in the libraries and archives in Augsburg and Dillingen/Donau. During my visits abroad I used to collect materials chiefly from the Fuggers' family archives in Donau/Dillingen. I realised that unless I set apart a few months exclusively for the collection of material from the archival repositaries in Lisbon and Donau/Dillingen I would not be able to do justice to my proposed work.

As usual Dr. José Blanco, the trustee of the International Service of the Gulbenkian Foundation, enabled me to work for a few months in the respective archives in Portugal and Rome with the help of a short-term grant awarded to me in 1992. The directors of the National Archives as well as the National Library of Lisbon were extremely kind in providing facilities for my work.

The generous help and hospitality extended by Dr. Michael Gorgas of the Zoologische Garten, Augsburg, made it possible for me to work in the Fuggers' family archives in Dillingen/Donau and in the Augsburg city archives. Thousands of pages of rare documents were photocopied and sent to India with the assistance of Dr. Gorgas. The interest shown by Dr. Gorgas, Mrs. Brigitte Gorgas and Frank Gorgas in my academic work inspired me to do it even faster. I enjoyed the friendly hospitality of Mr. Gottfried Fellner of the Pfarramt St. Peter, Dillingen, while staying in the town. The patient help given to me by Mr. Franz Karg in the family archives of the Fuggers in Dillingen/Donau is memorable.

The award of the National Fellowship to me by the University Grants Commission from 1 July 1993 for a period of two years enabled me to take two years off from the routine teaching and concentrate my attention on the finalisation of this work. I am greatly indebted to Professor A. Gnanam, the Vice-Chancellor of the Pondicherry University and to the U.G.C. for the affiliation of this fellowship to Pondicherry University.

Ms Joyce M., who assisted me in the publication of a couple of other works during the last four and a half years, took dictation and computerised the entire script and made it ready for printing. Ms Sussi George was, as always, ready to help me with her expertise in computers when I ran into any problems on my word processor. Dr. Michael Gorgas, the Director of the Zoologischer Garten, Augsburg, despite his busy schedule, went through the entire text and suggested relevant modifications. Frau Jutta Schweizer of his office took the trouble of going through the proof and correcting it. Similarly Professor Dr. Wolfgang Knabe hailing from Augsburg spent several hours with me discussing some of the details of the mercantile activities of the Fuggers. Dr. Joseph Palamattam, Herr Peter Jansenn and Herr Karl Sendker were extremely helpful to me during my stay in Germany in connection with this research.

I am deeply indebted to all of them and those who helped in various other ways. God bless them. I would like to express my special thanks to Manohar Publishers and Distributors for their promptness in publishing this work to an international standard.

Pondicherry,
30 July 1995

K.S. MATHEW

CHAPTER 1

INTRODUCTION

After the fall of Constantinople in 1453 to the Turks, the possibility of getting spices and other oriental commodities through the Red Sea was rendered difficult. Various political powers as well as merchants in Europe interested in amassing capital through trade and commerce looked for routes other than the one through Constantinople to reach the spice-producing areas in the East. In order to hold a strict monopoly over the routes and trade that would be discovered in course of time, it was necessary to get the approval of Pope, the supreme authority of Christendom. He was considered by the Catholic Europe capable of solving their political problems. Portugal managed to get a number of bulls issued by various Popes. The military Order of Christ that was in existence in Portugal had Infant Henrique as its Grand Master and this Order was given the jurisdiction over the new conquests in Africa and in the East by king Affonso V of Portugal. The king requested Pope Eugene IV to approve the donation made by him. Subsequently, on 9 January 1442, a papal bull entitled *Etsi Suscepti* was issued granting papal approval.[1] In view of the request made by king Affonso V, Pope Nicholas V issued the bull, *Dum Diversas* on 18 June 1452, permitting the king of Portugal and his successors to conquer and subjugate the kingdoms, principalities and lands of the infidels.[2] Thus, Portugal was fully equipped with papal authorisation to launch overseas expansion. The quest for sea-route to reach India from Europe became all the more strong after the fall of Constantinople to the Turks in 1453.

Pope Nicholas V himself came to the help of the Portuguese to keep off other powers from the areas discovered and conquered by them outside Portugal. He issued the bull called *Romanus Pontifex* on 8 January 1454 whereby he declared that the lands and seas discovered and to be discovered, possessed and to be possessed by Portugal would belong exclusively to her in perpetuity.[3] On account of this, the other powers were totally excluded from the areas brought under the Portuguese influence. The grant made by Pope Nicholas V through the above mentioned bull was confirmed by his successor Pope Calixtus III through another document *Inter Caetera* issued by him on 13 March 1455.[4] Both these bulls granting exclusive right over areas discovered and conquered by Portugal were confirmed by Pope Sixtus IV through the bull *Aeterni Regis* published on 21 June 1481.[5]

The Spanish monarchy that became strong after the marriage of Ferdinand of Aragon and Isabella of Castile in 1469 and especially after the *reconquista* and annexation of Granada in 1492 entered on the scene of explorations. The maritime activities of discovery sponsored by the Catholic kings of Spain to find a safe sea-route to India without trespassing on the areas demarcated for the Portuguese were conducted by sailing Northwestward across the Atlantic. No sooner did Columbus make the landfall in the Carribean and name it "West Indies"—a historical blunder—than the then Pope Alexander VI, the Spaniard granted Ferdinand and Isabella exclusive rights over the islands discovered to the west of Azores. The Portuguese who had already obtained unbounded rights and laid indisputable claims over the newly discovered territories interpreted this new sanction as an infringement of their rights and so remonstrated. The conflicting rights were finally defined by the treaty of Tordesillas in 1494 which described the meridian lying 370 leagues west of the Cape Verde Islands. The regions east of this divide were assigned to the Portuguese and those in the west to the Spaniards. This was subsequently approved by the Pope.

As soon as the controversy was settled through the good offices of the Pope, the Portuguese resumed their activities of maritime discovery in good earnestness. Their chief aim was to reach the sources of spices very much needed in Europe on account of the special diet and the lack of refrigeration to preserve meat during the winter season. But Portugal did not have enough finances to meet the expenses related to fitting out vessels for the discovery. Even when Pedro da Covilham was sent to India to discover a direct sea-route, Portugal had to depend on Bertholomeu Marchioni, a Florentine for loans. He was the most prominent among the foreign financiers having commercial establishments in Lisbon at the beginning of the sixteenth century[6] and had the greatest investment in Lisbon during the same period.[7] He established himself in Lisbon during the reign of D. João II. After a series of attempts to discover a direct sea-route connecting India with the Atlantic ports, Vasco da Gama, the undaunted Admiral of the Indian Ocean, reached Calicut on the western coast of India in 1498 and established commercial contacts with the port of Calicut, which was one of the important emporia in the east-west axis linking Malacca in the east with Alexandria in the west, one of the important Mediterranean ports, and finally with Venice.

Right from the very beginning, the Portuguese incorporated missionary aims into their overseas enterprise, presumably with a view to obtaining the approval of the Pope easily. Being satisfied with the performance of the Portuguese in the maritime activities, Pope Alexander VI issued a bull on 26 March 1500 granting the jurisdiction to the Portuguese king to appoint Apostolic Commissary with ordinary powers in places discovered by the Portuguese, from Cape of Good Hope up to India.[8]

The ecclesiastical sanctions enabled Portugal to discover, conquer and appropriate areas outside it without any political tangle. But just as before the discovery of the new sea-route by Vasco da Gama, Portugal had to look for the necessary funds to sustain the expensive enterprise involving hundreds of people and a distance of thousands of miles' voyage, besides inclement weather of the tropical area and totally different culture. In their attempt to find required finances they were constrained to open up avenues for other European financiers to come to their help.

The Portuguese king, who was in financial difficulties to continue the overseas enterprise, offered liberal concessions to all the merchant-financiers interested in joining him. He invited people from all over Europe to invest money in the project he placed before them. According to the scheme developed by him, the merchant-financiers were expected to fit out the vessels under the Portuguese banner. All the transactions in the East in general and in India in particular were to be done through the Portuguese officials in case of spices and other items of royal monopoly. They could also entrust to the India House (*Casa da India*) the commodities and cash to be exported to India for the purchase of the items they were in need of.[9]

Taking into account the details of the Portuguese enterprise on the Western coast of India, especially Malabar coast in the period between 1500 and 1506, an Italian observer in 1506 made the following calculations regarding the financial position of the Portuguese crown. The annual income of Portugal amounted to 350,000 ducats out of which 300,000 ducats were spent on the ordinary expenses of the kingdom. Consequently, only 50,000 ducats were at the disposal of the king for commercial enterprise in the East. Even though the salary of the crew and the officials was deplorably low by the standards of the period, an amount of 120,000 ducats was needed for fitting out about twelve ships a year including the expenses of the crew for fifteen months involved in the *carreira da India*. Another sum of 100,000 ducats was required for the purchase of commodities on the Malabar coast for eight to nine ships a year. Hence, the total investment needed for the conduct of trade was about 170,000 ducats more.[10] The king supplied only one-fourth of the total amount needed for the purchase of the commodities and the rest of the amount was to be arranged through the merchants and financiers. Commodities worth 25,000 ducats were imported into Malabar coast every year from Europe via Lisbon.[11]

On account of the financial problems faced by the king, a number of merchant-financiers from various parts of the world were invited by the king. The Italians, especially the Florentines, occupied an important place among the financiers who came forward to make capital of the situation.

Bertholomeu Marchioni, the Florentine financier, was the first foreigner to fit out a ship in 1500 in the fleet of Pedro Alvares Cabral to India.[12] His ship imported more than 25,967 kg of spices from the Malabar coast to Lisbon.[13] In view of the permission granted by the king in 1500, a consortium of merchants was formed under him and two out of the four ships sent to India in 1501 were owned by the consortium. Bertholomeu Marchioni appointed Fernando Vineti as the captain of his ship.[14] Again in 1502 he sent the ship San Tiago in partnership with the king to the Malabar coast under João de Bonagracia and the ship took a cargo of 1,10,163 to 1,15,409.9 kgs of spices half of which went to the king.[15]

Bertholomeu Marchioni had sent a ship with Giovanni da Empoli as the Factor to Malabar in the fleet of Affonso de Albuquerque in 1503.[16] He took part in fitting out ships to the Malabar coast along with the German financiers in 1505.[17] He advanced an amount of 1,82,811.93 *crusados* which could not be covered by the purchase of 3,56,773.6 kg of pepper and other items together with four ships, namely, *S. Jeronymo, S. Raphael, Leonarda* and *S. Vicente*. After all the transactions, about 30,578.13 *crusados* remained due to him from the king in 1507 when the letter of acquittal was issued.[18] Nardi, the employee of Marchioni, was sent to India in the fleet of Italian trading vessels in 1510 under the command of Diogo Mendes Vasconcellos. He attracted the attention of Afonso de Albuquerque as the most reliable factor in India. The governor praised him for his efficiency and trustworthiness.[19]

According to another letter of acquittal issued in 1514, the king owed a sum of 93,949.64 *crusados* to Bertholomeu Marchioni. He advanced the amount to the king both in cash and in bills of exchange in the account of the king in places like Rome, Flanders and Lisbon.[20] For quite a long period he continued to be one of the principal financiers and merchants of the Portuguese king in his trade on the Malabar coast. The ship *Anunciada* belonging to him took part in the export of commodities from India in 1519 and 1522.[21]

Francesco Corvinelli was a Florentine who took advantage of the new milieu. He commanded his own ship in the Portuguese fleet that left Lisbon for India in 1509. He was held in great esteem by the Portuguese and was appointed by Affonso de Albuquerque as the royal agent for the purchase, custody and despatch of all the goods obtained in the name of the king. He took his ship back to Lisbon loaded with spices from the Malabar coast in 1511.[22] Piero Strozzi, another Florentine who came to India in the fleet of Diogo Mendes Vasconcellos, was one of the factors in whom the Portuguese placed great trust. He was later appointed factor of the king for the entire Coromandel coast by the Portuguese governor Diogo Lopes de Sequeira.[23]

The two important groups of Florentine bankers, namely, Gualterotti and Frescobaldi, had their factories in Flanders and took active part in the trade in spices. They had shares in the fleet sent to the Malabar coast in 1505.[24] Filippo Gualterotti acted as the agent of Giovanni Francesco de Affaitati in Flanders and supplied copper to be taken to the Malabar coast by the Portuguese. Both Girolamo Frescobaldi and Filippo Gualterotti occupied, in the sixteenth century, an important position as financiers rather than as merchants.[25]

Girolamo Sernigi was another Florentine financier and merchant who had settled down in Lisbon at the time of the Portuguese discoveries.[26] He is referred to in the Portuguese documents by the name Hironimo or Jeronimo. He participated in fitting out a vessel to the Malabar coast in 1500 under Pedro Alvares Cabral.[27] His observations about the trade on the Malabar coast reveal the commercial interest he had in the Portuguese enterprise on the Malabar coast.[28] He came to India in 1510 commanding his own ship to participate directly in the trade.[29]

The Affaitati family was known for its banking activities in Cremona which was under Venice, and Giovanni Francesco de Affaitati, the head of the banking organisation, had established himself as a banker in Portugal before the discovery of the sea-route to India. He was a shrewd observer of trade in Lisbon and as soon as Cabral returned to Lisbon with the spices, he concentrated his attention on the trade with Malabar and began to invest in the trade in spices. He obtained the permission from the king to participate in the direct trade with Malabar in 1502 and sent Matteo de Bergamo as his Factor in the fleet of Vasco da Gama.[30] Though he tried to secure the monopoly of trade with India, the king did not give in and so he had to be content with that of the trade in spices with Flanders for a while[31] and concluded a number of contracts with the king regarding the purchase of pepper. He had his factories in Flanders, England, Seville, Valencia and Medina del Campo besides the one in Lisbon.[32] According to the contracts concluded with the king, he purchased 5,77,049 kg of pepper between 1508 and 1514.[33] He supplied copper to the Portuguese Factor in Flanders to be taken to the Malabar coast. Thus he provided the fleet that came to India in 1515 with 3,14,754 kg of copper.[34] The king of Portugal concluded a contract with him in 1516 according to which he supplied 6,29,508 kg of copper every year for a period of five years.[35] Filippo Gualterotti, a Florentine merchant, was his agent in Antwerp who saw that the stipulated amount of copper was supplied to the Portuguese factory. Thus the agent purchased 6,29,508 kg of copper from the Fuggers in 1516 and delivered the consignment to the Portuguese Factor, Sylvestor Nunes in Flanders.[36] Giovanni Francesco de Affaitati continued to be in Lisbon till his death in 1528 and then his nephew João Carlos de Affaitati took up the charge of the enterprise. Thus the Affaitati, who were known to the Portuguese by the corrupt forms of *Lafeta* or *Lafeita,* continued to be one of the important financiers and merchants in the Portuguese trade with the Malabar coast.

Lucas Geraldi, another Italian financier of importance in Lisbon, commanded immense respect.[37] He conducted business in Lisbon in partnership with Affaitati and often as his procurator.[38]

In addition to these financiers, there were others like a certain Genoese[39] who took part in sending a ship to India in 1500, Andrea Corsali who came to the Malabar coast in 1516[40] and Leonardo Nardi who sent a ship to India in 1518.[41] The Italians continued to be important financiers and merchants in the Portuguese trade even towards the end of the century. Giovanni Battista Rovelasca and others concluded a contract with the king of Portugal concerning the export of spices from the Malabar coast to Portugal in 1580.[42]

King Dom Manuel I granted to the German merchants special commercial privileges which were never before given to any one. Through his letter dated 13 February 1503, taking into consideration the request made by Simon Seitz in the name of Anton Welser,

Conrad Vöhlin and the firm of the Augsburg merchants, he permitted the German merchants and financiers to establish a house (factory) of their own in the city of Lisbon and to conduct trade under very liberal conditions. They were exempted from taxes of every sort on the commodities they wanted to purchase and export. Similarly they were authorised to take copper, silver, vermilion, quicksilver, brass and other items to any part of Portugal and her dependencies. These extraordinary privileges were granted for a period of fifteen years. The king added that though they were granted at the request of Simon Seitz in the name of the above merchants, any other German merchant was also entitled to the same privileges. Thus he opened up the field to all the German merchants and through these privileges attracted them to invest their money in the Portuguese trade with Malabar.[43]

As a result, several other German firms shifted their concern from Venice; closed down their *fondaco dei Tedeschi* and concentrated their activities on Lisbon. They discontinued visiting the Venetian market and began to send spices purchased from Lisbon to Antwerp, Bremen, Hamburg, Lübeck, Danzig, Augsburg, Nürnberg and Ulm, the last three of which were the principal cities of the *Suabic Leage.*[44] Besides, the Germans, under special conditions, were permitted to send their own ships to Malabar to purchase spices according to the treaty signed on 1 August 1504.[45]

Anton Welser, one of the sons of Lucas Welser, established a firm in 1496 in Augsburg in collaboration with his brother-in-law Conrad Vöhlin and Company. They concentrated their attention on the silver mines of Tyrol.[46] By 1503 he founded a factory in Lisbon with a view to taking part in the trade on the Malabar coast. It was Simon Seitz, the agent of the firm of the Welsers that obtained the privileges from D. Manuel in 1503 for the Germans as noted above.[47] Valentin Fernandes, a German, was appointed as the official mediator and interpreter (*Handelsagent und Vermittler*) between the Portuguese king and the German merchants. Lucas Rem remained in Lisbon from 1503 to 1508 as the Factor of the Welsers and thereafter his brother Hans Rem was given the charge of the factory.[48] They took part in the fitting out of the ships to the

Malabar coast in 1505 investing 20,000 florins.[49] This brought them a profit of 175 per cent of the amount invested. The factory of the Welsers was the earliest of the German houses in Lisbon.[50]

Since for a time the Welsers, like the others, did not get permission to trade directly with the Malabar coast, they entered into contracts with the king of Portugal to purchase a stipulated quantity of pepper at Lisbon to be taken to Antwerp and other places for resale and advanced considerable amounts to the king. The company paid 7000 *crusados* in advance for the three contracts regarding the purchase of pepper before 1516.[51] Moreover, they supplied the necessary metals such as copper and silver to the Portuguese factory at Antwerp to be taken to India. Lucas Rem with his brother Andreas Rem, Conrad Imhof and others were among the partners of the Welser Company.[52] The Welsers had well-established factories in Nürnberg, Danzig, Venice, Milan, Rome, Genoa, Freiburg, Berne, Zürich, Lyon, Saragossa, Antwerp and Lisbon.

Though the Welsers failed to get permission to trade in pepper and other spices directly with India they were allowed to trade in other commodities. The Welsers of Nürnberg had an agent named Hans Schwerczer who was in India in the 1530s looking after the business in diamonds and various types of precious stones in Vijayanagara and Goa. These items collected by Schwerczer from Goa and Vijayanagara were sent to Lisbon and from there to Antwerp, Augsburg and Venice for cutting, polishing and sale at a higher price. Imhof had partnership with Schwerczer without the knowledge of the Herwarts. He was in India in 1534 and left for Lisbon in 1536 with diamonds and other precious items collected from here with the idea of coming back.

When Schwerczer was ready to leave Lisbon for India the king's orders came on his way preventing everybody not having an household in Portugal from coming over to India. Therefore, he married a Portuguese lady of common origin and stayed there a year, so as to qualify himself to proceed to India. Subsequently, he resumed his commercial activities in the subcontinent of India in 1538. Sometimes Imhof looked after the interest of the Welsers in

India jointly with Schwerczer or singly in the absence of the latter.

Thus the Herwarts and Welsers, quite interested in conducting trade in diamonds and precious stones of different sorts, kept their agents in India who went to different parts of the subcontinent to procure the required items. Vijayanagara, which was a great centre of trade in diamonds, attracted their attention to a large extent. It was chiefly through Goa that the diamonds of the Deccan were exported by the German merchant financiers to Europe. The diamond mines of the kingdom of Golconda were connected with Goa through land routes via Hyderabad.

It was reported that the installations of the Herwarts in Lisbon used to cut and polish 365 precious stones at a time around this period.[53]

The Herwarts of Germany were specialists in precious metals, jewels and pearls of the East. Those of them residing in Lisbon had better contacts with India. They concluded a contract with Jorg Imhof, the son of Jorg Imhof from Rothenburg ob der Tauber according to which the latter agreed to serve Jorg Herwart, the son of Mathias Herwart of Augsburg, for a period of eight and a half years in India from 1 February 1526 till 1 August 1534. His long service in Lisbon for the Imhofs of Nürnberg and the Schwetz of Antwerp prompted the employer to appoint him for this task in India.

The Herwarts purchased a large variety of commodities from Europe and Africa through Imhof to exchange for the precious stones and jewels from India. They included red scarlet, knives, tapestry, brocades made in Cordova, black and red velvets, door curtains from Lisbon, red cloth and scarlatins from Toledo, velvet from Santarém, *vintecuatrins* from Covilhão, cloths from Castile, a special variety of ink (*tinta in Graa*) from Santarém, *trintena* from Valencia, black cloths, silver and gold items, wine, coffers from Flanders and France, glasses, jars, cups, *urinões* (chamber pots) from Lisbon, precious metals in bars, copper, quick-silver, money, textiles from Santarém, Toledo, and Valencia, luxury items from Italy especially Venice and the Netherlands, and a few items like swords from Moçambique.

He reached Goa and began to operate from there. In view of the commitment made by Jorg Herwart on 18 March 1524, a stipulated amount was handed over to Braz António Cristovão in Goa as reported by Imhof on 9 September 1527. Imhof continued getting several items sent through the ships reaching India from Lisbon. A few luxurious items of Venice such as *damas* with golden flowers and crowns, sateen with golden flowers and birds were among them. He used to receive money in India in the name of the Herwarts. He got velvets and golden flowers in Goa in October 1527 through the Portuguese officials of the ships arriving at Goa. The letter written by Imhof on 26 October 1527 at Goa makes mention of the receipt of cups, cans and guilded fountains.

A letter written by Imhof at Goa on 5 December 1527 refers to the use of bill of exchange in the transfer of money from Lisbon to Goa and vice-versa. A particular case in connection with Dona Guiomar Deça, the wife of the governor Lopo Vaz de Sampaio, is shown in this letter. Another case of the transfer of money from Goa to the Herwarts in Lisbon is brought out in a letter dated 10 December 1527 written at Goa by Imhof. Purchase of diamonds, rings with rubies, emerald, diamond table and various sorts of precious stones is also referred to in the same letter. He wrote on 25 December of the same year that he purchased from Goa garnet, small diamonds and rubies.

Sometimes Imhof moved from Goa to Cannanore and Cochin for procuring pearls, and several sorts of precious stones. He wrote on 2 January 1528 that he purchased pearls and rings with emerald from Cannanore. Imhof visited Vijayanagara from his station at Goa. It is seen that he spent a lot of time in Vijayanagara doing business in pearls without the orders of his employer, Herwarts. He was for over four years there till his death in Vijayanagara in 1540 and did not send reports about his activities to the Herwarts in Lisbon.

Next to the Welsers, Höchstetter had the most important business house in Augsburg and Ambrosius Höchstetter was at the head of the business in the early part of the sixteenth century.[54] They took part in sending ships to the Malabar coast in 1505 and invested an amount of 4000 florins for the same.[55] Later on, they concluded contracts with the Portuguese king for the purchase of pepper at the *Casa da India* and took the spices to their factory at Antwerp.

The Imhofs had a fairly important trading house in Nürnberg and Endres Imhof formed a consortium to which the Welsers of Augsburg belonged.[56] They had also a branch in Lisbon and an agent to take part in the Portuguese trade of the sixteenth century.[57] Ulrich Imhof and Michael Imhof represented the Imhofs in Lisbon for a time. They are known to the Portuguese writers by the name Imcuria.[58] The Imhofs too took part in fitting out the ships to the Malabar coast in 1505.[59]

Hirschvogel was another trading house of Nürnberg that too had associated itself with the Portuguese trade in the sixteenth century.[60] This firm also secured the same privileges granted to the other German firms by the king of Portugal and established a factory in Lisbon. The house of Hirschvogel had their agents in Lisbon like Lazarus Nürnberger who came to India and sent a detailed report to Michael Behaim, the brother of the famous Martim Behaim.

Lazarus Nürnberger was born in 1499 at Neustadt on the Aysch, a small village near Nürnberg. He left for Lisbon when he was fifteen years old to serve in the business house of Hirschvogel at Lisbon. Bernard Hirschvogel passed away on 23 October 1516 and so in view of the testament, Lazarus became one of the heirs of the property of Hirschvogel. He went to Germany in 1517 and left Neustadt on 16 January 1517 on his way to Antwerp.[61] On 25 February he boarded the vessel going to Lisbon where he reached on 17 March 1517. He left Lisbon for India on 2 April, on board *Agno Grandi* and reached Goa on 1 October 1517. After spending some time in Goa, he proceeded to the south and visited Bhatkal on 6 November 1517 which, according to him, was a very great town in the kingdom of Vijayanagara. The Portuguese had a factory there. He reported about the availability of precious stones and pearls and the commodities brought from Ormuz. He reached Cannanore on 20 November. He wrote about ginger, pepper, cardamom, cotton and cassiafistula which were available in Cannanore. The Portuguese king had a fortress with 200 soldiers to take care of it. He further visited the Portuguese fortress at Calicut and proceeded to Cochin where the Portuguese king had a very great fortress. The friendship of the king of Cochin as well as the availability of spices there are discussed by him in his report. He returned to Portugal from Cochin on 12 January 1518 in the annual fleet carrying pepper to Portugal.[62] He was found in Lisbon on 19 June 1518. During his absence Joachim Prunner assisted by Jorg Pock looked after the business of Hirschvogel.[63]

Jorg Pock was another agent of Hirschvogel who worked for them in India. He was born in Heidingsfeld near Würzburg and entered into the service of Hirschvogel of Nürnberg. He was trained in the house of Hirschvogel in Lisbon. Later in March 1520 he left for India in the Portuguese fleet of which Jorg de Brito was the captain-in-chief to look after the interest of the firm. In view of the standing instruction, money and material entrusted to Pock were handed over to the chief Factor Andre Diaz in Lisbon to be taken to India. After reaching India he started his activities in Goa. He had been to Cochin in 1522 in connection with the work entrusted to him by the employers as known from his letter written to Michael Behaim of Nürnberg. As Vijayanagara was known for precious stones, pearls and diamonds, he made a trip from Cochin via Honawar (Onor), Bangapur, Banavasi and Ranibenmur to the headquarters of the empire. He had made very interesting observation about the import of horses on a large scale into Vijayanagara. He visited Vijayanagara in its heyday under Krishnadeva Raya (1508 to 1530 A.D.). Though not in detail, he made mention of diamonds available in Vijayanagara. He worked for three years for Hirschvogel according to the terms and conditions of the contract. Erasmus Herwart, who had for a long time employed Erasmus Schleim of Regensburg in Lisbon, joined Hirschvogel in the enterprise through Pock. Pock was in India till his death in 1528 or 1529.[64]

Since pepper and other spices from India continued to be royal monopoly till the last quarter of the sixteenth century, the Germans could not purchase them directly from India. But trade in jewels, diamonds and precious stones was open to them. It is chiefly in this connection that the Germans established their contact with the western coast of India in the first half of the sixteenth century. The Herwarts of Germany who were also the members of the copper-syndicate of the Fuggers along with Paumgartner and Gossembrot were specialists in jewels and pearls of the East.

It was against this background of the German financiers like the Welsers, the Herwarts, the Imhofs, the Hirschvogel, the Hallers von Hallerstein, and the Heller of Frankfurt am Main that the Fuggers came forward to invest their capital in the overseas enterprise of Portugal. A change in the policy of the government offered them the opportunity to have direct contact with India in connection with the trade in pepper and other spices of the Orient.

The German merchants interested in purchasing Indian commodities like pepper and other items procured them at Lisbon in accordance with the terms and conditions of the contract. But a few firms like that of Melchior Manlich of Augsburg bought some of these items also at Allepo from the merchants from Armenia, Persia, Anatolia, Egypt and India.[65] The second half of the sixteenth century saw the liberal policy of the Portuguese king as far as trade in pepper and spices was concerned. The phase of "India contract" trade opened up during this period offered the German merchant-financiers a better opportunity for investment. The German merchants got the opportunity of purchasing the spices and other items directly from India in view of the contract signed on 29 November 1585.[66] The Welsers of Augsburg, a branch of the Fuggers under Philip Edward and his brother Octavian Secundus participated in the trade contract along with Giovanni Battista Rovelasca from Milan and Giraldo Paris, another merchant from the region of Aachen in Germany. The conditions of the contract were agreed upon by Giraldo Paris in the name of Rovelasca for a period of six years from 29 November 1585. They were ratified by the king of Portugal on 1 December 1585. The contractors took up the responsibility of sending 30,000 quintals of pepper every year from India to Lisbon and to fit out five vessels to India with necessary copper for exchange and money. Markus and Mathäus of the Welsers took 5/12 parts of the contract. The Fugger brothers, namely, Philip Edward and Octavian Secundus, took 3/12 parts of the contract. Ferdinand Cron, who was to play an important role in India, was sent as the representative of the Fuggers and Welsers.[67]

The Fuggers could be considered the most important merchant financiers wielding great influence in Europe during the sixteenth century on account of the capital at their disposal. They invested it in various productive activities, namely, mining, bills of exchange, floating loans and international trade. The rise of the Fuggers to the heights of capitalist enterprises was made possible in the wake of discoveries thanks to which large volumes of gold, silver, precious stones and other valuable materials were brought to Europe and were further taken to the oriental marts for the purchase of spices, pearls and other items that were in great demand in Europe.

Several studies had been done by scholars on the role played by the Fuggers in Europe, especially in connection with mining industry. The position held by the Fuggers in the financial transactions of the Holy Roman Emperor, Vatican, the rulers of Hungary, Denmark, Holland, Spain, England and Belgium is studied in detail by several economic historians of Europe. The importance of the Fuggers in the fairs of Antwerp, Frankfurt am Mains and other centres is also well discussed by historians. The mining of copper and the dealings in this metal done by the Fuggers has become an important object of research by many scholars. Similarly, the connection of the Fuggers with Spain is also well researched.

The Portuguese, who opened the sea-route connecting India with the Atlantic ports, revolutionised the maritime trade of India in the sixteenth century. The Fuggers played a very significant role in the trade conducted by the Portuguese with India. The Indian commodities, especially pepper, were purchased against the part-payment of copper. Portugal, though she initiated the exploitation of the commercial potentialities of India, did not have the necessary commodities or money for the acquisition of the much coveted pepper, pearls and precious stones from the East. It was stipulated that copper should be paid as part of the value of pepper to the merchants on the Malabar coast. So, the Portuguese had to look for someone who could supply the necessary quantity of copper. The

Fuggers, who had obtained monopoly of the copper mines of Tyrol, Schwaz, Hungary and other places against the advance of loans made to the Holy Roman Emperor and other needy kings, turned out to be the most influential persons who could come to the help of the Portuguese in supplying copper. It was estimated that approximately 30,000 quintals of copper were annually imported into India for the conduct of trade on the Malabar coast. Therefore, the Fuggers became quite an important group of merchant financiers for the Portuguese trade with India.

Apart from the supply of copper to the Portuguese, the Fuggers had their very important factory in Flanders. The Portuguese used to send spices from India to their own factory there itself. So, Flanders turned out to be the common place of mutual contact. The Portuguese agents managed to get loans as well as copper, silver and gold from the Fuggers through their agents stationed in Flanders. Initially the Fuggers were allowed to send their men to India for the purchase of commodities. When they, along with other German firms, tried to get the monopoly of direct trade with India the Portuguese king refused to comply with their request. However, he permitted them to enter on Europa-contract. This meant that the Fuggers through their agents in Lisbon could sign contracts with the officials of *Casa da India* in Lisbon for the purchase of a stipulated volume of spices against the rates fixed in advance by the king's officials. They were permitted to send the spices to other parts of Europe for sale. Often the Portuguese king obtained money in advance for the commodities which were contracted to the Fuggers. At the end of the transaction the accounts were settled.

In addition to the Europa-contract for spices, pepper and other commodities of royal monopoly, the Fuggers were allowed to have their agents in India to purchase pearls, diamonds and precious stones from various parts of the subcontinent, especially in Vijayanagara. These agents were allowed, in fact, to conduct trade in commodities that were not declared objects of royal monopoly.

As the Portuguese could not find sufficient means for keeping up monopoly over spices, pepper and other exotic items of the orient in the second half of the sixteenth century, Asia Contract was given to the European consortium. The Fuggers joined in this endeavour and agreed to send required money, copper and other materials with an understanding that they would buy the stipulated volume of commodities and transport it to Lisbon. Thus, they were involved in direct purchase on the coastal regions of India. They sent their agents who established factories in Goa, Cannanore, Cochin and Quilon for purchasing required merchandises. Their agents, besides being in charge of the purchases, were very important in the transmission of news regarding the other European competitors like the Dutch. In fact, the network of agencies for the collection of information from various parts of the world under the Fuggers was of immense importance in the sixteenth and the seventeenth centuries. A great corpus of information collected from various parts and preserved in different languages under the title *Fugger Newsletters* remains yet to be explored by the scholars. The service done by the agents of the Fuggers to the Portuguese activities in the East is significant.

The people of Augsburg and that of Germany in general celebrated the 500th anniversary of one of the stalwarts of the Fugger firm from June to September 1993. The present work was designed to coincide with this celebration. That famous business man who had international contacts of great importance was Anton Fugger. He was born on 10 June 1493 as son of Georg Fugger, the elder brother of Jakob Fugger, and Regina Imhof. Georg Fugger had been working with his brother Ulrich Fugger in their factory at Nürnberg. It was because of the contact with Nürnberg that he married Regina Imhof hailing from Nürnberg. When Georg Fugger died in 1506 Anton Fugger, who was then not even thirteen years old, had to enter into the business headed by Jakob Fugger, his uncle. He worked with the other two brothers, namely, Raymund and Ulrich. All the three got appropriate training in business. He was in Venice in the period after 1506 getting experience in the *Fondaco dei Tedeschi*. He came to the Fugger factory in Nürnberg in 1510 with a view to learning business there. From 1512 to 1514 Anton Fugger worked in Breslau to familiarise himself with the northeastern business of the Fuggers in the work of copper from

Hungary and its export to Western Europe and the region of the Eastern sea. He went to Rome in 1517 to handle an important work of Jakob Fugger with the Holy See in connection with the foundation of St. Moritz.[68] He extended financial assistance to the Papacy while he was in Rome and established close contacts with cardinals. He was associated with the preaching of indulgence and the collection of money for the papacy. Pope Leo X raised him to the status of papal Judge (*päpstlichen Ritter*) on 9 August 1519. He became the chief middleman for the Pope to get money from Switzerland and looked after the Fugger factory in Rome. With the election of Hadrian from Utrecht as pope, the collection of papal contribution once again came into the hands of the Fuggers.

He had been to Nürnberg in 1525 where Albrecht Dürer made a portrait for him. After the demise of Jakob Fugger on 29 December 1525, Anton Fugger took up the management of the firm at the age of thirty-two. The firm had been functioning since 1510 under the name *Jakob Fugger und Gebrüder Söhne*. The name remained unaltered till 1532 when it was transformed into *Raymundus, Antonius und Hieronymus, die Fugger, Gebrüder und Vettern*. Anton Fugger became the chief administrator of the firm after the death of Jakob Fugger. The other two partners were allowed to do anything only with the knowledge and consent of Anton Fugger. He married Anna Rehlinger, daughter of Hans Rehlinger, a patrician of Augsburg, and Anna Dietenheimer on 4 March 1527. The wedding was celebrated in the Cathedral church of Augsburg with solemn catholic ceremony. He had contacts with several parts of Italy such as Rome, Naples and Venice, Tyrol, Hungary, Spain, France, Slovakia, Scandinavian countries, the Netherlands, Poland and so on. Hence he was faced with stiff competition from the firms of Herwart, Pimel, Paumgartner and Höchstetter. According to the inventory of 1527, Anton Fugger had an asset of 16,02,319 gulden. Matthäus Schwarz was the chief accountant of the firm of the Fugger. Anton kept friendly relations with the famous humanist Erasmus and their friendship reached the highest point by 1530.

Anton Fugger had to take up the burden of the funds already extended to Charles V for the election to the position of Roman

Emperor. Similarly, Ferdinand of the Habsburg dynasty also got financial help in 1530 from the Fuggers for his attempt to become the king of the Romans. An amount of 365 845 gulden was given to Ferdinand. Besides, Ferdinand sold his annual income from Naples to Anton Fugger for 173 330 gulden. He kept close contact with Charles V, Maria, the Queen of Hungary, as well as Margaret the *Stathalterin* of the Netherlands. Anton Fugger had to get from Charles V of the Roman Empire an amount of 6,00,000 ducats in 1538 and from Ferdinand of Habsburg another amount of 6,00,000 ducats. He invested in landed estate too. He spent 20,000 gulden for land in Biberbach. Later he purchased land in Oberkirchberg, and invested 6,600 gulden in Donauwörth in 1536. In 1537 he purchased a village and the Glöt castle near Dillingen for 23,000 gulden. The purchase of the lordship of Babenhausen was also effected during this period. The castle and market of Babenhausen which belonged to the Duke of Würtemberg cost him 36,000 gold gulden. Anton Fugger's hold on money could be understood in the light of liabilities of Charles V and Ferdinand both of whom owed him 1,50,000 ducats and 8,00,000 gulden respectively in 1542. He advanced a further amount of 4,00,000 gulden to Ferdinand later. Anton Fugger took greater interest in expanding his activities in Italy, Spain, Antwerp and the far East rather than in Hungary and Eastern Europe since 1545. So, he intensified his interest in the quicksilver and zinnobar of Spain, business in gold in Antwerp and London.

His interest in defending the catholic faith against the Protestant revolution made him lend 2,00,000 ducats to the emperor in his religious fights in 1545. Thus it is clear that Anton Fugger invested the money in various activities including the defense of the catholic faith. The trust placed in him by the Pope and the Roman Emperor shows the importance of his hold on money during the troubled days of the Church. After having conducted such a worldwide and multifaceted business, Anton Fugger who brought the firm of the Fuggers to the greatest heights possible, expired on 14 September 1560 at the age of sixty-seven. According to his wishes, his body was shifted from Augsburg to Babenhausen to be buried in the church of the castle next to the tomb of his deceased wife.

Sufficient care has been taken in this study to highlight the role of the Fuggers' firm in the commercial revolution that took place after the discov ry of the direct sea-route connecting India with the Atlantic ports as well as the discovery of the Western hemisphere. As the overseas trade of the Portuguese loomed large in the era of the revolution, the international trade between India and Portugal is taken as the backdrop of this work. It was thought desirable to focus on the Fuggers in general instead of writing a monograph on Anton Fugger. The international dimensions of this German firm, especially in the context of the maritime trade of India and the Portuguese, has not been dealt in detail so far by any writer. Even the scholarly works of the German economists do not give adequate attention to the contacts of the Fuggers with India. So, this work was conceived as one that can fill up the gap and connect their attempts with the Portuguese commercial enterprises.

Apart from the 500th anniversary of the birth of Anton Fugger, the world, especially Portugal, is celebrating the 500 years of the discoveries by bringing out scientific works related to the encounter between Portugal and the East. It is the Portuguese who provided an opportunity to the German financiers to have direct commercial relations with the subcontinent of India. Therefore, it is considered worthwhile to study the enterprise of the Fuggers against the backdrop of the Portuguese discoveries and the subsequent establishment of overseas trade with India in particular and the Indian ocean regions in general. Studies on the overseas activities of the Fuggers in connection with the Portuguese expansion in the east exclusively have not been conducted so far. This renders the present study meaningful in the context of the celebration of the five hundred years of the discoveries by the Portuguese.

The nature and the dynamics of trade in the Indian Ocean regions at the close of the fifteenth century are discussed with a view to placing the involvement of the Fuggers in the Portuguese trade in a historical perspective. The maritime past of India and the brisk trade conducted with various parts of the world are highlighted to assess the changes brought about by the Portuguese in the sixteenth century. An attempt has been made to throw some light on the trade conducted by the Al-Karimi merchants as well as the Chinese contacts till the second half of the fifteenth century on the western coast of India. The fact that by the middle of the century there was a vacuum in the international trade because of the withdrawal of the Chinese as well as that of the Al-Karimi merchants is brought out. It was into this vacuum that the Portuguese stepped and established themselves by the turn of the sixteenth century.

Subsequently, attention is paid to the rivalries for establishing monopoly over trade in the Indian Ocean regions. No sooner did the reports regarding the availability of the much-desired spices and other oriental goods as well as the possibility of having direct maritime contact with India reach the Europeans than they vied with each other to establish contact with India. But the Portuguese before starting their overseas enterprise had equipped themselves with papal authorisation to keep other powers away from the areas discovered by them. The development of the claims put forward by the Portuguese against other West European powers forms part of a chapter in this work. This will explain why the German merchant financiers like the Fuggers and Welsers could not conduct direct trade with the subcontinent of India and had to wait for the permission from the Portuguese. Though the collaboration of the German financiers was essential on account of their hold on copper, quicksilver, gold and money, the Portuguese did not grant the permission to have direct trade with India in spices until the Spanish king Philip II took over as the king of Portugal. In fact, the Portuguese king kept pepper and spices as items of royal monopoly as long as he could. These details are discussed to highlight the participation of the Fuggers on a wider canvass.

Adequate emphasis is laid on the discussion about the rise of the Fuggers and the way in which they held sway over the financial activities in Europe. The Fuggers were not only the financiers of the Holy Roman empire as well as supporters to the papacy, but also were powerful industrialists and capitalists with large investments in fields like mining, banking, trade and bills of exchange. They owned large landed estates and conducted a number of social activities for the benefit of the poor. It may be said that their financial activities went beyond all the man-made boundaries.

Fuggers' involvement in trade with Portugal and through the Portuguese with India is something which deserves the attention of the scholars. This is done in one of the chapters of the present work. Details regarding the Europa- contract as well as the Asia-contract are furnished in the work. Perusal of the original contracts in Latin language and in Spanish helps one understand the importance of the Fuggers in the overseas trade conducted by the Portuguese with India.

Besides spices, pepper, diamonds, pearls and other rare items of the orient, exotic animals were taken from the Indian Ocean regions to Europe. Some of them were even taken to Germany where the Fuggers established a zoological garden. Dr. Michael Gorgas, the present Director of the Zoological Garden in Augsburg who has specialised in the study of the movement of animals, has contributed an article on the subject highlighting the role played by the Fuggers in developing zoological gardens.

The capitalistic nature of the activities of the Fuggers in the sixteenth century is emphasised in the concluding chapter of the work. Though this phase is taken as pre-capitalist, the activities of the Fuggers to a large extent evinced capitalistic enterprise. The revival of the trade in spices and pepper in the Mediterranean is also discussed to prove the fact that the Portuguese could not effect a strict monopoly over these items though the German financiers were kept off from direct trade with India for some time.

The invaluable collection of original documents in German, Spanish and Latin preserved in the Fürstl. und Gräfl. Fuggersches familien und - Stiftungsarchiv, Dillingen/Donau sheds considerable light on the activities and overseas enterprises of the Fuggers. Codex No. 46.1 and the following are of immense value. In fact, almost all the published material related to the Fuggers are carefully maintained in this Archives where excellent facilities for photocopying the material are available. This collection is the main source of information in the preparation of this work.

Fugger Zeitungen or "Fugger Newsletters" which formed part of the Fugger Library in Augsburg constitute a veritable mine of information. The collection of books and manuscripts of the library of Count Albert Fugger contained outstanding works in different languages and fields springing from 17,046 authors in 13,838 volumes. Emperor Ferdinand III purchased the library from Count Albert Fugger for 15,000 gulden in 1655 and the collection was transferred to Vienna. Among the "German Books Unbound" a large number of old manuscripts were included in this collection. The Fugger Newsletters are found under the section of the unbound German books and in their present form they comprise volumes 8949-8975 consisting of approximately 35,000 closely written pages. They furnish very significant information regarding trade and commerce in the sixteenth and seventeenth centuries and especially the financial transactions of the Fuggers in places like Antwerp, Middelburg, Hamburg, Frankfurt, Cologne, Venice, Rome, Paris, Constantinople and so on. Though most of the Fugger Newsletters are in German, Italian is well represented. They cover the period from 1568 to 1604. Reports sent from Antwerp (always called Antorf by the reporters of the Fuggers), Middelburg, Cologne, Venice, Lisbon, Madrid, Rome Constantinople, Lyons, Goa, Cochin and so on are contained in this collection. Copies of the Fugger Newsletters are also found in the Munich State Library besides Vienna Library. This collection covers the period from 1585 to 1595 and were culled weekly from the Fugger papers by the Augsburg Town councillor, Hans Mehrer, and sent by him to his brother-in-law, Stephen Fugger, who was the treasurer of Regensburg. Similarly as reported by Kleinpaul some of the reports prepared in Augsburg are found in the Leipzig University Library. Two volumes containing a selection of the Newsletters were edited by Victor von Klarwill under the title *Fugger-zeitungen: ungedruckte Briefe an das Haus Fugger aus den Jahren 1568-1605* in 1923 which was translated into English by Pauline de Chary with a foreword from H. Gordon Selfridge in 1924. The second series of the Fugger Newsletters was edited by Victor von Klarwill, the English translation of which was issued by L.S.R. Byrne in 1926.

The information furnished by Lazarus Nürnberger, Jorg Pock, Hans Mayr, Hans Schwerczer, Ferdinand Cron, Filippo

Sassetti and others who represented the firms of Fuggers, Welsers, Herwarts, Hirschvogel, Imhofs and Giovanni Battista Rovelasca in India in the sixteenth century are of great importance in the study of the Fuggers involvement in the international trade. The *Bratislava Manuscript Collection* containing the German translation of some contemporary works is also of importance for the study. This has been recently edited, translated and published.[69] The diary of Lucas Rem covering the period from 1494 to 1541 sheds a lot of light on the participation of the German merchant-financiers in the Portuguese trade with India. Lucas Rem was the son of Lucas Rem and Magdalena. He was born in 1481 and entered in the service of Anton Welser and Conrad Vöhlin in November 1499. Information about the three ships sent to India in 1505 by the German merchants in collaboration with the Italian merchants is given in this diary among other details of the German contacts.[70] Similarly, the report given by Belthazar Sprenger who was the writer in the ship *Leonarda* fitted out by the Germans in 1505 to India is also an important source of information for the present study.[71]

As the Germans had been closely associated with the Portuguese government in the sixteenth century, a number of Portuguese documents related to the involvement of the Fuggers in the overseas trade are kept in the Archivo Nacional da Torre do Tombo, Lisbon. *Cartas de Quitação del rei D. Manuel, Corpo Cronologico, Chancelaria de D. Manuel and Chancelaria de D. João III* are some of the collections which shed light on the subject. Special mention may be made of the *Fundo Geral* in the Bibliotheca Nacional de Lisboa. The copies of the privileges granted to the German financiers in general and the Fuggers in particular in the first decade of the sixteenth century are preserved in the library of the History of the City of Porto in Portugal. These documents are extremely useful in providing information regarding the early attempts of the Fuggers to participate in the trade with India. The Goa Historical Archives contain the famous collection called *Livro das Monções* and *Livro de Alvaras* related to the subject under discussion. The details of the three contracts and especially the Asia Contract are found in these collections.

The present work is, by and large, the outcome of a joint venture with Dr. Michael Gorgas, the Director of Zoologischer Garten, Augsburg, West Germany.

NOTES AND REFERENCES

1. Levy Maria Jordão, *Bullarium Patronatus Portugalliae Regum in Ecclesiis Africae, Asiae Atque Oceniae* (hereafter *Bullarium*), Tomus I, Olisipone, 1869, p. 20.
2. *Ibid.*, pp. 22-23.
3. *Ibid.*, pp. 31-34.
4. *Ibid.*, pp. 36-37.
5. *Ibid.*, pp. 47-52.
6. Sousa Viterbo, "Bertholameu Florentyn: Antigas relações commerciaes e maritimas de Portugal com a Italia", *Economista*, 24 October 1885, No. 951, pp. 1-2.
7. João de Barros, *Da Asia*, Decada I, Part I, Lisboa, 1777, p. 464.
8. *Bullarium*, p. 59.
9. For details on the organisation of trade, ref. Damião Peres, *Regimento das Cazas das Indias e Minas*, Coimbra, 1947.
10. Eugenio Alberi, ed., *Le Relazioni degli Ambasciatori Veneti al Senato*, Firenze, 1863, vol.15, p. 16.
11. *Ibid.*, p. 6.
12. Marino Sanuto, *I Diarii di Marino Sanuto: 1496-1533*, edited by G. Berchet R. Fulin *et al.*, Venice, 1897-1903, 58 vols., tom. IV, cols. 66-67; Jaime Cortesão, *A Expedição de Pedro Alvares Cabral e o Descobrimento do Brasil*, Lisbon, 1967, pp. 117ff.
13. Letter of Dominingo Pisani dated July 21 iv. 46 fl. 130v-131; Thomé Lopes, "Navegação as Indias Orientães escrita em Portugues por Thomé Lopes" in *Collecção de Noticias para a Historia e Geografia das Nações Ultramarinas que vivem nos dominios Portugueses ou lhes são vizinhas*, tom II, Nos. 1 and 2, Lisbon, 1812, p. 174.
14. Barros, *op. cit.*, Decada I, Part I, pp. 464, 473; Gaspar Correa, *Lendas da India.*, tom. 1, Lisboa, 1864, pp. 233, 235.
15. Sanuto, *op. cit.*, tom. V, col.131. Letter of Giovanni Francesco de Affaitati, dated 20 August 1503; Arquivo Nacional da Torre do Tombo (hereafter ANTT.) Chancel. de D. Manuel, liv. 46, fl.130ᵛ-131; Thomé Lopes, *op. cit.*, p. 174.
16. Giovanni da Empoli, "Viagem as Indias Orientães" in *Collecção de noticias para a Historia e Geografia das Nações Ultramarinas que vivem nos Dominios Portuguezes ou lhes são vizinhas*, tom. III, Nos. I & II, Lisboa, 1812, p. iii.

17. Leonardo da Ca'Masser, "Relazione di Leonardo da Ca'Masser", in *Archivio Storico Italiano*, Appendice, tom. I, Firenze, 1845, p. 23.
18. ANTT. Chancel. de D. Manuel, liv. 46, fl.130v-131r. For further details on Giovanni da Empoli ref. Laurence A. Noonan, *John of Empoli and his relations with Afonso de Albuquerque*, Lisboa, 1989.
19. Raymundo Antonio de Bulhão Pato, *Cartas de Affonso de Albuquerque* (hereafter *Cartas*), tomo. I, Lisboa, 1884, p. 404.
20. ANTT. Chancel. de D. Manuel, *op. cit.*, Livro 15, fl.90v; Livro V de Misticos, fl.119.
21. Luis de Figueiredo Falcão, *Livro em que se contem toda a Fazenda e Real Patrimonio dos Reinos de Portugal, India e ilhas Adjacentes e Outras Particularidades*., Lisboa, 1859, pp. 148, 150; Gaspar Correa, *op. cit.*, tom. 2, p. 609; Frei Luis de Sousa, *Anais de D. João* III, vol. I, Lisboa, 1951, pp. 138-39; Barros, *op. cit.*, Decada III, Part II, p. 99.
22. Noonan, *op. cit.*, p. 25.
23. *Cartas*, tomo. VI, pp. 408-410.
24. Richard Ehrenberg, *Das Zeitalter der Fugger* translated by H.M. Lucas as *Capital and Finance in the Age of the Renaissance*, New York, 1963, pp. 198-200.
25. *Ibid.*, p. 199.
26. E.C. Ravenstein, *A Journal of the First Voyage of Vasco da Gama*, London, 1898, p. 119ff.
27. Sanuto, *op. cit.*, tom. IV, col. 66.
28. For his account, ref. Biblioteca Riccardiana, Florence, Mss. Nos. 1910 and 2112b; Fracanzano Montalbodo, *Paesi Nuovamente Ritrovati & Novo Mondo da Alberico Vesputio Florentino Intitulato*., Venezia, 1597, Facsimile, Londom, 1916, pp. 68ff.
29. Falcão, *op. cit.*, p. 144.
30. William Brooks Greenlee, *The Voyage of Pedro Alvares Cabral to Brazil and India*., London, 1938, p. 118.
31. Herman Van der Wee, *The Growth of the Antwerp Market and the European Economy—Fourteenth-Sixteenth Centuries*, Vol. II, The Hague, 1963, p. 129.
32. For details about Affaitati, ref. A. Goris, *Les Colonies Marchandes Meridionales à Anvers de 1488 a 1567,* Louvain, *1925;* J. Denuce, *Inventaire des Affaitadi Banquiers Italiens à Anvers de l'anée 1566*, Antwerp, 1934.
33. ANTT. Chancel. de D. Manuel, Liv.46.fl, 155v; Liv. VI de Misticos, fl.176.
34. ANTT. Corpo Chronologico, I-24-89.
35. ANTT. *Ibid.*, I-19-111.
36. *Ibid.*
37. Prospero Peragallo, *Cenni intorno alla Colonia in Portogallo nei Secoli XIV, XV e XVI*, 2nd edition, Genova, 1907, p. 82.
38. Virginia Rau, *Um Grande Mercador—Banquairo Italiano em Portugal*,

separata da Estudos Italianos em Portugal, No. 24, 1965, pp. 4-5.

39. Sanuto, *op. cit.*, tom. IV, col. 66.
40. Giovanni Battista Ramusio, *Delle Navigationi et Viaggi*, Vol. I, 3rd edition, Valencia, 1563, fl.176[r]-188[v].
41. Sanuto, *op. cit.*, tom. XXVII, col. 641.
42. Archivo General de Simancas, *Secretarias Provinciales*, cod. 1571, fl. 14.
43. For a detailed study of the subject, ref. Johann Philipp Cassel, *Previlegia und Handelungfreiheiten, welche die Könige von Portugal ehedem den deutschen Kaufleuten zu Lissabon ertheilet haben*, Bremen, 1771. The document is reproduced by J. Denuce in *Archivo Historico Portugues*, Vol. VII, Lisboa, 1909, pp. 381-383; Bibliotheca Nacional de Lisboa (hereafter BNL) MSS. *Fundo Geral* No. 2771; Documentos Arquivados no Gabinete de historia da Cidade, *Boletim Cultural da Camara Municipal do Porto, Vol. XXXII*, Março- Junho, 1969, Fasc. 1-2, pp. 352-359.
44. E.A. Strassen/Alfredo Gandara, *Oito Seculos de Historia Luso-alemão*, Lisboa, 1944, pp. 133-34.
45. *Ibid.*, p. 138.
46. Richard Ehrenberg, *op. cit.*, p. 137ff.
47. J. Denuce, "Privileges commerciaux accordes per les rois de Portugal aux Flamands et aux Allemands-XVe siecles" in *Archivo Historico Portugues*, Vol. VII, Lisboa, 1909, p. 310ff.
48. B. Greiff, ed., *Tagebuch des Lucas Rem aus den Jahren 1494-1541*, Augsburg, 1861, pp. 8-9, 83.
49. Ehrenberg, *op. cit.*, vol. I, p. 138.
50. ANTT. C.C.I-25-75. For further details on Welsers, ref. K. Häbler, *Die Uberseeischen Unternehmungen der Welser und ihrer Gesellschafter*, Leipzig, 1903.
51. ANTT. C.C. I-19-111.
52. Ehrenberg, *op. cit.*, p. 139.
53. Herman Kellenbenz, "Neues zum oberdeutschen Ostindienhandel, insbesondere der Herwarts in der ersten Hälfte des 16. Jahrhunderts", Pankarz Fried, ed., *Forschungen zur schwäbischen Geschichte*, Sigmaringen, 1991, pp. 89-95.
54. Ehrenberg, *op. cit.*, p. 151ff.
55. *Ibid.*
56. *Ibid.*, pp. 168-71.
57. E.A. Strassen/Alfredo Gandara, *op. cit.*, pp. 141ff.
58. *Ibid.*, p. 141.
59. J. Denuce, *op. cit.*, p. 316; Joaquim de Vasconcellos, *Albrecht Dürer e a sua Influencia na Peninsula,* Coimbra, 1929, p. 25.
60. Joaquim de Vasconcellos, *op. cit.*, p. 25; Denuce, *op. cit.*, p. 316.
61. Miloslav Krasa, Josef Polisensky and Peter Ratkos, eds., *The Voyages of Discovery in the Bratislava Manuscript Lyc.515/8 (Codex Bratislavensis)*, Prague, 1986, pp. 36ff and 66ff.

62. Geneviève Bouchon, *Navires et cargaisons retour de l'Inde en 1518*, Paris, 1977.

63. The report prepared by Lazarus Nürnberger is preserved in the Library of Academy of Sciences of Bratislava. It was reproduced by R. Bishop Smith in 1974 as *Lazarus Nürnberger, being a photograph of the manuscript account of his voyage to India in 1517 and 1518 preserved in the Central Library of the Slovakian Academy of Sciences in Bratislava, Czechoslovakia,* Lisboa, 1974. This discovery was possible thanks to the article of J. Polisensky and P. Ratkos, "Eine neue Quelle zur Zweiten Indienfahrt Vasco da Gamas" in *Historica*, IX, Prague, 1964, pp. 53-67. Refer also Miloslav Krasa, *et al., op. cit.* For further details and the text in German together with an introduction and French translation, ref. Anne Kroell, "Le Voyage de Lazarus Nürnberger en Inde, 1517-1518", *Bulletin des Etudes Portugaises*, Paris, 1980, pp. 59-87.

64. Hedwig Kömmerling-Fitzler, "Der Nürnberger Kaufmann Georg Pock (+1528/9) in Portugiesisch-Indien und im Edelsteinland Vijayanagara", *Mitteilungen des Vereins für Geschichte der Stadt Nürnberg,* Band *55, 1967-68, Nürnberg*, 1968, pp. 137-184; Stadtarchiv Nürnberg, Behaimarchiv Nr.582(14); F.W. Ghillany, *Geschichte des Seefahrers Ritter Martin Behaim,* Nürnberg, 1853, pp. 120-122.

65. Hermann Kellenbenz, "From Melchoir Manlich to Ferdinand Cron; German Levantine and Oriental Trade Relations: Second Half of the Sixteenth and Beginning of the Seventeenth Century", unpublished paper presented at the seminar at Pondicherry in 1990, pp. 6-7.

66. MSS. Fürstl. u. Gräfl. Fuggersches Familien-und Stiftungsarchiv, Dillingen/ Donau (hereafter F.A.), No.46-1 fls.33-38.

67. For more details on Ferdinand Cron, ref. Hermann Kellenbenz, "Le front hispano-portugais contre l'Inde et le rôle d'une agence de renseignements au service de marchands allemands et flamands", *Studia*, No.11, Lisboa, 1963, pp. 263-289; Sanjay Subramanyam, "An Augsburger in Asia Portuguesa: Further Light on the Commercial World of Ferdinand Cron, 1587-1624", Roderich Ptak and Dietmar Rothermund, eds., *Emporia, Commodities and Entrepreneurs in Asian Maritime Trade, c.1400-1750*, Stuttgart, 1991, pp. 401-425; C.R. Boxer, "Uma raridade bibliografica sobre Fernão Cron", *Bibliofilia: De Bibliografia Luso-Brasileira,* Vol. XII, Numero 1, Janeiro-Março, 1971, pp. 323-344; K.S. Mathew, "German Merchant Financiers in Goa during 16th and 17th Centuries" in P.P. Shirodkar, ed., *Goa's External Relations*, Goa, 1992, pp. 32-56. For general information on Germans in India, ref. Amancio Gracias, "Alemais na India nos seculos XV a XVIII", *Boletim do Instituto Vasco da Gama*, No. 50, Goa, 1941, pp. 1-95; Bibliotheca Nacional de Lisboa *Colecção Pombalina*, No. 647, fls. 210-219; M.A. Hedwig Fitzler, "Der Anteil der Deutschen an der Kolonialpolitik Philipps II von Spanien in Asien", *Vierteljahrschrift für Sozial - und Wirtschaftsgeschichte,* 28, 1935, pp. 243-281.

68. Hermann Kellenbenz, "Anton Fugger" in *Lebensbilder aus dem Bayerischen Schwaben*, Band II, Augsburg, 1976, pp. 46ff.
69. Miloslav Krasa, *et al.*, *op. cit.*
70. B. Greiff, *op. cit.*
71. F. Kunstmann, *Die Fahrt der ersten Deutschen nach dem Portugieseischen Indien, München, 1861;* Franz Schulze, *Balthasar Springers Indienfahrt 1505-06*, Strassburg, 1902; the Latin manuscript without the name of the writer is preserved in the library of Giessener University; the German text of the diary "Die Merfart unn erfarung nüwer Schiffung and Wege zû viln onerkanten Inseln und Künigreichen..., wie ich Balthasar Sprenger sollichs: in kurzverschynen zeiten gesehen unn erfaren habe, gedruckt anno MDIX" consists of fifteen pages only. There are only four copies known to be existing; one in Munich, another in the Stadtbibliothek of Frankfurt a.M, the third in the royal library of Kopenhagen and the fourth in Wienna Library.

CHAPTER 2

TRADE IN THE INDIAN OCEAN REGIONS AT THE CLOSE OF THE FIFTEENTH CENTURY

J. C. Van Leur and a number of writers of the same strand of thought preferred to call the merchants of the Indian Ocean and the East Indies during the pre-industrial period pedlars and relegated the trade in that region to the background. [1] In tune with this idea some recent historians held the view that there was no structural change in the trade in the Indian Ocean regions till 1622 when Ormuz fell to the English and the Portuguese influence was wiped out from the Persian Gulf regions. The emergence of the East India Companies as active trading agencies subsequent to this event is considered the beginning of a new era by historians of this school as far as maritime trade was concerned. [2]

Immanuel Wallerstein, who speaks of the existence of "world-economies" before the sixteenth century which were transformed into empires like China, Persia and Rome, qualifies the period beginning with the sixteenth century as the period of "world-economy" in the proper sense of the term. He underlines the fact that the modern world-economy did not always progress in the direction of empires because of the techniques of modern capitalism and technology of modern science paving the way for thriving, producing and expanding without the emergence of a unified political structure. He affirms that the expansion of the sixteenth century meant economic expansion besides geographic. [3] It is concluded by him that the Indian Ocean regions were brought under the world-economy and capital accumulation was effected through extractive mechanism, market- oriented and profit-induced production decisions as well as accumulation of capital through appropriation of labour surplus. Thus, according to him, the trade and commerce in the Indian Ocean regions assumed capitalistic character in the sixteenth century.

Fernand Braudel, assigning an altogether higher status than that of pedlars to the merchants of the Indian Ocean regions prior to the emergence of the East India Companies, characterises the long-distance trade with capitalist aspects. He is of the opinion that all the merchants of the Indian Ocean regions prior to the sixteenth century could not be classified as pedlars. K. N. Chaudhuri, going a step further and subscribing to the view of Braudel, identifies capitalistic activities in the transcontinental trade which was in vogue from the rise of Islam. He says: "The history of maritime trade in the Indian Ocean from the rise of Islam to the end of our period (1750), it can be argued, is neither understood nor explained without explicitly taking into account the role played by capital in production and distribution."[4] He affirms that "capitalist principles strongly underpinned long-distance trade and economic production for non- local markets". Therefore, Chaudhuri seems to locate existence of capitalism, as far as the process of production and distribution are concerned, at the dawn of Islam, conquest of which, as Maurice Lombard suggests, restored the unity of two major economic units, namely, Indian Ocean and the Mediterranean areas.[5] He adds that the rise of the three great state systems of Asia, viz. the Ming (1368), the Ottoman (1453) and the Mughal (1526), represents the continuous attempts to do away with the power of the landed magnates through military and administrative means which enabled the state to centralise the distributive function. Milieu of this nature paved the way for a type of commercial capitalism which helped the great merchants act as bankers to the state and who converted the agricultural surplus into disposable income for the state and assignees. He underlines the fact that "the transcontinental trade of the Indian Ocean region operating through a network of commercial emporia benefited from the development of state capitalism and yet it remained firmly linked to an international order of economic specialisation".[6] Frank Perlin, writing on proto-industrialisation and pre-colonial South Asia, affirms the development of capitalism in India as in Europe at least from the sixteenth century. He writes, "I argue that India, like Europe, was affected by profound and rapid change in the character of its societies and economies, and state-forms, from at least the sixteenth century, and secondly that a fundamental aspect of that development was a local merchant capitalism which emerged independently of that in Europe, but with a common international theatre of societal and commercial changes."[7]

Thus, the emphasis is laid by a good number of historians of the Indian Ocean on the long-distance trade as the most important element of the commercial capitalism existing even before the discovery of direct sea-route connecting Indian Ocean regions, especially India with the Atlantic ports. The various dynamics of the long-distance and transcontinental maritime trade before the arrival of Portuguese on the Western coast of India shall be the focus of this chapter.

India, right from the dawn of her civilisation in the pre- historic period, had long-distance maritime contacts with various parts of the world as evinced by the achaeological findings of the Harappan sites. The Harappan cities, which came into existence towards the middle of the third millennium B.C., seemed to have commercial relations with Mesopotamia by sea. A number of typical seals from the Indus valley civilisation are found in Sumer at levels going back to 2300 to 2000 B.C. These seals which were found in large number in Mohenjo-Daro and Harappa are believed to have been used to mark the ownership of property. Every merchant or mercantile family, according to the scholars like A. L. Basham, had a seal. A number of typical Indus seals were found in Mesopotamia besides several products of the Indus regions. The archaeological findings in Mesopotamia prompted some historians to conclude that people of Harappan civilisation (2500 to 1750 B.C.) had trade and commerce with Sumeria. Cotton, the staple item of export from India, was presumably taken to Mesopotamia. Scholars like B. B. Lal and R. S. Sharma subscribe to the view that the trade the people of Harappan civilisation conducted with Mesopotamia was seaborne.

This suggestion is based on the findings of the excavations conducted at Lothal, not far from the Gulf of Cambay which was the inlet of the Arabian sea in the Gujarat coast. A dockyard, 216 metres long (north to south) and 37 metres wide situated to the east of the township of Lothal, one of the city sites of the Harappan civilisation, was discovered by the archaeologists.

A channel connected the dockyard of Lothal with Bhogavo river and the boats entered the dockyard through this channel during the high tide. B. B. Lal is of the opinion that the structure located near the dockyard of Lothal could be a warehouse where commodities of exchange were stored. The opinion that Lothal had long distance-maritime trade with other parts of the world is strengthened by the discovery of seals and sealings of the Indus style at the sites of Ur, Susa, Umma, Lagash and Tell Smar in West Asia and especially that of a sealing at Umma which was associated with a bale of cloth, evidently an export from India. Further, a seal, found in Lothal more or less same as those discovered at the contemporary sites of Barbar, Ras-al-Qala and Failaka in the Persian Gulf region, confirms the view that the commercial relations between the sites of Harappan civilisation and West Asia were at least partly maritime. A. L. Basham also subscribes to the view that the merchants of Harappan civilisation resided in Mesopotamia and that there were maritime trade contacts with West Asia which is now proved in the light of the findings at Lothal. D. D. Kosambi and R. S. Sharma are of the view that the merchants of the Harappan period had trade with Dilmun identified with Baharain in the Persian Gulf regions, which could be principally through maritime routes.[8] The flow of commodities from India to West Asia and some parts of Europe continued in the period after heyday of Harappan civilisation. Bharukachchha (Broach) in Gujarat was the chief port during the period between 600 and 320 B.C. which occupied an important place in the maritime trade of India with the West. An early Jataka story makes mention of ships sailing from the Port of Bharukachchha to Baveru, identified as Babylon. Sopara near Bombay was another port of great importance in the seaborne trade of India in the pre-Christian era. By the Mauryan times (321-185 B.C.) Tamralipti

(Tamulk) situated in the Ganges delta became the main port of the Ganga basin from where ships used to sail to Ceylon, Southeast Asia and Indonesia.

The seaborne trade of India reached great heights during the period between 200 B.C. and A.D. 300 especially on account of the trade conducted by the seamen of Roman Egypt. Egypt was annexed to the Roman empire in 30 B.C. The Roman trade with India was facilitated by the Roman conquest of Mesopotamia in A.D. 115 which was made a Roman province. The Roman Emperor Trajan conquered Muscat and explored the Persian Gulf. The use of monsoon known to the Arabs from the mid-first century B.C. was "discovered" by Hippalaus by the beginning of the first century A.D. The monsoon winds were used by the Romans for trade with India. The seaman's guide *Periplus Maris Erythraei,*[9] compiled in Greek by an anonymous writer in the second half of the first century A.D. was used by the merchants and seamen of Roman Egypt. The three important ports of the peninsular India, namely, Musiris known as Cranganore in the kingdom of Ceras on the Malabar coast, Korkai in the land of Pandyas not far from the modern Tuticorin on the eastern coast of India and Kaveripumpattinam at the mouth of the river Kaveri in the kingdom of the early Colas, are mentioned in Ptolemy's *Geography*. Strabo speaks of the embassy sent by the ruler of Pandyas to Augustus at Athens about 20 B.C. The early Colas profited greatly out of the seaborne trade, especially the one based on Kaveripumpattinam, their headquarters. The famous cotton products of Uraiyur found their way to various parts of the world through this port-town which was built up by the Cola ruler Karikala who flourished around A.D. 100. He founded Puhar and constructed an embankment of 160 km length along the river Kaveri.[10] A number of foreign merchants used to come and reside in this port-town. Tamil literature of the period called *Sangam* describes the layout of the city of Kaveripumpattinam, especially the two different sections occupied by the Indian and foreign merchants as well as the market place situated between these sections. The boats built at the coastal towns of the kingdom of the Colas were used for long- distance voyages to Malaya and Southeast

Asia. The Roman demand for spices drove the merchants of the Cola territory to Malaya, Java, Sumatra, Cambodia and Borneo. These merchants acted as middlemen for the Romans. Merchants from Kalinga and Magadha concentrated their commercial activities in Ceylon and Burma besides the trade on the eastern coast of India during the period from 200 B.C. to A.D. 300.

Another important centre of maritime trade of India from the first century B.C. to the second century A.D. was Arikamedu known to Periplus as Poduke near the modern Pondicherry. The extensive excavations conducted in 1945 and recent ones by a group of scholars from the United States in collaboration with the Archaeological Survey of India in the period from 1989 to 1992 unearthed a lot of material related to the commercial activities centred on Poduke. Besides being a port of call en route to Malaya and China, Poduke comprised a Roman settlement where certain commodities like muslins were manufactured. Pottery, glasswares, arretine and other wares, wine-amphorae and gold were brought to Poduke.[11] In the light of recent researches it is held that the peak period of the trade of Poduke with the Mediterranean was the first century B.C. The settlement here had two sectors, namely, an industrial sector and a port. Textile production seems to be one of the important industries. The recent excavations brought to light the existence of tanks which must have been used for dyeing textiles. Roman subjects resided in Arikamedu and so *terra sigillata* and wine-amphorae were brought for their use from the Mediterranean areas.[12]

Musiris on the Malabar coast had a flourishing trade with the Romans. Two Roman regiments were said to have been stationed at Musiris to protect their interests. It is concluded by the archaeologists that the Romans built a temple for Augustus at Cranganore. The other port-towns that had commercial relations with Rome during the Satavahana period (A.D. 106-220) were Amravati, Dharnikota and Nagarjunakonda on the eastern coast of India. The movement of Indian commodities to the west continued uninterrupted till 300 A.D. and then there occurred a setback in this direction of trade.

Satavahanas extended their power to the coastal Andhra. The lower Krishna and Godavari valleys reached high degree of economic prosperity during the second century A.D. with the expansion of their rule from the Western Deccan and the extension of the Mediterranean trade as concluded in the light of the recent researches. Immediate successor of Gautamiputra Satkarni (A.D. 106-130) called Vasisthiputra Pulumayi (A.D. 130-154) issued coins which were found in Andhra. The Satavahanas of this period attached great importance to the maritime trade of the eastern coast which prompted them to issue coins of the model of sea-going vessels depicting double masted ships. They profited very much from the Roman trade. The Iksvaku dynasty occupied the eastern part of the Satavahana kingdom, the deltas of the Krishna and the Godavari in the third century A.D. Even after the heydays of the Roman trade, the lower Krishna valley under the Iksvakus continued to prosper as centre of maritime trade. They issued coins which had great similarity with those minted by the Satavahanas. The extraordinary development of architecture especially Buddhist in Amravati and Nagarjunakonda speaks of the generous grants made by the merchants of the region involved in trade with South-East Asia and other parts of the world.

Even after the decline of the Roman trade, the subcontinent continued to conduct trade with various parts of the world especially because of the fact that Indian merchants driven to Southeast Asia on account of the greater demand of the Roman merchants developed commercial relations which they maintained even later. Indian settlements came up in Thailand, Cambodia, Java and Malaya. Ships from Tamralipti and Amravati were said to have sailed from Burma, Martaban and Indonesia. The south Indian ports sent vessels to Tenasserim, Trang, Straits of Malacca and Java. The Indian ships used to cross the China seas often. Besides Tamralipti, Ghantshala (on the Andhra coast) and Kadura on the eastern coast were the centres of trade of North India with Southeast Asia. The Pallavas of south India beginning with Mahendravarman I (A.D. 600-630) developed a navy and built dockyards at Mahabalipuram and Nagapattinam on the Coromandel coast.

The navy assisted in the maritime trade with Southeast Asian regions such as Kambuja (Cambodia), Champa (Annam) and Shrivijaya (Southern Malaya peninsula and Sumatra). The Pallavas extended their power to the northern part of Coromandel and conquered the territories under Iksvaku dynasty who held sway over the delta of Krishna and Godavari. The coins issued by the Pallavas, some of which were found in Kanchipuram, their head-quarters, have the bull on one side and a ship on the other which might indicate the continuation of maritime trade. Commercial boom of the eastern Andhra coast began to be replaced by the southern Coromandel under the influence of later Colas. Raja Raja Cola (A.D. 985-1014) and Rajendra Cola (1014-1044) created an environment conducive to the development of maritime trade. In fact Rajendra Cola conducted an overseas campaign against the Kingdom of Srivijaya. It is concluded by some of the historians that the campaign might have been for the protection of the Indian commercial interest from the interference of the Kingdom of Srivijaya. Cola king himself might have had his investment in trade with China which was going to be imperilled by the ruler of Srivijaya, whose intention was to keep his territory as one of the end-points of the trade so that he could get the profits. The ships from South India used to pass through the seas held by the kingdom of Srivijaya to China. Hence it is argued that if the campaigns of the Cola ruler were only on account of "the desire for overseas empire, this would have been followed up with Indian colonization of the areas annexed and an attempt to conquer more of the hinterland".[13] Since such a follow-up did not take place, the Cola incursion into Southeast Asia was considered forming part of the commercial enterprise.

The role played by the merchant guilds in the maritime trade of the peninsular India during the medieval period lends support to the view that the peninsular India continued its commercial activities with foreign centres of trade uninterruptedly. Maritime trade of this region was controlled by the merchant guilds like *manigramam* and *valanjiyar*. Some guilds like *Nanadeshi* having bases in South India and Sumatra were quite rich and influential. *Ayyavole* and *manigramam* were two important merchant associations of medieval South India engaged in both long-distance and local trade. *Manigramam* was involved in the trade at Quilon on the Malabar coast. They were active at Quilon from the ninth and early tenth centuries. This is corroborated by inscriptions of Sthanu Ravi. A Syriac document also makes mention of the arrival of a community of Syrian Christians under the leadership of the Syrian fathers Mar Sapor and Mar Parut at Quilon in 823. Quilon copper plates make mention of a certain Maruvan Sapir Iso, who is identified as Maran Sabr-Isho. Sthanu Ravi record gives clear indication that Quilon had important overseas trade during the ninth and tenth centuries. In fact, the port of Quilon is frequently mentioned in the Arab works as the important port where the Arab merchants used to halt on their way to southeast Asia. The fact that signatures in Pahlavi are appended to the Quilon grant of Sthanu Ravi corroborates the commercial relations Quilon had with Persia. *Manigramam* continued to be engaged in trade and commerce in the eleventh and twelfth centuries too.

The merchant guild of *Ayyavole*, on the other hand, was not situated on the coastal region as *Manigramam* but in the central Deccan plateau at Aihole, in the present-day Hungund taluk of Bijapur District. Aihole is located in the Doab region between Krishna and Tungabadhra on the banks of the Malprabha, a tributary of the Krishna. The merchants of *Ayyavole* association had branches both in Kannada and Tamil regions. [14]

These guilds conducted trade with foreign countries. The trade with southeast Asia under these guilds during the fourteenth century was quite significant. On account of the ever increasing demand for spices especially pepper available on the western coast of India, these guilds concentrated their attention on the spice-producing areas of the Malabar coast during the fifteenth century. [15]

Marco Polo, who visited Pandyan Kingdom in A.D. 1288 and 1293, left detailed narrative of the trade of South India especially of maritime trade. As described by him, Mahabalipuram, Kaveripattinam, Shaliyur and Korkai on the east coast of India and Quilon on the west coast controlled the seaborne trade to the East and West. Siraf on the Persian Gulf was the entrepot of the westward trade reaching up to Persia and Arabia. South India exported textiles, spices, drugs, jewels, ivory, horn, ebony and camphor to China as well as to West Asia. Horses in large numbers were imported into South India from Arabia and Persia as noted by Marco Polo.

The Deccan rulers always vied with each other for the maritime outlets both on the western and on the eastern coasts for the export of the surplus of the primary and secondary sectors of production as well as the import of some items like horses from West Asia and luxury articles needed for the rulers and nobles. The chief maritime outlets of the Deccan were situated on the Konkan and Coromandel coasts. A number of ports in these two regions catered to exports and imports of the coastal towns. The foreland which depended on these centres constituted chiefly West Asia, Europe and Southeast Asian regions. The political conditions of the Deccan, especially since the establishment of Vijayanagara empire around A.D. 1336, required large number of horses for the innumerable wars of conquests. The system of *naiks* and the duty imposed on them by the Vijayanagara emperor to assist him in the battles for expansion increased the demand for horses. The eagerness to get more horses is clearly expressed in the instruction given by the emperor of Vijayanagara who asked the officials to pay the full price of a horse even if a dealer, whose horse died on the way, brought only the tail of that horse as reported by Fernão Nuniz. [16]

A large number of horses were bought by the ruler of Vijayanagara costing four hundred to six hundred *cruzados* each. It was calculated that the emperor had more than 20,000 horses. [17] The travellers like Abd-er-Razzack,[18] Nicolo Conti[19] and Athanasius Nikitin[20] describe the on-going maritime trade of Vijayanagara in particular and of the peninsular India in general. While dealing with Calicut, Abd-er-Razzak says that Calicut was a perfectly secure harbour, like Ormuz. It brought together merchants from every city and from every country. Precious articles from various maritime countries like Abyssinia, Zirbad and Zanguebar were available in abundance at Calicut. At the time of the visit of Abd-er-Razzak, it had a large number of Hindus as residents and a sizeable number of Muslims who had two mosques for the Friday prayer. A lot of Muslims were reported to have come from the Red Sea area and stayed at Calicut without any restriction. The customs-house at Calicut used to look after the safety and security of the cargo as well as the rich merchants who visited the port of Calicut for the sake of trade and commerce. The freedom enjoyed by all those ships and merchants that came to Calicut was highly appreciated by Abd-er-Razzak. Vessels laden with pepper regularly left Calicut for Mocha. He found Vijayanagara city filled with various kinds of merchants and traders. Public sale of pearls, rubies, emeralds and diamonds in the city caught his attention. [21] By 1370 Madurai region, from where pearls were brought to Vijayanagara city, was conquered by the ruler of Vijayanagara empire.

Hasan Gangu (1347-1358), the Turkish governor of the Deccan under the Delhi sultanate, laid the foundation of the Bahamani Kingdom. As horses in large number were required for the kingdom, his successors developed better contacts with West Asia. Goa, which was a great centre of the import of horses from West Asia, was brought under the Bahamanis. Sultan Firuz Shah Bahamani (1397-1422) developed Chaul and Dabhol as centres of trade with Persian Gulf and Red Sea. Harihara II (1377-1406) wrested Belgaum and Goa from the Bahamanis with a view to conducting active trade with West Asia chiefly in horses. Conscious of the importance of Goa and Belgaum in the trade in horses, Khwaja Mahmud Gawan, the minister of the Bahamanis, captured the former in A.D. 1472 and the latter in 1473 from the Vijayanagara rulers.

The coastal towns of the Konkan were used for the export of diamonds, pearls and semi-precious stones available in various parts of the Deccan, especially from the region of Krishna-Godavari delta for which the rulers of Vijayanagara and Bahamanis fought unceasingly.

Bhatkal on the Canara coast was an important port through which horses from Ormuz were brought to the kingdom of Vijayanagara till the Portuguese established their sway over Goa and diverted the horses from Bhatkal.[22] A host of Muslim merchants were engaged in trade in this port city in the first decade of the sixteenth century as described by Ludovico di Varthema of Bologna.[23] Honawar (Onor) was another port which also served as an outlet for the Deccan. The local ruler, subject to the king of Vijayanagara, had several ships for surveillance of the port.

Diamonds, as well as precious and semi-precious stones available in the city of Vijayanagara attracted several merchants from far and wide. There were several diamond mines in the vicinity of the headquarters of Vijayanagara as well as in other parts of the Deccan. Besides the diamonds locally available, precious stones of different types from Pegu and Ceylon were brought to the city of Vijayanagara for sale. Pearls and seedpearls from Ormuz and Kayal situated in the neighbourhood of modern Tirunelveli were also taken to Vijayanagara. In fact a large variety of precious stones were in circulation in this town rather than anywhere else. Besides copper, quicksilver, vermilion, saffron, rose-water, great store of opium, sandalwood, aloeswood, camphor, musk and scented materials were also purchased by the foreign merchants from Vijayanagara. Similarly, pepper from Malabar was made available in the city of Vijayanagara for export.[24]

The economies of the Indian Ocean and the Mediterranean united in the Hellenistic times were split later into two rival worlds, the Roman-Byzantine and the Parthian-Sasanian according to some historians. These were again reunited by the Muslim conquest into a vast economic unit. "The centre of the Muslim world is located in the Isthmus region bounded by the Persian Gulf, the Red Sea, the Mediterranean, the Black Sea and the Caspian Sea."[25]

The aromatic goods of India, teak wood, peacock, fine textiles and other oriental curiosities found their way to the distant parts of Europe much prior to the rise of Islam through West Asian regions especially Red Sea and Persian Gulf. After a setback for a couple of centuries in this relation on account of political instability, the flow of commodities was revived in the wake of the domination of Islam over some parts of Africa and West Asia. The crusades provided a suitable opportunity to the Europeans for better appreciation of the oriental goods which subsequently enhanced in Europe the demand for spices and other items from the East. Merchants from Mocha, Turkey, Egypt, Persia and Ethiopia were among the important foreign merchants involved in the trade of pepper, spices and other commodities available on the western coast of India and supplied them to the Mediterranean ports from where the European marts received their share. [26] Moreover, there were merchants from Tunis at Calicut who were able to converse in Castilian and Genoese languages with the Portuguese under Vasco da Gama in 1498. [27]

The subcontinent of India had very active trade with China. Export of cotton fabrics, spices and drugs to China had already reached high watermark during the Sung Dynasty towards the end of the twelfth century. [28] The ports of Canton and Ch'uan-Chou flourished as the most important havens of foreign trade. Even when the southeastern and southern provinces of China passed into the sway of Mongols since 1227, external trade went on unaltered and perhaps with more vigour. A few more ports such as K'ingyuan (Ning-po), Shang-hai, and Kan-ju were also opened to foreign trade. In 1296 an order prohibiting exportation of gold and silver was issued along with the order restricting the trade with Quilon and Pantalayani on the Malabar coast. [29] This restriction indicates very clearly the fact that the ports on the Malabar coast had very active trade relations with China in the thirteenth century. The fourteenth century Chinese reports mention Quilon on the western coast of India having very flourishing trade. This was considered a principal port of all the lands of the western ocean by them. It was reported that a gold coin, *tangka* by name, was used in trade. Pepper, dry betel-nuts, jackfruit and coloured cotton stuffs were purchased by the Chinese from this port. Sapan-wood, frankincense, pearls, corals, butter and jasmine flowers were brought to Quilon. Cochin, another port north of Quilon, had also active trade in the fifteenth century as reported by the contemporary Chinese writers. Gold coin called *panam* was being used in the transactions at Cochin. Pepper was available in abundance at Cochin as reported by them. Kayamkulam, a small harbour between Quilon and

Cochin, had pepper in great quantity for export as noticed by the Chinese traders.

Under the reign of the third emperor Yung-lo (1402-24) attempts were made to establish commercial relations with the countries bordering on the Indian Ocean. A number of seaborne expeditions were sent between 1404 and 1433. The influential and Grand Eunuch Cheng Ho organised the first fleet from Ch'ang-lo in Fukien and reached Calicut. In fact this fleet consisted of sixty-two ships carrying 28,000 men. The enormous Chinese junks, that used to go up to the Persian gulf, began to frequent only the Malabar ports since the fourteenth century. [30] The Chinese merchants had a factory of their own at Calicut in the first quarter of the fifteenth century. [31] Gold coins called *panam* were used in Calicut for transactions. Large volume of pepper, coconut, ginger, mustard, coriander and melons were reported to be exchanged at Calicut. [32] It was called *Cina cota* in the local language. [33] The Chinese vessels between twenty and twenty-five in number used to visit Calicut with fine linen-cloth and brasswares and took spices in return till the first quarter of the fifteenth century. [34] But till the rise of the port of Calicut to such an importance, the main port visited by the Chinese junks was Quilon and frequent missions were exchanged between the king of Quilon and the emperor of China. [35] The works of Wang Ta-yuan (*Tao i chih lio* dated 1349), Ma Huan (*Ying yai shang lan* dated 1425-1432), Fei Hein (*Hsing ch'a shong lan* dated 1436) and Huang Shang-ts'eng (*Hsi yang chao kung tien lu* dated 1520) make mention of the Chinese trade conducted on the Malabar coast. The Chinese names of several items used in Malabar such as *cinacatti, cinavala* and *cinavedi* speak for the long Chinese contacts with the Malabar coast.

The voyages were stopped in 1433. There are indications that the Chinese, who had strong commercial relations with Calicut, withdrew from there in the first half of the fifteenth century because of some outrages committed by the people of the Zamorin. After taking revenge upon Calicut, they did not return to that port any more and shifted their activities to Nagapattinam on the eastern coast of India, according to the report given by a writer of the first decade of the sixteenth century. The new haven visited by the Chinese traders was in the Kingdom of Vijayanagara.[36] But there is no indication for the visit of the Chinese traders to the port of Calicut nor to the regions of the Bay of Bengal after 1439.[37] This state of affairs was after the abandonment of the expeditions in 1433 and on account of the attitude of the Ming Emperors who determined to close China's sea-coasts to foreign visitors placed an embargo on the trade of Chinese merchants to overseas regions.

A group of merchants named Al-Karimi were actively involved in the trade in spices with the Malabar coast. The Cairo Genizah papers shed considerable light on the long distance trade conducted by a community of merchants during the eleventh and twelfth centuries as well as on the economic organisation of the "Karim". The merchants of this organisation based on the Red Sea area are mentioned in the Egyptian records as having commercial relations with Indian Ocean regions. The important items purchased by them from India consisted of spices. It is held by some scholars that in the twelfth century the Karim was neither a guild of merchants nor a particular branch of international trade, but a kind of annual convoy or a seaborne caravan. They had very active trade relations with Calicut.[38] A few of the merchants from Cairo had settled down in Cambay and from there they came to the Malabar coast for trade.[39] This group from Cairo must have been undoubtedly the Al-Karimi merchants who wielded extraordinary influence in the period between the twelfth and the fifteenth centuries on the spice trade and established so to speak some sort of a monopoly over the trade between Yemen and Cairo where they had their headquarters.[40] Qüs, near Cairo, was in fact the entrepot of the Indian commodities in which the Karimis traded.[41] Ali Ibn Muhammad Kalyubi who died in 1492 was one of the rich Karimi merchants who had trade with Calicut in the second part of the fifteenth century.[42]

The Karimi merchants constituted an "organisation or corporation, an organised body of merchants closely knit together, a collective group of men who associated themselves for the pursuit of a common commercial goal—trade in pepper and spices."[43] The measures taken by Sultan Barsbay in the fifteenth century to establish a state monopoly over the spice trade in the Mamluk Egypt dealt a death-blow on the Karimi merchants and consequently a number of them left for India and settled down here. [44] When the fleet of Cabral reached Calicut, there were merchants from the Mamluk Egypt doing business in Calicut. [45]

Apart from the merchants of this organisation, there were other foreign merchants who traded in pepper and other spices available on the western coast of India prior to the arrival of the Portuguese. Merchants from Mocha, Tenasserim, Pegu, Ceylon, Turkey, Egypt, Persia and Ethiopia were among the foreign merchants who frequented the port of Calicut, the most important centre of trade on the western coast of India during the fourteenth and the fifteenth centuries. [46]

Another important group of merchants who made fortunes out of trade in spice with the Malabar coast was the Italians of Genoa and Venice, the latter being the most prominent among them. Though they had no direct relation with the Malabar coast, they purchased these oriental commodities at the hands of the Muslim merchants at Beirut, Alleppo, Alexandria and Constantinople to distribute them to the various parts of Europe. The consternation caused by the discovery of the direct sea-route by the Portuguese and the establishment of Portuguese trade on the Malabar coast knew no bounds and the Venetians watched doggedly the developments in the East hoping that the Portuguese trade would not continue. [47] Their trade in spices was the nourishment and sustenance of the Republic of Venice. [48] Venice itself was a very important commercial centre and its prominence went on increasing ever since the mortal remains of St. Mark were transferred from Egypt to Venice in the ninth century. [49] They had established themselves in Constantinople and other important places where they could trade in spices and other oriental commodities. When Constantinople was conquered by the Turks under Mohammed II in 1453, they intensified their activities in Alexandria and Cairo even outdoing the competing Genoese. They considered the spice trade one of the major branches of the international trade and became the sole suppliers of these and other Indian commodities to the central and eastern Europe.[50] Though the Florentine, Genoese, and Catalan merchants had colonies in Alexandria, Damascus and other centres of Levantine trade, and had some part in the spice trade, they were not parties to be reckoned with in comparison with the Venetian traders and their major role in the trade of oriental commodities.

Thus the people from all over the world interested in trade had their share in the trade on the Malabar coast and nobody claimed or fought for any sort of monopoly over it. The participants were not in the name of any government; they did business in their individual or collective capacity. It is understandable that respective governments had taken measures to afford security to the traders while they were in the territories concerned. Thus the Karimi merchants in Egypt had sometimes convoys from the government to protect their ships laden with merchandise.[51] In Calicut too, whenever a few merchants came to take in cargo, the king used to appoint a Nair to protect them, and a *chatim* clerk to keep the accounts and a broker to arrange the needed commodities.[52] This sort of a treatment was given to all the foreign merchants without any preference or discrimination.

Al-Karimi merchants were chiefly instrumental in reaching the commodities of the Orient especially the spices and pepper produced in the Indian subcontinent to the Mediterranean ports from where they were taken to various parts of Europe.[53]

The commodities from India were taken to several parts of the world through different routes. One could distinguish a land route and two sea-routes used since the time of crusades to carry the oriental commodities to Europe, especially to the Western Europe.[54] The land route from India took the direction of the areas of Persian Gulf, Bassorah, Baghdad, Aleppo and then through the regions of the gulf of Alexandretta (Iskenderum), Ankara, Constantinople (Istambul) and from there to other parts of Europe. But, since the land route was liable to extraordinary risks on account of political reasons and piracy, the sea-routes were preferred and they became more important in course of time.

The main sea-routes that were used for the purposes of trade in the oriental commodities before the arrival of the Portuguese were two: one through the Persian Gulf and the other through the Red Sea. Pepper, ginger and various other oriental commodities were shipped to Ormuz from the Malabar coast and things needed for exchange in that area were left there. Then the rest of the commodities were shipped to Bassorah on the bank of the Euphrates whence a part was transported by caravans to Armenia, Trebizonda and Tartaria and the other to the cities of Aleppo, Damascus and finally to Beirut on the Mediterranean. The Venetians,[55] Genoese and Catalans who were the masters of trade in spices purchased the commodities from this city and carried them to other parts of Europe for resale.[56] In certain cases, the merchants from Germany, Hungary, Flanders, France and other parts beyond the Alps went to Venice to purchase the spices.[57]

The other route through the Red Sea had occupied a more important place in the period before the arrival of the Portuguese. The commodities from Calicut and other ports on the Malabar coast were taken to Aden on the Red Sea side and from there to Djeda (Jeddah) near Mecca.[58] The merchants paid customs duties in Jedda to the Sultan and then the commodities were loaded in smaller vessels to be shipped to al-Tur near mount Santa Catharina, otherwise called Suez[59] and the customs duties were paid here too. Then by means of camels hired at four *crusados* each the merchandise was transported to Cairo[60] where again taxes were paid to the Sultan. Sometimes, the Karimi merchants who dominated the spice trade between the twelfth and fifteenth centuries in the area from Aden to Cairo, their headquarters, made use of another shorter route. Instead of taking the cargo to Suez, they stopped at Qusair on the Egyptian side of Red Sea and from there by means of camels and slaves the commodities were transported to Qüs, an important commercial centre of Egypt next to Cairo at that time.[61] Then the merchandise was sent to Cairo through the Nile in barques. This diversion from Qusair reduced duration of transport by land.

From Cairo the commodities were taken in barques through the Nile to Alexandria, with a halt at Rossetta[62] where customs duties were paid to the Sultan once more. Then the camels carried the things from Rossetta to Alexandria where the spices were sold to the

European merchants from Venice,[63] Genoa, Marseilles and Barcelona. From Venice the merchandise found its way to Germany, Flanders, France, Hungary and so on as noted above.[64] The Sultan of Egypt was reported to have received 600,000 *crusados* every year by way of customs duties levied from the traders in spices.[65] So it is easy to understand the exorbitant prices of these commodities in Venice and upon re-export, in other parts of Europe.

The merchants on the Malabar coast made use of the sea-route to reach Cambay in the North, Ceylon, Maldive Islands, Pulicat on the Coromandel coast and the ports of Orissa. They used *catures* and *tones*[66] to ship the merchandise to these ports. At the end of the fifteenth century about 400 cargo boats were found engaged in trade.[67] Keeled ships with a capacity of one thousand to one thousand and two hundred *bhars* were built in Calicut during the days of its prosperity. They were constructed without any nails but only with thread and coir. At least fifteen of these ships were used to take spices every year during the monsoon to the Red Sea, Aden and Mecca.[68] The merchants from the Malabar coast navigated generally for eight months a year, i.e. from September to the end of April,[69] with their merchandise to various places.

There were also land routes from the Malabar coast to the Coromandel through which spices were taken and rice was brought back to Malabar. The commodities from the Malabar coast were sent on the back of bulls through Aryankavu pass near Punalur in the south and through Kanjirappilly, to the Coromandel coast.[70]

Various sorts of spices and other commodities were collected by the merchants from the important entrepots on the Malabar coast, either directly from the cultivators or from the local merchants. Several merchants frequented the port of Cannanore to purchase pepper, ginger, cardamom, myrobalans, canafistula, zerumba and zedoary.[71] The merchants from Cannanore themselves traded with Cambay, Ormuz, Coromandel, Dabhol, Chaul, Banda, Goa, Ceylon and the Maldives.[72] The other ports like Nileshwaram, Baliapattam, Dharmadam and Madayi which belonged to the kingdom of Cannanore were not so important as the port of Cannanore itself.[73] The next entreport to the south of Cannanore was Calicut which, according to the Chinese writers of the fourteenth century, was the "most important of all the maritime centres of trade. . ." and "principal port of the Western Ocean".[74] "Almost all of India was said to be coming together in Calicut."[75] It was reported to be bigger than Lisbon towards the end of the fifteenth century.[76] Merchants from various nations had established their factories there since it was the greatest entrepot where spices produced in Malabar and those brought from the Southeast Asian countries were in abundance.[77] Oriental commodities flowed from here to all parts of the world through different routes.[78] Thus the port of Calicut by the end of the fifteenth century, when Vasco da Gama landed there, occupied an unparalleled position on the Malabar coast in the matter of trade.[79] It was compared to Bruges in Flanders by Dom Manuel I in his letter to Queen Isabella of Castile, his mother-in-law,[80] and to Venice in Italy.[81]

Cranganore lay further south of Calicut. It was well known to the merchants of the Middle East and the whole of Europe in the past though by the time the Portuguese reached India, it was in a decadent state on account of the emergence of other ports like Cochin, Calicut and Quilon. However, it was one of the centres from where coconuts and pepper were exported to Cairo, Persia, Syria and other places[82] and fairly good trade was being conducted there. The port of Cochin which had an abundant supply of pepper[83] is situated further south on the same coast. Pepper was brought from the interior parts to the port for the merchants coming to purchase it.[84] Kayamkulam, still further south of Cochin, supplied pepper, coconuts, betelnuts and liu fish to the merchants.[85] A certain amount of trade was conducted here by the end of the fifteenth century.[86] Quilon, to the south of Kayamkulam, furnished dry betelnuts, coloured cotton stuffs, sapan-wood, frankincense, pearls, coral, butter and jasmine flowers all of which were brought to Quilon which acted as an entrepot.[87] The native products of Quilon offered for sale were coconuts, liu fish, betelnuts and pepper. Though Quilon occupied an important place in trade especially with China before the rise of Cochin and Calicut, it was not in a flourishing condition when the Portuguese arrived on the Malabar coast.

Thus it is evident that Cochin was not a port of any importance till the end of the fifteenth century as far as trade in spices and pepper with the West was concerned. In fact Calicut was the chief port for the export of these items. Quilon, Kayamkulam, Cranganore and Cannanore served as satelite ports of supply.

Gujarat on the north western coast of India was another important region which had international trade and commerce during the period prior to the arrival of the Portuguese. It had well-established long-distance trade with Malacca in the Southeast Asian regions and with the eastern coast of Africa as well as the centres of trade in the Persian Gulf and the Red Sea areas at the time when Vasco da Gama, the Admiral of the Indian Ocean, reached the western coast of India. When he landed at Moçambique in 1498, he came across a number of merchants from Gujarat selling cloths, cloves, pepper, ginger, pearls, silver rings, and rubies. Similarly, he met several Gujarati merchants who resided in Melinde and conducted trade.[88] One of the Gujarati merchants at Melinde met Vasco da Gama and offered to supply whatever spices the Portuguese wanted. But the ruler of Melinde made it very clear to him that Gujarat did not produce the spices, but it was only a centre of transit trade where pepper and other spices from Calicut were available. It was added by the same ruler that because of an arrangement of this sort, spices supplied by the Gujaratis were dearer than those available at Calicut.[89]

Khambath, currently known as Cambay, was considered the metropolitan port-city of the kingdom of Gujarat which was known to the Portuguese as kingdom of Cambay or Cambaya from the name of the town of Cambay or Khambath.[90] The close commercial link of Khambat with Eden in the west and Malacca in the east was graphically described by the Portuguese writers of the first quarter of the sixteenth century.[91] Khambath was the emporium par excellence on the coastal Gujarat in the international seaborne trade connecting Malacca with Alexandria through Calicut, Eden, Jeddah and Cairo during the period prior to the establishment of direct maritime trade via Cape of Good Hope at the turn of the sixteenth century.

Khambath, as noted above, was the most important emporium of Gujarat prior to the arrival of the Portuguese. It was a halting place and an important entrepot in the East-West axis of the international maritime trade connecting Malacca with Cairo. Malacca, which is located at the limit of the monsoons, could not be reached by the merchants from Cairo and other ports of the Red Sea as well as Perisan Gulf areas in a single monsoon. The ports of Gujarat especially Khambath provided the best place for the merchants from the west to halt and do business. It was reported by a contemporary writer that the city of Khambath itself sent one ship every year to Malacca with a cargo of 70,000 to 80,000 *cruzados* during the first quarter of the sixteenth century. [92] Malik Gopi, one of the ministers of Muzaffar Shah II of Gujarat, was known to the Portuguese as the chief merchant of this city. Several ships laden with commodities sailed from Khambath to Eden, Ormuz, the regions of the Deccan, Goa, Bhatkal, all over Malabar, Ceylon, Bengal, Pegu, Siam, Pedir, and Pase besides Malacca. It was estimated that there were a thousand Gujarati merchants in Malacca besides four or five thousand Gujarati seamen who frequented Malacca regularly. They had their *shabandar* who was their chief and looked after their well-being. [93] The relation between Malacca and Khambath was such that the contemporary Portuguese writer concluded that Malacca could not live without Khambath and Khambath without Malacca. He reiterated saying that "if Cambay were cut off from trading with Malacca, it could not live, for it would have no outlet for its merchandise". [94] This statement of Pires regarding the dependence of Khambath on Malacca could be considered an exaggeration and paradoxical since Pires himself speaks of other important outlets for the port-town. Perhaps, as K. N. Chaudhuri concludes, the dependence of Malacca on Khambath was more intense than that of Khambath on Malacca. [95]

Khambath held such an important position not only because it was just a centre of transit trade but also because it provided a variety of commodities produced in Gujarat. Silk and cotton textiles of different kinds, carnelians, indigo, lac, pachak, catechu, wormwood, tincal, cotton, soap, dressed hides, leather, honey, wax, wheat, barley, millet, sesame-oil, rice, butter, meat and coarse pottery which were brought from various parts of Gujarat and the neighbouring countries were exported from here to various parts of the world till the first quarter of the sixteenth century. [96] Cloves, mace, nutmeg, sandalwood, seed-pearls, some porcelain, musk, lignaloes, gold, white silk, tin, damask, coloured silks, and birds were in return taken to Khambath after paying 6 per cent customs duties. [97] Before the channel of Malacca was discovered, the Gujaratis used to trade with Java going round the southern part of the island of Sumatra, and also collecting the products of Moluccas from Grisee.

The merchants from Khambath conducted trade with the regions of the Deccan, Goa, and Malabar coast. The importance of the Gujarati merchants in trade with Malabar is attested by the Portuguese writers who spoke about the appointment of Gujarati merchants of Calicut to train the newly arrived Portuguese merchants in commercial practices in 1500 by the Zamorin of Calicut.

The commercial relations Khambath had with the west till the first decade of the sixteenth century were equally important as those with the south and the southeastern parts. Raisins, opium, rosewater, gold, silver and horses brought to Eden from Zeila and Barbera and the islands of Suakin and Arabia were imported into Khambath from Eden. The merchants from Cairo took their commodities to Tor and from there to Jeddah and further to Eden and subsequently to Khambath. During their halt at Khambath, those items that had great demand and fetched good prices were sold and the rest were taken to Malacca. The merchandises brought from Italy, Greece and Damascus to Cairo such as arms, scarlet-in- grain, coloured woollen cloths, coral, copper, quicksilver, vermilion, nails, silver, glass and other beads and golden glassware were brought to Khambath by these merchants. Opium, rosewater and liquid storax from Mecca were imported into Khambath by the merchants coming from there. Those of Eden brought great quantity of opium, raisins, madder, indigo, rosewater, silver, seed-pearls and other dyes to Khambath. [98] Horses, silver, gold, silk, alum, vitriol, and seed-pearls were imported into Khambath from Ormuz. In return,

Khambath provided rice, wheat, soap, indigo, butter, oils, carnelians, coarse pottery, cloths of all kinds for trade with Zeila, Barbera, Socotra, Kilwa, Malindi, Mogadishu and other places in Arabia. The commodities brought to Khambath from Malacca such as cloves, nutmeg, mace, sandalwood, brazilwood, silks, seed-pearls, musk, and porcelain were also sent to the west either in the ships belonging to the Gujaratis or in those of the merchants from there.[99]

A glance at the composition of commodities of export and import in the period prior to the arrival of the Portuguese will be of relevance to assess the role of copper furnished by the German merchant financiers in the sixteenth century to the Portuguese for the conduct of trade with India.

Commodities of various sorts were involved in the international maritime trade of India till the end of the fifteenth century. The merchants coming to Malabar coast purchased pepper, ginger, cinnamon, cardamoms, myrabolans, tamarind, canafistula, precious stones of every kind, seed-pearls, musk, amber, rhubarb, aloes-wood, cotton, sealing wax, jewels, almiscar, benzoim, incence, silk-clothes, preserves, cloves, nutmegs, mace, sandalwood, brazilwood, porcelains and a number of various other products. [100] All these items were not produced in Malabar, but brought here from other places like Malacca, Ceylon, Pegu and so on. Calicut served as a great entrepot. [101] One could add coconuts, copra, coconut oil, betel, betelnut, jaggery (palm sugar), arecanuts and coir to the list of commodities exported from the Malabar coast during this period.[102] The Chinese merchants also purchased liu fish, jasmine flowers and corals from the Malabar coast. [103]

The commodities imported into Malabar from other parts of the world were also many. Things like copper, quicksilver, vermilion, coral from the regions of the Western Mediterranean, [104] saffron, carpets, porcelaine, tin from China, [105] coloured velvets, rose-water, knives, coloured camlets, gold, silver, [106] madder, raisins, opium, scarlet-in-grain, coloured woollen cloths, glass beads, [107] brass, [108] and horses[109] were imported into Malabar by various merchants with the idea of purchasing spices from here. The Venetians sent damask, glass-wares and coral among other items via Alexandria and the middle eastern ports. [110] Horses in large numbers were imported from Persia to Cannanore to be taken to Vijayanagara and other kingdoms of South India. [111] A horse in the early sixteenth century cost 800 *pardaos* and each *pardao* consisted of 335 *reis.* [112] The king of Cannanore got twenty-five ducats for every horse as customs duties. [113] Rice too was imported to Malabar from Goa and Vijayanagara for the area between Manjeswaram and Tanore, and from Kalinga (Orissa) via Coromandel for the area south of Tanore. [114] The people of Quilon area depended on the rice brought from Orissa for their food. [115] The Chinese merchants imported into Malabar gold, silver, copper, ironwares, coloured satins, white silk, cotton stuff, blue and white porcelaine, beads, musk, quicksilver, camphor, black tassels, cardamoms and cloves. [116]

It can thus be concluded that the Indian subcontinent had a very flourishing trade at the end of the fifteenth century when the Portuguese under the leadership of Vasco da Gama reached the port of Calicut. The Indian Ocean regions were opened to everyone interested in trade and commerce and there was no political power which asserted any sort of monopoly and restricted the movement of merchant marines. In fact, the rulers of the subcontinent of India encouraged merchants from any part of the world to come and conduct trade with various parts of the country. We find that there was a continuity in the external trade which flourished from the prehistoric period till the pre-modern period or late medieval period of Indian history. It is also worth noting that the trade that was in vogue in the fifteenth century was the long-distance trade involving bulk goods meant for daily consumption. It cannot be stated that the trade was solely in items of luxury but it was of long haul. Moreover, it is unhistorical to classify the merchants of this period as pedlars since they were having large investments in long-distance trade and were dealing in bulk goods. In fact, there was a very systematic trade network during this period comprising distant parts of the world like Malacca in the southeast and Cairo in the west.

NOTES AND REFERENCES

1. J. C. Van Leur, *Indonesian Trade and Society—Essays in Asian Social and Economic History,* The Hague, 1955, passim.
2. Niels Steensgaard, *The Asian Trade Revolution of the Seventeenth Century: The East India Companies and the Decline of the Caravan Trade*, London, 1974, p. 114.
3. Immanuel Wallerstein, *The Modern World System*, New York, 1974, pp. 16, 102.
4. K. N. Chaudhuri, *Asia before Europe: Economy and Civilisation of the Indian Ocean from the Rise of Islam to 1750*, Cambridge, Cambridge University Press, 1990, p. 384.
5. Maurice Lombard writes about the centre of the Muslim world: "It was therefore set at the intersection of the two major economic units: the Indian Ocean area and the Mediterranean area. These two territories, united in Hellenestic times but later split into two rival worlds, the Roman-Byzantine and the Parthian-Sasanian, were now reunited by the Muslim conquest, so as to form a new, vast territory which was economically one." *The Golden Age of Islam*, trans. J. Spencer, Amsterdam, 1975, pp. 9-10.
6. K. N. Chaudhuri, *op. cit.*, p. 387. On the Emporia trade and the East-West axis connecting Malacca with Venice in the long-distance trade, ref. K. N. Chaudhuri, *Trade and Civilisation in the Indian Ocean: An Economic History from the Rise of Islam to 1750,* Delhi, 1985, pp. 98-118.
7. Frank Perlin, "Proto-Industrialisation and Pre-Colonial South Asia", *Past and Present*, No. 98 (1983), p. 33.
8. For identification of Dilmun with Baharain, ref. S. N. Kramer, "Dilmun, the Land of the Living", *Bulletin of the American School of Oriental Research*, No. 96 (1944), pp. 18-28; P. B. Cornwall, "On the Location of Dilmun", *Bulletin of the American School of Oriental Research*, No. 103 (1946), pp. 3-11; P. B. Cornwall, "Two Letters from Dilmun", *Journal of Cuneiform Studies*, No. 6 (1952), pp. 137-145; G. Bibby, "According to the standard of Dilmun", *Kuml*, No. 20 (1970), pp. 349-53. For a detailed study of the external trade of the Harappan civilization, ref. Dilip K. Chakrabarti, *The External Trade of the Indus Civilization*, Delhi, 1990.
9. The date of the composition of the *Periplus of the Erythraean Sea* is fixed as A.D. 60. The author must be an Egyptian Greek, a merchant active in trade who personally made the voyage to India. Ref. Wilfred H. Schoff, transl., *The Periplus of the Erythaean Sea: Travel and Trade in the Indian Ocean by a Merchant of the First Century*, New Delhi, 2nd edition, 1974.
10. For details about Kaveripumpattinam, ref. Natana Kasinathan, ed., *Seminar on Marine Archaeology*, Madras, 1992.
11. For further information on Roman contacts ref. Wheeler, Krishna Deva and Ghosh, *Ancient India*, No. 2, 1946; E. H. Warmington, *The Commerce*

between the Roman Empire and India, Cambridge, 1928, Vimla Begley and Richard Daniel de Puma, eds., *Rome and India: The Ancient Sea Trade*, Wisconsin, 1991. Articles by Vimla Begley, "New Investigations at the Port of Arikamedu", *Journal of Roman Archaeology*, Vol. 6, 1993, pp. 93-108; Mortimer Wheeler, *Rome beyond the Imperial Frontiers*, London, 1954; P. Z. Pattabiramin, *Les fouilles d'Arikamedou (Podouke)*, Pondicherry, Paris, 1946, J. M. and G. Casal, *Site urbain et sites funéraires des environs de Pondichéry*, Paris, 1956; Fr. L. Faucheux, *Une vieille cite indienne pres de Pondichery: Viropatnam*, Pondicherry, 1945.

12. Vimla Begley, "New Investigations at the Port of Arikamedu", *Journal of Roman Archaelogy*, Vol. 6, 1993, Michigan, pp. 93-107.
13. Romila Thapar, *A History of India*, Vol. 1, Penguin, 1972, pp. 196-197.
14. Meera Abraham, *Two Medieval Merchant Guilds of South India*, New Delhi, 1988, pp. 13-53.
15. *Ibid.*, pp. 66ff.
16. Vasundhara Filliozat, *The Vijayanagar Empire as seen by Domingos Paes and Fernão Nuniz*, New Delhi, 1977, pp. 87-88.
17. João de Barros, *op. cit.*, Decada II, part 1, Lisboa, 1977, p. 210; Ludovico di Varthema, *The Itinerary of Ludovico di Varhema of Bologna from 1502-1508*, London, 1928, p. 51.
18. He visited Vijayanagara in 1443; ref. R. H. Major, ed., *India in the Fifteenth Century*, London, 1857, pp. 1-49.
19. R. H. Major, *op. cit.*, pp. 3-39. He visited Vijayanagara in 1420.
20. *Ibid.*, pp. 3-32. He visited Vijayanagara in 1470.
21. *Ibid.*, pp. 13-24.
22. Duarte Barbosa, *The Book of Duarte Barbosa*, Vol. 1, New Delhi, 1989 (reprint), p. 18; Tomé Pires, *The Suma Oriental of Tomé Pires*, Vol. 1, New Delhi, 1990 (reprint), pp. 61-62.
23. Ludovico di Varthema, *op. cit.*, p. 49.
24. Barbosa, *op. cit.*, Vol. 1, pp. 202-203.
25. K. N. Chaudhuri, *Asia before Europe*, p. 385.
26. Montalbodo, *op. cit.*, p. 94; Varthema, *op. cit.*, p. 151; Prospero Peragallo, *op. cit.*, p. 31.
27. Damião Peres, ed., *Diario da Viagem de Vasco da Gama*, Vol. 1, Porto, 1945, p. 59.
28. W. W. Rockhill, "Notes on the Relations and Trade of China with the Eastern Archipelago and the Coast of the Indian Ocean during the Fourteenth Century" in *T'oung Pao*, Vol. XV, Leiden, 1914, p. 419.
29. *Ibid.*, p. 425.
30. Conde de Ficalho, *Viagens de Pedro da Covilham*, Lisbon, 1898, p. 89.
31. Montalbodo, *op. cit.*, p. 162.
32. *Ibid.*, pp. 447-460.
33. Garcia da Orta, *Coloquios dos Simples e Drogas da India*, Vol. I, Lisboa, 1891, p. 205.

34. Montalbodo, *op. cit.*, p. 71.
35. W. W. Rockhill, *op. cit.*, pp. 430-443.
36. Antony Vallavanthara, *India in 1500 A.D. —The Narratives of Joseph the Indian*, Mannanam, 1984, p. 199.
37. Haraprasad Ray, "An Enquiry into the Presence of the Chinese in South and Southeast Asia after the Voyages of Zheng He in Early Fifteenth Century" in K. S. Mathew, ed., *Mariners, Merchants and Oceans*, New Delhi, 1995, pp. 97-110.
38. S. D. Goitein, "New Light on the Beginnings of the Karim Merchants" in *Journal of the Economic and Social History of the Orient*, Vol. I, p. 181; K. N. Chaudhuri, *Trade and Civilization in the Indian Ocean*, pp. 59-60.
39. Tomé Pires, *op. cit.*, pp. 41-42.
40. Walter J. Fischel, "The Spice Trade in Mamluk Egypt" in *Journal of the Economic and Social History of the Orient,* Vol. I, Leiden, 1958, pp. 162-163.
41. Walter J. Fischel, "Über die Gruppe der Karimi-Kaufleute" in *Analecta Orientalia*, No. 14, Studia Arabica, Rome, 1937, p. 74.
42. Gaston Wiet, "Les Marchands D'Epices sous les Sultans Mamlouks" in *Cahiers D'Histoire Egyptienne*, Serie VII, Fasc. 1, Cairo, 1955, p. 128.
43. Walter J. Fischel, "The Spice Trade in Mamluk Egypt", *op. cit.*, p. 165. For further details regarding the nature of the Karimis and the true composition of the group one could consult the following studies: Gaston Wiet, *op. cit.*, pp. 81-135, wherein the writer gives about forty-six Karimi merchants among other details regarding their activities; E. Ashtor, "The Karimi Merchants" in *Journal of the Royal Asiatic Society of Great Britain and Ireland,* London, 1956, pp. 45-46, wherein he proves that people other than Muslims were included in the group called "karimi"; S. D. Goitein, *op. cit.*, pp. 175-183, wherein the writer draws on the Cairo Geniza documents. See also Ibn Iyas, *Journal d'un Bourgeois du Caire,* tanslt. by Gaston Wiet, Paris, 1955.
44. Eliyashu Ashtor, "The Venetian Supremacy in Levantine Trade: Monopoly or Pre-colonialism?" in *The Journal of European Economic History,* Vol. 3, No. 1, Rome, 1974, pp. 21, 27.
45. Montalbodo, *op. cit.*, p. 94.
46. *Ibid.*, Varthema, *op. cit.*, p. 151; Prospero Peragallo, *op. cit.*, p. 31.
47. Girolamo Priuli, *I Diarii di Girolamo Priuli*, Vol. II, pp. 156, 174, 187.
48. *Ibid.*, pp. 306-307.
49. Ernst Samhaber, *Merchants Make History*, London, 1963, p. 104.
50. Eliyashu Ashtor, "The Venetian Supremacy in Levantine Trade", *op. cit.*, p. 17.
51. E. Astor, "The Karimi Merchants", *op. cit.*, p. 52.
52. Barbosa, *op. cit.*, Vol. II, p. 77.
53. A. H. Lyber, "The Ottoman Turks and the Routes of the Oriental Trade" in *The English Historical Review*, No. CXX, October 1915, p. 579.

54. A. H. Lybyer, *op. cit.*, p. 579.
55. Girolamo Priuli, p. 238.
56. João de Barros, *op. cit.*, Decada I, parte II, pp. 177-178.
57. Girolamo Priuli, *op. cit.*, Vol. II, p. 156.
58. Damião Peres, Diario. . ., *op. cit.*, p. 98; Montalbodo, *op. cit.*, p. 94.
59. Barros, *op. cit.*, Decada I, Parte II, p. 178.
60. Damião Peres, *Diario. . .*, *op. cit.*, p. 101.
61. W. J. Fischel, "The Spice Trade. . . ", *op. cit.*, pp. 162-163.
62. Damião Peres, *Diario. . .*, *op. cit.*, p. 101.
63. Fernão Lopes de Castanheda, *Historia de Descobrimento e Conquista da India pelos Portugueses*, Livro II, Coimbra, 1924, pp. 318-322.
64. Barbosa, *op. cit.*, Vol. II, p. 77.
65. Damião Peres, *Diario. . .*, *op. cit.* p. 101.
66. James Hornell, "The Sailing Craft of Western India" in *The Mariner's Mirror,* Vol. 32, Cambridge, 1946, pp. 195-216.
67. Tomé Pires, *op. cit.*, pp. 75-83.
68. Barbosa, *op. cit.*, pp. 76-77.
69. Ludoviço di Varthema, *op. cit.*, p. 153; Montalbodo, *op. cit.*, p. 94.
70. F. C. Danvers, *The Portuguese in India*, Vol. I, London, 1966, p. 346; Nycolão Gomçallves, *Livro que trata das cousas da India e do Japão*, Andelino de Almeida Calado, ed., Coimbra, 1957, p. 47.
71. Barbosa, *op. cit.*, Vol. II, p. 83; Varthema, *op. cit.*, p. 124.
72. Barbosa, *op. cit.*, p. 81.
73. Tomé Pires, *op. cit.*, Vol. I, p. 77.
74. Rockhill, *op. cit.*, p. 454.
75. Montalbodo, *op. cit.*, p. 162.
76. Montalbodo, *op. cit.*, p. 68 and B. Greiff, *op. cit.*, p. 122.
77. Tomé Pires, *op. cit.*, p. 78; Archangelo Garavallense (transl.), *Itinerariu Portugallesiu e Lusitania in Indiã et inde in Occidentem et demum ad Aquilonem*, Milano, 1508, p. 38.
78. Damião Peres, *Diario. . .*, *op. cit.*, p. 98; Richard Eden, *The First Three English Books on America*, 1511-55, Birmingham, 1885, p. 20.
79. Montalbodo, *op. cit.*, p. 162; *Cronica do Descobrimento e Conquista da India pelos Portugueses*—Codice anonimo, Museu Britanico, Egerton 20901, Coimbra, 1974, p. 9.
80. W. B. Greenlee, *op. cit.*, p. 41.
81. "Copia de Uma Carta de el-Rei de Portugal enviada ao Rei de Castella acerca da viagem e successo da India", reproduced by Prospero Peragallo, *op. cit.*, p. 13.
82. Barbosa, *op. cit.*, p. 90; Tomé Pires, *op. cit.*, p. 83; Montalbodo, *op. cit.*, p. 155.
83. Rockhill, *op. cit.*, pp. 449-452.
84. Tomé Pires, *op. cit.*, p. 83.
85. Rockhill, *op. cit.*, p. 446.

86. Tomé Pires, *op. cit.*, p. 80.
87. Rockhill, *op. cit.*, p. 448.
88. Fernão Lopes de Castanheda, *op. cit.*, Livro I, pp. 17, 29.
89. Gaspar Correa, *op. cit.*, tomo 1, parte I, pp. 33-34, 57.
90. João de Barros, *op. cit.*, Decada IV, part I, pp. 533-637. For further details on Cambay ref. M. N. Pearson, *Merchants and Rulers in Gujarat*, Delhi, 1976, pp. 19-20; K. S. Mathew, *Portuguese and the Sultanate of Gujarat, 1500-1573*, Delhi, 1986, pp. 11-13.
91. "Cambay chiefly stretched out two arms, with her right arm she reaches out towards Aden and with the other towards Malacca, as the most important places to sail to, and the other places are held to be of less importance." Ref. Tomé Pires, *op. cit.*, p. 42; Surendra Gopal, *Commerce and Crafts in Gujarat: 16th and 17th Centuries*, Delhi, 1975, pp. 22-74.
92. Tomé Pires, *op. cit.*, pp. 43, 269-70. ". . . those from Cairo and Mecca and Aden cannot reach Malacca in a single monsoon, as well as the Parsees and those from Ormuz, and *Rumes*, Turks and similar peoples such as Armenians, at their own time they go to the kingdom of Gujarat, bringing large quantities of valuable merchandise; and they go to the kingdom of Gujarat to take up their companies in said ships of that land, and they take the said companies in large numbers. They also take from the said kingdoms to Cambay, merchandise of value in Gujarat from which they make much profit. Those from Cairo take their merchandise to Tor, and from Tor to Jidda, and from Jidda to Aden, and from Aden to Cambay, where they sell in the land things which are valued there, and the others they bring to Malacca, sharing as aforesaid."
93. Castanheda, *op. cit.*, Livro III, p. 133.
94. Tomé Pires, *op. cit.*, p. 45.
95. K. N. Chaudhuri, *Trade and Civilization. . . op. cit.*, p. 109.
96. *Ibid.*, p. 45.
97. *Ibid.*, p. 270.
98. *Ibid.*, p. 45; K. S. Mathew, "Trade Economy of Coastal Gujarat in the Sixteenth Century", *Journal of the Oriental Institute*, Vol. XXXIV, Nos. 3-4, Baroda, 1985, pp. 201-215.
99. *Ibid.*, p. 44.
100. Montalbodo, *op. cit.*, pp. 94, 161; Duarte Barbosa, *op. cit.*, Vol. II, p. 77; Tomé Pires, *op. cit.*, pp. 43, 78; Prospero Peragallo, *op. cit.*, p. 31.
101. Damião Peres, *Diario. . . op. cit.*, Vol. I, p. 98; Girolamo Sernigi in Montalbodo, *op. cit.*, p. 69.
102. Tomé Pires, *op. cit.*, Vol. I, pp. 82-84.
103. Rockhill, *op. cit.*, pp. 445-461.
104. E. Ashtor, "Venetian Supremacy. . . ", *op. cit.*, p. 47.
105. Montalbodo, *op. cit.*, p. 162.
106. Barbosa, *op. cit.*, p. 77.
107. For details about glass beads and their use, ref. W. G. N. Van der Sleen,

"Ancient Glass Beads with Special Reference to the Beads of East and Central Africa and the Indian Ocean" in *The Journal of the Royal Anthropological Institute of Great Britain and Ireland*. Vol. 88, Part II, July-December 1958, pp. 203-217.

108. Montalbodo, *op. cit.*, p. 70.
109. Richard Eden, *op. cit.*, p. 15.
110. G. Berchet, *Del Commercio dei Veneti nell'Asia*. Venezia, 1864, p. 13.
111. Varthema, *op. cit.*, p. 124; Rockhill, *op. cit.*, p. 462.
112. Tomé Pires, *op. cit.*, p. 58.
113. Varthema, *op. cit.*, p. 124.
114. Tomé Pires, *op. cit.*, Vol. I, pp. 76-77.
115. Fei Hsin, "Hsing Ch'a sheng lan" in Rockhill, *op. cit.*, pp. 448-449.
116. Rockhill, *op. cit.*, pp. 445-462.

CHAPTER 3

EUROPEAN RIVALRIES FOR THE MONOPOLY OF TRADE

The Portuguese, intent on obtaining exclusive right for the overseas trade in the east and proprietary claim over the lands and seas to be discovered in course of time, equipped themselves with papal bulls which permitted them to discover, conquer and appropriate whatever area they liked. Whenever they were challenged by anyone in connection with their claim, they referred to the papal authorisation and argued for their exclusive right. Therefore, it will be worth examining the tenor of papal bulls adduced by the Portuguese in this regard.

The organised plan for the overseas expansion of the Portuguese was executed by the Military Order of Christ which received ecclesiastical approval from Pope John XXII on 15 March 1319. [1] The Portuguese kings Edward and Affonso granted the jurisdiction over the conquered territories to the Military Order of Christ and its grand master, Infant Dom Henrique, which was confirmed by Pope Eugene IV through his bull *Etsi Suscepti* issued on 9 January 1442.[2] Subsequently, king Affonso V of Portugal obtained authorisation from Pope Nicholas to conquer the kingdoms, principalities as well as lands occupied by non-Christians anywhere in the world and bring them to subjection. All their possessions in terms of movable and immovable goods could be appropriated by the Portuguese. They were also permitted to enslave the enemies of Christ perpetually in the light of the bull *Dum Diversas* issued by Pope Nicholas V on 18 June 1452.[3]

A document of great significance on the basis of which the Portuguese argued for exclusive right over overseas possessions, especially in the Indian Ocean regions, was issued by Pope Nicholas V on 8 January 1454. The papal bull entitled *Romanus Pontifex* is rightly interpreted as the sheet-anchor of Portuguese imperialism by some historians. The Pope appreciated the overseas activities of Dom Henrique, the uncle of Affonso V, the king of Portugal who since 1419 promoted, to a large extent, the salvation of souls and glory of God, the Creator. The opinion of Prince Henry the navigator that the Ocean up to India was not crossed by any body from Europe and that Indians worshipped the name of Christ was held in great esteem by the Pope. He shared the view of the prince that the Portuguese could circumnavigate the African continent and with the help of the Indians who were reported to be believers in Christ, they could bring to subjection not only the Muslims but also all the others who did not believe in Christ and were not affected by the religious tenets of Muslims. The possibility of preaching the name of Christ to the non-Christians because of the extraordinary pains taken by the Portuguese was highly commended by the Pope. Therefore he permitted them to invade, conquer and appropriate territories and kingdoms of all those who were outside the Christian faith and reduce them to perpetual slavery. Unlimited power in this regard was granted to Dom Henrique, the king Affonso and all his successors. This was done by the Pope *motu proprio* within the fullness of his apostolic power and wisdom as he himself made it clear in this bull. The Pope further approved the Portuguese monopoly of navigation and trade and extended it to India. Others were forbidden to interfere in any way with the Portuguese monopoly of discovery, conquest and trade under the penalty of excommunication.[4]

The Portuguese, keen on making known to others the full purport of the Papal largesse, organised a public proclamation of the bull in the Sé Cathedral, Lisbon on 5 October 1455 before a large congregation. The foreign communities like the French, English, Castilians, Galicians and Basques were invited to witness the ceremony wherein both the Latin original and the Portuguese translation were made available to the public. This was a calculated move to make others keep off the areas of the Portuguese interest.

The monopoly over the Indian Ocean regions claimed by the Portuguese was further buttressed by Pope Calixtus III through his bull *Inter caetera* issued on 13 March 1455.[5] Confirming the order of Pope Nicholas V, the new Pontiff conceded to the Order of Christ under Prince Henry, the spiritual jurisdiction over the areas conquered and to be conquered by the Portuguese. The grand prior of the Order was given the power to nominate the incumbents to all the benefices both spiritual and temporal. Thus the Order of Christ was given a very extensive jurisdiction overseas. On the death of Prince Henry in 1460, the king Affonso was made the Grand master of the Order of Christ through the bull *Dum tuam* issued by Pope Pius II on 26 January 1460.[6]

The Portuguese wanted to tighten their authority over the area between Cape of Good Hope and the subcontinent of India by acquiring the authority to nominate Apostolic Commissar. So they approached Pope Alexander VI who issued the bull *Cum sicut* on 26 March 1500 granting the right to the Portuguese king in view of the request made through the Cardinal of Lisbon.[7]

The king of Portugal, Dom Manuel I who was known as the "Grocer King of Europe", decided to obtain the papal sanction for the conduct of trade and commerce with the Muslims and other non-Christians and to exonerate his predecessor as well as himself from the sins committed by them in doing it. This was thought to be indispensable for asserting the absolute monopoly of trade with the Indian Ocean regions inhabited chiefly by Muslims and Hindus. In fact, all those who traded with Muslims and other non-Christians without special permission from the Pope incurred grave sin as well as the penalty of excommunication. Hence, the Portuguese kings John II and Manuel I, who established commercial relations with Muslims and Hindus in their overseas enterprises were deemed to have committed serious sins and incurred ecclesiastical censure. Accordingly, Dom Manuel I supplicated before the Pope for remission of sins committed by him and his predecessor as well as his subjects. Pope Julius II listened to the petition sympathetically and issued the bull *Sedes Apostolica* on 4 July 1505 making arrangements for the remission of sins and the reparation. Every one who incurred ecclesiastical censures by conducting unauthorised trade with Muslims and Hindus was given the permission to choose for himself a confessor who would recommend the penance to be performed for such sins. The Pope issued an order of this nature solely in view of the fact that the Portuguese trade and commerce with the people of Guinea and India brought salutary effect to Portugal and the church at large, and promoted salvation of souls and the glory of God. He further absolved all the sins committed by the kings of Portugal.[8] The same Pope issued another bull *Desideras ut nobis* on 2 April 1506 permitting Dom Manuel to conduct trade with Muslims and Hindus since the desire of the king was born out of his interest for the salvation of souls.[9]

With the permission given by the Popes, the Portuguese went on intensifying their overseas activities in the East and came to clash with the Spaniards who too were interested in attempts of this sort. Finally they had to come to terms regarding the limits of the sphere of their activities and an agreement was reached. Dom Manuel wanted to buttress this treaty with the approval of the Pope and therefore he approached Pope Julius II who through his bull *Ea quae* dated 24 January 1506 ratified it.[10] Thus the possible clash and encroachment on the part of the Spaniards were averted and the sphere of influence of the Portuguese was kept jealously away from the Spaniards.

The Portuguese rulers were quite keen on seeing that their feats were brought to the notice of the Popes and making others understand that whatever they did in the east was with the sanction of the Pope. This was calculated to guard their conquests away from the encroachment of others and to confirm their monopoly. As soon as they conquered Malacca, the most important emporium of international maritime trade which connected the East with Venice in the East-West Axis of emporia trade, this was brought to the knowledge of the Pope Leo X. The fact that Affonso de Albuquerque, after his conquest of Goa, brought the coveted emporium of the east under the Portuguese was announced to the cardinals in the consistory. Through the bull *Significavit nobis* issued on 5 September 1513 the Pope thanked the king Manuel of Portugal.[11] Thus Portuguese rulers always tried to show a religious touch for their activities as the pioneers of Christian faith with a view to keeping away others from interfering with their valuable acquisitions. To enhance this feature of their feats in the east, they obtained from Pope Leo X the authority to bring all the ecclesiastical institutions and benefices in the areas captured and to be captured from the non-Christians under the vicar of Thomar, the seat of the military Order of Christ. [12]

By giving a religious colour to the overseas enterprise, the Portuguese ran the risk of the encroachment of the clerics on the jealously guarded monopoly of trade. The clerics, enjoying the special privilege from not being judged and prosecuted by the civil authorities as well as exempt from freight charges, entered into trade and commerce with India as it was very profitable. This was considered an infringement of the monopoly of the Portuguese king and detrimental to the finances of the kingdom. So the king petitioned to the Pope for a favourable disposal of the case. Since the Pope was aware of the fact that the Portuguese trade and commerce were beneficial to the church at large in ways more than one, he issued an order on 27 April 1521 whereby the chief chaplain of the king was given the faculty to punish clerics in minor orders for offences of this type. [13]

The Portuguese who were thus protected by the papal authority from any infringement of their all-pervading authority over the Indian Ocean regions were rendered extremely powerful to dictate the price of spices in the international market. They did not have any competitors. Hence it was notified to the Popes that they were exploiting the situation and were amassing wealth through excessive profit in the trade in spices. Italians as well as people from the rest of the christendom made representations to the Pope to interfere in this matter. Therefore, Pope Clement VII issued an order to king John III of Portugal on 9 April 1524 asking him to reduce the profit he used to make from the trade in spices and bring down the sale-price.[14]

The close interaction of this nature between the papacy and the Portuguese kingdom emboldened the clerics to derive profit from trade and at the same time cling on to the clerical privilege of not being under the secular laws. This brought about great fiscal problems to the Portuguese crown. So, king Sebastian approached the Pope for necessary provisions in this regard. Pope Pius IV issued a bull on 4 October 1563 admonishing the clerics and permitting the Portuguese crown to judge the clerics involved in trade and commerce without ecclesiastical intervention.[15] The privilege so far enjoyed by the clerics was done away with. The Portuguese crown benefited a lot from this in putting into effect their monopoly and plugging all the possible loopholes even by bringing the recalcitrant clerics under the royal orders.

Apart from taking steps to guard the newly discovered territories and maritime trade in the Indian Ocean regions from other powers with the assistance of the ecclesiastical authorities, some important steps of secular nature were taken by the Portuguese king as well as the writers under the orders given by him. After the discovery of the sea-route connecting India with the Atlantic ports and the establishment of commercial relations by Pedro Alvares Cabral, Dom Manuel, the king of Portugal, augmented his grandiloquent title in 1501 by adding a new epithet, which ultimately read: "Lord of navigation, conquest and commerce of Ethiopia, Arabia, Persia and India" (*Senhor da Navegação, Conquista e commércio da Ethiopia, Arabia, Persia e India*).[16] Subsequently Vasco da Gama, who had been to India for the second time, introduced a device whereby the ships plying in the Indian Ocean regions were constrained to take a pass from the Portuguese authorities lest they should be captured and confiscated by them. This was initiated in 1502 for the first time.[17] Though the payment for the pass (*cartaz*) was only nominal in the initial stages, in course of time such ships were bound to visit the stipulated ports under the Portuguese power and pay customs duties for the items carried in the ships as it will be discussed later. Assumption of the title and the insistence on the obligation of purchasing *cartaz*, a humiliating one as far as the Indian merchants, nobles and rulers were concerned, were two important steps taken by the king in the direction of asserting his supremacy over the Indian Ocean regions.

The Portuguese claim for monopoly over trade and navigation

in the Indian Ocean regions was justified in a very graphic manner by a Portuguese historian, João de Barros, in the first half of the sixteenth century. His argument is summarised below for a better understanding of the position taken by him and other Portuguese writers of this period. First of all, the assumption of the title *Senhor da Navegação, conquista, e commércio da Ethiopia, Arabia, Persia, e India* is explained by him. The king rightly assumed the title in the wake of the discovery of the sea-route by Vasco da Gama and especially after the return of Pedro Alvares Cabral. In fact, the king took possession of whatever was discovered and was conceded and granted to him by the supreme pontiffs. This grant was made because of the large expenditure incurred by Portugal both in terms of bloodshed, sacrifice of lives of the Portuguese and discovery undergoing sickness and dangers as well as works of thousand sorts.

Dom Manuel I, the king of Portugal, took the title because the supreme pontiffs beginning with Pope Eugene IV and Pope Nicholas V to Pope Sixtus IV granted to Portugal everything from Cape Bojador till the end of the east that would be discovered by the Portuguese. Entire India, islands, seas, ports, fisheries and so on were clearly included in the papal donations. The king ordered Vasco da Gama and Pedro Alvares Cabral to discover three things which none of the kings of Europe cared for, nor tried to discover. He wanted to take possession of these three things which were very essential in the whole of the Orient. He discovered the navigation of the unknown seas through which people travelled from Portugal to India in the east; he took possession of the route of navigation through navigating in it. The king discovered the lands inhabited by the "idolatrous gentiles" and "heretical Muslims" to be able to conquer and take away these lands from their hands who were unlawful holders since they denied to God the glory due to Him as Creator and Redeemer. Hence, the king assumed the title over these lands. He discovered the trade in spices which were dealt by those "infidels". Just as he was the lord of the route and of the conquest of the land, it was fitting that he be the lord of trade of that region.

Barros added that there was no need for any further justification for these titles assumed by the king other than the early apostolic grants. These titles based on the papal grant were again confirmed by the right of usucaption and prescription, as the jurists put, of more than fifty years of possession as seen in the process of the Portuguese history. Here the writer refers to the undisturbed and pacific possession of the land for a stipulated period which gave proprietary right through the legal title called prescription.

As far as navigation was concerned, the power of the Portuguese fleets in the oriental regions was so great that with the naval power of this nature Portugal could be the lord of the seas. This made both the Hindus and the Muslims ask for certificates of safe conduct called *cartaz* from the Portuguese officials posted in India so that they could peacefully and securely send their ships. If an infidel, from places where there were no Portuguese fortresses or with which the Portuguese had no friendly relations, was found, he could be rightfully captured as in a just war.

The Portuguese writers of this period recognised the fact that seas had to be regarded as open to every one since there was no other public passage. They held that a Christian through faith and baptism was brought under the jurisdiction of Roman Church and thereby he was subject to Roman law. They further held the view that the common right of passage in the seas for navigators and the obligation of respecting the property of those navigating in the seas were applicable only to Europe and that too only to Christians. Portugal and other kingdoms directly under the Pope observed this law not because they were subject to the imperial law as feudatories, but because these laws were just and agreeable to reason which was considered the mother of law.

The Muslims and Hindus were not considered to be privileged to enjoy the advantages of the laws observed by the Portuguese since they were outside the law of Christ which was the true one to be respected and held in esteem by every one under pain of eternal fire. The Hindus and Muslims were not members of the evangelical community though they were in potency and on the way as long as they were alive and were capable of entering into it. Evidently they lost the common right referred to above because they did not accept Christian faith. Further, even those who received that faith were not entitled to this right in the oriental regions because, before the Portuguese entered India, and took possession of it, none of them had acquired any property by way of inheritance or conquest. So, no body, except the Portuguese, had any right in India. This state of affairs was based on the natural principle and common law according to Barros.

With regard to the title of conquest, Sofala, Quiloa, Mombaça, Ormuz, Goa, Malacca and Moluccas with all the islands were already brought under the jurisdiction of the Portuguese king before the end of the first half of the sixteenth century. Besides, the city of Diu and Bassein with the lands attached to them in the kingdom of Gujarat were also in the possession of Portugal. Similarly, Chaul, Bhatkal and all those areas where Portugal had fortresses and officials for administration had been under the Portuguese king. Quiloa and Mombaça had been given up on account of sickness and lack of any good results. Islands of Socotra and Anjediv being not essential were also left out. Moreover, there were other areas, the ports of which were in friendly relations with the Portuguese and received the Portuguese vessels as though Portugal was their ruling power.

The title of trade was also due to the king of Portugal. This was clear from the fact that several ships carrying spices and commodities of other sorts used to reach Portugal from India every year. Commercial relations of this nature presupposed the agreement of two contracting parties which entailed peace, friendship and observance of the terms of the contract. Beyond this general convention, Portugal had trade with India in three ways. First, trade was conducted with the conquered areas of the Indian Ocean regions by establishing commercial relations with the local people as vassals with their lords whose revenue for entry and exit belonged to the Crown of Portugal. Secondly, the Portuguese concluded permanent contracts with the local kings and rulers regarding the prices of commodities purchased and sold by the Portuguese as it was done with the kings of Cannanore, Chale, Cochin, Quilon and Ceylon. They were the lords of all the spices available in India. The said contract was only for the supply of spices to the officials of the

Portuguese king stationed in his factories in India for the annual fleet going over to Portugal. The commodities other than spices were free to be purchased by the Portuguese privateers and local people at any price mutually agreed upon by the seller and buyer. Thirdly, the Portuguese merchant vessels plied through all the parts of the Indian Ocean conforming themselves to the practice of the place and exchanging commodities with the local people at prices agreed among themselves. [18]

The monopoly claimed by them in the light of the papal bulls and other legal presumptions prompted them to keep the entire Indian Ocean regions under their control through the introduction of passes (*cartazes*), the establishment of well-fortified fortresses in strategic places and *cafila*. Of all these, the most important for the Portuguese and most humiliating for the Indians was the system of passes which shall be discussed first.

The background against which the passes began to be insisted upon provides some idea about its working. After Pedro Alvares Cabral met with a serious rebuff from the Zamorin, the king of Calicut from whom the Portuguese in a high-handed fashion demanded exclusive rights to trade with Calicut, Vasco da Gama reached the Malabar coast in 1502 with a fleet of fifteen well-equipped ships ready to fight against his rivals in this region. As the rulers of Cannanore, Cochin and Quilon were, for various reasons, sympathetic towards the Portuguese, Vasco da Gama decided to spare the ships belonging to those three kingdoms from attack. The Portuguese Admiral placed the demand before the Zamorin that he should expel all the Muslim merchants, both Indian and foreign, from Calicut and not a single Muslim should be permitted to have any relations with any port in his kingdom. There were about 5000 Muslim families residing in Calicut itself at that time. The Zamorin stated in unequivocal terms that his port and kingdom would always remain open to everyone and thus he turned a deaf ear to the Portuguese request. So, fierce naval battles were fought in this region and the Portuguese, with a view to sparing the vessels of the above-mentioned kingdoms, introduced an expedient under which those ships that were not to be attacked were required to carry a certificate duly signed by the Portuguese authorities, namely, the royal factor, or the captain of the fortress. This certificate was called *cartaz* and it was issued first time in 1502 as mentioned above.

Later, the Portuguese officials were detailed to guard the coastal regions with a view to preventing other ships from conducting trade with any part of India and they were asked to capture and confiscate all the ships that were not equipped with *cartazes.* [19] Merchants and rulers interested in sending their commodities to various places like Ormuz, or coming to the different ports of India were constrained to take *cartazes* from the Portuguese as they found it necessary, and this became a regular practice. [20] The captain of the respective fortress or the official of the factory issued *cartazes*. Lopo Soares, the governor of Portuguese India, ordered in 1518 that there should be a register in which all the *cartazes* issued from time to time could be entered and this book was to be shown to him whenever he desired to consult it. The *cartazes* were to be made out by the writers of the factory who were entitled to have a share in the perquisites, but they were to be signed by the authorities of the factory or fortress. [21] At times an amount of five *pardaos* for each *cartaz* was charged to the parties concerned. [22]

A *cartaz* thus issued contained the reference to the circumstance in which it was given. The name and tonnage of the ship, name and age of its captain, the port of embarkation as well as disembarkation, and the approximate date of departure were also indicated in the *cartaz*. Mention was made of the arms and ammunitions carried in the ship and the items that were prohibited to be transported were also declared. Lastly the names of the writers and of the issuing authority were given along with the date of issue. [23]

The insistence on the obligation of taking *cartazes* for the vessels belonging to rulers and merchants as well as the strict naval surveillance instituted to implement the system effectively called for international resistance. On account of the humiliating treatment meted out, the Zamorin of Calicut came forward to muster support for a global confrontation. He was rather upset with the high-handedness of the Portuguese who wanted that the merchants from Mocha, Tenasserim, Pegu, Ceylon, Turkey, Egypt, Persia, Ethiopia and Gujarat who used to frequent the port of Calicut should be kept away from his port.[24] The flourishing trade brought significant revenues to the exchequer of the Zamorin. By the arrival of the Portuguese, things began to take a turn altogether different. They sacked the city in 1500 and insisted on the expulsion of all the Muslim merchants from Calicut.[25] Vasco da Gama in 1502/03 insisted that the Zamorin should not allow any Muslim vessel to anchor off any of his ports or to have relations of any sort for trade.[26] Since the Zamorin did not accede to the demands of the Portuguese, they bombarded the city and captured a number of vessels.[27] As a result of the frequent attacks of the Portuguese and the strict watch kept on the movement of the vessels in the Indian Ocean, the trade that flourished for several years in the port of Calicut was dislocated; the merchants fled to other places. Besides, the Portuguese established cordial relations with the other kings like those of Quilon, Cochin and Cannanore where they constructed their factories and fortresses in due course of time. This was a great blow to the prestige of the Zamorin who held sway over all the kings on the Malabar coast. So, he wanted to retaliate the Portuguese, and as he, on his own, was not powerful enough to take the bull by the horns, he sent envoys to Q'ansawh al-Ghawri, Sultan of Cairo, Malik Ayaz, the governor of Diu and to the ruler of Gujarat beseeching their help to form a united front against the Portuguese.[28]

The kingdom of Gujarat too held a pre-eminent position in trade before the arrival of the Portuguese. Many of the Gujarati merchants had their settlements in Calicut, Cannanore and Cochin. The most important of them was the one at Calicut.[29] The Gujaratis, who were compared to the Italian merchants in the matter of trade in spices, extended their trading operations up to Malacca in the south.[30] They took spices and other commodities to the African coast too. Now that the Portuguese began to establish their authority over the Indian Ocean and forbade other ships to navigate in this region, the Gujarati vessels could not go to the ports on the Malabar coast to take cargo to Gujarat and finally to Mocha where they reaped great profit from the trade. Muhammad Shah, the Sultan of

Gujarat, had appointed Malik Ayyaz as the governor of Diu who took up the cause of the Gujarati merchants. As soon as he got the complaint from the Zamorin regarding the harassment of the merchants by the Portuguese, he sent word through the merchants from Mocha to the Sultan of Cairo offering his cooperation in evicting the Portuguese from the Indian Ocean. [31]

Q'ansawh al-Ghawri, the Sultan of Cairo who held sway over Egypt till 1517, had been interested in retrieving the loss. He started to suffer ever since Portuguese appeared in the Indian Ocean regions. He had his authority over the various centres of trade in West Asia like Jeddah, Mocha, Suez, Cairo, Alexandria, besides Beirut, Allepo and Damascus which were very important port-towns through which the commodities from the Orient passed to the European marts. He drew large revenues by way of customs duties on the commodities of trade. His annual income from this source was calculated to be 600,000 ducats. [32] As the Portuguese began to plunder as well as capture all the Arab ships in the Indian Ocean regions and prevented the flow of spices through the Red Sea and the Persian Gulf, trade in these centres of trade under the Sultan of Cairo dwindled and his source of income dried up. So, he decided to make common cause with the aggrieved parties in India and sent his ambassadors to the Zamorin in 1501 asking him not to receive any more Portuguese vessels in his port. [33]

Another group of merchants who were very badly affected by the monopoly imposed by the Portuguese in the Indian Ocean regions was the Venetians who purchased spices and other oriental commodities at Alexandria, Damascus and Beirut and sold them at various centres of trade in Europe. They made great profit through the trade in oriental goods. They had their representatives in Cairo too, the headquarters of the Sultan. Though they had rather friendly relations with the Portuguese till the discovery of the direct sea-route connecting India with the Atlantic ports, the Portuguese enterprise in the East was described by the contemporary Italian writers as the death-knell of the Venetian trade and consequently the ruin of Venetian prosperity. [34] The Venetian diarists, from the time they knew of the arrival of the Portuguese at Calicut, bewailed the imminent ruin of the Venetian Republic that could be caused by the Portuguese trade in the East and the possibility of the merchants from Flanders, Hungary, France, England and Germany going to purchase spices from Lisbon rather than from Venice. [35]

Right in 1499 the Venetians came to know of the success of Vasco da Gama's voyage in discovering the direct sea-route. Then onwards they began to plan out ways and means to obstruct the Portuguese attempts in the East. Through the letter sent from Bruges and Antwerp the Venetians came to know of the arrival of two Portuguese ships at Flanders loaded with pepper from the Malabar coast. Venetians published in 1501 the letter of Il Cretico (Giovanni Matteo Cretico), a special secretary of Domenico Pisani, the Venetian ambassador to Spain and Portugal, sent to Lisbon to express the condolence over the demise of the infant son of D. Manuel II. Cretico wrote in detail about the fleet of Alvares Cabral to India and the possibility of obstructing the trade of the Mamluks with India and thereby causing harm to the Venetian traders. [36] Pietro Pasqualigo himself made it clear to the Venetians that the Portuguese enterprise would be a great blow to the Venetian trade. [37] They instigated the Sultan to take measures against the Portuguese and threatened him saying that they would not send any more galleys to Beirut and Alexandria which would naturally deprive him of large revenues by way of taxes on the commodities purchased and sold by the Venetians. As they did not get sufficient cargo from Beirut and Alexandria in 1502, they sent a letter to the Sultan in October 1503 informing him that unless he took some serious steps to do away with the Portuguese trade in the East, they would withdraw from Alexandria and Beirut and thus he would forfeit the income he could derive from them by way of customs-duties in the light of the agreement already concluded. The Venetian galleys returned from Alexandria without any spices at all in 1504, something unheard of in the recent past. [38]

Thus, in view of the messages the Sultan of Cairo received from the Zamorin of Calicut, the governor of Diu as well as the Venetians, he decided to take some serious steps in 1504. He sent Frei Maurus de'Spanha, a member of the Franciscan mendicant order, residing in Jerusalem, to the Pope asking him to do the needful to dissuade the Portuguese from continuing their commercial activities in the East. He made it very clear that if the Portuguese were not contained by the Pope and were not prevented from sending their ships to India, he would destroy the holy Sepulchre of Jesus Christ and the Monastery of Mount Sinai together with the Church. [39] Pope Julius immediately directed the envoy sent by the Sultan to the king of Portugal with a copy of the letter of the Sultan and another letter from himself asking him to put an end to further attempts in the Indian Ocean regions. [40] But the king sent a reply to the Pope assuring him of the security of the Holy Sepulchre and his intention to send more ships to India. The Franciscan friar returned to the Sultan with the impression he got from the Pope and the king of Portugal. Though the reply from the Pope was not at all satisfactory, the Sultan did not hasten to execute the threat. On the other hand, he made arrangements with the Zamorin of Calicut and the ruler of Gujarat to face the Portuguese menace in the East. Moreover, he appointed Amir Hussayn, or "Mir Hocem" of some of the Portuguese writers like Barros and Castanheda and "Agacem" of Correia, the governor of Jeddah as the captain of the fleet to be sent to India to fight against the Portuguese in collaboration with the other disgruntled powers. [41]

The reaction of the Venetians to the high-handed activities of the Portuguese in the East against their interest in the trade in spices is best illustrated by their alliance with the Sultan of Cairo. Apart from threatening to withdraw the Venetian merchants from the ports of the Sultan and instigating him to take steps against the Portuguese, they collected information about the Portuguese commercial activities through various means. They sent a spy in the name of Ca' Masser to Portugal in 1504 who spent two years in Lisbon and submitted a report to the Venetian senate. [42] The eagerness of the Venetians to be informed of the affairs of Portugal and especially of the probable abandonment of the new enterprise, if it came through at all, could be understood from the report of Vincenzo Quirini, who on a mission to Castile went up to the frontiers of Portugal to extract information about the Portuguese trade.[43] Therefore, they tried to divert the attention of the Portuguese from the Indian Ocean regions and keep themselves busy in Europe. In tune with this line of thought they, being informed that the Turks had made preparations to attack some of the Venetian possessions in Greece, sent a deputation to the Pope in 1501 requesting him to intercede with the king of Portugal to get some help to fight against the Turks in the Mediterranean. The Pope contacted the king of Portugal through the papal Nuncio and consequently the king, after having made necessary consultations, sent thirty *naos* and caravels to help the Venetians. The fleet under João de Menezes left Lisbon on 15 June 1501.[44] Doctor Pietro Pasqualigo had already been in Lisbon as a special emissary of the Republic of Venice with the plea for help against the Turks, and delivered his formal address to king Manuel on 20 August 1501. In his address he thanked the king in the name of the Venetian Senate for having consented to help them against the Turks and declared that he was sent to Portugal by the Senate with the special mission of expressing gratitude. He also tried to play on the religious sentiments and vanity of Dom Manuel as a protector of the true catholic faith and added that the most important need of the time was to fight against the enemy at close quarters rather than the one in the far away land, meaning thereby the "attempts against the Muslims" in India.[45]

One could see the two-fold aim of the embassy, namely, to divert the attention of Dom Manuel from the East and to concentrate it on the Mediterranean regions thereby serving the interests of the Venetians, i. e. to destroy the Turks who challenged the Venetian trade in the Mediterranean and to dissuade the Portuguese from the newly established trade with India. This is further strengthened by the fact that the Venetian delegation while at Lisbon contacted the few men brought by Cabral from the Malabar coast to Portugal and tried to convince them that the Portuguese king did not have as much money as the Venetians and that the king depended on the foreigners to find necessary funds to fit out the fleet to India.[46] The hidden interest of the Venetians to see that the Portuguese commercial activities in India were nipped in the bud could be understood further from the attitude they took towards the papal emissary. At the threat pronounced by the Venetians, the Sultan of Cairo communicated a message to the Pope as discussed above. The envoy sent by the Pope, perturbed by the message of the Sultan, reached Venice. The Venetian Senate, aware of the fact that the Sultan had already taken some steps against the Portuguese as desired by them conducted a meeting and sent a letter of approval very secretly to the Sultan and externally sympathised with the message brought by the papal emissary.[47] This should be viewed against the one and the same Christian faith shared both by the Portuguese and the Venetians and their allegiance to Pope.

The international rivalries for trade in the Indian Ocean regions during the first quarter of the sixteenth century reached their climax by 1508. Elaborate preparations were made both in India and abroad to oust the Portuguese from the Indian Ocean regions. The Venetians who declared that the Portuguese attempts in the East were of more consequence to them than the Turkish attack on their possessions supplied carpenters, caulkers, and artillery to the Sultan to prepare for the encounter with the Portuguese. The fleet consisting of 2,000 men under Amir Hussayn proceeded from the Red Sea with the destination of Diu to join forces with the men of Malik Ayyaz and the other rulers of the western coast of India. Maymamme, the envoy of the Zamorin to the Sultan of Cairo, was also in the fleet under Amir Hussayn.[48] On the Indian side, Malik Ayyaz led the fleet comprising the men from Gujarat, Bijapur, Ahmednagar and Calicut. The combined forces proceeded to Chaul where the Portuguese fleet under Dom Lourenço, the valiant son of Francisco de Almeida, was found.[49] The Zamorin of Calicut had sent about forty ships to the north to participate in the naval confrontation.[50] The battle took place in January 1508 and the Portuguese were utterly defeated; their leader Dom Lourenço died in action; a number of the Portuguese were taken captives by Malik Ayyaz and despatched to the Sultan of Gujarat.[51]

The Venetians who sent two vessels and supplied necessary articles for the fleet to attack the Portuguese at Chaul were informed of the defeat of the Portuguese squadron. Their joy knew no bounds when they were informed that the Portuguese fleet were put to flight and a number of the Portuguese were taken in captivity. [52]

The Portuguese Viceroy, Dom Francisco de Almeida, did not leave the Muslim powers unavenged for the death of his beloved son. Though Affonso de Albuquerque, who was to succeed him, showed readiness to take revenge upon the victorious fleet of Amir Hussayn and Malik Ayyaz, Almeida himself took up the challenge and proceeded to the North from Cannanore on 12 December 1508 with nineteen vessels consisting of 1200 men among whom there were 400 men from Malabar coast itself. The Zamorin in the meantime had sent the necessary communication to Amir Hussayn in Diu regarding the preparations that were going on in Cannanore and Cochin against the combined contingent.

The Viceroy, after having avenged Dabhol for the help extended to Amir Hussayn and Malik Ayyaz, proceed to Diu and reached the destination on 2 February 1509. The contingent of Amir Hussayn, consisting of the Egyptians, Venetians and others in cooperation with the Indian fleet composed of the soldiers of Malik Ayyaz and the Zamorin, confronted the Portuguese in Diu and fought desperately. The Zamorin had sent one hundred *paraos* to Diu despite the vigilant blockade of the Portuguese. They defeated the enemies mercilessly and put Malik Ayyaz and his men to flight. Subsequently a treaty of peace and friendship was reached when Malik Ayyaz surrendered. [53] The Portuguese captives of the battle of Chaul were set free and the terms of peace were agreed on 3 February 1509. Malik Ayyaz agreed to give tributes to the king of Portugal. Thus the Portuguese managed to assert their sway over the Indian Ocean regions by courting victory over the international front which gave them more confidence.

The acquisition of Goa, an important centre of trade in horses and a variety of other goods, around 1510 and the subsequent conquest of Malacca in 1511 by Affonso de Albuquerque gave them a commanding position in the Indian Ocean. They were by then in a better position to insist on the system of *cartazes* which was an efficient instrument in implementing the monopoly and supremacy over the maritime trade of the Indian Ocean regions.

The Portuguese saw to it that the obligation of taking *cartaz* was incorporated in the treaties signed by the Indian rulers and the Portuguese king. The king of Calicut agreed in a treaty signed by him on 26 February 1515 that all the vessels visiting the port of Calicut with the exception of those belonging to his territory and those of the kingdoms of Cannanore and Cochin would take the *cartazes* from the Portuguese officials lest they should be attacked and confiscated. Further arrangements were also made regarding the sharing of the income from the issue of the passes. Half of the income was assigned to the Zamorin and the other to the Portuguese king.[54]

They compelled Bahadur Shah of Gujarat, the most commercialised region of the subcontinent of India, to accept the system of *cartazes* under the terms and conditions of the treaty signed on 23 December 1534. The vessels leaving the kingdom of Gujarat for the straits of Mocha or any other interior parts thereof were bound to go first to Bassein and take *cartazes* from the Portuguese officials posted there and on their return voyages, these ships were required to go to Bassein and pay customs-duties. Violation of this amounted to the confiscation of the ships by the Portuguese which would be considered booty of a just war. The Sultan of Gujarat agreed not to remonstrate about such a step taken by the Portuguese.

Those ships that left the kingdom of Gujarat for places other than the straits of Mocha were also bound to collect *cartazes* from the Portuguese officials at Bassein against a nominal payment of a *tanga* each. These vessels were, however, free to move anywhere they wanted, without having any other obligation. It was also agreed that no warship should be constructed in any ports of the Kingdom of Gujarat or any other region which, in future, the Sultan might acquire. Those ships that were already manufactured were not allowed to make any further voyage.[55]

The insistence on *cartazes* was further repeated in the treaty signed by the same Sultan on 25 October 1535 in connection with the surrender of a site in Diu to the Portuguese for the construction of a fortress. According to the terms of the treaty concluded at the time of the surrender of Bassein, it was agreed that all the ships should visit the port of Bassein to pay the customs-duties to the Portuguese. The new treaty stipulated that henceforth the ships should visit Diu to pay the duties. [56]

A number of other local rulers were also constrained to accept the system of *cartazes*. The king of Cannanore used to collect *cartazes* for more than ten ships a year and sent them laden with commodities to Cambay and Ormuz. He was at times permitted to import horses to the Malabar coast. [57] The ruler of Tanur on the Malabar coast, who was friendly with the Portuguese from the first decade of the sixteenth century, obtained *cartazes* from them for his ships. [58] The Zamorin of Calicut too agreed to collect *cartazes* from them for his ships and it was also stipulated that all those vessels from Ormuz, Gujarat, Malacca, Sumatra, Pegu, Tenasserim, Bengal, Coromandel, Ceylon, Jafnapattam and Chaul coming to Calicut should carry the Portuguese *cartazes*. The Nizam Shah of Ahmednagar, in the light of the terms of the treaty signed on 22 April 1539, collected *cartazes* from the Portuguese for his ships and Hussain Shah (1553-65) obtained *cartazes* from them in 1561 for the ships with a view to importing horses. [59]

The Zamorin of Calicut obtained *cartazes* from the Portuguese during the time of Afonso de Noronha, the viceroy of Portuguese India (1550-54), for sending his ships. The ruler of Tanur and Chale on the Malabar coast purchased *cartazes* in 1550 from them to send their ships to Mocha. The Adil Shah of Bijapur and Nizam Shah of Ahmednagar sent three ships to the Straits of Mocha in 1563 with the *cartazes* issued by the Portuguese. [60] The Zamorin in fact obtained permission around 1568 from them to send two ships every year to Mocha with 300 *bhars* of pepper. [61] He got *cartazes* for five ships every year around 1598 to be sent to West Asia. [62]

Even the emperors like Akbar the Great, and Jahangir took *cartazes* from the Portuguese to send their ships to the regions of the Red Sea in connection with the pilgrimage. The circumstance under which the Portuguese agreed to issue a free *cartaz* every year to Akbar and his successors and the financial implication of it explain the hold the Portuguese had on the movement of ships in the Indian

Ocean regions. The Mughal Emperor Akbar, looking for a maritime outlet and attracted by the wealth of coastal Gujarat, encountered the Portuguese when he came down to Surat and established personal contacts with them.[63] Subsequently, Akbar signed a *firman* on 18 March 1573 presumably at Broach instructing the captains, governors, administrators and other officials working especially in Surat, Broach, Naussari and Velodra (Vadodara) in the province of Gujarat not to disturb the Portuguese in their possessions like Diu. It was further enjoined on them that they should not favour the Malabar pirates but on the contrary they should extend help to the Portuguese. No harm should be done to the Portuguese. In case slaves belonging to the Portuguese took refuge in any part of the area belonging to the Mughal territory of Gujarat, they were to be judged according to the law and to be returned to the master.[64] Issue of so friendly a *firman* in favour of the Portuguese who had a few establishments only on the coastal regions by a mighty land-based emperor like Akbar shows the power the Portuguese had in the Indian Ocean regions. This was definitely an acknowledgment of the Portuguese claim of supremacy and confession of the debility of the empire in naval power.

This is further testified by the request made by the officials of the Emperor to Antonio Cabral who provided the vessels of the Mughal emperor with *cartazes*. Cabral was requested to make special mention in the pass (*cartaz*) of extraordinary attention to be paid to this particular vessel and the important persons travelling to Mocha which was done readily by him. It was further agreed that every year a free *cartaz* would be issued to an imperial ship leaving for Mocha from Surat according to the desire of the Emperor Akbar and the ship furnished with the pass would be exempted from customs-duties on her return to the Gujarat coast. This practice continued even after the death of Akbar so much so that Jahangir and his successors were regularly given the free *cartaz* and mention was made in such passes that this was done according to the custom in vogue.[65]

A glance at the financial implication of the free *cartaz* gives an idea of the significance of the monopoly claimed by the Portuguese and also depth of indebtedness of the Mughal emperors to the Portuguese. According to the prevailing terms and conditions agreed upon both by the Sultans of Gujarat and the Portuguese authorities, all the vessels leaving or reaching Gujarat coast were bound to report at the customs-house at Diu for paying the duties. The revenues of the customs-house at Diu were farmed out to the highest bidder during this period. Therefore, the farmers of the revenue of the port of Diu, being aware of the free *cartaz* issued to Emperor Akbar, demanded a reduction of 18,000 *pardaos* from the amount due from them per annum. They justified their demand showing the details from the books of the customs house at Diu. So the finances of Portuguese India suffered a loss of 18,000 *pardaos* solely because of the free pass issued every year to Akbar. It is calculated that this was further aggravated by another decrease of 5,000 *cruzados* per year in the income of the Portuguese. The residents of Cambay, who used to proceed to Mocha in their own vessels numbering between twelve to fifteen, were bound to reach Diu every year on their return voyage to pay the customs duties. In view of the fact that the ships of Akbar returning from Mocha were exempted from paying customs duties, these merchants from Cambay began to load their rich cargos of gold, silver, brocades, coral and other commodities into the imperial ship at Mocha. In fact the customs house at Diu used to get large revenues from such costly items before the issue of free *cartazes*. On account of the change of the situation, a great loss in revenue was inflicted on the customs house and subsequently on the finances of Portuguese India. Thus they lost much more than the revenue that could be collected from a single ship returning from Mocha. They could not do anything since they were bound by the agreement made with Akbar in 1573.[66] It was reported that a ship belonging to Akbar which returned from Jeddah to Goga in 1577 brought gold and silver worth 600,000 *cruzados* besides coral, brocade and other items according to the logbook kept in the ship.[67] Here one gets further insight into the financial implications of the free *cartaz* issued to the Mughal emperor as well as the amount of income the Portuguese used to collect through the system of *cartaz*.

The monopoly of trade implemented through the system of *cartazes* was much more vigorously inflicted on the nobility and the merchants involved in overseas trade. The merchants of Cochin, like Cherina Marakkar, used to purchase *cartazes* from the factory at Cochin to send their merchandise to Ormuz. Malik Gopi, the great merchant governor of Surat, collected *cartazes* for his ships to be sent to Malacca and other regions of the Southeast Asia. In return for defending the cause of the Portuguese at the court of Champaner in Gujarat, Malik Gopi insisted that the Portuguese should issue *cartazes* for the Gujarati ships to trade with Malacca and the surrounding areas. Later Amir Gopi, his son otherwise called Mircopi, collected twenty *cartazes* at a time from the Portuguese for his ships to be sent to Dabhol around 1533.[68] Despite his inveterate enmity towards the Portuguese, Khwâja Safar, the merchant governor of Surat in the kingdom of Gujarat, purchased *cartazes* from the captains of Bassein and Diu for his ships to be sent to Suez and Jeddah.[69] Khwaja Shams-ud-din Giloni, the administrator of Asad Khan, the governor of Belgaum in the kingdom of Bijapur, had trade with Malacca, Jedda, Ormuz, Diu and the Moluccas, and he sent even pepper, an item of royal monopoly under the Portuguese, to West Asia in the ships equipped with *cartazes* issued by the Portuguese.[70] Abu Bakar Ali, the uncle of Adiraja (Ali Raja?) of Cannanore on the Malabar coast, obtained *cartazes* from the Portuguese to send his ships with commodities to various parts of India and abroad and he himself instructed his people to continue this practice. So the merchants of Cannanore pursued this religiously and in 1546 the Muslim merchants sending their ships to Mocha were found carrying the *cartazes* from the Portuguese.[71]

The number of merchants purchasing *cartazes* went on increasing as the Portuguese sphere of influence and might spread far and wide. Both Indian and foreign traders collected *cartazes* from the Portuguese officials in Cochin, Cannanore, Goa, Chaul, Bassein, Daman and Diu. This practice continued to be in vogue even in the second half of the eighteenth century and there were instances of *cartazes* being issued to various merchants of Mangalore, Barcelor, Bedrur, Bidanur, Condapur, Honawar, Karwar, Goa, Rajapur,

Surat, Broach, Goga, Kutch and Kutch Mandovi for their ships to Bassora, Ormuz, Aden, Bengal and Congo.[72] Even the Armenian merchants purchased *cartazes* from the Portuguese for their vessels.[73]

The monopoly claimed by the Portuguese was challenged in practice by the rulers and merchants occasionally. This was chiefly because the Portuguese insisted on the delivery of commodities at the price fixed at the dawn of the sixteenth century. The Zamorin of Calicut, displeased with the price offered by the Portuguese, sent forty-two of his vessels loaded with pepper to Diu in 1523.[74] Adiraja of Cannanore had a very important trade in pepper with the Lakshadweep around 1568 and dispatched his ships in contravention to the Portuguese restrictions as war had broken out between himself and the Portuguese in 1559.[75]

The attitude of some, at least of the private Indian merchants, was the same. Despite the risk of being captured by the Portuguese, they sent their ships laden with commodities to various places where they could obtain a better price. Regardless of the stringent measures adopted by the Portuguese towards such attempts, ships loaded with spices appeared in the Red Sea around 1513. About this time twelve or thirteen ships carrying pepper and other merchandises left the Malabar coast for Mocha and Aden. Also in the same year almost the same number of vessels were found ready to proceed to the same destination. Mohammed Massary, the chief merchant of Calicut, sent spices loaded in three vessels from Calicut to Cairo in 1513. Small vessels carried pepper to Chaul and Diu from the Malabar coast in 1520, unmindful of the Portuguese system of *cartazes*. The merchants from Jeddah came to Calicut to purchase pepper even though there were two Portuguese fortresses in its vicinity and the local merchants supplied the required quantity of pepper. This risk was taken by them because the gains were quite attractive and worth the trouble, as they themselves confessed.[76] Large quantities of pepper were taken to the Coromandel coast through the interior parts of South Kerala on bullocks and as headloads. Vilinjam, Aryankavu and Puthura were some of the places through which this "unauthorised" traffic was carried on.[77]

Around 1547, it was reported that the local merchants sent several ships loaded with pepper to Mocha and they never cared to collect the *cartazes* from the Portuguese officials. [78] The practice of the local merchants breaking the Portuguese monopoly and sending ships to various ports in India and abroad without *cartazes* continued in the second half of the sixteenth century also. It was estimated that out of the 60,000 quintals of pepper produced annually in the area between Calicut and Cape Comorin, only 15,000 quintals were delivered to the Portuguese factories and the rest, that is three-fourths, were taken "illegally" to other parts. [79] This bears out the fact that trade of considerable magnitude was being conducted in the Indian Ocean regions by the merchants and rulers despite the monopolist and prohibitory measures adopted by the Portuguese. Only one-fourth of the total produce of pepper reached the Portuguese factories in India in spite of the desperate attempts made by them. In other words, the Portuguese attempts to implement strict monopoly through the system of *cartazes* did not bear the required fruit.

The Portuguese, right from the first decade of the sixteenth century, established fortresses in strategically important places to prevent others from encroaching upon the area claimed by them and to keep up the monopoly. Dom Manuel appointed Francisco de Almeida in 1505 as the first viceroy to India and enjoined upon him the duty of constructing well-fortified fortresses at Anjediva, Cannanore and Cochin.

The fortress at Ormuz, the construction of which was initiated on 24 October 1507 by Affonso de Albuquerque, was the key to the Portuguese possessions in the East. The town of Ormuz was conquered by Affonso de Albuquerque in 1515 and subsequently the fortress too was completed. The entry to the Persian Gulf was thus controlled by the Portuguese till May 1622 when it was lost in the encounter between them and Shah Abas assisted by the English.

Another strategically important centre in the international maritime trade was Diu where the Portuguese started a fortress in 1535 in view of the treaty concluded between them and the Sultan of Gujarat. This gave them a stronger hold on the movement of the ships from Western India to West Asia. A fortress was already in existence in Daman under the Sultan of Gujarat. This was ceded in February 1559 to Dom Constantino Bragança, the Portuguese viceroy. Incorporated in the administration of Daman was the modest fortress of Sanjan south of Daman besides a small fortified centre in Danu. The captain had a well-fortified residence in this place. With a view to controlling the movement of the vessels, the Portuguese established fortified settlements in Tarapor and Sirgam further south of Daman. Similarly the fortification at Mahim or Quelme Mahim was also designed to implement the Portuguese monopoly over the Western coast of India. This too was under the administration of Daman. Another fortress which became the headquarters of the northern region was that of Bassein which was surrendered to the Portuguese by Sultan Bahadur Shah in view of a treaty concluded on 23 December 1534. Later by 1556 the fortresses of Asseri and Manora were annexed to the territory of Bassein through the efforts of Francisco Barreto, the governor. The places like Thana in Salsette, Maim, Caranja and Agassim situated near *Ilha de Vacas* (otherwise known as Island of Cows) had also fortifications and were attached to Bassein.

Chaul occupied an important position on the western coast of India and the creeks were of great help for the merchants interested in evading the Portuguese supremacy. Therefore, the Portuguese governor, Diogo Lopes de Sequeira, built a fortress in Chaul in 1521 with the approval of the Nizam Shah of Ahmedanagar, one of the offshoots of the Bahamani kingdom in the Deccan. *Morro de Chaul* or the ramparts of Chaul situated opposite to the fortress of Chaul across the creek helped the Portuguese to control the entry of the other ships to the creek.

In view of the contract with Adil Khan a factor was appointed to Dabhol to issue *cartazes* to the ships leaving the port to other parts.[80]

Goa, which was occupied by the Portuguese in 1510, was of great importance in implementing the monopoly of maritime trade. Therefore, a couple of fortified centres in Goa were established after its conquest. Aguada, Rachol and Bardes had fortied centres meant for the defence of the area as well as the control of the movement of ships. The castle of Rachol in Salcette was constructed in 1535. The fortifications in Bardes were raised by D. Afonso de Noronha I, the viceroy (1551-54), on the ruins of a castle of Adil Khan of Bijapur.

The Portuguese viceroy, Dom Francisco de Almeida, got a fortress constructed in the Island of Anjediv further south of Goa, though it was abandoned after some time.

As the ports of Canara were important in the maritime trade of India, the Portuguese established their strongholds in its coastal regions. Onor, or Honawar of the modern times, was conquered by the Viceroy Dom Luis de Ataide in 1569 and a fortress was established there. Sivapa Naique, the ruler of Ikkeri, took possession of it in 1654. A factor was appointed to Bhatkal on the Canara coast to issue *cartazes* to the ships moving in the Arabian sea. This was done in the first half of the sixteenth century. Dom Luis de Ataide, the viceroy, constructed a fortress at Barcelore known otherwise as Barkur in 1568. This was in the possession of the Portuguese until it was conquered by Sivapa Naik of Bednur in 1652. Cambolim near Barkur had a Portuguese fortification since 1629.

Mangalore, which was the place from where the merchants used to send ships loaded with spices to West Asian regions avoiding the Portuguese naval surveillance, was chosen by Viceroy Dom Antão de Noronha for a fortress, and construction began in January 1568.

Cannanore, further south of Mangalore, was right from the beginning of the sixteenth century hospitable to the Portuguese especially since the local ruler was very sympathetic to them in the context of trade. So, under the instructions given by Dom Manuel, the king of Portugal, Dom Francisco de Almeida, started the construction of a fortress in 1505 and completed it in 1508.

Affonso de Albuquerque who understood the need of having a chain of fortresses for the implementation of the Portuguese monopoly over the Indian Ocean regions could not leave Calicut free. So, he made some diplomatic arrangements whereby a new Zamorin well-disposed to the Portuguese was seated on the throne. A treaty of peace and friendship was signed in 1513 whereby permission was accorded to open a fortress at Calicut. But this was abandoned in 1525 on account of continuous frictions between the Zamorin and the Portuguese. Later, through the good offices of the Portuguese governor Nuno da Cunha a fortress was constructed at Challe in 1531 near Calicut and arrangements were made for the issue of *cartazes* for the ships.

Cranganore, which was an important centre of trade of the Romans in the early century of Christian era, served as entrance for Zamorin to Edappally and Cochin. Francisco de Almeida suggested in 1508 that it would be good to have a fortress there on account of the availability of pepper. In the light of an agreement made in 1536 with Martim Affonso, purveyor of finances, the Portuguese under the instructions given by the governor Nuno da Cunha constructed a fortress which was christened Fort St. Thomas.

Cochin, which was the commercial headquarters of the Portuguese for several years, had a fortress since 1503. This was constructed at the mouth of the Edappilly river with timber under the supervision of Francisco de Albuquerque. Later with the arrival of the viceroy in 1505 this was converted into a masonry structure with strong fortifications. This fortress housed several institutions and the administrative offices.

There were constant contacts between the Malabar coast and the Coromandel through land routes from Quilon, which was an important centre of trade before the rise of Calicut and attracted the Chinese merchants. The Portuguese interested in establishing a water-tight monopoly of maritime trade started a factory at Quilon in 1503 and later in 1519 a fortress.

The Portuguese were interested in pearls and decided to effect a sort of supremacy over pearl-fishing. Therefore a small fortress was set up at Manar in an island belonging to Ceylon by Lopo Soares Dalbergaria in 1518. This island was later acquired by Dom Constantino in 1560. A captain was appointed for the pearl fishery coast of India by the Portuguese so that the Portuguese authority could be exercised. Besides, another captain was stationed in the

Coromandel coast of the subcontinent of India who controlled trade from Pulicat and San Thome since 1522. *Cartazes* were issued by him for the ships. In fact there is evidence pointing to the existence of a Portuguese office at Pulicat from where *cartazes* were issued in 1530. In course of time the Portuguese established other settlements at Nagapattinam, Porto Novo and Devanampattinam where there were Portuguese captains to control the trade. These steps were meant to extract as much volume of commodities as possible and also to control the maritime trade. Even those merchants from the Coromandel who used to go to Southeast Asian regions as well as those coming from there to Coromandel were bound to take *cartazes*. They were not satisfied with Coromandel and so they extended their influence to Chittagong and Hugli where too they opened their establishments. [81]

Thus the Portuguese established a number of fortresses and factories on the eastern as well as western coasts of India to control the movement of ships and assert their supremacy over the Indian Ocean regions. The insistence on *cartazes* through diplomacy and force of arms could be considered the characteristic feature of their policy. Besides, they had established naval surveillance in these regions. Regular patrolling of the sea was done by detailing well-equipped ships in different zones. Ships devoid of *cartazes* were attacked and confiscated by such ships on surveillance.

As noted above, the division of the world by Portugal and Spain among them was done through the treaties of Alcaçovas and Tordesillas (1494) which was approved by the Popes. The French disputed the exclusive rights claimed by the Portuguese and the Spaniards over the newly discovered lands and those to be discovered. They stated that the approval of the Popes in this matter could not be held valid unless there was a permanent settlement of the Europeans in the discovered lands. They maintained that mere trade would not suffice to establish claim over any discovered land. In other words the French were keen on evolving a new idea of colonialism. They insisted on actual possession of the discovered land and permanent settlement as the foundations on which the claim should be based. Areas where there was no permanent occupation should be open to trade for everyone. Moreover, they did not want to extend the claim to areas that were not discovered. Three French ships appeared off Diu in July 1527 probably with the idea of establishing commercial relations with India. [82] They therefore approached the Pope for clarification of the bull *Inter Caetera* issued by Pope Alexander VI which divided the world among the Portuguese and the Spaniards. Francis I of France managed to get a new bull issued by Pope Clement VII in 1533 which defined in clear terms the intent of the bull *Inter Caetera*. The new papal pronouncement made it very clear that the order of Pope Alexander VI was valid only for the lands till then discovered, not for the lands to be discovered. Thus the French secured the papal approval to discover new areas and appropriate them by dislodging the claim of the Portuguese and the Spaniards. Without coming into confrontation with the Portuguese directly, they concentrated their attention on opening an alternative route to India through the western hemisphere which brought them accidentally to New France and for a long period they were actively involved in this region. They took up the direct enterprise with India through Cape of Good Hope only towards the second half of the seventeenth century though the background was prepared for a new theory of colonialism and papal approval was obtained.

But the Dutch challenged the arguments put forward buttressing their claim for supremacy over Indian Ocean regions based on the legal titles explained above and especially the validity of the papal bulls for the monopoly of trade and the insistence on *cartazes*. The first doctrinal and systematic exposition rejecting the Portuguese claims for supremacy over the Indian Ocean regions came from the side of the Dutch scholar Hugo Grotius who was called upon to find justification for the capture of a Portuguese ship and its confiscation in the East.

Presumably the wave of protestant revolution that was striking roots in the Low Countries and the inveterate enmity of the Dutch towards the Spanish Crown prompted them to call the papal bulls in question and to flout the Portuguese supremacy. This was aggravated by the fact that the Spanish king, who since 1580 was also the king of Portugal, prohibited the sale of spices to the protestants. Hugo Grotius, with a view to justifying the capture of the Portuguese galleon, *Santa Caterina*, published in 1608 his *Mare Liberum.*[83] He refuted the arguments of the Portuguese writers and denied that the Portuguese could have sovereignty over the East Indies on account of the title of discovery. Because, as India was famous for centuries before the arrival of the Portuguese and merchants used to come to India by sea to find means to escape poverty, the Portuguese could not say that they had "discovered" India.

> Quid quod ne reperisse quidem Indiam
> ullo modo dici possunt Lusitani,
> Iam ab Horatii tempore
> Impiger Extremos currit mercator ad Indos
> Per mare pauperiem fugiens.[84]

Even granted that they had discovered it, it did not bring about the possibility of appropriating it as long as it was not *res nullius*, or "no man's land" unoccupied by any one. The famous theologians like Thomas Aquinas and the Spanish writer Victoria held that on the basis of religious beliefs no infidel could be deprived of his possessions and so the proprietary right of the infidels could not be taken away by the Portuguese.

As noted above, the Popes had issued a number of bulls granting the Portuguese right to the territories already discovered or to be discovered. The Portuguese writers like João de Barros made much of the papal grants. But, Hugo Grotius very clearly denied the right of the Portuguese to the oriental lands based on the papal bulls. Because, the Pope could not have any temporal authority and even granted that he could have, he had nothing to do with the infidels and to expropriate them in so far as they did not belong to the Church. He refuted the argument that the Portuguese had right to India on the basis of war and conquest, except in the case of Goa. The Indians being unbelievers could not be subjugated by force just because they were infidels. Nor could they be justified in saying that they fought the Indians for the sake of spreading the Christian faith, because the Portuguese were amassing wealth even to the neglect of their religious duties. [85]

Grotius refuted also the theories regarding the right claimed by the Portuguese for the dominion over the Indian Ocean since the titles such as papal donation, occupation, and prescription or custom did not hold good in this regard. In the same way, claim to the monopoly of trade based on the titles of occupation, papal donation and prescription had been denied. Thus Grotius argued that trade with India as well as the right to navigate in the Indian Ocean should not be considered a monopoly of the Portuguese but on the contrary it should be open to all. [86]

The English, going a step farther than the merchant adventurers of the Levant Company, also established the English East India Company and acquired foothold in some of the port towns of India. The English mind too was not ready to accept the arguments put forward by the Portuguese and the Dutch as the final verdict on the subject and so jeopardise their commercial interests. William Welwood published the booklet *An Abridgement of all the Sea-Lawes* in 1613 providing the theoretical background for the British claims to the dominion of the sea. John Selden defended the right of the British crown to appropriate the seas as well as the land and refuted the ideas expressed in *Mare Liberum*. His tract entitled *Mare Clausum* was written in 1617 or 1618 attacking the Dutch position. In 1619 Welwood wrote another book entitled *De Dominio Maris Juribusque ad Dominium Praecipue spectantibus Assertio brevis ac Methodica.* This too argued against the proposition of Grotius.

The Portuguese took up the challenge and Frei Serafim de Freitas came up with his *De Justo Imperio Lusitanorum Asiatico* published in 1625 from Valladolid. Freitas upheld the right of the Portuguese to the East Indies especially Indian Ocean regions on the basis of the freedom to propagate the Christian faith in non-Christian areas and thus evaded the objections raised by Grotius. He admitted that the Pope did not have direct jurisdiction over the infidels in India, but he affirmed the indirect jurisdiction. The Pope, being the universal pastor, had the right and duty to send missionaries to the areas of unbelievers and force the infidels to hear the word of God preached by the missionaries. He could also insist upon the infidel rulers not to impede the preaching of the missionaries and promote conversion of the people even by waging war against the rulers. Thus the Pope had indirect jurisdiction over the infidels. Freitas added that the Pope who had such a jurisdiction over the infidels and the right to send the missionaries could delegate the power to any particular nation of his choice as he did in the case of the Portuguese and he was empowered to restrict the right of navigation to these areas only to a certain nation as missionaries were to be taken by ship. Moreover, the Pope also had the power to assign the monopoly of trade to these people and exclude others since the missionary activities needed money for their survival. This was the fundamental argument Freitas had to offer in support of the validity of papal grants to the Portuguese in regard to their jurisdiction on the infidels of India, the navigation thereof and the commerce with India against the objections raised by Grotius. He added that the papal grants regarding these points would not have any relevance if they were prescinded from the missionary activities and that the king of Portugal could not claim the monopoly if he did not send missionaries to India.

Similarly, regarding the occupation of the Indian Ocean which, by its nature, was not a thing to be occupied, he seems to have admitted the possibility of quasi-possession or quasi- occupation by reason of the privileges granted by a sovereign authority such as Pope for the sake of the activities of the propagation of faith, since he had jurisdiction all over the world. Therefore, one could acquire the right to prevent any one from causing trouble to the peaceful navigation of the occupant of the ocean. The explanation given for the system of *cartazes* in the Indian Ocean was also based on the papal grants, which implied that nobody else should navigate in the Indian Ocean without the permission of the Portuguese. As the Arabs from the beginning of the entry of the Portuguese in the Indian Ocean tried to oust them and destroy their properties by inciting the oriental rulers, it was necessary for the Portuguese to introduce such measures with a view to curbing their dangerous attempts. This step was necessitated also by the fact that the Turks and the Egyptians were helped by Christians themselves who lost sense of their common faith and fought against the Portuguese.

He held that the right of the Portuguese to navigate in the Indian Ocean was founded on the title of occupation before any one else, prescription and custom, because they discovered India and had occupied it though it was known for centuries. The activities of Bartholomeo Dias in 1493 to find out the direct sea-route to India via Cape of Good Hope and the final attempt of Vasco da Gama in 1497 are adduced to corroborate the fact of discovery. [87]

Thus one could conclude that the strongest point for Freitas to prove the Portuguese right to monopoly of trade and navigation in the Indian Ocean lay in the duty and right to propagate the Christian faith delegated exclusively to the Portuguese by the Pope. This is at the same time the weakest point in his argumentation. [88]

The English, jealous of the capital accumulated by the Portuguese through trade, went beyond argumentation and captured some of the Portuguese ships and took them to London for spoils ever since the unification of the Portuguese and Spanish crowns in 1580. The five vessels leaving Lisbon for India in 1591 were escorted by eleven well-armed Dutch ships with Portuguese and Spanish soldiers for fear of the English attacks. It was reported that despite the security offered by the accompanying ships, the English might worry them.[89] A Portuguese ship, leaving Calicut for Lisbon with a cargo worth a million ducats, was captured by the English in 1592. Moreover, two other ships returning from Calicut to Portugal were being chased by the English in the same year. A report from London sent by the agents of the Fuggers makes mention of the capture of Portuguese ship by the English near Azores. This was one among the five ships that left Calicut for Lisbon. It was taken to London with the cargo. Out of the five ships that left Calicut only one reached Lisbon safe.[90]

Another report from Antwerp dated 3 October 1592 refers to the capture of three ships from Calicut by the English. The cargo of these ships was estimated to be worth 300,000 ducats. The Portuguese ship *Santa Maria* carrying spices was taken by the English to Portsmouth. The cargo of this ship consisted of 8,000 quintals of pepper among other things. [91]

Thus various powers interested in establishing trade in the Indian Ocean regions fought among themselves, and tried to get the matter settled through the intervention of the Popes and also through formulation of theories. In fact, apart from such rivalries we do not come across any important armed confrontation till the second half of the seventeenth century. The Portuguese to a considerable extent managed to keep other powers away from the Indian Ocean regions for some time. It does not mean that they managed to establish a very effective monopoly over the trade in this region. The trade going through West Asia to the Mediterranean regions could not be totally exterminated. They managed to keep the powerful Italian and German merchant financiers under their flag without giving them a free hand in trade with India. The association of the Fuggers with the Portuguese in their overseas enterprise could be very well understood against this backdrop.

NOTES AND REFERENCES

1. The Military Order of Christ which got the papal approval in 1319 was the successor of the Military Order of the Templars established in Jerusalem in 1119 to fight against the infidels. The Templars settled themselves in Tomar not far from Santarém in Portugal since 1159. Pope John XXII through his bull *Ad Ea* dated 15 March 1319 granted papal recognition to this new Military Order of Christ. Ref. Levy Maria Jordão, ed., *Bullarium. . .*, Tomus I, pp. 2-6. The same site was later occupied by the Military Order of Christ in 1356. If the declared aim of the Templars was to fight against the Muslims, the new Order of Christ was to play a significant role in the overseas and maritime expansion of Portugal with their headquarters at Tomar. The members of the Templars were incorporated into this new Order which finally was secularised in 1789 and continued only as a honorific order.
2. *Ibid.*, p. 21.
3. *Ibid.*, pp. 22-23.
4. *Ibid.*, pp. 31-34.
5. *Ibid.*, pp. 36-37.

6. *Ibid.*, p. 39.
7. *Ibid.*, p. 59.
8. *Ibid.*, pp. 60-61.
9. *Ibid.*, p. 73.
10. *Ibid.*, p. 70.
11. *Ibid.*, pp. 81-82.
12. *Ibid.*, pp. 98-99. Bull "Dum Fidei" issued by Pope Leo X on 7 January 1514.
13. *Ibid.*, pp. 122-123.
14. *Ibid.*, p. 137.
15. *Ibid.*, pp. 206-207.
16. João de Barros, *op. cit.,* Decada I, parte 2, p. 11.
17. Gaspar Correa, *op. cit.,* tomo 1, p. 298.
18. Barros, *op. cit.,* pp. 11-19.
19. *Ibid.*, Decada I, part 2, p. 21; Decada II, part 1, p. 181.
20. Marino Sanuto, *op. cit.,* tomo IV, col. 367.
21. J. H. Cunha Rivara, ed., *Arquivo Portuguez Oriental*, fasiculo V, part I, New Delhi, 1992 (reprint), pp. 30-31.
22. Historical Archives of Goa (hereafter HAG), MSS, codex no. 3027, fol. 21v.
23. HAG, MSS, codex no. 1043. fl. 50.
24. Fracansano Montalbodo, *op. cit.,* p. 94; Ludovico di Varthema, *op. cit.,* p. 151; Prospero Peragallo, ed., "Carta del Rei D. Manuel ao Rei Catholico Narrandolhe as Viagens Portuguesas a India desde 1500 ate 1505" in *Centenario do Descobrimento da America*, Lisboa, 1892, p. 31.
25. Thomé Lopes, *op. cit.,* tom. II, Nos 1&2, p. 187; João de Barros, *op. cit.,* Decada 1, part 2, p. 49.
26. *Cronica. . .*, p. 33.
27. Report of Giovanni Francisco de Affaitati in Marino Sanuto, *op. cit.,* tomo V, col. 129.
28. Gaspar Correia, *op. cit.,* tom 1, p. 746, Fernão Lopes de Castanheda, *op. cit.,* livro II, p. 384.
29. "Copia de uma carta de el-rei de Portugal enviada ao Rei de Castella acerca da Viagem e successo da India" in *Centenario do Descobrimento da America*, p. 29; Duarte Barbosa, *op. cit.,* Vol. 2, pp. 86-87.
30. Tomé Pires, *op. cit.,* Vol. 1, p. 45.
31. Gaspar Correia, *op. cit.,* p. 746.
32. Alvaro Velho, *Roteiro da Primeira Viagem de Vasco da Gama,* edited by Fontoura da Costa, Lisboa, 1969, p. 6.
33. Girolamo Priuli, *op. cit.,* Vol. II, p. 185.
34. *Ibid.*, Vol. I, p. 153; Vol. II, p. 156; Castanheda, *op. cit.,* pp. 381, 383; For further details, refer Visconde De Souveral, *Apontamentos sobre as antigas relações Politicas e commerciães de Portugal com a Republica de Venezia*, Lisboa, 1893.
35. Rinaldo Fulin, ed., *Archivio Veneto,* Vol. XXI, part I, p. 160; Priuli, *op. cit.,* p. 156.

36. Montalbodo, *op. cit.*, pp. 142-145.
37. *Ibid.*, pp. 145-147.
38. Priuli, *op. cit.*, Vol. I, p. 153; Vol. II, pp. 175, 197, 207, 335.
39. Barros, *op. cit.*, Decada 1, part II, pp. 183-86; Priuli, *op. cit.*, Vol. II, p. 335.
40. Priuli, *op. cit.*, Vol. II, p. 353; *Alguns Documentos do Archivo Nacional da Torre do Tombo*, Lisboa, 1892, pp. 135-138; Barros, *op. cit.*, Decada I, part II, p. 184.
41. Priuli, *op. cit.*, p. 405; Barros, *op. cit.*; Decada II, part I, p. 231; Castanheda, *op. cit.*, p. 384; Gaspar Correa, *op. cit.*, p. 748; Damião de Gois, *Cronica do Felicissimo Rei D. Manuel I,* part II, Coimbra, 1953, pp. 85 ff.
42. Leonardo da Ca'Masser, *op. cit.*, tom II, p. 36.
43. Eugenio Alberi, *op. cit.*, pp. 4 ff.
44. F. M. da Costa Lobo, *A Acção diplomatica dos Portugueses nos seculos xv e xvi , destinada a realização de descobertas e conquistas*, Lisboa, 1937, p. 139.
45. Donald Weinstein, *Ambassador from Venice Pietro Pasqualigo in Lisbon, 1501,* Mineapolis, 1960, pp. 47-48.
46. Cronica. . ., p. 29.
47. Priuli, *op. cit.*, Vol II, pp. 335, 342-43.
48. Castanheda, *op. cit.*, p. 384.
49. Barros, *op. cit.*, Decada II, part I, p. 181.
50. Shaykh Zaynud din, *Tuhfat-al-Mujahidin,* translated by David Lopes as *Historia dos Portuguêses no Malabar*, Lisboa, 1898, p. 40.
51. Relying on the evidence from the works of Wajih ad-Dayba and Castanheda, *op. cit.*, livro I, p. 254 and also Haji al-Dabir, Denison Ross proves against the statement of Barros *op. cit.*, decada II, part I, pp. 181ff; Correa, *op. cit.*, tom I, pp. 762-771; Ferishta, *History of the Rise of the Mahomedan Power in India*, Vol. I, Delhi, 1981, p. 204, and *Mirati Sikandari* that the fight at Chaul took place in January 1508, not in April 1507. Ref. Denison Ross, "The Portuguese in India and Arabia between 1507 and 1517", *The Journal of the Royal Asiatic Society of Great Britain and Ireland,* London, 1921, pp. 547, 550.
52. Ca'Masser, *op. cit.*, p. 36; Rinaldo Fulin, *op. cit.*, p. 205.
53. Damião de Gois, *op. cit.*, part II, p. 132; Barros, *op. cit.*, p. 293; Antonio Brasio, *Uma carta inedita de Valentim Fernandez*, Coimbra, 1959, p. 20; R. B. Serjeant, *The Portuguese off the South Arabian Coast: Hadrami Chronicles,* Oxford, 1963, pp. 44-45. It is interesting to note that only a few oriental writers like Sheik Zeinuddin in his *Tuhfat ul-Mujahidin* make mention of the defeat of Malik Ayyaz. Ref. David Lopes, *op. cit.*
54. *Cartas. . .*, tomo II, pp. 448-452. Evidently the income mentioned here could not be merely the payment for the purchase of *cartazes*, but on the other hand it could be the taxes levied on the cargo exported or imported as stipulated in the terms and conditions of the *cartazes*.

55. Simão Botelho, "O Tombo do Estado da India" in Rodrigo José de Lima Felner, ed., *Subsidios para a Historia da India Portugueza*, Lisboa, 1888 (hereafter *Subsidios*) pp. 134-138; Julio Firmino Judice Biker, ed., *Collecção de Tratados e Concertos de Pazes que o Estado da India Portugueza fez com os Reis e Senhores com quem teve Relações nas Partes da Asia e Africa Oriental desde o Principio da Conquista até ao fim do seculo XVIII* (hereafter *Tratados*), Lisboa, 1881, tomo I, pp. 63-65; Diogo de Couto, *Da Asia*, Decada IV, Parte II, Lisboa, 1778, pp. 316-317.
56. Simão Botelho, *op. cit.*, fol. 180v.
57. ANTT, MSS, Nucleo Antigo, no. 891.
58. *Cartas. . .*, tomo I, p. 321.
59. Simão Botelho, *op. cit.*, pp. 115-117; ANTT, Corpo Chronologico (hereafter CC), 1-105-75.
60. ANTT. CC. 1-105-75; ANTT. CC. 1-83-90; ANTT. CC. 1-107-38.
61. Archivum Romanum Societatis Jesu (hereafter ARSJ), Codex Goa 38, fols. 352-375.
62. Diogo de Couto, *op. cit.*, Decada xii, p. 239.
63. It is construed by the contemporary Persian chroniclers that the Portuguese were found in Surat at the invitation of the Mirzas to fight against the forces of Akbar. The Portuguese presumably interested in fishing in the troubled waters of Gujarat gladly reached Surat with a view to appropriating it as they came forward in 1535 under the pretext of helping Bahadur Shah of Gujarat against the emperor Humayun and occupied Diu. But on realising that Akbar had an invincible array, they resorted to diplomacy and the Portuguese governor sent an ambassador to Emperor Akbar for establishing peace and friendship. It is also held by some other chroniclers that Akbar himself had sent an envoy to Goa asking the Portuguese governor to send some persons to meet him at Surat. This attempt on the part of Akbar to send his envoys to the Viceroy at Goa could be on account of the interest Akbar had in being friendly with the Portuguese in the context of the pilgrimage of the members of his harem as well as his mother and other relations to Mocha. Ref. Abu-l-Fazl, *Akbar Nama*, New Delhi, 1977, Vol. III, p. 37; Diogo de Couto, *op. cit.*, Decada ix, Lisboa, 1786, pp. 64-87.
64 Diogo de Couto who was later appointed by Dom Philip, the king of Portugal, as the first keeper of the Archives (*Torre do Tombo*) in Goa collected the *firman* issued by Akbar from some one in Goa and showed it to the Viceroy (Dom Francisco Mascarenhas?). Later it was deposited in the Archives. Couto says that this *firman* was written on paper of high quality and sealed by the hanging seal of Akbar. In fact Couto expresses his surprise as to how this document reached the man in Goa. He, however, did not know the name of the person. The full text of the *firman* in Portuguese translation is provided by Couto. Ref. Couto, *op. cit.*, Decada x, pp. 62-84.
65. Goa Historical Archives, MSS. codex no. 1043. fl. 50.

66. Couto, *op. cit.,* Decada ix, pp. 86-87.
67. *Ibid.*, pp. 300-304.
68. *Cartas*. . . tom 1, p. 49; Correa, *op. cit.,* tomo II, pp. 215, 354, tomo III, pp. 543-544.
69. K. S. Mathew, "Khwaja Safar, the Merchant Governor of Surat and the Indo-Portuguese Trade in the Early Sixteenth Century", *Proceedings of the Indian History Congress*, Kurukshetra, 1982, p. 237.
70. K. S. Mathew, "Khwaja Shams-ud-din Giloni: A Sixteenth Century Entrepreneur in Portuguese India" in Roderich Ptak and Dietmar Rothermund, eds., *Emporia, Commodities and Entrepreneurs in Asian Maritime Trade, C. 1400-1750*, Stuttgart, 1991, pp. 364-65.
71. Armando Cortesão e Luis de Albuquerque eds., *Obras Completas de D. João de Castro*, Vol. II, Coimbra, 1976, pp. 110-111, 447.
72. HAG Mss. Codex no. 1363, fol. 48; Codex no. 1063, fols. 31, 34^{v}, 35, 41^{v}, 42; Codex no. 1363, fols. 48^{v}-69, 50, 47, 51, 49, 53^{v}-54; Codex no. 1063, fols. 37^{v}, 3; Codex no. 1363, fols. 139, 90, 92^{v}; Codex no. 1063, fols. 27, 27^{v} 28, 30, 37, 39; Codex no. 1363, fols. 45^{v}-46, 52, 58, 74^{v}-75, Codex no. 1083, fols. 28^{v}, 29; Codex no. 1363, fols. 91^{v}-92, 95, 197.
73. HAG Mss. Codex 1063, fols. 38^{v}-39, 45; Codex 1363, fols. 47^{v}-48.
74. Sanuto, *op. cit.,* Vol. xxxvi, col. 514.
75. ARSJ. Goa-38, fol. 370.
76. *Cartas*. . ., tom 1, p. 180; tomo III, p. 50, tomo. IV, p. 179, tomo vii, p. 174, tomo I, p. 126.
77. *Ibid.*, tomo. VII, p. 175.
78. Cortesão e Albuquerque, *op. cit.,* p. 44. 7
79. Josef Wicki, ed., "Duas Relações sobre a Situação da India Portuguesa nos anos 1568 e 1569", *Studia*, 8, 1961, p. 155.
80. *Subsidios*. . ., p. 244.
81. For a detailed study of the fortresses the following works could be consulted. *Subsidios*. . . ; Panduronga S. S. Pissurlencar, *Regiments das Fortalezas da India*, Bastora, 1951; Jean Aubin 'Le, "Orçamento do Estado da India de Antonio de Abreu", *Studia*, Vol. 4, Lisboa, 1959, pp. 169-289.
82. João de Barros, *op. cit.,* Decada IV, Part I, Lisboa, 1777, p. 583; Fernão Mendes Pinto, *Peregrinação*, Vol. I, Lisboa, 1957, pp. 46-63.
83. The Portuguese ship Santa Caterina was captured by the Dutch naval commander Heemekerck in the straits of Malacca in 1602. It was taken to Amsterdam and the proceeds of the sale of the cargo in the ship were passed on to the assets of the Dutch East India Company. Hugo Grotius was requested to give his opinion on this matter and he wrote a book in 1604-05 entitled *De Jure Praedae.* Chapter XII of this book was published anonymously in 1608 under the title *Mare Liberum sive de Jure quod Batavis competit ad Indicana commercia dissertatio*. The text with the English translation is published by Ralph van Deman Magoffin and James Brown Scott under the title *The Freedom of the Seas or the Right which belongs to the Dutch to take part in the East Indian trade*, New York, 1916.

84. Hugo Grotius, *op. cit.*, p. 12.
85. *Ibid.*, pp. 13, 16, 20-21.
86. *Ibid.*, pp. 45-46, 22-44, 47, 60, 65, 66-68.
87. Frei Serafim de Freitas, *De Justo Imperio Asiatico dos Portugueses*, Lisboa, 1961, Vol. II, pp. 90-91, 113-114; 93-94, 121, 150, 126, 106-107, 172-173.
88. C. H. Alexandrowicz, *An Introduction to the History of the Law of Nations in the East Indies, 16th, 17th and 18th Centuries*, Oxford, 1967, p. 70.
89. Victor von Klarwil, ed., *The Fugger News-Letters: Second Series*, London, 1926, p. 221.
90. *Ibid.*, pp. 239-240.
91. *Ibid.*, pp. 240-241.

CHAPTER 4

THE FUGGERS' HOLD ON MONEY AND MATERIAL IN EUROPE

The meteoric rise of the Fuggers from an obscure position to the phenomenal hold on money and material needed for the trans-continental trade is worth examining. From the profession of farmers the Fuggers gradually entered into weaving, business, mining and banking. Their emergence as leading bankers occurred simultaneously with the expansion of overseas trade with Asia as well as with the western hemisphere. Historians trace the lineage of the Fuggers to Hans Fugger hailing from a small village called Graben in Lechfeld, south of Augsburg. He moved from Graben to Augsburg and commenced his work in 1367 with the weaver named Widolf on the Kreuzgasse in Augsburg.[1] It is noted in the tax register of the imperial city of Augsburg that the Fugger arrived ("Fucker advenit") in 1367.

The city of Augsburg offered him chances to liberate himself from the clutches of the feudal set up of his village and become free as the old adage goes: *Stadtluft macht frei*. Augsburg named as *Augusta Vindelicorum* founded by the Romans in 15 B.C. during the reign of Caesar Augustus was strategically located on the high land between the Lech and Wertach rivers.[2] It was the capital of the province of Raetia. Christianity was brought to this city in the fourth century by Afra who was martyred and became the patron saint of the city. One of the important bishops of Augsburg called Ulrich became the second patron of the same urban centre. He joined forces with the king Otto I in A.D. 955 to defeat Magyars in the battlefield of Lechfeld. Augsburg grew as an important market, a centre for trading rural and urban products. It started with wool and linen-weaving. Around A.D. 1500 Augsburg had a population of

20,000. The number of weavers amounted to 2500 against 700 in 1466. Melanchthon, the sixteenth-century Reformer, compared Augsburg with Florence which was one of the centres for the emergence of early capitalism like Venice, Milan and Genoa. He wrote: "Augsburg is the German Florence and the Fuggers rank with the Medici".[3]

Hans Fugger seeking fortunes came to this city at a time when the artisans organised themselves in guilds and were taking steps to assume control of the government combining political and economic destinies in their own hands which they did in 1368, a year after his arrival. He did not come to the city empty-handed. He, in fact, paid the "admission fee" to the civic community from his own funds.

He married Klara Widolf, the daughter of Widolf. After the death of Klara Widolf, Hans Fugger married a certain Elisabeth Gfattermann, the daughter of Andreas Gfattermann, a business man from whom he received the inspiration to sell his own goods at various fairs like those of Nürnberg, Ulm, Donauwörth and Frankfurt rather than depending on others to come to his aid. In fact, his relations with Widolf made him an accomplished weaver and owner of a number of looms. The contact with Gfattermann, on the other hand, encouraged him to enter into trade and commerce. Probably he knew the importance of trade as seen in the adage: "A trade in hand finds gold in every land". Towards the end of his life, he was the proprietor of three houses in the city of Augsburg, besides the ancestral one in Graben, fifty looms in and around the city and a few vehicles drawn by horse to carry the merchandises to various centres of Fair. The famous firm of the Fuggers began with the humble but steady rise of Hans Fugger who died in 1408.

The successors of Hans Fugger did what they could to enhance the prestige of the family. They became members of the most distinguished guilds of the city, namely, those of the merchants and weavers which had an important role in the management of Augsburg. The membership in these guilds added prestige to their name. Jakob Fugger, one of the sons of Hans Fugger, became the master of the Weavers' Guild though he ceased to be a weaver. The members of the family dealt exclusively in the trade in spices, silk, and woollen materials based on Venice for a long time. Andreas, one of the sons of Hans Fugger, was very rich and was respected highly by others. The Emperor Frederick III of the Holy Roman Empire granted arms to Lukas, the eldest son of Andreas, in 1467. The arms consisted of a golden roe deer on a blue ground. It was an appropriate symbol for the volatile and ambitious Fugger. Andreas Fugger is remembered as the founder of the branch of the Fuggers called *Fuggers von Reh* or Fuggers of the Roe deer.[4] This branch lost its importance by 1494 when Lukas, the last son of Andreas, died and most of them turned out to be handicraftsmen or entered in the service of their better-off cousins, namely, the Fuggers of the Lilies. Until the seventeenth century they were found in the southwest and east of Germany. They were later known as Fukier in Warsaw.

Jakob, the younger son of Hans Fugger, became the founder of another branch of the Fuggers known as *Fugger von Gilgen* or Fuggers of the Lily. Their arms depicted a flowering Lily on a golden and blue ground. He was known as the masterweaver, alderman and merchant. He married Barbara Bässinger, the daughter of a goldsmith and mintmaster. Ulrich, Georg Markus and Jakob II who later became known as "Jakob the Rich" were his children. Jakob the elder died in 1469 leaving the charge of business to his eldest son Ulrich.[5] He dealt in transit trade with textiles and spices.

The branch of Fuggers of Lily which became prominent took its origin from Jakob I, the master of the Weavers' Guild of Augsburg, one of the sons of Hans Fugger as noted above. His matrimonial relations with the daughter of Bäsinger, the master of Augsburg mint, brought him in contact with the mining industry in Tyrol which, in course of time, paid high dividends. After the death of Jakob Fugger I, his sons, Ulrich, George and Peter, continued the traditional business of the family. When Peter died in 1473, the other two brothers persuaded another son of Jakob I who came to be known as Jakob Fugger II (1459-1526).

The Fuggers reached the zenith of their glory under Jakob Fugger II, known as Jakob the Rich, who was the grandson of Hans Fugger. He was interested in becoming a member of the clergy and so he received a canonry in the monastery of Herrieden in Franconia with a prebend of four silver marks. He was the tenth son of his parents. Despite the earnest interest to become a cleric and the initial studies in Latin and other related subjects, he had to give up the idea and take up business at the sudden demise of two of his brothers as noted above. He was required to look after the branches at Nürnberg and Venice. The Fuggers had a factory and an office in the German business house at Venice, *Fondaco dei Tedeschi*. The oriental goods were brought to Venice to be taken to various parts of the world. He went to Venice in 1477. Jakob Fugger and Ulrich Fugger got acquainted with their business at Venice and acquired mastery over it through their representatives, namely, the Köler brothers. They were introduced in Venice to the businessmen from Köln, Worms, Nürnberg, Lübeck, Regensburg, Ulm, Rheinland and Ravensburg. Jakob Fugger learned there the double entry system of book-keeping and use of Arabic numerals in calculation. He familiarised himself with the business in saffron, a novelty in the German cuisine, and other spices. The knowledge and experience he obtained in Venice broadened his outlook and helped to diversify the scope of his business.

He learned the primary lessons of modern business methods and got acquainted with the early capitalistic tendencies. Venice was away by ten days' journey by land from Augsburg. There were forty-four banks, goldsmith workshops, 16000 weavers producing silks, linen and cotton at Venice during this period. He concentrated his interest from 1477 on the *Fondaco dei Tedeschi*, containing warehouses, offices and home away from home. He learned new banking methods and the way in which profit could be made through business. He returned to Augsburg in 1479.

After spending approximately five years in Augsburg, he left for Innsbruck, the most important trading post of the firm. Archduke Sigismund resided in Innsbruck, the capital of Tyrol. Sigismund, was the son of Frederick IV known as "of the empty purse". The rich mines of Schwaz were owned by Sigismund who had forty illegitimate children to support and was always in financial crisis. He did not have any legitimate issue. Jakob Fugger went out of his way to

Jakob Fugger the Rich
(ALBRECHT DÜRER)

help Sigismund by advancing loans whenever he wanted and obtained valuable securities, rights over the mines and various trading privileges. On the abdication of Sigismund, Tyrol fell to his cousin Maximilian I, the son of Emperor Frederick III and Eleonore of Portugal. Jakob Fugger was always ready to extend loans to Maximilian who was born in the same month and year as he himself.

During another visit to Venice, Jakob Fugger met a man called Thurzo, a member of the influential Austrian family, who was an engineer engaged in silver and copper mining in Hungary. Thurzo pointed out to him the importance of mining and added that the princes (*Fürsten*), dukes (*Herzöge*) and counts (*Grafen*) would be beggars before the engineer if he were a Fugger. Jakob Fugger and his brother went on acquiring more buildings in Augsburg for the better conduct of business in Antwerp, Lisbon, Madrid, Venice, Rome and Pressburg without paying any heed to the suggestion given by Thurzo.

When Jakob Fugger became a partner in trade and three of them carried on trade together, it was agreed that the male heirs and descendants should leave the property in common for business and the female members would be given dowries. This was designed to keep the Fugger business undivided. He married Sybille Artzt on 9 January 1498. As he did not have any children, he established a partnership with his nephews Hieronymus, Ulrich, Raymund and Anton on the death of his brothers George and Ulrich in 1506 and 1510 respectively. The business continued to be known as *Jakob Fugger and Nephews* till his death on 30 January 1526.

Jakob Fugger II gave a new dimension to the business by entering in fields so far untrodden by his predecessors such as bills of exchange and mines which brought greater profits. The business in bills of exchange was already initiated by his father in the middle of the fifteenth century. He developed this branch and brought more profits about which detailed discussion will be made below.

Jakob Fugger II who headed the merchant dynasty decided to build an imposing structure in Augsburg which would be a noble residence and at the same time fitting headquarters of the firm. The house on the Rindermarket was too small for this business. He, therefore, purchased a complex of buildings on the Weinmarket in the heart of the city, on the old Roman road. In conformity with the civic regulations the house of the Fugger was fitted with a number of façades. Interior was adorned with Hans Burgkmair's frescoes mixed with Gothic and Renaissance styles. This house known as *Fuggerhaus* became the palace of a merchant dynasty, and the headquarters of the firm. Matthäus Schwarz, the chief book-keeper, worked with Jakob Fugger in this house. When Jakob Fugger assumed control of the firm in 1510 his share of the company capital was 80999 florins whereas it amounted to 667,790 florins in 1525. It is calculated that he made an average annual profit of 15.7 per cent. Martin Luther, who challenged the doctrine of the Catholic church by placing 95 theses on the door of the castle church in the university town of Wittenberg in Saxony on 31 October 1517, was interrogated by Cardinal Cajetan in the Fuggerhaus in 1518.

Apart from the diversification of business, he entered in various fields of activities related to religion and social work. He got constructed the church of St. Ann enriched with statues and decorations. This was planned in 1509 and was consecrated in 1518. Sebastian Loscher was the architect. The panels around the organ were designed by Jörg Breu. Albrecht Dürer designed the tomb for Ulrich and Georg Fugger. A tomb was prepared probably by Hans Burgkmair in the same church for Jakob Fugger. The Carmelite monks of St. Ann were bound to celebrate mass every day in the mortuary chapel of Jakob Fugger and to expose the blessed sacrament for adoration every Thursday, to sing *Salve Regina* on Saturdays and to conduct Eucharist procession on first Thursday of the month. The Carmelites began to move towards the Lutheran ideology in the wake of protestant reformation. As the Lutherans obtained this church during the Protestant Reformation, Jakob Fugger II instructed his nephews to bury him in another church occupied by the Catholics. Even the St. Moritz church, next to the Fuggerhaus and under their patronage, was influenced by the Lutherans.

Jakob Fugger donated generously for the construction of several other churches. His liking for architectural beauty is evinced in the construction of one of the existing Fugger houses in the Weinmarket at Augsburg. Just as Leonardo da Vinci and Erasmus of Rotterdam represented arts and sciences respectively, Jakob Fugger represented commerce of his period. He patronised Albrecht Dürer, one of the well-known painters of the time. The portraits of the Emperor and Jakob the Rich were painted by him.

The concern he had for the socially downtrodden is witnessed till today by the development of *Fuggerei* which is one of the premier institutions of charitable works in Europe in the first quarter of the sixteenth century. Jakob the Rich deposited an amount of 15,000 florins in 15ll for the endowment in the account called "St. Ulrich". He purchased an artisan quarter in the suburb of the city along with a tract of land in the "Kappenzipfel" in 1514. He made an agreement in 1516 with the city that he would provide decent, cheap and comfortable accommodation for deserving citizens of Augsburg. Fifty-two houses were completed by 1523. The *Fuggerei* was financed by the "St. Ulrich" account and turned out to be a mini-town inhabited by artisans. Each family got a separate apartment in the *Fuggerei*. The founder of the *Fuggerei* had laid down the condition that the beneficiaries should daily recite a *Pater Noster, Ave Maria* and *Credo* for the founder and the members of his family.

The progress made by the Fuggers under the able guidance of Jakob the Rich prompted several revolutionaries like Ulrich von Hutten and Martin Luther, the Augustinian monk, to write against them. Hutten used his satire against the Roman curia and the financial capital, the pope and his banker in Augsburg, namely, the Fuggers.[6] The sort of monopoly established by the Fuggers in Indian products and the trade in metals also came under the attack of Hutten. He pleaded that the Fuggers should be driven out of Germany.[7] Hutten considered the monopoly held by the Roman church, the dynastic monopoly of the Holy Roman Emperor and the economic monopoly of the Fuggers damaging. He attacked the monopoly of the Fuggers in Indian merchandises and circulation of coins lacking intrinsic value.[8]

The method by which Jakob Fugger and his associates made money came under the severe attack of Martin Luther who referred back to the medieval prohibition of taking interest. He declared that a great evil has befallen the German nation in terms of taking interest for loans. He expressed his surprise how God could permit a single person like the Fugger to amass large amount of money to the neglect of other Germans.[9]

Jakob Fugger reacted to the accusations levelled against him by his opponents like Martin Luther and Ulrich von Hutten in his characteristic manner. He got his position justified with the help of thinkers and rulers. St. Moritz church in Augsburg was under the patronage of the Fuggers. With a view to getting theological support for his taking interest on loan which was prohibited by the medieval church, he appointed Johannes Eck, a scholastic theologian and University professor in Ingolstadt, as the parish priest of St. Moritz. The theologian had propounded his idea that the ban on taking interest placed by the Church was obsolete and meaningless. He expressed his views long back in the disputations in Bologna, Vienna and Augsburg much before the controversy was initiated by Martin Luther. Hence Jakob Fugger found a support for his activities in Johannes Eck which prompted him to have him as the parish priest of St. Moritz. The theologian stated that interest-taking as such was not usury, and he defended that the rate of 5 per cent interest was quite acceptable. He added that the exchange brokerage did not fall within the definition of usury. He earned the sobriquet *Apostolus mercatorum* for his defence for the merchants and financiers.

Jakob Fugger did not forget to obtain the opinion of humanists and publicists in support of his capitalistic endeavours. His fellow-citizen Konrad Peutinger, a city clerk of Augsburg, knew the importance of the tax paid by the merchant houses of the city. He advocated free entrepreneurship, free economy and free trade against the backdrop of stricter spiritual, intellectual and political tutelage striking root in the wake of Lutheran Reformation. He defended the merchant houses and the Fuggers against the anti-monopoly movement of the Reformation and the ideas propounded by Martin Luther and Ulrich von Hutten.

The firm of the Fuggers had a number of agencies all over.

Fugger House on Maximillia Street

Lisbon, Seville, Madrid, Saragossa, Paris, Lyon, London, Helsingör, Malmö, Danzig, Riga, Reval, Narva, Torun, Poznan, Warsaw, Cracow, Lemberg, Kieve, Breslau, Teschen, Leuscheau, Neusohl, Vienna, Ofen, Pest, Sibiu, Cluj, Maribor, Agram,Trieste, Veniced, Padua, Milan, Genova, Pisa, Florence, Naples, Rome, Bolzano, Innsbruck, Munich, Nürnberg, Fulda, Hohenkirchen, Zwickau, Magdeburg, Berlin, Hamburg, Lübeck, Strasbourg, Frankfurt on Main, Mainz and Cologne were some of the trading posts in Europe. All these centres were connected with the headquarters at Augsburg through a network of communications. Correspondents appointed in various places kept him abreast with day-today information.

Raymund Fugger I (1489-1535) was the father of Georg Fugger II. He was the founder of the Raymund-line of the Fuggers and was really a good merchant. He was the counsellor of the Roman Emperor. But the actual running of the family business after the death of Jakob Fugger the Rich, was solely in the hands of Anton Fugger I.

After the demise of Jakob the Rich, the entire business passed on into the hands of his nephews who were his partners since 1510. But he realised that one of his nephews, Hieronymus, was not to be entrusted with the business as he did not show any interest. So according to the second will prepared on 22 December 1525, Raymund and Anton, the other two nephews, were to continue the business. But as Raymund was not able to undertake business trips, the entire business was to be conducted at the will and pleasure of Anton Fugger (1493-1560) under whom the firm reached its zenith of glory.

The firm which was under the name *Jakob Fugger and Nephews* continued to be guided by Anton Fugger. Raymund Fugger I (1489-1535) and Hieronymus Fugger died in 1535 and 1538 respectively. So, Anton Fugger took his nephews Hans, Jakob, Georg, Christopher and Raymund into business in 1538 and the firm was henceforth known as *Anton Fugger and Nephews*. He was the son of Jakob Fugger's elder brother Georg and was designated as crown prince disregarding the claims of his elder brothers Markus and Raymond and the sons of Jakob's eldest brother Ulrich, Hieronymus and Ulrich. He had his training in Augsburg and in the trading posts like Nürnberg, Breslau, Cracow, Vienna, Budapest and Schwaz as an ordinary "trade clerk". He spent six years in Rome. Soon after assuming charge of the firm, he conducted a general survey of the assets and liabilities. The account books of the various trading posts like Venice, Rome, Antwerp, Nürnberg, Breslau, Schwaz, Bozen, Fuggerau, Vienna, Leipzig, Hohenkirchen, Ofen, Neusohl, Cologne and Frankfurt on the Main, agencies in Spain and the headquarters at Augsburg were examined by the auditors. Ownership of the mines in Hungary was restored in 1526. He was made count of the Holy Roman Empire in the same year by Charles V who obtained successive loans from Anton Fugger, in 1526 for his fights against the Turks, in 1527 for financing Archduke Ferdinand's election as king of Bohemia and Hungary, another loan in 1529 for defending Vienna against the Turks. Further loans were advanced by Anton Fugger to Charles V in 1530 for his coronation as Holy Roman Emperor in Bologna and Ferdinand's election as king in Frankfurt in 1531, for the support of the campaign against Würtenberg in 1534, for the fight against Tunis and Algiers in 1535 and to prepare for the confrontation with France in 1538.

Anton Fugger obtained rights to saline mine deposits in Transylvania and the imperial right to mint. The lease of the *maestrazgos* in Spain was renewed during his time and the Hungarian leases were extended. Anton Fugger remained more loyal to the Emperor than to the Pope. This was clear from the fact that he made money out of the sack of the papal city of Rome by the imperial forces. This, in fact, paved the way for the closing of the Fugger office in Rome after the departure of the imperial soldiers.

Anton Fugger invested in the business with South America since 1532 when he got the licence to colonise Chile and southern Peru from the Spanish king. But this was not vigorously followed up after the first ship wrecked. He withdrew from this endeavour gradually. By 1536 he got involved in the negro traffic or slave trade between Africa and America. Fugger agent in Santo Domingo made large profit from the human cargo and the merchandise brought back from the Spanish colonies.

Anton Fugger

He was in full control of the management of the firm without being accountable to anybody. After realising that the Fugger firm had a lot of liabilities and large sums were to be recovered from those who took loans from them, he adopted a policy of caution. Instead of advancing more money he began to try all means to recover what was due from the debtors. Anton Fugger became rather disillusioned by 1546 since his nephews did not show great interest in the business and so he went to the extent of thinking of giving it up. However, the firm had the largest business capital ever held till then by a single firm. In 1546 it had the working capital of five million guldens, the greatest asset ever the Fuggers had till the date. The headquarters were removed temporarily from Augsburg to Schwaz in the same year on account of the troubles in Germany. As his associates were not as active as his predecessors the business began to decline after 1550. Anton was also partially responsible for this state of affairs since he had a passion for making money for his own interest. Frequent loans to the Emperor for his wars and the impossibility to recover them created a situation quite detrimental to the well-being of the firm. Sometimes, even disregarding the unwillingness of his nephews he took over the business on his own account as in 1552. Anton Fugger became quite worried about the large number of creditors to whom payment had to be made and the financial crisis on account of mismanagement at Antwerp by his agent Örtel around 1557. In 1558 he wrote: "The creditors are many. A man might shudder to think of them." He found himself unable to pay them off.

As his sons were too young to take up the business, he approached his nephews one by one to continue the work after his death. Finally he laid down that Hans Jakob (1516-1575), one of his nephews, should assume the responsibility together with Markus, the eldest son of Anton Fugger, without altering the name of the company for six years more. He died on 14 September 1560 full of anxiety about the future of the firm. He thus worked for half a century in this business and was the sole director for thirty years. He was described by a Florentine man as the "real prince among the other merchants".

The third generation of the Fuggers was not very successful in business. Hans Jakob Fugger along with Markus resumed the work left by their predecessor. Hans was more preoccupied with things other than business. He conducted his wedding ceremony at the Bavarian Court in Munich in May 1560. On his arrival at the ancestral house at the Weinmarket, Hans Fugger took steps to improve it. Planning and building started immediately. The walls of his chambers were adorned with beautiful hangings of gilt leather especially made for him in Venice. Alessandro Trevisio of Treviso from the Court of the Duke Albert of Bavaria, a famous artist, took up the work. Famous Amsterdam painter Frederick Sustris and his assistant Antonio Ponzano were entrusted with the work of decorating large rooms in the house with frescoes. They worked for four years and completed the masterpiece which remains to this day declaring to the world the greatness of the Fuggers. Hans Fugger built up a world famous library in the Fugger mansion at Augsburg. The name of the firm continued to be the same for a longer period than what was intended by Anton Fugger. But the international contacts were becoming less valuable and the "Fugger Bonds" lost importance after the death of Anton Fugger on account of the decline in the credibility of the firm. The firm took an amount of 300,000 florins as loan from Spanish usurer Juan de Curiel della Torre at 10 per cent interest in 1563. This is an indication of the weakness of the firm. It became weaker still on account of the fact that Hans Fugger had taken large loans both on his own account and that of the firm. He had to leave Augsburg in 1563 finding himself totally unable to clear his loans. All his property including his castle of Taufkirchen was handed over to his creditors. He had a debt of more than one million florins on his own account. At last it was agreed that he would leave the firm and the partners would take upon themselves all the liabilities of the firm and his debts in Augsburg. Finally Hans Jakob Fugger entered in the service of the Duke Albert of Bavaria and moved to Munich. He died in 1575 leaving his descendants unable to come up any more.

Georg II (+ 1569) and Raymund Fugger, his brothers, died in 1569 while Christopher Fugger, last of his brothers, took up Hans

Auszug aus der Genealogie des Fürstlich und Gräflich Fugger'schen Hauses

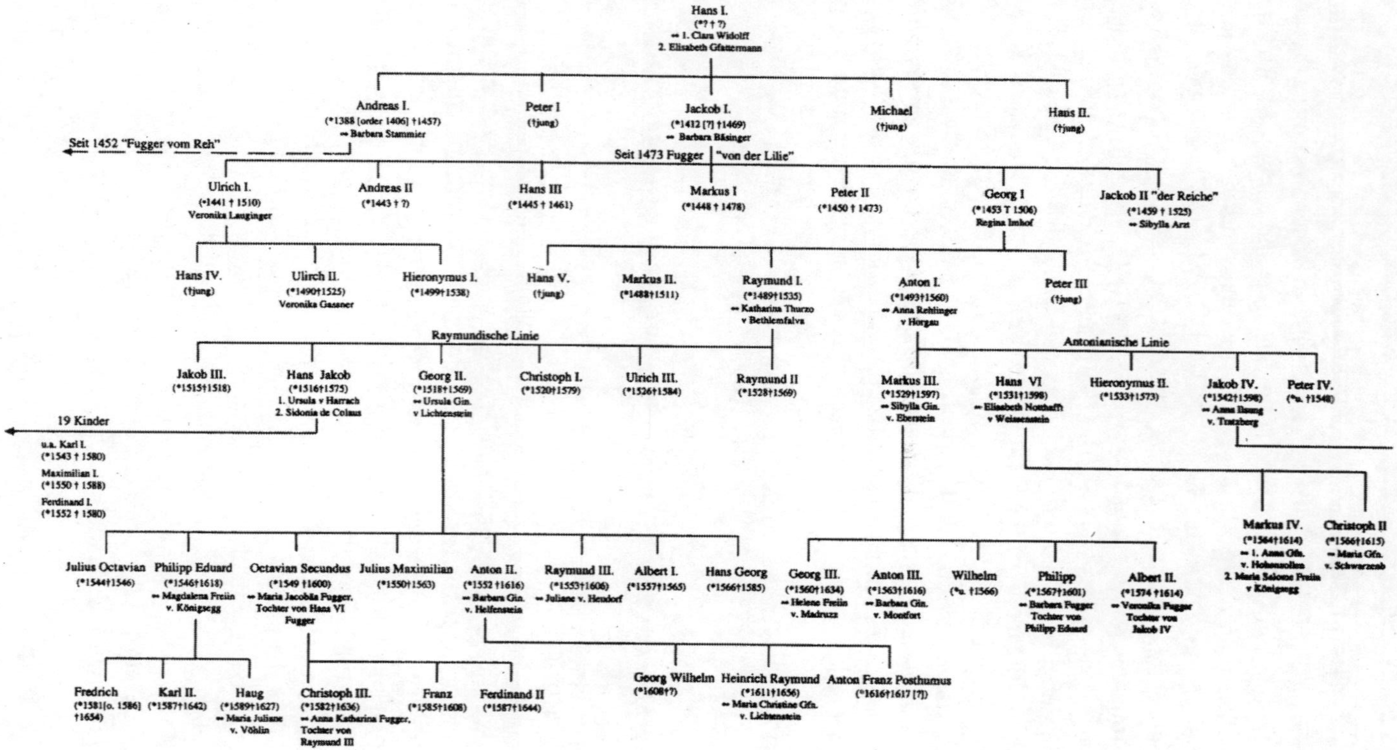

Jakob's part in 1572 and left the firm in quarrel. He expired in 1579. Markus Fugger, the elder son of Anton Fugger, had to assume the management of the firm on his own since the other brothers refused to do it. A considerable part of the private fortune which Anton Fugger had already withdrawn from the business was brought into it. Now on the business was carried soley by the three sons of Anton Fugger, namely, Markus, Hans and Jakob, and it functioned under the name *Marx Fugger and Brothers*. Markus Fugger handed over the business in 1591 to his brother Hans who further passed it on to his son Hans in 1597. Anton Fuggers three sons passed away in 1597.

Philipp Eduard (1546-1618) and Octavian Secundus Fugger (1549-1575) were the sons of Georg Fugger II who died in 1569. Both of them were brought up in Ingolstadt under the care of Hieronymus Ziegler and Nikolaus Everhardus from 1555. Philipp Eduard visited the universities of Dole, Basel, Padua, and Bologna. Octavian Secundus was admitted in the University of Bologna in 1561. Both of them studied jurisprudence and Latin classics in Bologna up to 1565. Later they went to Rome and stayed in *Collegium Germanicum* to deepen their knowledge as desired by their parents. Philip Eduard Fugger went back to Augsburg in 1567 and Octavian Secundus in 1568. When the latter went to Louvain for further studies, the former took up the training in the Fugger factory at Antwerp till 23 August 1569. Count Philipp Eduard Fugger (1546-1618) was another lover of books and he added great deal to the library established by Hans Fugger.[10]

Octavian Secundus too had his training in the factory at Antwerp up to 1573. Both of them learnt to be on their own. Subsequently they got permission from Markus III (1529-1597) and Hans VI Fugger (1531-1598) to administer their inherited asset by themselves from 1 January 1574. Their younger brothers, Raymund III (1553-1606) and Hans Georg (1566-1585), assisted them. Thus 1574 marked the beginning of a new life for Philipp Eduard and Octavian Secundus Fugger. They finally decided to enter into the group of the merchants involved in the import of pepper into Europe from India.[11] "Georg Fuggerische Erben" functioned from the house of Philip Eduard Fugger at Augsburg. It had its factors in

Madrid, Lisbon, Goa, Hamburg, Köln, Frankfurt/Main and Venice. Philip Krel was the most important of the factors the Fuggers had in Madrid, where he worked from 1580 to 1595. The firm was very pleased with the activities of Krel so much so that when he died on 4 September 1595 in Spain both Philip Eduard and Octavian Secundus showered praises on him for the services he rendered to the firm. During the period of Asia contract (1586-1591) it had factories also in Lübeck, Amsterdam, Middelburg and Antwerp besides a few correspondents at Genoa, Lyon and Vienna.[12] The firm had Philip Litscher as one of its factors in Madrid from 1590. During the period of the pepper contract (1586-1591) Hans Jakob Krel and Hans Ulrich Bechler looked after the interest of the Fuggers in Lisbon while Hans Christoph Manlich was taking care of the business concern of *Markus Matthäus Welser und Gesellschaft* (Markus Matthäus Welser and Company). At times Manlich received a lump sum from Philip Eduard and Octavian Secundus Fugger every year for the help he used to extend to the *Georg Fuggersche Erben*. As the head of the Fuggers branch in Lisbon, Joseph Hartlieb looked after the business in Lisbon from 1589. Though there arose some difference of opinion between Hartlieb and *Georg Fuggersche Erben* on account of the *Europa- Kontrakt* by 1591 this was not very apparent and began to sink. After 1591 he was made the solicitor rather than the factor for the Fuggers in connection with the Asia Contract. The firm had Ferdinand Cron as its factor in Goa from 1586 to 1591 of which further details will be provided in the following chapter.

Hans Eberlin took up the work from 1593 to 1595 as the chief account of this firm after Bechler. He visited the Fugger Factories in Lisbon and Madrid and died in 1598. During his absence of four years in Spain and Portugal, Daniel Krel, the brother of Philip Krel, the factor of the Fuggers in Spain, substituted him in the central office in Germany. He was succeeded by Arbogast Nachtreub in 1598 as chief accountant who died in 1609. Later, after the liquidation of the firm of *Georg Fuggersche Erben* he worked with Philipp Eduard in Augsburg. This firm had several other assistants like Hans Ulrich Bechler, one of the sons of Hans Bechler, who was associated with the commercial activities from 1594. Hans Jakob Krel (1565-1628), one of the sons of Daniel Krel, worked in the Fuggers factory at Lisbon from 1586 to 1589. Later, from 1599 to 1600 he was found in the central office at Augsburg.

The firm of *Georg Fuggersche Erben* had Hans Ulrich Bechler, the son of Hans Bechler, as their agent in Lisbon from 1583 to 1588. From 1594 he worked in the central office of the firm at Augsburg till his death on 16 March 1589. Bechler had already worked with Georg Fugger II and accompanied Octavian Secundus to Louvain. He had worked in Madrid from 1548 to 1593 in the Fuggers' factory in place of the factor Jobst Walther. Hans Jakob Krel (1565-1628), the son of Daniel Krel, was an accountant from 1586 to 1589 in the Fuggers' factory in Lisbon. Later, from 1599 he worked in the central office of the *Georg Fuggersche Erben*, which was at the house of Philipp Eduard Fugger at Augsburg.

The Fuggers and the Holy Roman Empire

Astute as the Fuggers were, they prepared the theological ground to get rid of the ecclesiastical punishment for those who gave loan on interest. The Church had issued orders to declare as heretic those who collected interest which prevented many from enhancing their capital through loans. The financiers could not thrive under dispensation of this nature. So, the Fuggers and other influential merchant-financiers of Augsburg took the help of a theologian named Johannes Eck, of the University of Ingolstadt, in 1514 to prove the thesis that Christians could take moderate interest of 5 per cent for the loans advanced to others as mentioned earlier. Though the university of Bologna accepted this thesis, the universities of Leipzig and Vienna refused to do it until the imperial council came down heavily upon them. Thus the Fuggers obtained civil recognition for usury and the practice became common. The avenues for enhancing capital were thus wide open to the Fuggers without being objects of ecclesiastical censure. The imperial crown itself provided them with golden opportunities.

The relation with the ruler of the Holy Roman empire in some sense helped the Fuggers to accumulate capital through the establishment of their hold on silver and copper mines but to a large extent it undermined the financial position of the Fuggers on account of loans extended to the Emperor from time to time. During times of need, the Emperor approached the Fuggers for large sums of loan which he could not repay. The Fuggers found it delicate to decline the request of the Emperor. This weakness of the Fuggers was exploited by Habsburg rulers, especially in the context of the religious wars. The various phases of the relation between the Fuggers and the Holy Roman Emperor shall be discussed in a historical perspective.

Ulrich Fugger did business with the Habsburgs, or the house of Austria in 1473. The emperor Frederick III on his way to Trier in connection with the marriage of his son Maximilian with Maria, the daughter of Charles the Bald, the ruler of Burgundy, obtained good clothes and silks from Ulrich Fugger. In fact Ulrich Fugger was recommended to the Emperor as an honest and sound man by Charles Rebwein, the chancellor of the Emperor. He provided the Emperor, his son and his suite with clothes of the best variety without expecting any payment. As a mark of his appreciation for the business he did in cloth and silks with Ulrich Fugger, the Emperor gifted the coat of arms of lilies to him. This is considered to be the first business with the Emperor. Thus the relation is traced back to 1473. As the house of Austria was in the process of adding Burgundy, the Netherlands, Spain, Bohemia and Hungary to their realm, the Fuggers got a golden opportunity to expand their enterprise in to the ever growing Empire. In return for the services of court financiers, they obtained solid securities in terms of mines to be worked, prerogatives in metal tradings with silver, copper, tin and mercury in Tyrol, Carinthia, Thuringia, Bohemia, Slovakia and Spain. They acquired the right to mine silver from Schwaz as security for a loan advanced to Archduke Sigismund residing in Innsbruck, capital of Tyrol in 1487. The Archduke ruled Tyrol as the son of Frederick IV, the emperor of Holy Roman empire. He was always in financial difficulties on account of which he approached the Fuggers for loans. In return for the money advanced, the Archduke handed over mining rights to the Fuggers and eventually abdicated. Tyrol was assigned to his cousin Maximilian who restored the unity of Habsburg territories. His son Philip the Handsome married Joan of Castile, heiress of Spain. By 1489 they obtained virtual control of the rich mine of Tyrol.

Jakob Fugger I, one of the sons of Hans Fugger who married the daughter of Bäsinger, the mint master of Augsburg, got interested in the mining industry in Tyrol by the middle of the fifteenth century. Bäsinger went to Hall, the centre of the growing mining district of Tyrol because of which the Fuggers too started showing interest in the mining industry in Tyrol. Jakob II or Jakob the Rich who was busy in trade in spices, silks and woollens made a decisive change in the business in 1487 when, together with the Genoese Antonio de Cavallis, he advanced a sum of 23,627 florins to Sigismund, the Archduke of Tyrol. This amount was given against the security of the mortgage of the silver mines of Schwaz and the whole of the province of Tyrol. If the money was not duly and punctually repaid, the silver from the above mentioned region was to be handed over to the creditors.

The indebtedness of Sigismund became greater on account of another large sum of loan given by the three Fugger brothers namely, Ulrich, Georg and Jakob, in 1488. An amount of 150,000 florins was advanced to the Archduke against the entire output of silver from Schwaz at a very low price till the debt was cleared. The Fuggers themselves owned mines in Tyrol and Carinthia which became increasingly important in course of time. As mentioned elsewhere, the influential Austrian family of Thurzo put the idea of entering into mining industry while he met him in Venice.

Maximilian was the son of Emperor Frederick III and Eleonore of Portugal and was born in the same year and month as Jakob Fugger II. Both of them depended on each other for money, mining rights, trading prerogatives, social privileges and political influences. Maximilian became coregent with his father Emperor Frederick III in 1486. On the death of the latter in 1493 he became emperor on his own. He was fond of Augsburg and often visited the Golden city. He spent 182 days at Augsburg in 1500. He obtained the sobriquet of "Mayor of Augsburg".

The Fuggers had very close contact with Emperor Maximilian

I of the Roman Empire. Sigismund, the Archduke, handed over the Government of Tyrol to Maximilian I in 1490. Maximilian I got possession of Tyrol and became the Emperor too in due time as mentioned earlier. Jakob Fugger II and Maximilian I probably first met at the Frankfurt *Reichstag* (Diet) where the former was found taking part in the Frankfurt Fair. As a prince, Maximilian used to visit the house of the Fuggers at the Weinmarket in Augsburg and was familiar with their financial position. He re-established his contacts with the Fuggers in 1492. As he was a spendthrift and used to luxurious life-style, he needed more and more money. Being a bad manager of funds he had to approach the Fuggers for a loan in 1492. He had also been engaged in military campaigns against France and Venice. Matthäus Lang, the adviser to the Emperor, visited the Fuggers' office in Augsburg several times and requested them to be bankers of the Emperor in return for the rights the latter would give to the Fuggers over the copper mines of Tyrol. Jakob Fugger recalled to his mind the suggestion made by Thurzo. He entered into some agreement with the Emperor regarding the mines in Tyrol against the stipulated payment made to him.

Probably, the loan was given by the Fuggers to Maximilian against the silver production of Tyrol. It is found that they had a claim of 40,000 florins on the silver from Tyrol in 1494. Against the wish of the Fuggers, Maximilian tried to pledge the silver to a Nürnberg consortium. But the Fuggers declined to release their mortgage. The Emperor had to lead an expedition in 1496 to Italy. Despite persistent requests from the Emperor the loyal cities declined to extend any financial assistance to him. At last the Fuggers came to his rescue by furnishing 121,600 florins on the security of the copper mines of Tyrol. The Fuggers being aware of the inability of the Emperor to repay the amount kept half of the sum offered for satisfying the claims they had on silver. Therefore, in effect the Emperor got only 13,000 florins besides another deduction made by the State Government for its own use.

The counsellors of Maximilian explained to him that every florin borrowed from the Fuggers put him under greater indebtedness to them and that they would have a major say in the running of the empire if things continued to be so. Maximilian attempted a counter move in 1498 through a copper syndicate. The Fuggers strongly resisted it as an encroachment on private enterprise. The syndicate was broken in a year's time to the greatest displeasure of the emperor.

The Fuggers were again constrained to advance another amount of 27,000 florins to the emperor on the security of silver. Maximilian had to wage war against Switzerland in 1499. But he did not have sufficient funds with him and consequently he requested the Fuggers to make fresh advance against the copper from Tyrol. The Emperor sent his trusted man, Georg Gossembrot, to persuade the Fugger to give loan on the security of copper from Tyrol. They agreed. This was in fact protested by Gossembrot who tried to have the monopoly of the copper market. Thus the Fuggers became the masters of trade in copper as well as silver on account of the financial crisis the Roman Emperor was going through. Their chief occupation in the subsequent years continued to be in the trade in silver and copper. The Habsburgs had, as the best security, the feudal lord's share of copper and silver production.

The dependence of the Roman Emperor on the Fuggers became more and more pronounced as he started further enterprises, especially in the wake of the ten years' war in Italy (1508-1517). As the general taxes of the empire were not enough he was allowed to raise loans from the business houses in 1507. Since he did not have strong security except the mortgage of the Crown lands, he, as the Count of Kirchberg and Lord of Weissenhorn, mortgaged the revenues of these regions to the Fuggers for 50,000 florins. Because the mortgage was never released the Fuggers became the proprietors of these lands. They became the lords of the county of Kirchberg and the town of Weissenhorn in 1507. Maximilian could not get himself anointed and crowned by the Pope in Rome according to the custom prevailing since the time of Charlemagne and Otto the Great. He did not succeed in reaching the Eternal city on account of the hostility of Venice. So, with the help of the Fuggers he declared himself as the "Roman Emperor Elect" at Trent on 4 February 1508. Therefore, Jakob Fugger could be considered an Emperor-maker. In view of the requirements of the war the amount already collected was not enough and, therefore, in 1508 he approached the Fuggers for another loan of 8,000 florins from them against the right to farm salt at Hall and Tyrol. Further, an amount of 128,750 florins was taken from the Fuggers as loan on the security of the silver and copper production. Though the League of Cambrai gave 170,000 ducats payable at distant places like Rome, Florence and Antwerp, the amount he wanted immediately in Germany could not be realised except through the bills of exchange issued by Jakob Fugger. A transaction of this magnitude in such a short time through bills of exchange speaks of the financial potentialities of the Fuggers. They made great profit through the arbitrage of the bills.

Maximilian started war against Venice with the money advanced by the Fuggers who had a vital link with Venice in trade. This could have dealt a fatal blow to the Fuggers. But, Jakob Fugger, shrewd as he was, negotiated peace that settled the war which neither side could win. He received commercial privileges both from the Emperor and from the Doge.

Grateful as he was to the Fuggers, Maximilian came out to help the Fuggers in a difficult problem in 1509. Melchior von Meckau, Prince-Bishop of Brixen, had invested a lot of money with the Fuggers very secretly outside the reach of the Pope and the Emperor. Prince-Bishop and Cardinal Melchior von Meckau died in Rome in March 1509. Large amount invested by him with the Fuggers brought sizeable interest. The investment amounted to 152,931 florins in 1509. Compared with the trading capital of the Fuggers which was only 198,915 florins, this was a considerable sum. Though this amount was kept in secrecy, on the demise of the cardinal the news leaked out and reached the ears of several people including Martin Luther. The Fuggers were involved in the sale of indulgences, and they had financed the recruitment of the Swiss Guard. The Fuggers had received the concession for the papal mint on account of the financial assistance extended to the recruitment of the Swiss guards. So Martin Luther attacked the Fuggers very vehemently. Pope was in a dilemma. The cardinal should not have possessed such a huge sum which was to be handed over to the church. Being aware of the steps taken by the Pope to claim the assets of the late cardinal, Jakob Fugger appealed to Maximilian for help and apprised him of the fact that the loss of such a huge some would bring about the ruin of the Fugger bank. In other words, if Jakob Fugger had to part with an amount of this magnitude, the Emperor would not have any chance of getting loan from the Fuggers. Maximilian issued a decree prohibiting the transfer of the assets before the case had been settled. The problem was solved taking into account the interest of the Fuggers. The papacy in Rome, Jakob Fugger and Maximilian stood to gain from this. The Fugger bank did not collapse, but on the contrary went on making headway. The Diet met at Augsburg in 1510 and celebrated the victory. Jakob Fugger was elevated to the nobility of the Holy Roman Empire on 8 May 1511 which was totally unprecedented. No merchant had so far been given nobility though coats of arms were given to those merchants who had rendered valuable services.

The Emperor developed a crazy idea of becoming Pope in 1511. He decided to borrow 300,000 ducats from the Fuggers through his agent Paul von Lichtenstein to bribe the Cardinals for his election to the papacy. The interest itself was calculated to be 100,000 ducats. The Fugger bank in Rome was supposed to hand over the loan to the envoys of the Emperor. The Emperor had agreed to accept the loan on conditions that were extremely beneficial to the Fuggers. Though this remained a pious wish it speaks for the dependence on, and confidence in, the Fuggers, as far as the Emperor was concerned. Jakob Fugger gave a loan of 12,000 florins to the Emperor in 1514 against the revenues of Tyrol and 32,000 florins against the lordship of Biberbach. The Emperor pressed Jakob Fugger for further loan in 1515. But he declined saying that in the same year large sums to the tune of 300,000 florins were already advanced to him on the security of silver and copper. It was also added that a great part of the loan was not repaid. The Emperor had pledged silver for seven to eight years to come. Similarly, copper was also pledged for four years. As the production of these metals sank, the debts were delayed. Once again the Emperor persuaded Jakob Fugger to advance an amount of 40,000 florins in conjunction with Höchstetter on the security of the copper from Schwaz for the years 1520-1523. The price fixed for 100 weights of copper was 4.5 florins. Again a loan of 10,000 florins was advanced on the security of silver and a grant of customs privileges. Thus, one can conclude that the Fuggers were very close to the Roman Emperor and that they had reached great heights in financial dealings.

When the Emperor received a lump sum of 100,000 florins at the time of his grandson's release from tutelage whereby interference in the government of Netherlands was stopped, the money had to be transferred from Antwerp. The Fugger agents in Antwerp facilitated the transfer. In 1516 the Fuggers advanced a sum of 20,000 florins to the Emperor.

The material wealth and possessions of the Fuggers were further enhanced on account of the grants of land made by the emperor who wanted money from them. Lang was sent again to the office of the Fuggers. In return for the amount required by Maximilian, Jakob Fugger was given the earldom (*Grafschaft*) of Kirchberg on Iller with a castle (*Schloss*) and sixty villages, the lordship (*Herrschaft*) of Weissenhorn with nineteen villages, and the lordship of Pfaffenhofen on the Roth with twelve villages. All these were against a payment of around two million German marks (about 50,000 Gulden). It is reported that towards the end of his life the Emperor was forced to borrow from the Fuggers profusely even "to eat".

Maximilian I was keen on placing his grandson, Charles V, Duke of Burgundy and king of Spain on the throne. There were two other contenders for the same, namely, Francis I of France and Henry VIII of England. As the seven electors were not unanimous and some of them were liable to be bribed, the election to the throne could be manipulated and the candidates came forward with the offer of money.

The attempts made by Maximilian I to get his grandson Charles of Spain elected as the Emperor through the financial assistance of the Fuggers show the power wielded by Jakob Fugger. Two loans to the tune of 2,000 florins and 1,000 florins were already given to the Emperor by Jakob Fugger in 1518, being aware of the pathetic condition of the aging Emperor. Yet Maximilian approached for a very large sum to bribe the electors of Germany. Charles V had already several financial dealings with the Fuggers through their agent Wolf Haller at Antwerp when he ruled only the Netherlands. This was recognised by Charles V when he took up the reins of Spain in 1517. In fact, the same Haller travelled from Antwerp to Spain in 1519 for some financial transactions between Charles V and the Fuggers in the context of the election. Charles declared his plan to become the king of the Romans at whatever cost it might be. As soon as this was disclosed, Francis I of France came forward to spend three million *livres*, half of his annual income. Therefore, Charles had to bargain with the German electors who wanted payment in hard cash rather than promises. While the negotiations were going on Maximilian died on 12 January 1519. Immediately Francis doubled the amount he promised to the electors with a view to increasing the demands on Charles. The Fuggers stood by the House of Austria and extended support to Charles. The representatives of Charles reported time and again that the electors would give credence only to the promises of Fuggers if they were to vote. Therefore, Francis I tried to woo the Fuggers to his side and asked them to accept a bill of 300,000 écus from him. Yet the Fuggers remained loyal to Charles. In fact, everyone was nervous regarding the possibility of the South German financiers shifting their loyalty to Francis I. The Swabian League too insisted that the South Germans should not entertain any request from Francis I for credit or bills of exchange. Therefore, it was made clear that Francis would get no support from the South Germans. Charles, however, had to raise an amount of 720,000 florins for the election. Helpless as he was, he turned to the Fuggers for new loans. Being aware of the fact that repayment was not forthcoming and large sum by way of arrear was pending, they gave vent to their grievances. At last, the Fuggers provided a sum of 543,000 florins, the Welsers 143,000 florins and the Genoese and Florentine merchants an amount of 165,000 florins to Charles V in connection with his election. Thus, the election of Charles V to the Imperial Crown of Holy

Roman Empire was chiefly due to the generosity and loyalty of the Fuggers.

The Emperor did not pay back the amount to the merchant financiers who helped him without any limit in his election. He transferred the claims of the Fuggers in part to Tyrol and in part to Spain in 1521. The indebtedness of the Emperor to the Fuggers prevented him from taking any steps against them even on the face of popular demands. There were complaints about usurers, abuse of monopoly, speculation and profiteering. Therefore, the matter was raised in the imperial Diet and in 1523 the fiscal arm of the imperial council of Regency brought out an indictment on the houses of merchants in Augsburg, prominent among whom were the Fuggers. Monopoly and illegal mercantile practices adopted by the Fuggers came for the common attack. It was rumoured that based on the discussions in the Diet, capital of individual firms would be restricted to 50,000 florins and the number of branches of such houses would be limited to three. These suggestions would have dealt a fatal blow on the business house of the Fuggers. Emperor Charles was in a fix not knowing what to do in such a situation. Being aware of the harm that could be done to his firm, Jakob Fugger wrote to the Emperor in early 1523 that the Fuggers remained always loyal to the House of Austria and he and his cousins supported his claim for the Imperial Crown.[13]

In 1523 the Fuggers received very little of the claim of 415,000 florins on Tyrol. But nothing was paid on the claim transferred to Spain. Jakob Fugger became impatient since no full repayment of the huge loans advanced to the Emperor was forthcoming. He wrote a very strong letter to the Emperor.[14] He made it clear that the Fuggers in general were always loyal to the House of Austria and to fulfil the desires of the late Emperor Maximilian to make Charles V the Roman Emperor they had undertaken tremendous risk by advancing huge amount. He added that it was well known that Charles V would not have received the Imperial Crown had there not been the help of the Fuggers. He was selfless, and unmindful of the advantages that could accrue to him from the proposed bond with Francis I, he supported the cause of Charles V. This letter was handed over to him in Valladolid on 24 April 1523. Further Jakob Fugger reminded him of the outstanding loan taken at the Diet of Worms to the tune of 152,000 ducats.[15] Subsequently, the repayment of the loans increased though in 1530 an amount of 112,200 florins was due to the Fuggers from the Emperor. The Emperor ordered the fiscal authorities not to take any steps against the monopoly. The reminders of Jakob Fugger met with the expected results and the proceedings were dropped. The other merchant-firms also benefited from this.

The Emperor was in further financial crisis in 1524. Charles V needed money since he was at war with France. Francis I of France had regained Milan, which the Emperor wanted to take back. The Fuggers seem to have come to the aid of the Emperor by advancing the required loan.[16] The money sent by the Fuggers reached the Emperor on the decisive battle at Pavia. The Emperor won the battle. On the day the Emperor received the news of the victory at Pavia, 10 March 1525, he confirmed the privileges of the monopolists. Subsequently on 12 May 1525, he issued the edict of Toledo placing the great merchant firms under imperial legal protection. This was evidently the expression of gratitude the house of Austria had towards the Fuggers and explains the dictum *do ut des*. Till the death of Jakob Fugger II on 30 January 1526 he remained loyal and ready to help the Emperor in moments of his financial crisis.

Almost the same attitude towards the Holy Roman Empire was kept up by Anton Fugger who succeeded Jakob the Rich. When Charles came back to Germany in 1530 after his engagements in Italy he found himself in financial trouble. He was interested in getting his brother Ferdinand elected as the king of Romans. Even in the transfer of large sums of money from Spain to the Emperor, the help of the Fuggers was sought. The Emperor had to bring 250,000 crowns of the French ransoms and 150,000 ducats already granted by the Cortes. Besides, the Fuggers and the Welsers paid equivalent of these amounts to the Emperor part of which was used by them for the election of Ferdinand. The money was secretly brought to Fuentarabbia, on the Spanish frontier and an agent of the Fugger received it to be finally handed over to the Emperor. This transaction was done clandestinely to avoid interference of the Spaniards who were not very happy to see that large sums of money were taken out of Spain. The Fuggers seem to have advanced large sums on the *cruzada* granted to the Emperor in 1529 by Pope Clement.[17]

Raymund, Anton and Hieronymus Fugger agreed in 1530 to pay an amount of 275,3330 florins for the election of Ferdinand, the brother of Charles V, as king of Rome. A part of it was for the Archbishop himself and another to the elector of Brandenburg and the next to the Count of Palatine. The amount was delivered in the account of Ferdinand at 10 per cent interest. It is to be noted that the Fuggers themselves had to take loans from their friends and other merchants at an extremely high rate of interest to satisfy the need of the Emperor. Ferdinand agreed to repay a part of the loan in the Netherlands in five annual instalments and another part on Neapolitan annuity of Ferdinand. Yet another part was to be repaid through silver from Schwaz. The remaining part of the liability was to be paid to the Fuggers by allowing them to take over the Mark of Burgau for 10,000 florins at which Bishop of Augsburg held it. The Fuggers paid an annuity of 7000 florins to the Archbishop of Mainz on the security of the revenues from the Joachimsthal mines and the salt pans of Hall.

The balance sheet of the Fuggers in 1530 shows that Charles V owed 112,000 gulden from the time of his election and his brother king Ferdinand had to pay the Fuggers not less than a million gulden. On account of the liability of the Emperor to the Fuggers, Raymund, Anton and Hieronymus Fuggers were given the title of nobles by the Emperor on 14 November 1530 besides large number of immunities. In fact, the Emperor went so far as to permit them to take the title of Count or *Freiherr*, though they did not assume at that time.

The Emperor waged war with France in 1536 in which the Fuggers helped him substantially. They granted 100,000 ducats to the emperor as loan on the 14 April at 14 per cent interest which was to be paid in two instalments, namely, May and June. This was against the gold or silver to be imported from the western hemisphere.

The supply of silver and gold was so plenty that the mints did not know what to do with the large inputs. The Emperor found himself again in financial problem and so in 1537 he took another loan of 100,000 ducats from the Fuggers at 14 per cent interest. In return, the Fuggers were allowed to hold back the rent of *Maestrazgos* as surety. The loan was to be repaid in two instalments from the Spanish revenues.

Again in 1537 the Turkish menace compelled king Ferdinand to equip himself with armaments for which he had to take a loan of 83,000 florins from the Fuggers. According to the balance sheet of 1539, the Fuggers had to get an amount of 200,000 florins from the Emperor. They granted two more loans to king Ferdinand in 1540 and 1541. The alliance of the Turks with France compelled Charles V and his brother Ferdinand to look for more money to face the threat. The Fuggers came forward to help the Habsburg brothers by raising loans in Antwerp. The Queen *Statthalterin* Maria collected 250,000 crowns from the Fugger and Welser in the Netherlands for the Emperor. He himself raised a loan of 100,000 ducats from the Fuggers for Italy before 1544.

Being aware of the fact that financial transactions with the Emperor were detrimental to the firm because of the inability of the Emperor to repay, Anton Fugger showed reluctance to advance further loans to him. Still the Fuggers often came forward to help the Emperor. In 1546 the Emperor Charles V decided to wage war on the Protestants. He required money for the encounter with them. So, he decided to raise loans of 150,000 to 200,000 ducats at the lowest interest from the Fuggers or the Welsers. He approached the Fuggers and obtained an amount of 122,477 florins on 27 January and 20,000 ducats on 15 February 1548. It was reported that the Fuggers were tired of giving loans to the Emperor. When Charles conquered the Elector of Saxony on 15 May 1546 he had concluded negotiations with Anton Fugger for a loan of 60,000 florins. Again on 1 August 1548 the Fuggers lent the Emperor an amount of 150,000 ducats against a share of Neapolitan revenues at 12 per cent interest. This was besides the three loans granted at Ulm and Wittenberg during the war against Schmalkalden which started in

1546. This amount was not paid back till 1551. In April of the same year the Emperor asked for further loans from the German merchants. The Fuggers, just for the sake of getting the previous loans repaid, issued bonds to be discounted by Wolff Haller von Hallerstein in Antwerp at 11 per cent instead of ready cash. The Fuggers' share amounted to 70,000 florins. It seems that they did not advance any more loans till 1551.

In October 1551 the Emperor borrowed large amounts from Augsburg at 12 per cent interest in return for the gold and silver expected from the western hemisphere. The firm *Anton Fugger and Nephews* in its own name got interested in this deal and advanced 33,000 ducats. Anton Fugger on his personal account invested 20,000 ducats. Again by the end of the year 1551, the Emperor approached the Augsburg merchants for fresh loans. But they declined to oblige him.

In February 1552, Maurice, the Elector of Saxony with the help of the French king challenged the Emperor. Charles V at that time was in Innsbruck without having any financial resources. He tried to raise funds. But the merchants of South Germany did not show any inclination to help him. Queen Mary of the Netherlands managed to get some money from the Fuggers through their agent at Antwerp. The emperor threatened by his enemies went on negotiating with Anton Fugger for some time. Helpless as he was, the Emperor at last through an autograph letter called him to Innsbruck in haste. As the army and the garrison of the fortresses were not paid, the emperor did not get any solid support from them. Anton after reaching Innsbruck started negotiations with Erasso, the Emperor's secretary. In the meantime Maurice attacked Emberg on 19 March as a result of which the Emperor along with Anton Fugger had to flee to Villach in great haste. In May Innsbruck itself was attacked by Maurice. Threatened from various sides, the emperor tried to raise funds in Augsburg, Ulm, Nürnberg, Strasburg and even in Venice. Most of the south German and Venetian merchants sided with the enemies of the Emperor. Anton Fugger was the only one who saved the Emperor in such a sad plight. Negotiations started in Passau towards the end of May 1552. Anton

Fugger granted 400,000 ducats, an enormous sum indeed. He did it even to the displeasure and disagreement of his nephews who were partners in the firm. At last Anton Fugger had to take it over on his own.[18] Matthäus Örtel, the agent of the Fuggers in Antwerp, made the payment to the Emperor through the Queen-Regent of the Netherlands. Thus Habsburg, especially the emperor and his brother Ferdinand, owed a lot to the loyalty of the Fuggers who became, to a large extent, poor on account of the deal with the Emperor. The total amount due to the Fuggers from the Emperor amounted to 273,161 ducats in February 1552.

An amount of 540,000 ducats was advanced as loan to the Emperor in Spain by the agent of the Fuggers, Matthäus Örtel, after 1552. In the autumn of 1555 Fugger himself advanced an amount of 112,000 ducats to the Emperor. After a long-drawn-out and relentless battle against the protestants Charles V made peace with his opponents. The Peace of Augsburg was declared on 25 September 1555 in the council hall of Augsburg. The "Augsburg Confession" was given equal religious rights with the Roman Catholic Church. Princes were given the right to determine the religion of their own territories—*cujus regio, ejus religio*. Both the protestants and the catholics were recognised in Augsburg. Further, an amount of 70,000 ducats was advanced in 1556 to the Emperor, a part of which was against the guarantee of the output of the silver mines of Guadalcanal discovered then. Charles V formally abdicated in 1556. His son Philip II inherited the crown of Spain with all its colonies, Naples, Milan, the Franche-Comte and the Netherlands. Ferdinand I, his brother who had already assumed the title of German king and ruled the Austrian hereditary provinces Bohemia and Hungary, became the Holy Roman Emperor. Örtel advanced a sum of 430,000 ducats in 1557 against the import of gold and silver from America. Charles V to whom Anton Fugger remained loyal died in 1558 in the Spanish monastery of San Jeronimo de Yuste where he was leading a retired life after Ferdinand took over the reins of the Empire. Thus instead of waiting for the repayment of the amount already advanced, the Fuggers went on granting new loans to the House of Austria and the wealth of the Fuggers was pumped dry by Erasso, the secretary of the Emperor. As reported by Örtel, the Fuggers had advanced 1.5 million of gold to the Emperor in one year and a half. But the House of Austria was not adequately grateful to the service rendered by the Fuggers who lost a lot on account of the dealings with the emperor, his son as well as his brother. However, one can understand the financial power of the Fuggers in the sixteenth century and get an insight into the indebtedness of the Emperor and his dynasty to the Fuggers.

The Fuggers and the Papacy

The Fuggers being devout Catholics had close contact with the Church. They had a factory in Rome which was described as the "Fugger Bank" as early as 1500. It had a lot of financial dealings with the Roman Curia as well as the individual princes of the Church. Some of the bishops and cardinals with a view to keeping their assets away from the Pope and the Emperor deposited large unaccounted sums of money with the Fuggers who kept these investments very secretly without bringing to the notice of any body else. The case of Melchior von Meckau, Prince Bishop of Brixen, which is referred above is a classical example.

They had interest in the lease of papal mint. Pope Julius II deposited large sum to the tune of 100,000 ducats in the Fugger Bank in 1507. Similarly in 1509 the same Pope invested huge amount collected in the year of Jubilee in the Fugger Bank in Rome. They sold a diamond in 1510 to the Pope for 18,000 ducats. Because of their connection with the Roman Curia they were categorised among the merchants of the middle ages called *Campsores Romanam curiam sequentes.*

The bishops in Germany made use of the Fuggers' connection in Rome and sought their help in the dealings with the Roman Curia. The Archbishops had to pay in hard cash to the Roman curia for their confirmation and the pallium. The young Hohenzollern Albrecht of Brandenburg who was the Archbishop of Mainz since 1515 led a life of luxury. He held numerous ecclesiastical benefices like the archbishopric of Magdeburg and the position of administrator of the Halberstadt episcopate. He needed money to pay to the Pope for the pallium, insignia of the Archbishop. He took a loan of 29000 florins from Jakob Fugger for the payment to be made to the Roman curia. The papacy in turn permitted Albrecht to sell indulgences to tide over his pecuniary difficulty. Half of the proceeds of the sales was to be remitted to the Holy See and the other half to be retained by him.[19] An amount of 29000 florins was paid to the Roman curia by Jakob Fugger through his agent at Rome. This was furnished against the payment of a certain amount as interest under the periphrasis "Trouble, Danger and Expense". As the archbishop would not be in a position to repay the amount from his usual revenues, he had to have recourse to some other means. The Fuggers again helped him at Rome as their money was involved. On payment of 10,000 ducats Pope Leo X granted to the Archbishop of Mainz the right of being General Commissary for Saxony and other parts of Germany in connection with new Jubilee Indulgence then declared by the Pope.

The Archbishop appointed Johann Tetzel, the Dominican to preach the indulgence and collect money. He is said to have made the statement: "when the cash clinks in the box, the soul jumps out of purgatory". He was accompanied by an agent of the Fuggers who kept the key of the Indulgence chest. The chest was opened in the presence of the agent of the Fuggers and the entire amount was handed over to Andreas Mattstedt, who was the Fuggers' agent in Leipzig. Half of the proceeds was paid to the Roman Curia and the other half was taken over by the Fuggers as interest and part-payment of the capital advanced by them to the Archbishop.

The Fuggers helped the papacy in fighting out the protestants in Germany especially in the confrontation with the Schmalkalden. The Emperor of the Holy Roman Empire declared war against the Schmalkaldian League. He issued orders to his son Philipp in Spain in 1546 to raise funds for the war. As the Emperor could not get any money from Italy, he had to depend heavily on the German financiers. Though the protestant democratic party prevailed in the city of Augsburg and the Schmalkaldian League was supported by the patricians of the city, the Fuggers remained firm in their relations with the Roman Church. Anton Fugger came forward to support the Emperor in his fight for the Catholic faith even to the great dislike of the Augsburg Council. He lent large sums to the Emperor. The Fuggers' farm house was threatened to be destroyed by the supporters of the League. Anton Fugger managed to get the Augsburg Council to the side of the Catholics against the protestant princes. The protestant democratic party was rendered helpless in obtaining forced loans from the Catholic merchants of Augsburg. By 1546 the Emperor became master of South Germany. Anton Fugger mediated for his native city against the wrath of the Emperor and at the same time remained profoundly loyal to the Catholic faith so much so that he was held as a model. In addition to the various loans already advanced, he furnished to the Emperor in January and February with two loans of 122,477 florins and 20,000 ducats respectively.

The Fuggers and the Spanish Crown

Charles, the future Roman Emperor and the grandson of Maximilian I, had several financial dealings with the Fuggers when he was ruling only the Netherlands. Wolff Haller, the Fuggers' agent in Antwerp, had close contact with him. Charles took over the government of Spain in 1517. When he set out for Spain in 1517, he handed over to his envoy Courteville and the Imperial treasurer Villinger bills of 94,000 florins on the Fugger so that they might bring the electors to elect him. As the electors wanted ready cash, the bills were not of any use. Here came in Maximilian who knew how to handle the situation. Haller had done a lot for him after his taking over the reins of Spain and especially at the time of his election as the successor to Maximilian. As the agent of the Fuggers, he made a trip from Antwerp to Spain in 1519 to carry out monetary transaction in connection with the election. The German electoral princes would not have elected Charles the king of Spain as Roman Emperor had not the Fuggers supported the cause with their money.

As mentioned in the context of the relations between the Fuggers and the Roman Empire, a large sum was advanced by the Fuggers for the election of Charles to the imperial throne.

For the first time in 1524 the Fuggers took lease of the revenues of the Spanish Crown from three ecclesiastical orders of Knights, namely, Sant Jago, Calatrava and Alcantra. The king of Spain was the grand master of these orders. In fact the Fuggers held lease of the *Maestrazgos* from 1525 for almost a century or so with some interruptions. This lease served as the basis for their long-standing business in Spain.[20] This offer included the mercury mines of Almaden. As mercury or quicksilver was necessary for the separation of silver from the ore in which it is usually embedded, this helped the Fuggers in their dealings in silver. In fact the Fuggers supplied silver to the Portuguese king for his trade and commerce in the East. Thus the surety became handy for the Fuggers. Though the newly elected emperor did not pay back the amount he received from them, they got remuneration both in cash and kind from the lands occupied by these orders. Similarly, the products of the quicksilver mines of Almaden as well as those of the silver mines of Guadalcanal came into their possession. They took over the management of the mines as well as farms temporarily. Representatives were stationed in various districts under a chief agent at Almagro. In course of time a chief director was appointed at the Court to look after the entire business of the Fuggers in Spain.

Anton Fugger in his private capacity had a lot of dealings with Spain which turned out to be a gigantic enterprise after the incident of Villach. When Charles' son Philip came from Spain to the Netherlands, Anton Fugger saw to it that large quantity of silver was sent secretly with him in the ship. Silver worth 200,000 ducats was brought to Antwerp in 1553 as ordered by Anton Fugger. Philip of Spain married Queen Mary of England who through Gresham managed to get money brought from Spain. The Fuggers' agent Örtel collected the money from Spain and delivered it to Gresham at Antwerp. Philip of Spain got the government of the Netherlands from his father, Charles V, in 1555. Mathew Örtel, in the name of the Fuggers, undertook to deliver a sum of 400,000 ducats to king Philip in Spain for paying the salary of the soldiers of the king. A bond on secure revenues for everything he owed to the Fuggers was given by the king. This also included the interest of 12 per cent.

The Fuggers paid an annual rent of fifty million *maravedis* (approximately 135,000 ducats) for the *Maestrazgos*. At the end of the three years they got a profit of 2,200,000 *maravedis* which scarcely amounted to the interest on the capital. They held the *Maestrazgos* till 1635 with a few interruptions. The election debts were transferred to Spain and so the lease of the *Maestrazgos* served the purpose of paying them off.

King Philip of Spain by 1558 owed a large sum to the Fuggers. According to the general statement of that year, they had to get an amount of 1,660,809 ducats from him only on account of the dealings in the Netherlands. Besides, the king had taken silver from them which, including the fourteen per cent interest, amounted to 762,262 crowns. It was calculated that the Fuggers' claim on the Spanish crown amounted to three million ducats in 1560. The total capital of the Fuggers at this time amounted to two million only. This shows the depth of the indebtedness of the Spanish crown to the Fuggers.[21] By 1604 the Fuggers had to get five and a half million ducats from Spain of which five millions were to be recovered from the Crown itself.

The Fuggers and Naples

The Emperor Charles V put his brother Ferdinand in charge of the administration of the German dominions. The great burden of the debts from the time of Maximilian I including the loans advanced by the Fuggers for the election of Charles V was imposed on Ferdinand. However, the important revenues in Naples were also transferred to him. Ferdinand mortgaged them to the Fuggers who in 1524 gave the former 25,000 florins and 20,000 ducats. In 1525 an amount of 59,562 ducats was granted by the Fuggers. They went on advancing large amounts even to the tune of 400,000 ducats against the mortgage in Naples. Tyrol belonging to the German dominions was already mortgaged to the Fuggers much before 1521. The delays in the repayment for the amount advanced in Naples put the Fuggers in trouble and in 1546 they cut their losses and the Genoese came forward.

THE FUGGERS AND HUNGARY

The Fuggers started contacts with Hungary in 1495. The trade in copper started in this year was gradually extended to working the large copper mines in Neusohl and other places. Here it is worthwhile to recall the suggestion given to Jakob Fugger at Venice by the engineer Thurzo, a member of an Austrian family, with whom the Jakob Fugger established matrimonial relations and entered into mining activities. Jakob Fugger and Thurzo along with other business firms of Augsburg formed syndicates in 1498 and 1499 to control the copper sale in Venice. They simultaneously sent the Hungarian copper to Antwerp through Danzig. When the Portuguese king established his factory in the Netherlands and wanted copper for his overseas trade, the Fuggers supplied Hungarian copper through their agent in the Netherlands. In fact Jakob Fugger understood the importance of his enterprise in Hungary and so even when his nephew, George Thurzo, urged him to give up the risky Hungarian business, he did not yield, but added that he would win so long as he was able and continued it.

Anton Fugger was rather cautious in extending financial assistance to Ludwig, the king of Hungary. However, in extreme need he helped him. He granted an amount of 50,000 florins to him. Had Anton Fugger been little more generous towards him, as reported by his agent, Ludwig would not have been defeated and killed in the fight with Ferdinand of Austria who won the crown of Hungary against the national candidate Zapolya.

The establishments of the Fuggers in Neusohl in Hungary continued to be flourishing under Anton Fugger. In forwarding Hungarian copper to Antwerp from the Baltic, they had contacts with Denmark. In 1530 Anton Fugger had to get an amount of 258,400 florins from Hungary which constituted the old debt from the king.[22]

The Fuggers and the Crown of England

In 1552 the Fuggers had a claim of 123,047 *livres* from the crown of England. Thomas Gresham, the agent of the crown, went to Antwerp to raise funds for the repayment of the amount due to the Fuggers. Christopher Dawntsey, the new agent of the English, approached the Fuggers' agent at Antwerp in 1553 repeatedly for collecting loans. Gresham managed to take a loan of 10,000 pounds from Hans Fugger at Antwerp in 1559 for Queen Elizabeth of England.

The Fuggers and the Crown of the Netherlands

The Court of the Netherlands entered into financial transactions with the agent of the Fuggers in Antwerp. In 1516 Bernhard Stecher in the name of the firm of the Fuggers advanced an amount of 27,000 pounds to the Court on the guarantee of the city of Antwerp for a year. This loan was given at 10 per cent interest. The amount was not repaid in the stipulated time since the Netherlands had to spend a lot of money for the journey of Charles to Spain to take over its government in 1517. Again in 1518 a further sum of 38,000 pounds more had to be lent for the payment of the garrisons. A large sum of money borrowed by the *Statthalterin* Margaret in the Netherlands by 1529 was transferred to Italy by the Fuggers to help the Emperor Charles for his battles there.

In 1542 Queen *Statthalterin* Maria borrowed a sum of 250,000 crowns from the Fuggers and the Welsers for the Emperor. This was besides the amount of 100,000 crowns the emperor collected as loan from the Fuggers in Spain for his Italian engagements. Further in March 1552, the queen succeeded in getting from the Fuggers at Antwerp some more money.

The Fuggers in Antwerp

During the course of the expansion of financial transaction and international trade, the Fuggers were attracted to Antwerp which had a favourable situation for world trade. From the beginning of the fourteenth century it had two fairs a year. Merchants from Italy, England and the Hansa towns frequented this market and the fairs. Its growth was very slow till the middle of the fifteenth century. The Mediterranean cities which controlled the Levantine trade and the Hansa towns that had monopolistic trade over northern Europe had important trade relation with Bruges but in 1442 the international trade in commodities and the dealings in bills and money so far concentrated on Bruges were shifted to Antwerp. The emergence of Antwerp as one of the important centres of trade was on account of the combination of political, economic and other causes.

As the foreign merchants flocked together to Antwerp after 1442 the Fuggers too directed their attention to this centre of trade. Their involvement in the business of Antwerp became quite important especially after the opening of the sea route to India by the Portuguese. Right in the first decade of the sixteenth century the Fuggers entered into trade at Antwerp which, in due course of time, added a new dimension to the commercial activities at Antwerp. The factory, the Fuggers had in Antwerp, had been dealing only in commodities. In 1508 it had its own house where pepper and copper were traded. They conducted large-scale business in pepper and copper at Antwerp for several decades. Portuguese, Spanish, English and German merchants who used to visit the centre only during the fairs began to settle permanently there. East Indian products and English cloths were the chief items that were traded in Antwerp in comparison to the trade of Bruges. The commodities from the East were formerly brought to the Levant and were taken to various directions. After the Portuguese had established trade with India, these commodities by and large flowed to Lisbon and then to Antwerp. The king of Portugal sold the cargo coming from the East as a whole to the rich syndicates of merchants who obtained monopoly in the sale of these commodities. They saw to it that the whole trade was concentrated at Antwerp so that they could control the price. So the entire cargo they received at Lisbon was brought to Antwerp. Similarly, the English managed their trade in cloth by directing the whole output for sale to Antwerp. Copper from

Hungary, which used to be taken to Venice formerly, began to be taken to Antwerp especially since the Fuggers established themselves in Antwerp and entered into the business of copper.

The Fuggers were attracted to Antwerp also on account of the fairs and *bourses*. There were two fairs, one in the spring popularly known as *Whitsundite* and the other in autumn called St. Bavon's, vulgarly known as *Bamas* or *Pamas*. Besides, two other fairs were added which continued to be important till the forties of the sixteenth century. There were the Cold market at Christmas and the Easter market which began at Candlemas. By the third decade of the sixteenth century the Fuggers possessed a large factory with house, garden, stabling much furniture and important stocks of goods at Antwerp. Their establishments at Amsterdam were not very important.

Similarly *bourses* of Antwerp attracted the Fuggers. *Burse* which formerly came into existence in Bruges, was not a *bourse* in the modern sense of the term meaning a meeting place of all the merchants. Originally the *Burse* of Bruges was only the meeting of the Italians who had their consular houses in the *Bourse* Square. It was chiefly used for dealing in money and bills of exchange while the trade in commodities was held in the warehouses or large *Halles*. The government set up merchants' *bourse* in Antwerp close to the Great Market in the English or Wool Street. Public weighing place and the money changers' banks were established here for facilitating trade and commerce. Antwerp *Bourse* was set up primarily for trade of the people from all nationalities and languages. Business was done there with the help of brokers handling several languages. Similarly, dealings in bills and money loans (deposits) were also carried out in *bourse*. The Antwerp *bourse* was the first international or world *bourse*.

Pepper brought from India under the monopolistic supervision of the king of Portugal, as mentioned above, was sold to the large syndicates by the Portuguese king. These syndicates who got the monopoly of further sale at second hand used to advance large amounts to the king of Portugal. They regulated the price of pepper at Antwerp *bourse*. Arrival of new cargo from the East via Lisbon set the new price at Antwerp. In fact the interest of the large syndicates and the arrival of the new import were the chief factors in the fixation of the price of pepper at Antwerp *bourse*. This situation provided ample opportunities for speculation. This was very important since the price of pepper determined the trend in most of the markets.

The Fuggers' agent in Lisbon used to purchase pepper from Lisbon and send it to Antwerp where the factor saw to the sale of the same. Factors stationed at Antwerp like Kornard Meutting or Mutinck from 1507, Felix Hanolt (1510-13), Bernhard Stecher (1513-1520), Wolff Haller (1517-22), and Hanolt (1521) had been involved in the trade of pepper. Subsequently it developed to great heights during the first four decades of the century and excelled all other centres in Europe. It was reported in a memorandum of 1564 that the men of Antwerp had "eaten out of their trade" the merchants of the other towns. One may say that it was the city of Antwerp, not the men of the city, which had "eaten" the other towns. Because, this city attracted merchants from other towns which lost their importance on account of the phenomenal growth of Antwerp. Spices from the east and copper from Hungary and Tyrol were sold by them at Antwerp. They were in constant touch with the agent of the Portuguese king at Antwerp in connection with the transactions in copper and pepper besides bills of exchange. During the forties of the sixteenth century they began to borrow money regularly on the Antwerp *bourse* on deposit.

The Fuggers and Florence

Anton Fugger in his eagerness to make money entered into contact with the Duke of Florence. In 1553 he brought from Duke Cosimo an annual sum of 10,000 ducats from the Duke's Neapolitan revenues for 100,000 ducats.[23] Negotiations were carried out by the agent of the Fuggers in Venice and the officials of the Duke under the instructions given by Anton Fugger. They lent to the Duke an amount of 75,000 *scudi* at an interest of 12 per cent in 1554. They sold a jewel to him for 23,600 *scudi* at the same time.

The Fuggers in Venice

Venice occupied an enviable position in the international trade. The Venetians outdid the other trading nations at the end of the fourteenth century and at the beginning of the fifteenth century. The Levantine trade of other European nations declined at the beginning of the fifteenth century and the Venetians emerged as the most powerful traders in this branch of international trade. They considered trade in spices as the most lucrative trade and tried to be the suppliers of these items to the central and eastern Europe. So, they maintained regular galley services to the important ports of Egypt and Syria. The Venice-Alexandria line became prominent since 1346 and that of Beirut since 1374. They had their establishments in Constantinople till 1453 when it fell to the Turks under Mohammed II. Subsequently they intensified their activities in Cairo, Alexandria, Damascus, Beirut and Allepo. Though the Florentine, Genoese and Catalan merchants had colonies in Alexandria, Damascus and other centres of the Levantine trade, and had some part in the spice trade, they were not parties to be reckoned with in comparison with the Venetian traders and their major role in the trade of oriental commodities.[24]

The significant role played by Venice in the international trade attracted the Fuggers to Venice where they established a permanent factory and an office. By 1484 they had their own chambers in the famous *Fondaco dei Tedeschi* in Venice established by the German merchants way back in 1288. Besides, pepper and other oriental goods, saffron brought to Venice in the fifteenth century was purchased by the Fuggers and supplied to various centres of Europe. On account of the emergence of Lisbon as the chief centre of the supply of the spices, the Fuggers like other German firms shifted their interest to Lisbon and Antwerp in the sixteenth century.

The Fuggers in Denmark

They had their establishments in Denmark and functioned only for the sake of facilitating the movement of copper from Hungary and from the Baltic to Antwerp.

THE FUGGERS AND THE MINING INDUSTRY

The Fuggers, especially since the time of Jakob Fugger, diversified their activities. Hans Fugger who was an agriculturist turned out to be a weaver. Then he entered into the trade. Jakob Fugger while in Venice was given the suggestion by the Austrian Thurzo to enter into mining industry which according to him would be much more profitable. Though initially Jakob Fugger was unwilling to tread new grounds of opportunities offered to him by Maximilian I, Charles V, Ferdinand and Philipp took him and his successors to large scale mining especially of silver and copper. The mining industry started by the Fuggers in Hungary, Spain, and Tyrol was of great importance in the context of the overseas maritime trade. During the sixteenth and seventeenth centuries metals, especially copper, played a significant role in the international trade.

The Fuggers established very significant contact with mining in Hungary which was closely connected with Nürnberg market. The products from Hungary were taken to Nürnberg, Augsburg, Frankfurt, Leipzig, Köln, Aachen, Venice, Antwerp, Amsterdam and Hamburg.[25]

The mines of Almaden in Spain supplied them with quicksilver essential for works of silver.[26]

Jakob Fugger bought the output of the copper mines of Tyrol in 1494 and copper from Tyrol was sent to Nürnberg and Venice. Copper from Tyrol was transported through the Inn to Bavaria for further distribution to other centres like Lindau, Strassburg, Italy, Switzerland, and the marketing centres of the Netherlands.[27] The joint venture with Thurzo at Krakau since 1494 gave further opportunities for development of the business in copper. Krakau played an important role as the staple-centre for this metal under Thurzo and the Fuggers. This was connected with Lublin, Lemberg, and other centres in the east. Copper and bronze were taken via Poland to Moldau.

They began exploiting the mines in Hungary in 1491. Before long they had *de facto* monopoly over copper in Europe especially over the outputs of the mines in Mansfeld in Thuringia, Neusohl in Slovakia and in Rottenberg and Schwaz in Tyrol. Besides, the

Fuggers had metal processing industries in Hochkirchen in the Thuringian forest, in Fuggerau near Villach in Carinthia and Teschen in Bohemia.

The Fuggers and the Dealings in Money

As we have already seen, apart from supplying copper, silver and gold to the Portuguese as well as other powers of Europe the Fuggers entered into the profitable business of giving loans on interest, and bills of exchange. When the Church was not in favour of charging interest on loans, the Fuggers through their contacts with the Holy Roman Emperor and some of the theologians managed to get it ratified that reasonable interest could be charged against loans advanced. Large sums were advanced to the Emperor Maximilian, Charles V and various other rulers of Europe as it has already been noticed. The Fuggers collected interest from all of them. Similarly it was discussed that the money from one place to another was transferred by them through the medium of bills of exchange at various places.

Besides the head office at Augsburg, the Fugger firm had several factories in various parts of Europe when Anton Fugger took charge of it. Some of the factories were in Bozen, Hall in Tyrol, Schwaz, Vienna, Leipzig, Hochkirch in Silesia, Breslau, Neusohl in Hungary, Nürnberg, Frankfurt-on-Main, Köln, Antwerp, Amsterdam, Denmark, Venice, Rome, Spain and Lisbon in Portugal.[28]

The Fuggers turned their attention to Lisbon in 1503 and obtained special privileges from the Portuguese king to conduct trade in oriental commodities, the details of which will be discussed in the next chapter.

Thus it may be concluded that the Fuggers rose to great heights of economic activities from their humble position of weaver. Their hold on money rendered them greatly influential so much so that the Emperor of the Holy Roman empire came forward to see that the greatest stumbling block in the financial dealings was removed. The scholars were constrained to theologise for the benefits of the

Emperor as well as those of the Fuggers. The church had to legalise interest on loans; the avenue was thus opened for the Emperor to take unlimited loans from the Fuggers and the latter got an opportunity to enhance their capital through advancing money. The relation of this nature paved the way for their hold on copper and silver mines. These metals played an important role in the age of merchant capital especially since the dawn of the sixteenth century.

The weakness of the Fuggers to decline the requests of the Emperor of the Holy Roman empire for large sums of money as loans and the inability of the latter to repay the same undermined the financial position of the firm and finally paved the way for their decline. Moreover, their extraordinary religiosity and their involvement in the catholic reformation to counteract the Lutheran one could be considered another factor leading to their gradual vulnerability.

NOTES AND REFERENCES

1. *Hei, Grüss di Gott, Ländle - Der Fuggerzug geht über Land vom Bayernweber zum Handelherrn*, Kempten (Allgäu), 1961, pp. 3-9.
2. This city got its name from the Emperor Augustus of Rome whose legionaries were stationed here. They built it as fort in 15 B. C. for military purposes. In course of time it developed as a major centre of trade on account of its location at the end of the Via Claudia Augusta. The fort became the capital of the province Raetia. It was connected with Italy and Gaul (France).
3. Franz Herre, *The Age of the Fuggers*, Augsburg, 1985, p. 19.
4. The coat of arms of this family contained the figure of roe or small kind of European deer.
5. Jakob Fugger, the elder wore a fur cap as the sign of prosperity. A copy of the lost original of his portrait is preserved in the Babenhausen castle.
6. Hutten wrote: "Open your eyes, you Germans, and see who is robbing you here at home, destroying your reputation abroad, who bears the blame for all your misfortune, all your grievances. Look at them, those despicable indulgence-vendors, heinous traders in grace, dispensations, absolutions and all kinds of bulls, who have set up their market in sacred things in the Church of God—from which He once Himself drove out dealers whose wares were of trivial value. These are the master craftsmen of all delusion, inventors of all guile, it is they who are the fathers of the servitude and

bondage of the people." Franz Herre, *op. cit.*, p. 67.

7. "Have not the Fuggers already attempted by every means admissible to exclude all other merchants from trade with Indian products, extracting gold and silver from good Germans for imported goods which are unnecessary or damaging to health and morals? Must it not therefore be the will of all honest Germans, including right-thinking merchants, that, the sooner the better, these people be driven out of our fatherland?" Franz Herre, *ibid.*, p. 67.
8. "Is it not robbery when they innundate Germany with a coin lacking the intrinsic content? And is it not robbery to have acquired almost the same monopoly over indulgences, prebends, dispensations and other papal privileges as they hold over Indian merchandise, when they flood all Germany with these Roman and Indian trinkets, extracting good money from their fellow-citizens." Franz Herre, *ibid.*, pp. 67-68.
9. "The greatest evil that befell the German nation is interest-taking. How can it possibly be just and the will of God that a single man—Fugger—should amass such a pile of royal money? I do not know how with one hundred florins twenty can be added in a year even one more each for florin. . . . For money is not fruitful of itself, it neither bears nor begets more money, for it is sown like grain. It cannot simply be sold by shrewdness. And therefore this present trade with money is wrong and against God, corrupting and sucking dry the country and its people. . . . Fugger and his like must be curbed." Franz Herre, *ibid.*, p. 68.
10. Klarwil (1926), *op. cit.*, pp. vii-ix.
11. Reinhard Hildebrandt, *Die Georg Fuggersche Erben: Kaufmännsche Tätigkeit und sozialer Status 1555-1600*, Berlin, 1966, pp. 22-43.
12. *Ibid.*, pp. 85-86.
13. "Most noble Majesty, All-powerful Emperor, most Gracious Lord! Your Majesty will be in no doubt of the loyalty and devotion with which I and my cousins have served the House of Austria in the interest of its welfare and prosperity; for which reason we allied ourselves to His Majesty Emperor Maximilian of praiseworthy memory as a humble subject in obtaining the crown of Rome for Your imperial Majesty against many and several princes who placed their confidence and trust in me and perhaps no other person; that afterwards, after negotiations with Your Majesty's commissioners, for the purpose of achieving the said end, we advanced a large sum of money, which I provided not from my own funds or those of my cousins, but, at great detriment to myself, from other good lords and friends, so that Your Majesty might be raised to high honour and prosperity." Ref. Franz Herre, *op. cit.*, p. 72.
14. A portion of the famous letter of Jakob Fugger addressed to the Emperor is reproduced here: "Your imperial Majesty doubtless knows how I and my kinsmen have ever hitherto been disposed to serve the House of Austria in all loyalty to the furtherance of its well-being and prosperity; wherever, in

order to be pleasing to Your Majesty's Grandsire, the later Emperor Maximilian, and to gain for Your Majesty the Roman Crown, we have held ourselves bounden to engage ourselves towards diverse princes who placed their trust and Reliance upon myself and perchance on no Man besides. We have, moreover, advanced to your Majesty's agents for the same end a Great Sum of Money of which we ourselves have had to raise a large part from our Friends. It is well known that Your Imperial Majesty would not have gained the Roman Crown save with mine aid and, I can prove the same by the writings of Your Majesty's agents given by their own hands. In this matter I have not studied my own Profit. For had I left the House of Austria and had minded to further France, I had obtained much money and property such as was then offered to me. How great a Disadvantage had in this case accrued to Your Majesty and the House of Austria, Your Majesty's Royal Mind well knoweth." Ref. Richard Ehrenberg, *op. cit.*, p. 80.

15. "To this day Your Majesty is indebted to me for the sum of money which Your Majesty borrowed from me at the Diet in Worms, on security of the county of Tyrol. But from this I am not yet repaid in full, therefore, Your Majesty still owes me 152,000 ducats. . . . And so it is my most humble appeal and request to Your Majesty graciously to consider my loyal and humble services which have brought such honour and prosperity to Your Majesty, and to give orders that the sum of money advanced by me be paid in full with interest and without further delay. I humbly request to be permitted to be of further service to Your Majesty. . . . Your Majesty's most obedient servant and subject, Jakob Fugger." Franz Herre, *op. cit.*, p. 73.
16. *Ibid.*, pp. 80-81.
17. *Cruzada* was the name given for crusade-bulls to the kings of Castile by the popes to fight against the moors. One could buy indulgence under this.
18. Richard Ehrenberg, *op. cit.*, p. 108.
19. The medieval church substituted indulgences for acts of penance for the temporal punishment due to sins committed by human beings. Indulgences consisted in the common fund of merits acquired by the Church through Jesus and His saints. These indulgences could be obtained by persons on earth through the participation in crusades or by making pilgrimage to Rome during the jubilee years announced by the church. The first Jubilee was declared in 1300. The papacy needed money for the rebuilding of St. Peter's and other monuments. Pope Julius II entrusted Bramante with the work of rebuilding St. Peter's and Raphael with the task of painting the Stanze and Michaelangelo with the duty of decorating the Sistine chapel. The extraordinary expenditure involved in these activities of construction demanded large sums of money. So Pope Julius II dispensed an indulgence. The Medici Pope Leo X extended it. The bull of dispensation issued by the Pope declared that the cathedral of St. Peter was to remain as the testimony of the *Universa Christiana Republica*.

20. Hermann Kellenbenz, *Die Fugger in Spanien und Portugal bis 1560*, München, 1990, Part I, p. 68.
21. Richard Ehrenberg, *op. cit.*, p. 116.
22. *Ibid.*, p. 93.
23. *Ibid.*, p. 109.
24. Eliyahu Ashtor, "The Venetian Supremacy. . . . ", *op. cit.*, pp. 5-53.
25. Hermann Kellenbenz, *Schwerpunkte der Kupferproduktion und des Kupferhandels in Europa 1500-1650,* Wien, 1977, pp. 331-333.
26. Hermann Kellenbenz, "Schwäbische Kaufherren im Tiroler Bergbau, 1400-1650", *Beiträge Schwaben Tirol*, Rosenheim, 1989, pp. 208-210.
27. Hermann Kellenbenz, *Schwerpunkte. . .*, *op. cit.*, p. 333.
28. Richard Ehrenberg, *Renaissance: A Study of the Fuggers and their Connections*, New York, 1963, p. 89.

CHAPTER 5

THE FUGGERS TURN TO TRADE WITH INDIA

The Fuggers' participation in the maritime trade of India in the sixteenth century can be considered in the general framework of the German participation and within this, three different phases can be distinguished. In the first, the Fuggers participated in the fitting out of the three vessels to India with a view to establishing direct commercial relations with India. As the king of Portugal became rather apprehensive about the fact that he would forfeit the monopoly over the trade in the Indian ocean regions, he did not give in to the proposal to permit them to have direct relations with India. On the other hand, the Fuggers like other German and Italian firms entered on contract with the king of Portugal for the purchase of pepper and spices at the India House in Lisbon against the price fixed by the king and to sell these commodities in other parts of Europe. Similarly, they supplied copper, silver and quicksilver to the Portuguese king and advanced money for the purchase of the commodities at the India House. By the end of the second decade of the sixteenth century the interest in the purchase of spices and pepper in Lisbon began to dwindle on account of their involvement in establishing direct relations with the Southeast Asian countries where these items were available in plenty.

In the second phase, the Fuggers concentrated their attention chiefly on the supply of copper to the Portuguese king and the trade in pearls, precious metals and diamonds. Similarly advancing of money to Portugal continued. However, the involvement was not as active as in the first two decades, especially after the demise of Jakob Fugger the Rich.

The third phase saw the participation in the Asia Contract as well as the Europa Contract of the "Georg Fuggersche Erben" under the guidance of Philipp Eduard Fugger and Octavian Secundus. They entered on contract with the Welsers. Regular factors were appointed in Lisbon as well as India to look after the various aspects of the Asia Contract as well as later on for Europa Contract.

We shall start with the general shift of interest on the part of the German merchant financiers from Venice to Lisbon and their growing interest in Lisbon. The movement to Portugal was motivated by their eagerness to participate in the maritime trade of India. We shall also discuss the concentration of their attention on the factory in Antwerp which was the chief centre of meeting between the Portuguese agents and the Fuggers.

Germans had already been in Lisbon towards the end of the fifteenth century with very strong settlement of their own. Jobst von Hütter (probably from Flanders), the father-in-law of Martim Behaim, had a palatial building in an area in Lisbon which is now known as Rossio. This served as a guest house for the Germans and was the central point in Lisbon for their relations with Portugal. Hieronymus Münzer from Nürnberg who visited Lisbon in 1494 and 1495 reports about the famous house of Hütter as well as about the German ship called *Bernhard Fechter* from Danzig. He saw about thirty German bombardiers in a warship bearing the name of the Queen. Similarly he came across German artillery men at Alcaçar do Sal. Münzer visited Lisbon several times at the invitation extended by king John II in the context of cosmographic information. Both Martim Behaim (1460-1507) and Münzer had been together in Lisbon and obtained information from Diogo Gomes about the discovery of Guinea and of the islands in the western ocean. [1] Diogo Gomes who was the chief of the palace at Sintra organised a report for Behaim. [2]

Valentin Fernandes, from Moravia was a printer, interpreter, and writer in geography who was also employed by a noble man of Queen D. Leonar. He was in Lisbon since 1482 and translated the report of Marco Polo into Portuguese and published it in 1502. Similarly, he translated from Latin into Portuguese the book of

Nicolaus Veneto and the letter of Jeronimo Santo Estevam. [3] He became the chamberlain to Queen Eleanor and was appointed as royal agent by the king Manuel to negotiate with the German merchants in 1503. He got interested in the Portuguese voyages and so produced a codex containing twelve travel accounts, which he copied from 1506 to 1511. Martim Behaim is said to have assisted him in the preparation of the collection. [4]

The Germans in Lisbon comprised three groups, namely, craftsmen, bombardiers and merchants, and they had their own associations connected with the churches of St. Dominic and Our Lady of Conception. [5] The brotherhood of St. Bartholomeu (*Bartholomäusbrüderschaft*) played an important role in the life of the German settlers in Portugal. On account of the special permission given during the time of king D. Diniz (1279-1325) a chapel in the name of St. Bartholomeu was established. A group of German merchants got themselves associated with this brotherhood centered around this chapel.

The second group of German residents in Lisbon founded in 1414 another association called the Brotherhood of Holy Cross and St. Andrea. They had a chapel in the Dominican church. Most likely this chapel was initially with the Flemish people and in the sixteenth century it was dominated by the Germans. However, the Germans, the Flemish, the Dutch and those from the Hanseatic towns were found in this brotherhood.

The third group of the Germans in Lisbon consisted of bombardiers who were connected with the chapel of St. Bartholomeu. They played an important role in the colonial expansion of the Portuguese and so the Portuguese king gave special privileges to them especially in the second half of the fifteenth and sixteenth centuries in the context of the battles waged in Asia and Africa. Affonso de Albuquerque, the founder of the Portuguese empire in the east, wrote to D. Manuel, king of Portugal, on 25 October 1514 that half of the bombardiers to be stationed in various places in India should be Germans. His appreciation of the German bombardiers was so much so that he gave permission to build a chapel for the Germans in Goa.

The Germans, therefore, were in a better position to learn of the importance of direct sea-route connecting India with the Atlantic ports which was discovered by Vasco da Gama in 1498. Moreover, the details given by Dom Manuel I, king of Portugal, to the Catholic kings of Spain were also brought to the knowledge of the Germans. Availability of various articles like pepper, cinnamon and pearls (*Edelstein*) in India was disclosed by Dom Manuel, the king of Portugal, through his letter written on 26 August 1499. [6] The German merchant financiers who were interested in trade in these items wanted to come to India. The "Grocer king" found himself unable to exploit the vast commercial potentialities of the orient discovered by Vasco da Gama, the admiral of the Indian Ocean. Right in 1500 the king had to seek the help of financiers and there were two ships owned by private merchants in the fleet consisting of twelve ships under Pedro Alvares Cabral that came to Calicut. [7] On 29 June 1500 he issued an order permitting native as well as foreign merchants to fit out their own ships to India. [8]

Nicolaus de Rechterghem hailing from Aquisgrana or Aachen stationed in Antwerp sent in 1501(?) to Germany the first consignment of pepper brought by the Portuguese from India to the Flemish town of Antwerp. The Germans had the opportunity to have the good surprise of getting pepper of which they had several unfounded pieces of information. Suddenly they decided to have direct access to spices by going over to Lisbon and avoiding Antwerp. Their attempts were further encouraged by the information circulated in Europe about the first and second voyages of Vasco da Gama. A German trade-agent was on board a Portuguese ship sent to India in 1502 according to the anonymous report of the second voyage of Vasco da Gama. The details of the second voyage of Vasco da Gama to India in 1502 were also brought to the notice of the German merchants at Augsburg and Nürnberg. In fact there were other reports about the success of the Portuguese voyages of discovery and trade.

Two texts of the report on the second voyage of Vasco da Gama to India, one in German and the other in Portuguese, are preserved in the National Library of Vienna. Both these reports are anonymous. The manuscript containing these reports was in the possession of Philippine Welser and in 1665 it was brought from the castle of Ambras to the library of the Kaiser in Vienna as stated by Christine von Rohr.[9] Hans Mayr, who came to India in the fleet of 1505 as one of the officials of the German group of merchants, was in the service of Valentin Fernandes in 1502. Moreover, another German report about the second voyage of Vasco da Gama is found among the documents in the Bratislava collection.[10] Karl Otto Müller came across a few documents related to trade with India after the first voyage of Vasco da Gama. They were preserved in the family archives of Paumgartner, an Augsburg merchant.[11]

The German merchant financiers decided to take advantage of this situation and came over to India for trade in the coveted items of the orient. Simon Seitz, the factor of Welsers along with Scipio Löwenstein and Lucas Rem left for Lisbon via Lyon in December 1502. With accustomed humaneness Simon Seitz in the name of Anton Welser and Conrad Vöhlin (Filim) and in the name of the company of the noble merchants of the royal city of Augsburg and other German towns approached the king of Portugal in February 1503. He explained the request of the German merchants to establish a house of the company to trade in various commodities in the Portuguese kingdom. They asked for some privileges and favours from the king of Portugal. Taking into account the fact that they came from the imperial city of Augsburg under the Roman empire Maximilian I, who was his nephew, the king Dom Manuel decided to grant the privileges and favours requested by them. In fact the king mentioned that privileges of this type were never granted to anybody till that date, not even to his own Portuguese subjects.

They were given the permission to conduct trade, sell or purchase whatever commodities in Portugal as well as in territories under the Portuguese directly or through their factors or employees. They were allowed to take silver by land or sea to Portugal and the areas under it without being obliged to pay taxes or levies of any kind. They were authorised to sell it to anyone they liked and to take back to the place of their choice whatever remained unsold without paying anything for exit. Further, the king permitted them to take to Portugal or its territories lead, copper for minting, vermilion, quicksilver, and equipment of various types for ships without paying anything except the 10 per cent. However, they were empowered to take back whatever commodities that were not sold. They obtained the authorisation from the king to buy, in retail or wholesale, spices, brazilwood and any other commodities brought from India or other areas recently discovered, without paying any tribute or tax while taking the commodities out of Portugal. It was also agreed that the German merchants could build their own houses within the city of Lisbon or outside the walls in any place purchased by them just as the Flemish merchants were allowed. But they were exempted from search by the customs officials.

The merchants were asked to select an agent to deal in the commodities. This person was bound to confer with other agents of the city and enter the details of sales and purchases in the books and inform them of the profit derived. The German merchants were given the right to see that their merchandise was processed fast in the customs house at Lisbon. Similarly, the silver brought by them for minting would be taken care of in the mint prior to that of others. These extraordinary privileges were granted to them for a period of fifteen years through the order issued by the king on 13 February 1503. It was further added that though these privileges and immunities were granted in view of the request made by Simon Seitz, the same were extended to any other group of German merchants and to any German individual merchant interested in conducting trade and commerce in Lisbon. [12] These merchants tried their best to obtain the exclusive right to trade in spices with India. But Dom Manuel, the Portuguese king, wanted to keep for himself the trade in spices, pepper and drugs. [13]

As stipulated in the grant of 13 February 1503 an agent was to be appointed who would act as a middleman between the king of Portugal and the German merchant financiers. Valentin Fernandes was the most acceptable person to discharge this duty and so he was given this job. Dom Manuel through his order issued on 21 February 1503 conferred this position on him. He was supposed to be in charge of all the transactions in the Lisbon market between the German merchants and the Portuguese. He was given the necessary conditions to discharge the duties effectively. He was authorised to draft the contracts, and any other documents for the trade, and translate them into Portuguese or Latin from the language of the Germans.

The king mentioned that there were already twelve agents in Lisbon. One more had to be added on account of various factors such as the establishment of the merchant houses of the foreigners, increase in trade and commerce as well as the contract concluded with Simon Seitz in the name of the German company of merchants. Valentin Fernandes, who was the *escudeiro* of the house of the Queen and sister of the king and known for his expertise in language and ability to serve the kingdom well, was proposed by the company of the German merchants who concluded a contract with the Portuguese king for trade in spices and drugs. He was entitled to the same benefits as the other twelve. Besides, being an agent he was empowered to publish all the writings and contracts the Germans concluded with the Portuguese or among themselves. The translations he made into Latin or Portuguese were considered valid before the Portuguese king if they were duly signed by Valentin Fernandes. The king's Chancellor was asked to issue necessary orders whereby Valentin Fernandes's signature was affixed in the book of the chancery. The aldermen and other officials of the city of Lisbon were commanded by the king to permit Valentin Fernandes to discharge his duties duly and to obtain the usual perquisites as the others. Valentin Fernandes affixed his signature in the book of the chancery. [14]

As individual German merchants too were invited by Dom Manuel through the order issued on 13 February 1503, Jakob Fugger sent his agent Markus Zimmermann, or Marx Zimmermann popularly known to the Portuguese as Marco Alemão to the Portuguese king in the autumn of 1503. [15] In view of representation made by Zimmermann further privileges were granted by the king on 3 October 1503/1504 in favour of the Fuggers. [16]

The Fuggers, who individually got the privileges to conduct trade in spices and other oriental goods, started their factory in Lisbon. When the German firms of the Welsers and Vöhlin came forward to fit out the ships to India in view of the contract signed in 1503, the Fuggers too joined them. They invested 4,000 *crusados* while the Welsers and Vöhlin group 20,000 *crusados* each, Höchstetter 4,000 *crusados*, Gossembrot 3,000 *crusados*, Imhof 3,000 *crusados* and Hirschvogel 2,000 *crusados*. The Florentines also came forward with an amount of 31,400 *crusados*. One-fourth of the total investment was made in metal and the rest in hard cash. The consortium consisting of the above-mentioned firms fitted out three vessels to India under the Portuguese flag, namely, *S. Jeronimo, S. Rafael* and *Leonardo* in the fleet of Francisco de Almeida. [17] Hans Mayr was the writer in the ship *S. Rafael* and Baltazar Sprenger in the ship *Leonardo.* [18] Thirty per cent of the total worth of the spices brought to Lisbon was to be given to the Portuguese king. Yet the dividend for the various participants was quite an enormous gain. Without any loss the three ships of the German merchant financiers brought to Lisbon 13,800 quintals of spices. The Portuguese king had apprehension that such a great quantity of spices would bring down the prices in the European market. So it was ordered that the cargo brought should be left in the India House (*Casa da India*) in Lisbon. Further it was decided that if the merchants wanted to buy the spices they could do it against an annual state loan. The price of the spices, especially pepper and ginger, would be fixed in advance. The sales price was hiked by at least two to three *crusados* over the purchase price. Thus the king tried to lessen the high cost for the annual fleet to India. Against all these odds the profit accrued to the German entrepreneurs was quite high. It is calculated that they got a profit of 175 per cent in view of the investment they made in 1505. Like other German merchant financiers, the Fuggers had Markus Zimmermann as their agent in Lisbon.

There is no explicit evidence regarding the participation of the Fuggers in the next fleet under Tristão da Cunha that left Lisbon in 1506. Nor is there anything contrary to it. Hence, it could be assumed that the Fuggers continued to be associated with the Portuguese fleets that departed from Lisbon regularly for India. Since the order of 1 January 1505, purchase of all spices whether they belonged to the king or private persons had to be done only in

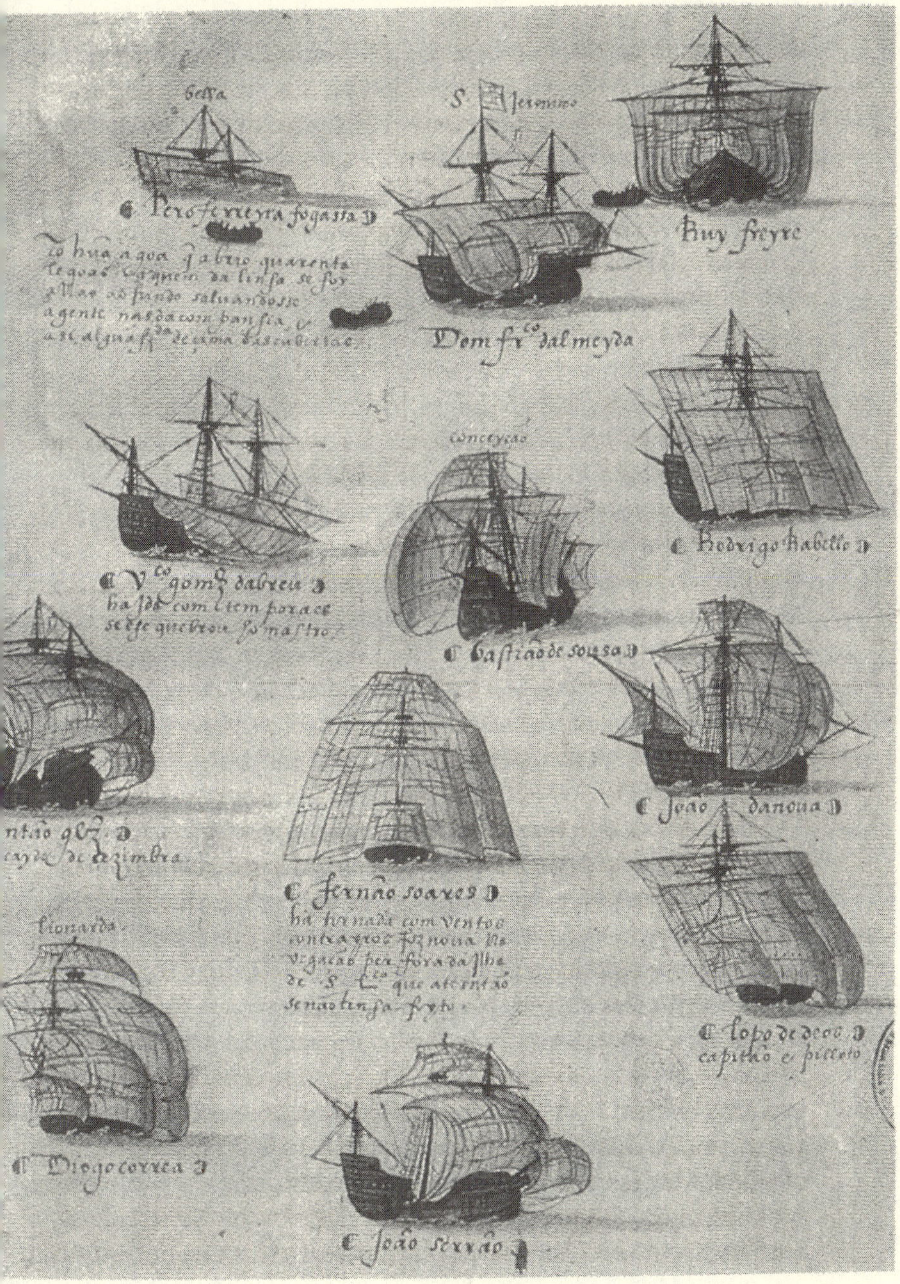
Pero ferreyra fogassa
Ruy freyre
Dom fr^co dalmeyda
Rodrigo Rabello
Bastião de sousa
João danoua
Fernão soares
Lopo de deos
capitão e pilloto
Diogo correa
João serrão

the factory at Lisbon from the chief factor of the king. [19] The price of a quintal of pepper was thereafter fixed at twenty-two ducats. When the Fuggers wanted to have direct trade with India the king did not give in but on the other hand insisted on the royal monopoly over pepper. [20] The Portuguese factor in Antwerp was expected to look after the problem of sale price. In fact the German merchant financiers did not find the system of monopoly and fixation of price by the Portuguese as a welcome step. The Fuggers' agent Markus Zimmermann must have violently reacted against this step at Lisbon in favour of the firm he represented. Quite unexpectedly Markus Zimmermann in Lisbon had to face Hans von Schüren hailing probably from Rheinland who wanted to take up the work from him for the Fuggers. But the former had to refuse the suggestion and he continued the business. He had the support of the factor of Imhof. Hans von Schüren was found again in Lisbon in 1511. He was closely connected with the Iberian business in Antwerp along with Georg Herwart, another representative of the Fuggers. He was the illegitimate offspring of the Augsburger Herwart and was conversant with the Portuguese language excelling all other German agents. The Fuggers' business was closely connected with the brothers Diego and Cristobal de Haro—the former worked in Antwerp and the latter in Lisbon.

In fact Valentin Fernandes who was in Lisbon for a long time extended great help to the Fuggers' business in general and to their agents in particular. As mentioned earlier the Germans had organised themselves in Lisbon with their own chapel. Hans von Schüren faced some problems in Lisbon. He, however, established contact with Tomé Lopez who discharged an important function in the India House in Lisbon and concluded some agreement regarding the sale of spices. [21] At the same time the Fuggers conducted exchange in precious metals with the Portuguese. On 10 April 1513, Tomé Lopez reported about the transport of gold to Rouen, the proceeds of which were to be sent to Lisbon through bills of exchange. Lopez spoke with the Fuggers' agents about this. But they were not for sending the gold to Rouen. Yet they envisaged another possibility whereby their factor in Antwerp "Felys" could undertake a part of the consignment. Therefore, the Fuggers' agents in Lisbon were able to give 5,000 or 6,000 *crusados* to the Portuguese. The Portuguese government in 1514 was bound to give 700,000 *reis* to Valentin Fernandes for printing "*Ordenações do reino*" which was paid in spices. Then he got pepper for 400,000 *reis* and also cloves. The Fuggers and the Imhof purchased the remaining fifteen quintals of pepper from him on 20 October 1514. [22]

It was decided by the Portuguese king to post his own factor in Antwerp so that he could control the price of the oriental commodities brought to Europe and to conduct the dealings in metals like silver and copper. In view of the changed situation, there was no need for the German merchant-financiers to keep their factors in Lisbon. Large volume of spices was brought to Antwerp and only the rich merchant firms could cope up with the situation. The Portuguese king was in great need of finances to continue the commercial enterprise with the East for which he needed money as well as metals for exchange. Either individual firms of business people or a consortium concluded contracts for the purchase of pepper and other commodities from the East against large loans advanced to the king of Portugal. The contract was made against the price mutually agreed. Thus the Portuguese king managed to keep the price rather stable.

Tomé Lopez was sent to Antwerp as the representative of the king of Portugal. In early 1515 he contacted Maximilian, of the Holy Roman empire. In the same year the Fuggers came into contact with him at Augsburg who concluded a copper-pepper contract. The king of Portugal wanted 5000 to 6000 quintals of copper from the Fuggers for the next year's fleet to India. Therefore Jakob Fugger immediately decided to contact the Emperor in connection with the copper mining. Being convinced of the fact that the Portuguese king needed large quantity of copper and that copper fetched high price in India, he argued with the Emperor for larger supply. Fugger came out with the suggestion to Tomé Lopez that he could purchase from the Portuguese an amount of 15,000 quintals of pepper per year for a period of six years. Tomé Lopez, in fact, wished to get a contract for large volume, namely, 30,000 quintals. [23]

Tomé Lopez died in July 1516 and was succeeded by Rui Fernandez de Almada who took charge as Portuguese factor in Antwerp. The Fuggers demanded more price for the copper, namely, twenty-eight shillings as reported by the new Portuguese factor at Antwerp in his letter dated 6 February 1517 addressed to the king of Portugal. They sold silver in Lisbon for forty-three shillings. The factor was instructed by the Portuguese king to purchase 6000 to 8000 quintals of copper as seen in the letter dated 2 March 1517. But he could not get the required quantity on account of its shortage. By 13 July, Rui Fernandez managed to purchase 6000 quintals of copper from the Fuggers at twenty-eight shillings per quintal.[24] The Fuggers purchased pepper in return for the copper and sold it to Bohemia and Hungary besides the various parts of Germany.

Rui Fernandez from Antwerp proceeded to Augsburg and Munich and met Jakob Fugger. He succeeded in persuading the Fugger to conclude a contract to supply, besides 12,000 quintals of copper, whatever quantity the Portuguese king desired at twenty-eight shillings per quintal. Though Höchstetter and Lucas Rem were the competitors of the Fuggers in the business of copper, the Fuggers continued to maintain good relations with the Portuguese king on account of their copper-business in Hungary and Sweden besides that of Austria. They exported copper to Italy and France by land. About 10,000 quintals of copper were used in Nürnberg and approximately 5000 to 6000 quintals were exported to Flanders every year of which 4000 quintals were regularly sold to the Portuguese king. In fact, Rui Fernandez advised the king to get copper primarily from the Fuggers themselves on account of their command over business in copper and the consistency of Jakob Fugger who kept his word. Similarly, Fernandez reported to the king that the Fuggers could let 10,000 to 20,000 *crusados* slip within an hour. In fact, Rui Fernandez was willing to sell pepper to the Fuggers for twenty-four *crusados* a quintal. Before Fernandez left for Antwerp in January 1520, he discussed with Fugger the possibility of hiking the price of copper. Fernandez reported to the king of Portugal that Jakob Fugger was the most important person in Germany and that he had great command over the kings and nobles so much so that nobody could think of living without him. Everyone wanted to be a friend of Fugger. If he were not there Charles V would not have been elected Emperor on 28 June 1519 because the king of France offered him an interest of 20 per cent for the money he proposed to take as loan from Fugger. But Jakob Fugger replied that he would not like to have anything to do with Francis I of France. But on the contrary he promised all the electors and wrote to them to elect Charles V as the Emperor. They had great trust in him and they followed what he suggested. The Emperor wrote to him several times. He would rather like to have Jakob Fugger with him than four princes of Germany, because no German does anything without money. If the king of Portugal wanted to have any negotiation with Germany it was better to have with him. He added that all the Dukes and electoral princes visiting Augsburg used to go to meet him at his residence and spend the time with his wife as a sign of their respect towards him. [25] The importance of the Fuggers is brought out by Rui Fernandez saying that as long as he lived, the Emperor could rule well. He underlined the fact that if anybody wanted large quantity of copper or better copper, he could have it only from the Fuggers. He added that there was great demand for spices in Germany, Hungary, Poland and Russia. He made mention of the insecurity of the traders on account of fear generated by the robbers. The business in spices, according to his opinion, suffered a lot from this. In fact the people in Nürnberg requested Rui Fernandez to contact the king of Portugal for writing to the king of Castile (Charles) to see that security was provided to the trade in spices, especially pepper, in Nürnberg. He referred to the instructions given by the Emperor to all the responsible persons to do the needful to instil into the hearts of the merchants a sense of security and promote trade and commerce. [26]

The way in which the Fuggers obtained large volume of spices against the supply of copper was not liked by all. The German merchants complained to Rui Fernandez that the king of Portugal sold the entire spice and pepper only to one or two Germans. In fact the German merchants had their factor in Lisbon throughout the year so that they might get the opportunity to purchase these items.

But in the meantime, someone came in between and purchased every thing for himself. They suggested that merchants from all over the world should be invited to Lisbon and sales should be done on retail so that every one could get something rather than selling on a wholesale basis to one or two merchants. This was expected to help the price go up. The opinion of the German merchants was transmitted by Rui Fernandez through his letter written from Antwerp to the king of Portugal. He pleaded further that even if the entire consignment received in Lisbon was not sold out in the same year, and remained for the next year, all the merchants from various parts of Europe would come to Lisbon. When the commodity was sold to many persons it would be used widely which would be much more beneficial to the Portuguese kingdom according to his views.

Despite these suggestions to the king of Portugal on the side of the Portuguese factor, the Fuggers managed to conclude a copper contract for three years from 1521 at twenty-eight shilling per quintal.[27] The Portuguese king always maintained the hope that he would be able to sell the entire volume of pepper to the Fuggers probably to the tune of 30,000 quintals. Fuggers were expected to dispose of the dowry of 30,000 quintals of pepper planned by the Portuguese king to be offered in three instalments starting in September 1521 for the marriage of his sister Isabella of Portugal with Charles V of Spain.[28] Though this plan did not materialise, it indicates the trust Dom Manuel, the king of Portugal, had in Jakob Fugger and his ability to hold on to the trade in pepper brought from India. It becomes clear that the Fuggers played an important role in the sale of pepper during the period from 1515 to 1521 and that Venice which was the main competitor for Portugal sank into abysmal insignificance during this period as far as trade in pepper was concerned. The Portuguese markets in Lisbon and Antwerp were frequented by the Germans, Italians, New Christians (converts from Jewish religion) and the *Burgalesen*.

The Fuggers for some time after 1521 did not show great interest in the purchase of pepper from Lisbon. Because, they did not have their own man in Lisbon after Georg Herwart who served their interest as the agent at Lisbon for a long time and could not get along with them. Moreover, Jakob Fugger himself had his eyes on the international spice trade under the Spanish leadership which sent mariners to Moluccas. In fact, Jakob Fugger invested an amount of 10,000 ducats in the second expedition to Moluccas sent in 1522.[29] However, on account of the significant position occupied by the Fuggers in the business of copper, they were always given great importance in the matter of pepper trade.[30]

Portugal was the most important client of the European copper market. It needed copper as material for coins, arms and ammunition, fitting out of the vessels and above all as commodity of exchange. A quintal of copper costing fourteen *crusados* could fetch twenty-four *crusados* if minted into coins.[31] According to the terms of agreement with the king of Cochin in 1503 regarding the fixation of the price of pepper, a quintal cost three *crusados*. Three-fourth of the price was to be paid in cash and one-fourth in copper which amounted to 2. 62 kilograms of copper.[32]

Copper from Europe fetched a huge profit for the Portuguese when it was used as commodity of exchange. One quintal of copper purchased at Antwerp for 4. 5 *crusados* and brought to India cost at the most nine *crusados* including the freight charges. A quintal of copper was sold at fourteen *crusados* in India. Thus the Portuguese were able to make a profit of five *crusados* at least by way of the sale of copper. Therefore the Portuguese officials stationed in India used to write to the king of Portugal to send copper regularly to India.[33] In fact there was great demand for copper on the coastal towns of Gujarat and so in the early part of the sixteenth century large volume of copper brought to the Malabar coast was despatched to Gujarat along with pepper and silk to purchase cloths of various sorts, indigo, sealing wax, gold and silver coins and a sort of shining stone which could stop bleeding (*alaqueca*).[34] On account of the greater demand for copper in Gujarat, Affonso de Albuquerque, the Portuguese governor, wrote to the king in 1513 informing him of the short supply of copper in the factory at Cochin and asking him to despatch large volume of copper from Europe to India.[35] He mentioned that he had approximately only 1,000 quintals of copper in the factory of Cochin. Affonso de Albuquerque in his letter dated 4 December 1513 informed the king of the request made by the Sultan of Gujarat to start a Portuguese factory at Diu and to send more copper to Gujarat. The Sultan wrote to him that every year at least 40,000 quintals of copper would be needed in Gujarat and each quintal of copper could be sold at 18 *xerafins.*[36]

The profit that was reaped by the Portuguese in the use of copper as material for minting coins was still greater. Though the price of copper varied between twenty-five and thirty *soldos* a quintal,[37] a quintal of copper (52. 459 kgs) cost at the most 4. 5 *crusados* in Europe. Even if almost the same amount was considered to be the freight charges of a quintal of copper imported to Malabar, the total cost of a quintal of copper could be at the most nine *crusados* when it reached Malabar as noticed above. There were cases in which Cherina *Marakkar* of Cochin, and a certain Jew purchased copper at more than fourteen *crusados* a quintal.[38] The merchants of Quilon and Kayamkulam paid only fourteen *crusados* a quintal of copper.[39] However, the minimum price of a quintal of copper could be taken as fourteen *crusados*. Hence the profit per quintal was five *crusados*, if copper was sold as it was, while a quintal of copper minted in coins fetched twenty-four *crusados.*[40] As noted above, an average of 4000 quintals of copper was imported into Malabar annually in the first decade of the sixteenth century and this would bring at least 20,000 *crusados* as profit. In the period subsequent to it, the import of copper was at least 6000 quintals and the profit would reach a minimum of 30,000 *crusados*. Since minting began in Goa in 1510 and later in Cochin, one could undoubtedly conclude that the profit went higher than that. Moreover, it is to be noted that copper was sold at a higher price in Cambay and large quantities of it were taken to that side.

Thus the great demand for copper in the overseas enterprise of the Portuguese compelled them to be associated with the Fuggers who occupied the most prominent place in the business of copper. Thus the cooperation of the Fuggers was inevitable for the Portuguese to continue their activities of trade with India, because copper was the most important commodity of exchange in the subcontinent of India. V. M. Gondinho came to the conclusion that about 3000-

12000 quintals of copper were imported into India during the sixteenth century.[41] The Fuggers got copper from various places like Mansfelder, Schwaz, Tyrol, Hall, Bohemia, Poland and Slovakia. It was calculated that Schwaz itself produced 25,000 to 30,000 quintals of copper every year for the Fuggers while Mansfelder provided 16,000 quintals out of which 10,000 quintals were needed for the metal work in Nürnberg and remaining 6000 quintals were sent to Antwerp.

As Jakob Fugger was interested in the trade in spices and the exchange of copper for pepper, he kept a factor in Lisbon from 1503. The then factor Markus Zimmermann represented the Fuggers in Lisbon up to the arrival of Hans von Schüren in 1511. Georg Herwart too worked along with him in Lisbon as representative of the Fuggers. From the time the Portuguese king appointed his factor in Antwerp and began to dispose of the spices and pepper on wholesale at Antwerp, the importance of the Fuggers' factory in Lisbon declined. Yet according to the musterbook kept by Matthäus Schwarz, the Fuggers had a firm representation in Lisbon through their factory there in 1516. Jakob Fugger gradually shifted his interest from spice-trade to the expedition to Moluccas as mentioned above.

The Fuggers' factory in Lisbon lost its meaning under Anton Fugger. But he could not leave the place totally unattended since the capital city of Portugal was also the centre of trade in pearls and diamonds. Moreover, the king of Portugal was the most important client for copper. So, even if there was no permanent factor for the Fuggers in Lisbon there was always somebody who took care of the interests of the Fuggers in Lisbon. There was Ulrich Ehinger in 1522 in Lisbon to represent the Fuggers. Later Veit Hörl, the representative of Herwart, served the Fuggers' interest in Lisbon and Spain. Hörl stayed in Lisbon from 1531 to deal in diamonds and pearls for the Fuggers. He had also done some service for the Fuggers in the matter of bills of exchange. In the same year Christoph von Stetten, representative of Herwart, came in contact with the Fuggers who according to the wish of the latter sent money from Lisbon to Flanders. Later Christoph Raiser, who was in the service of Herwart, left Lisbon to represent the Fuggers in Seville. Occasionally the Fuggers did the purchases in Lisbon through Nicolas Jenoval, a French man who represented the Fuggers in Paris.

A new phase in the business developed in the middle of the century. Jobst Veit and later Bonaventura Schweicker served the Fuggers in Lisbon during this period. New pepper contracts were concluded with João Rebello, the Portuguese factor in the Netherlands on 16 September 1547 when "Joam Suycart" served as the factor of the firm *Anton Fugger and Nephews*. He obtained special privilege for a year to be exempted from tax. Later Hans Bechler represented them in Lisbon. He concluded contracts with the Portuguese government for the supply of copper in large quantity. He collected money from the Portuguese government for the copper and brass supplied to them and forwarded it to the chief factory of the Fuggers in Spain.

At the beginning of 1551 Johann von Schüren left for Lisbon to help Bechler in his activities there. At times there were possibilities for fitting out the fleet to India. The Portuguese king needed wheat, copper and material for ships from the Fuggers. According to the plan of the Portuguese government, the Fuggers were expected to supply a stipulated quantity of materials for the ships destined to India and Brazil. During his stay in Lisbon Schüren identified diamonds, rubies and pearls worth 30,000 ducats though he could not finalise the deal. [42] Schüren had written to Augsburg on 16 March 1551 from Lisbon on this subject. At the same time he had made use of his stay in Lisbon to have closer contact with, and to finalise details of the service of Bonaventura Schweicker who did not want to represent Anton Fugger any more. Schüren at last assessed the jewels of Nuno da Cunha and sent the particulars to Anton Fugger. He also came across beautiful diamonds, rubies and especially a big diamond table and a grain of ruby embedded in an Indian ring besides a beautiful emerald. Thus he provided details of the pearls and other valuable items available in Lisbon to his master Anton Fugger. A few days after the departure of Schüren, Bechler was found again in the service of the Fuggers and he was replaced by Thomas Miller. During these years Matthäus Schwarz and Anton Fugger worked together as seen in the inventory of 1553. In the subsequent years the role of the Fuggers' factory in Lisbon became less important.

As noted earlier, the interest of the Fuggers in pepper declined by 1516 but the supply of copper in large quantities continued since Portugal needed it very badly for the trade with India and the Fuggers were considered the best suppliers. However, during this period they developed their interest in pearls, diamonds and precious stones, of which reports were sent by the agents of the Fuggers in Lisbon to Augsburg.

Asia Contract

Though the Portuguese king did not permit anybody else to trade in pepper and a few items of spices which were reserved for the king of Portugal as monopoly items, the king found that several persons were violating his orders and entering into several malpractices. Therefore, king Sebastian (1557-1578) issued an order in 1570 whereby trade in pepper so far held under the royal monopoly was thrown open to private traders. [43] Though the major South German firms like the Fuggers tried to get the Europa Contract of pepper, the Portuguese king rejected their overtures and awarded the contract in 1575 for five years to Konrad Roth, an ordinary merchant of Augsburg. To the bewilderment of the business world Roth himself took up the contract from king Sebastian of Portugal and sent Gabriel Holzschuher to India. As the enterprise was beyond his own resources he sold three-eights of his contract to Giacomo dei Bardi and Company of Italy.

A substantially new orientation was given to the spice-trade conducted by the Portuguese crown on 1 March 1577. The king issued the new ordinance regarding the trade of pepper, drugs and merchandise of India (*Regimento de trato da Pimenta, Drogas e Mercadorias da India*) permitting the private merchants to import to Portugal spices from India under the Portuguese flag. Thereafter either a single business house or a consortium of several firms could conclude a contract with the Portuguese crown for a couple of years. The private merchants (*contratadores*) were bound to arrange a stipulated number of ships—at least five or six—to buy a definite quantity of pepper and spices in view of the mutual agreement at the fixed price in India. These commodities were to be brought to Lisbon at their own expense and risk and they should deliver these items at the India House in Lisbon at the price once again mutually fixed along with a lumpsum amount for the expenses for fitting out the ships. The conditions of the Asia Contract of 1578 provided the basis for the Asia Contract concluded after the union of the Portuguese Crown with that of Spain under Philipp II of Spain without any substantial change. The sale of the commodities brought to Lisbon was to a large extent similar to the Europa Contract which, in contrast to the Asia Contract, did not last for more than one or two years. Both these contracts could be combined in the same hand as in the case of Konrad Roth in 1578.

However, there were some differences between the Asia Contract and the Europa Contract. The Asia Contract did not give any liberty to contractors in the choice of commodities to be purchased and they tried to import into Lisbon as much volume of pepper as possible. While the contractors of the Europa Contract had the freedom of choice and were not bound to enhance the volume of export from Lisbon, Asia Contract involved approximately an amount of 200,000 florins per year; the Europa Contract entailed an amount of 800,000 florins.

Konrad Roth (1530-1610), who had already concluded Europa Contract with the Portuguese Crown in 1575, tried to unite both Europa Contract and Asia Contract in 1578 by concluding an agreement with Portugal and sold seventeen shares and a half to the Portuguese and Italian merchant financiers. He devised means to control the price of pepper in Europe and founded the *Thüringische Handelsgesellschaft des Pfefferhandels zu Leipzig* which took care of the sale of pepper in the Netherlands, Hungary, Bohemia and Poland. The remaining territories of pepper trade were to be looked after by the Portuguese and Italian partners. Konrad Roth had to face a lot of problems arising from the side of Friedrich II, the king of Denmark and Sweden. The raw materials, wheat and weapon needed for Portugal from the region of Leipzig for the spices sent to that area were not easily obtainable. Moreover, Roth could not keep the monopoly effective as well as the market price under control for the spices since the flow of spices through Cairo, Alexandria and Venice was not totally stopped. [44] Often the required quantum of pepper could not be obtained from India. It seems that the contract obliged Roth to import at least 30,000 quintals of pepper every year from India to Portugal. The five ships that left Lisbon on 4 April 1579 reached Goa on 10 October, and finally proceeded to Cochin to load pepper. Roth had one establishment in Goa and another at Cochin for the trade in pepper. His agent Holzschuher was accompanied by four young Germans to look after the business. The Germans had established good relations with the king of Cochin who helped in delivering pepper in six weeks' time. Yet it was difficult to collect more than 20,000 quintals of pepper for the fleet of 1579 as shown by Holzschuher in his letter dated 10 January 1580 addressed to Sixtus Adelgaiss, a merchant of Augsburg.[45]

The details of the consignment of 1580 are given below:[46]

(Cargo of four ships from Calicut in India which arrived at Lisbon in 19 August 1580)

	cwts.
Pepper (all sorts)	20,777
Cloves	2,863
Mace	343
Nutmegs	444
Cinnamon	248
Ginger	203
Ginger for preserving	600
Tufted cloves	470
Indigo	235
Wax	235
Resin	27
Raw silk	87
China silk	1. 2
Incense	3. 2
	arobas
Amber	2,826
Small pearls	1,696

Roth became bankrupt by 1580 and thereafter the Asia Contract was taken over by Giovanni Rovelasca, an Italian merchant from Milan. [47] Approximately 5,500 to 8000 quintals of pepper were taken from India to Portugal in a ship besides other commodities as a report from Lisbon dated 30 July 1582 points out. [48] Rovelasca appointed Filippo Sasseti, the Florentine humanist, to look after the business in India from 1583. He spent his time in Cochin and Goa from 1583 to 1588 till his death. [49]

Giovanni Battista Rovelasca, hailing from Milan through Gerhard Paris (Giraldo Paris) of Aachen, submitted his proposal for the Asia Contract on 29 November 1585 to king Philipp II of Spain (1527-1598) who ruled Portugal from 1580 in connection with pepper trade with India. Cristóbal de Mora (1538-1613), who was the member of the Royal Council of State of Spain and Portuguese by birth and who worked as the comptroller of finances (*vedor de fazenda*), conveyed the acceptance of the proposal by the king on 1 December 1585. Nuñes Alvares (+1586), the Secretary of State for Portugal, checked the document and signed it on 5 December 1585. Giraldo Paris signed the contract on 15 February 1586 for himself and for Rovelasca. This was ratified by the king two days later. Accordingly Giraldo Paris bound himself for the next six years to fit out five ships with 24,000 ducats and to send an amount of 170,000 ducats to India every year to purchase 30,000 quintals of pepper in India. He was obliged to take care of the transport of the pepper to Lisbon and pay a fixed tax of five and two-thirds of ducats to the Portuguese king. In short he took up the entire responsibility of this business. On delivering the pepper in the India House (*Casa da India*) an amount of 12 ducats per quintal along with the 24,000 ducats spent for the fitting out of the ships was paid by the king to the contractor so that further arrangements could be made for the next fleet to be sent to India.[50] The freight charge per quintal was calculated as four *crusados*.

The money taken to India was kept in the Franciscan convent at Cochin lest it should be diverted to any purpose other than the purchase of pepper.[51]

It was further stipulated in the terms of the contract that spices and other items worth 12,000 ducats should be brought from India for the united government of Portugal and Spain without any taxes.[52]

The Fuggers' interest in spices became renewed in the context of the Asia Contract of 1585. However, Philipp Eduard Fugger and his brother Octavian Secundus Fugger were fully aware of the problems faced by Konrad Roth which were discussed not only in Augsburg, but also in Köln, Frankfurt and Antwerp. Hans Fritz in Köln expressed very clearly scepticism of the mercantile world about the viability of the scheme. Yet the family firm of the Fuggers at that time under Anton I was not indifferent to enter into partnership with Roth though the common business remained withdrawn. Already in 1585 Philipp Eduard and Octavian Secundus had discussed the details of a collaboration between the Welsers and Fuggers and Philipp Krel, the Fuggers' factor in Madrid, was informed of it. Markus, Matthäus Welser and Company took up 5/12 shares of the new Asia Contract. The "Georg Fuggerschen Erben" (Georg Fugger's heirs) took 3/12 shares in this contract from the Welsers who presumably did not have sufficient funds to keep the entire share received.[53] Thus, one-fourth of the Asia Contract was given to the Fuggers. Philipp Eduard and Octavian Secundus invested an amount of 48,500 *crusados* as their first instalment of the share in 1586 for the purchase of spices and the fitting out of the ships and insurance. In the subsequent year (1587) their contribution was 5:4 for the insurance of the ships. But in 1589 they left insurance of the ships unattended to. The Fuggers had Philipp Krel as their factor in Madrid and later Joseph Hartlieb as their own factor in Lisbon from 1589. Eduard and Octavian Secundus sent Hans Jakob Krel, the nephew of Philipp Krel and Philipp Litscher, in 1590 to Lisbon to assist Hartlieb to look after the business in Lisbon. From 1591 Johann Eberlin worked in Lisbon as the factor of the Fuggers.

The important duty to be performed by the officials of the Fuggers stationed in Lisbon consisted in handing over the stipulated sum of money to the India House (*Casa da India*), to arrange sea-worthy and strong ships and to see to the disposal of the import at the rate fixed with the king. Often there were a lot of problems in this regard. The Portuguese crown naturally tried to sell the imported pepper at the highest price possible mostly in the form of a Europa Contract. There was only a period of four to five months to complete the sales. As pepper used to be brought to the European market via Cairo and Alexandria in a considerable volume, the price of pepper in Lisbon naturally went down. The potential purchasers of pepper did not want to purchase pepper and other spices at any high price. Therefore, the Portuguese crown wanted to dispose of pepper as soon as possible. The contractors were naturally the victims in such difficult situations. They were often not able to find purchasers in so short a period and to get the money for the next trip. Therefore, without any surety, they had to arrange money by paying interest. The agents in Lisbon had therefore a very tough work to be performed. Similarly, the factors in India too had very difficult task before them.[54]

The problems started with the very purchase of pepper which was totally different from what was generally understood by those who did not have the first hand knowledge. The local producers used to adulterate the crop to get higher profit since the fixed price was far below the current market rate. Better commodities were purchased first by the Moors and the traditional Arab merchants at considerably higher price and were taken to Tartary, Arabia and China as reported by Cron, the agent of the Fuggers. The local rulers were willing to deliver pepper at the fixed rate only when the Portuguese were ready to help them in their constant fight among themselves. The Portuguese on their side were not sympathetic to such demands and so the local rulers did not care to see that the stipulated volume of pepper was delivered on time against the fixed rate. This naturally created insurmountable difficulty to the agents of the Fuggers as well as those of the others.

Another difficulty faced by the agents stationed in India emanated from the disorganisation prevailing in the Portuguese colonial administration. Cron himself reported that the soldiers were not properly paid and sometimes they had to live on the proceeds of the plunder which left very little time for the exercise of their duty. The garrison at Barcelor, for example, in 1587 did not get any pay for the last five years and were put to great difficulty. Cron and his colleagues were often afraid that such soldiers would demand the money under the "service of the Portuguese king" which they kept with them for the purchase of pepper or would seize the commodities already offered or send them away to find some money for their livelihood. The problem of piracy was not so frightening as this.

Cron was conscious of the bane of corruption rampant in the Portuguese colonial administration right from the Viceroy down to the lowest echelon of bureaucracy. He added that there was not a single official of the king who kept himself away from attempts to make himself rich at whatever cost it might be so much so that even the Viceroy would strive to become king. The difficulties arising from situations of this nature for non-Portuguese merchants were still greater especially on account of the jealousy of the Portuguese nationals in general and of the nobility (*fidalgos*) in particular.

Finding the sea-worthy vessels in right time to carry pepper to Lisbon from the Indian shores was of great significance for the smooth running of the Asia Contract. The vessels that were manufactured in Portugal became quite weak after three voyages. Some of them like the *Reliquias* sank in the sea with the entire cargo. On the top of these difficulties, there was the misuse of selling some offices like those of pilot to the greatest bidder. Cron speaks of the sale of the post of a pilot of a ship for 400 to 600 ducats. As a result the ships' personnel were not often from those trained in seafaring, but people following the professions of tailor, farmer and worker in the stall.

Under these circumstances it was almost impossible for the contractors of the pepper trade to arrange 30,000 quintals of pepper every year for the trip to Lisbon. Yet, Cron made the necessary adjustments in different places like Cochin, Cannanore, Calicut and Quilon which were the important centres of trade, for obtaining as much pepper as possible. Almost always the amount for pepper had to be paid in advance and Cron had to wait for the arrival of the ships from Lisbon every year with money. Sometimes he had to buy pepper at rates higher than those agreed upon. Therefore, the people in Lisbon used to doubt about the purchase price in India. Cron had tried his level best to take advantage of the difference of price between purchase in India and sales in the India House in Lisbon, so that the Fuggers might be in a position to reap better profit.[55]

The consortium of the merchant financiers including the Fuggers fitted out five ships, namely, *S. Thomé, S. Felipe, Buen Jesu, Reliquias* and *Salvador*. An amount of 194,000 ducats in 400 sacks which again were packed in ninety-seven packets was loaded in the ships at Lisbon. Though preparations were made to leave on the 15 March 1586, they set sail only on 12 April on account of the bad weather.

The cash was loaded in the ships in the following manner:[56]

Name of the ship	*For pepper*	*For the repair of ships*
S. Thomé	35,200	8,000
S. Felipe	35,200	4,000
Buen Jesu	33,200	4,000
Reliquias	33,200	4,000
Salvador	33,200	4,000
for pepper	170,000	
for the repair of ships		24,000
Grand Total		194,000 ducats

The total amount sent to India was strictly in conformity with the terms of the contract signed on 15 February 1586.

Rovelasca had several Portuguese and Italian personnel to look after the business in India. Besides them, two Germans, namely, Gabriel Holzschuher and Markus Wolspunter, and Jan Galan, a Dutch man, were sent to India. They took up the responsibility of arranging money for the purchase of pepper. With a view to getting the stipulated quantum of pepper they established five factories south of Goa: Honor (Honawar), Barzelor (Barkur), Mangalore, Cannanore (Kananur) and Calicut. Each factory had two factors, one appointed by the consortium and the other by the king. But both were to be paid by the contractors. The comptroller of finance under the Portuguese king supervised the entire purchase. As the Portuguese did not have any influence beyond the coastal line, the contractors had to face a lot of problems in obtaining the required quantity of pepper and to bring it from the hinterland to the port. The difficulty was enhanced on account of the diversion of spices to Persia, Arabia and other places by land. The best variety of pepper grew in Canara. The harvest season started around Christmas. Though the contract obliged them to import 30,000 quintals of pepper to Portugal they could not succeed in getting the stipulated volume in the first year of their contract. By the end of 1586 they managed to get only 14,592 quintals of pepper. In January 1587 four ships were ready to leave for Portugal. Only two ships were lucky enough to reach Lisbon in August 1587. Ship *S. Thomé* left Cochin on 9 January 1587. The two ships named *S. Thomé* and *Nostra Señora de Concepcion* had only 10,368 quintals of pepper besides other spices. Out of this, 640 quintals were considered waste. The agents of the consortium with great difficulty managed to purchase and load 14,592 quintals of pepper at a higher rate. But *Reliquias* sunk into the sea with a consignment of 1638 quintals of pepper on leaving Goa for Lisbon. The ship *S. Salvador* came into East African coast due to emergency in the sea. The fifth ship *S. Felipe* did not reach Goa at all. But it was held up at Moçambique. Another ship which left Portugal had to go back from Azores on account of the English freebooters. Thus out of 194,000 *crusados* only 164,979 *crusados* were brought to India. Usually 71 per cent of the total volume of pepper purchased in India reached Portugal excluding the waste.[57]

As soon as the contract for the direct export of pepper from India was concluded, the Welsers and Fuggers began to look for a reliable person to represent them in India. Ferdinand Cron (1559-1637) was at that time 28 years old. He was recommended by Cardinal Archduke Alberto to be sent to India. Ferdinand Cron was appointed the chief factor for the Fuggers in India from 1587. He was assisted by Christian Schneeberger. As the latter became sick, they sent Sebastian Zangmeister and Gabriel Holzschuher to India in 1589.

In 1587 five ships, namely, *S. Francesco, S. Alberto, Nostra*

Señora de Nazareth, S. Antonio and *Santa Maria* left Lisbon for India. Two of them reached Goa in September and *S. Antonio* reached in October. Ferdinand Cron (1559-1637) and Christian Schneeberger, who were in charge of the Fuggers' business, boarded the ship *S. Antonio*. Cron was in the Iberian peninsula from 1580. He reached India in 1587 and had been in Cochin as well as Goa looking after the business of the Fuggers. After establishing a German factory at Cochin for the Fuggers he left for Goa where he was received cordially by Dom Duarte Meneses, the Viceroy at Goa. The Governor Manoel Sousa Coutinho (1588-1591) too had been helpful to him in his attempt to procure pepper for the Fuggers and Welsers. As he himself narrates in his apology written in the 1620s, the governor helped him to raise 29,000 *xerafins* from local sources for the purchase of pepper during the rainy season for the ships that used to leave for Portugal in December or early January. The volume of pepper exported every year ranged from 27,000 to 30,000 quintals as reported by him.

As there was no rain in the summer of 1587 the harvest of pepper was very poor. They were, however, lucky enough to get 22,963 quintals of pepper according to the statement made by Philippo Sasseti, an Italian factor. The details of the cargo of 1588 are given later (p. 179).[58]

According to the statement made by Filippo Sasseti (1540-1588), a Florentine agent of Giovanni Battista Rovelasca at Cochin, on 23 January 1588 about 4,500 quintals of commodities were yet to be sent to Lisbon. There was a waste of 6.5 per cent for the total volume of pepper imported to Lisbon.[59]

Again in April 1588 five ships as usual were made ready to be sent from Lisbon to India under the terms of the contract. In a few weeks later the long-awaited war between England and Spain broke out. Therefore, only by the end of May these ships left Lisbon for India. Four of these ships returned to Lisbon on 16 September 1589 safe and sound and imported 24,163 quintals of pepper and other spices. The fifth ship, *S. Thomé,* with 5,877 quintals of pepper on board reached up to Port Natal on the south African coast without being able to reach Lisbon.[60] Out of the 30,042 quintals of pepper

Volume	*Commodities*		
	Quintal	*Arroba*	*Arratel*
Pepper	22,963	3	29
Cinnamon	1,735	0	00
Indigo	1,627	2	00
Sealing wax	289	0	00
Cloves	162	0	00
Mace	28	0	00
Nutmeg	212	0	00
Dry ginger	118	1	00
Ginger in conserve (pickle)	1,362	2	00
Alaqueque	90	0	00
Azeure (orpiment)	13	2	00
Legno Santo (?)	26	2	00
Camphor	9	0	00
Benzoin	24	0	00
Borax	7	0	00
Wax	77	0	00
Ebony	193	3	00
Cowry shells	462	0	00
Incense	12	2	00
Spanish wax	92	0	00
Musk	250 ounces		
Silk	733 boxes		
Sacks and cloths	1271 boxes		

Received in Lisbon on 13 August 1588.

Ships	*Quintal*	*Arroba*	*Arratel*
St. Francisco loaded with pepper from Onor	5,958	2	5
Nazareth with old pepper from Quilon	2,498	1	18
St. Alberto with pepper from Bracelor (Barcelor)	6,265	3	2
St. John Baptist with old pepper from Quilon and new from Cochin	2,693	2	5
St. Antony de Capitania with old pepper from Cochin	5,547	2	31
Total	22,963	2	29

sent from India 80.4 per cent reached Europe. Besides, there was a waste of 4.7 per cent. The contractors were able to place a demand of 382,400 *crusados* before the Portuguese administrators of finance.

The relatively initial success in loading the ship with a rather satisfactory consignment in India during 1588 and 1589 caused slump in the price of pepper in Lisbon. This downward tendency of the fluctuation of the price of pepper was strengthened by the report that 30,000 quintals of pepper via Cairo and Alexandria were expected. Philipp Eduard and Octavian Secundus were afraid that the Venetians would buy more pepper for Venice from Alexandria rather than from Lisbon. They suspected the Portuguese for a clandestine deal in pepper with the Arab merchants in India. The Portuguese officials, despite the unfavourable market conditions, tried their level best to sell the pepper at an enormously high rate. But they could not find anyone willing to purchase. The Crown needed money very badly so that the members of the Asia Contract could send the required money in the fleet of 1590 to India. The Fugger brothers believed that the import of large quantity of pepper into Lisbon would bring down price and the Europa contractors would be the sufferers. The Portuguese officials themselves tried with the Asia contractors to conclude the Europa Contract too with a view to keeping the price steady. But nobody came forward in 1590.

Again and again the Fugger brothers instructed their factors in Lisbon as well as in Madrid to fulfil the terms of the contract through the Portuguese Crown. They were asked to sell the pepper brought from India and to arrange the money for sending to the East.

On account of the troubled situation the India fleet did not leave Lisbon till May 1590. It was too late for the ships to reach Goa in the same year. One of the ships, *Santa Cruz* broke into pieces at the time of departure from Lisbon. The other ships, *Nostra Señora de Concepciòn, S. Cristóbal* and *S. Juan Battista,* had almost fallen in the hands of the English freebooters and returned to Lisbon because the wind was not favourable for further voyage. The ship *S. Antonio,* with Mateo de Albuquerque, the new Viceroy, on board was driven to Brazil and reached Goa only in the next year.[61] The participants of the Asia Contract for the following months had to make it clear that payment of hard cash by force could not be possible in the situation prevailing at that time for pepper. The suitable time of departure by then was over. However, of the fleet that left Lisbon in 1589 four ships returned to Lisbon from India in September 1590 with 23,682 quintals of pepper, cloves and mace. The ship *Madre de Dios* had to face the English pirates near the Cape of Good Hope on her return journey to Portugal. Later the ship coming from Calicut was reported to have been taken to Portsmouth in 1592. It had 200 barrels containing large quantity of pearls, jewels and gold in bullion besides large volume of spices such as 4500 quintals of pepper, cinnamon, nutmegs, mace and cloths which must have fetched over £200,000. This was reported to be of 1500 tons with thirty-six brass guns. There were ninety sailors and numerous passengers aboard the ship. The value of the ship was calculated far above a million. The spices themselves were considered to be worth one million. It had besides gold costumes, Calicut linen and Chinese silk. The same letter mentions that the Portuguese ship coming from India and burnt off the Azores was named *Santa Cruz*. A letter dated 13 October 1592 at Antwerp indicates that the Queen had issued strict orders on pain of severe punishment for the return of all the property of the Calicut ship brought to England. What had already been sold must be reported at Court and paid for. It was hoped that by those means the jewels and other valuables would disappear. It was thought also that the price of pepper would not come down, especially as the pepper on the *Santa Cruz* was lost.[62]

The ships that left Lisbon in May 1590 reached Goa after a delay of one year. Therefore, there was no import of spices to Portugal in the autumn of 1591. Though at least two ships were expected none reached Lisbon from India. The Portuguese government wanted to extend the contract by one more year on account of the absence of import in one of the years of contract as mentioned earlier. But the Fugger brothers along with the Welsers took objection to it.

Another set of five ships besides the one meant for Malacca left Lisbon for India on 4 April 1591. This was the sixth and last year of the contract. On account of the fear from the English navigators these five ships were escorted by eleven well- armed ships from the Netherlands with Portuguese and Spanish soldiers on board. Not much cash was carried due to the expected troubles. It was feared that the English would attack these ships.[63] They set sail from India in January 1592 with 34,000 quintals of pepper, 3,500 quintals of cloves, 1,600 quintals of cinnamon, 549 quintals of mace and 2,500 quintals of indigo. But they all did not reach Lisbon. The ship *S. Cristóbal* landed at Lisbon in the autumn of 1592 with 8,438 quintals of pepper. *Santa Cruz* caught fire in the fight against the English freebooters. It was reported from London that the Portuguese captain's ship coming from Calicut was captured by the English pirates and this was said to have had a cargo worth a million *ducats*. The same English pirates were stated to be chasing two other ships which were coming from Calicut. The letter from London dated 13/23 September 1592 gives further details about the ships captured by the English pirates. The Viceroy and his suite were in the ship which was of 1,500 to 1,600 tons. It was captured near Azores. The English could not take the ship easily to London because of the fact that there were fifty small Spanish vessels surveilling the French coast. It was further reported that out of the five vessels returning from Calicut only one had arrived at Lisbon, one caught fire, one captured and the fourth was said to have been lost while the fifth was eagerly awaited.[64] Another report dated 3 October 1592 originating from Antwerp refers to news reaching Zeeland from England that the Portuguese ship going from Calicut to Lisbon captured by the English was taken to London. The crew, passengers, nobles and the Viceroy were allowed to disembark on the island of Corvo in Azores.[65] A missive from Antwerp dated 3 October 1592 speaks of a letter from Zeeland regarding the capture of three ships from Calicut to Holland, Zeeland and Hamburg. It was surmised that this would create antagonism between Holland, Zeeland and England. The letter added that the Queen of England would be requested to return the ships and the cargoes and that in the meantime a greater portion of the property could be stolen causing great loss to the traders. It was estimated that the three ships carried cargo worth 300,000 *ducats*.[66]

Capture of the ship *Santa Maria* going from India to Europe by the English was mentioned in a letter from Middelburg dated 9 October 1592. The ship was taken to Portsmouth. Half of the cargo in the ship was stolen by the warships. It had 8000 quintals of pepper and a large quantity of cinnamon, cloves and indigo.[67] Details about the capture of a ship from Calicut are furnished in a correspondence from Antwerp dated 11 October 1592.[68] A report from Middelburg dated 18 November 1592 refers to the capture of two caravels from India which were captured by the English and taken to Plymouth. The value of these ships was estimated at £200,000. The Viceroy along with his family and all the fortune he had were on board. A lot of pepper too was found in the same ship. It was calculated that there would be a glut of pepper since there were already 6000 quintals of pepper stored in Amsterdam.[69] Cloves worth £6000 carried in the said ship were sold off. The Queen stopped further sale of the merchandise in the ship with a view to fixing the price at which the cargo could be sold. She wanted to get a higher price.[70]

Nothing was further heard of the ships *Buen Jesu, S. Bernardo* and *S. Luiz*. Presumably they must have sunk into the sea on their return journey.[71] *Madre de Dios* at last was taken to England with 7101 quintals of pepper after the encounter with the English ships near Cape of Good Hope. Despite the efforts made by Philipp Eduard and his brother right from 20 August 1589 the ship was not released by the English and finally after three years of their attempts they had to accept the fact in 1592 and left the matter. Sebastian Speidel and Bartholomäus Schorer from Germany who were in London could not achieve anything substantial in this case. Even the two letters written by the Roman Emperor addressed directly to Queen Elizabeth I of England did not bring about the desired fruit of getting the ship released. Philipp Eduard and Octavian Secundus Fugger (+ 31 August 1600) reacted to this by avenging the English merchants in Regensburg. The attempts made by the Fugger brothers to get back the ships did not meet with any success till 1598. The agents of the consortium were later called back to Europe. But Ferdinand Cron, the agent of the Fuggers, continued in India for a longer time involving himself in a variety of activities.

Cron, the agent of the Fuggers, continued to be in India for thirty-seven years and involved in various fields. He bought shares in the contract for the Portuguese pepper monopoly. Ferdinand Cron married Dona Maria Leytoa, the daughter of a nobleman in Goa in 1592 during the viceroyalty of Mathias de Albuquerque. This matrimonial relationship paved the way for his getting citizenship in Goa. As a result, he was able to enter into the administration of the city as well as the House of Mercy (*Hermandade da Santa Misericordia*). Cron extended personal and financial assistance to the Viceroy for the battles waged in the northern part of Western India by the Portuguese. He reported that during the tenure of Count of Vidigueira, the admiral, he had again given a lot of money on credit to the Viceroy for various needs of Portuguese India. Cron used to get letters from the Fuggers and Welsers by land and, in the light of the information contained in them he went on apprising the Portuguese in India about the movements of the Dutch. Since the Dutch were keen on entering into the Oriental trade and to oust the Portuguese from the Indian Ocean, the service rendered by Cron was of great importance. He, residing at Goa, informed the Portuguese officials about the departure of four ships from the Netherlands to Malacca intended to discover the trade of the south. The letters regarding this matter were written in Augsburg in 1597 as he described and were sent to Goa via Venice to Ormuz. They were received by Cron on 9 May 1598 and were subsequently handed over to the Viceroy. The Viceroy ordered a fleet to be sent in September from Goa to the south under the general command of Gutierre de Monroy.

Cron continued his good services in Goa. When Ayres de Saldanha became the next Viceroy and eleven ships of the Dutch reached Goa in 1604, Cron helped the Portuguese Viceroy by giving 6,000 *xerafins* to fit out a fleet against the Dutch and to chase them up to Cape Comorin. The Comptroller of Finances and the Secretary of State in Goa were adduced as witnesses to the service rendered by Cron.[72] Similarly, in view of the letters received in 1605 from Augsburg via Venice, Cron briefed Andres Furtado de Mendonça about the preparation being made in the Netherlands to send a fleet to Malacca. The Viceroy took the necessary precaution in this matter based on the information passed on by Cron. On 15 March 1606 Cron received further information from Germany via Venice regarding the departure of the Dutch fleet to Malacca. Martin Alfonso de Castro, the then Viceroy after consulting Dom Alexis de Meneses, decided to raise funds to send ships to face the threat in the south. Cron came forward with a large sum as help to the Portuguese. Again in 1607, Cron passed the message on to Dom Alexis de Meneses which he received through the letters sent by land from Lisbon and Venice. He informed the Governor about the eleven Dutch ships found near Moçambique. Cron supplied a large amount to the Portuguese Governor to make preparations for any confrontation with the Dutch.

As Cron rendered a lot of service to the Portuguese and was a resident married man of Goa (*morador y casado*), the king issued orders granting him the title of nobility with a monthly payment of 12,000 *reis* (*Fidalgo de sua casa com dois mil reis de moradia por mes*) on 10 December 1609. He received the habit of the Order of Christ and also that of a Knight (*Cavellero*) with an emolument of 20,000 *reis* per month as ordered by the king. Cron went on advancing money to the Governors and Viceroys during the time of troubles. Later, in 1611 Cron became the sole agent in Goa for the courier service between Asia and Europe and he took the responsibility of sending letters from Goa to Lisbon. The importance of the correspondence handled by Cron can be understood clearly against the backdrop of the hostile attempts of the Dutch and the English in the Indian Ocean.[73] Cron survived in India despite the law promulgated in 1605 against the foreigners living in India, Brazil, Guinea, São Tomé, Cape Verde, Azores and Madeira. He was exempted from being expelled from Goa chiefly because of the wealth and respect commanded by him in Goa. He managed to see that his daughters were married to highly placed persons like Dom Pedro de Almeida with the captaincy of Diu as dowry. One of his daughters after becoming a widow was remarried to Diogo de Melo de Castro, the Captain-General of São Tomé de Mylapore (1625-1534). Dom Manuel de Sousa married his other daughter called Dona Maria who, later as a widow, entered in the convent of Santa Monica.

These matrimonial relations with the influential noblemen of Portuguese India give some idea of the position occupied by Cron in Goa.

He was held in great esteem by the Spanish Crown and was appointed in 1611 by the Spanish Queen Dona Margarida as her procurator in Asia. Later, he was given two voyages to Japan from the proceedings of which he was able to help the construction of the Augustinian Monastery at Madrid near the Royal palace. He was also allowed to sell the voyages granted to him and make money. Sometimes, he purchased indigo from Sarkhej and Byana as well as cinnamon from Ceylon with the part of the proceeds from such transactions and sent them to Europe. He donated considerably for the Chapel of St. Francis Xavier in Goa. He went so far as to set up a Capuchin monastery in one of his orchards near Goa. He was closely associated with the various institutions like *Santa Casa de Misericordia* till 1620. He also took part in the trade in textiles. On account of a lot of scandals in his association with the Viceroys and officials of Portuguese India, he was forced to leave Goa in 1624 for Lisbon and in 1627 he moved to Madrid. He continued in Madrid as a person of some importance till his death in 1637.[74]

The contract of pepper transport and trade concluded with the consortium of the German and Italian merchant financiers in 1586 continued to operate till 1593 and then began the contract with Thomas Ximenes, Heitor Mendes, Jorge Roiz Sulis e Elvas concluded in 1592 which lasted till 1597. The trade in pepper with India was further conducted directly by the Portuguese Crown from 1597 to 1607.[75]

Europa Contract of 1591

Hartlieb, the agent of the Fuggers in Lisbon, wrote to the Fugger brothers on 23 March 1591 about the insistence of the Portuguese king to conclude the Europa Contract. The Welsers, Giovanni Battista Rovelasca, Giraldo Paris, Thomas and Andree Ximenes as well as Francisco and Pedro de Malvenda had purchased a certain quantity of pepper from the Portuguese king which was supposed to be the part payment of the debt the king owed to them. Though the Fugger brothers clarified in their correspondence that Hartlieb had nothing to do with the sale of pepper in Europe they had to accept it by force from the Spanish king. The other partners of the Europa Contract of 1591 were those who had been known for their business especially in cash, with the Spanish king. The contract was concluded on 8 April 1591 for a period of two years. The firm of Thomas and Andrea Ximenes of Portugal took twelve out of thirty-two shares, the Fuggers took seven in the name of *Georg Fuggersche Erben,* the Welsers five, Giovanni Battista Rovelasca and Giraldo Paris four and the Spanish business house of Francesco and Pedro Malvenda four shares. After a short while the Ximenes purchased two shares more from Malvenda. Thus a combination of several nationals took part in the Europa Contract of 1591.[76]

The Fuggers sent pepper from Lisbon to Hamburg and Lübeck in the ships that brought wheat and other things to the Atlantic ports. Hamburg itself got 48.3 per cent of the pepper sent by the Fuggers in 1591 while Lübeck got 23.4 per cent and the balance of 28.3 per cent was sent to Amsterdam. Gilis de Greve, Dominikus van Uffeln und Cornelis de Hertoghe hailing from the Netherlands were the agents in Hamburg for the Fuggers. Along with the Hamburger brothers Bartholomäus and Lukas Beckmann as well as Martin Entzisberger, they formed the commission for the sale of spices. The Fuggers took up the contract just for less than a year. They got only a profit of 4.7 per cent for the pepper sent to Hamburg and Lübeck. In all, they obtained only 4 per cent over the capital they invested in the Europa Contract of 1591. The factor in Lisbon was instructed to dispose of the shares to anyone at the earliest. After a long period of bargain Ruy Lopez d'Evora along with Thomas Ximenes purchased the shares of the Fuggers.[77]

The Portuguese Crown made a sizeable profit from this business. A quintal of pepper delivered at the India House for sixteen *crusados* was sold for more than thirty-six *crusados*. The shareholders of the Europa Contract fixed forty to forty-two *crusados* per quintal as its sale price. Therefore, the profit that accrued to them was not very significant. The difficulties that were faced during the course of the year made the Fuggers sell seven out of the thirty-two shares to certain Lopo Ruiz d'Evora in Lisbon. Nicholas and Simon Ruiz d'Evora were the agents at Antwerp for the Portuguese shareholders of the contract. They had played a still better role in the pepper and spice trade in the subsequent years.

Several groups of financiers were closely connected with the business in pepper in Europe especially Ximenes and the Welsers. From the correspondence of the Fuggers it was made clear that their interest in pepper trade was waning by the end of the century.[78]

The opportunities provided by the discovery of the direct sea-route connecting India with Europe were gainfully made use of by the Fuggers beginning with Jakob Fugger the Rich. The investment in the copper and silver mines paid good dividend to the Fuggers during the sixteenth century. As soon as the pendulum of the international maritime trade began to sink in the direction of Lisbon, the Fuggers shifted their establishments from Venice to Lisbon. But on realising that the Portuguese King did not want to give up the monopoly of trade with India they concentrated most of their attention on the factory at Antwerp where pepper, spices and other Oriental commodities were made available for sale. The period beginning with the dawn of the sixteenth century offered the Fuggers the best opportunity to rise as big merchant-financiers so as to control the Holy Roman empire as well as the international market. Everyone right from the Emperor to the theologian had to dance to the tune of the Fuggers since they had hold on money and material. Therefore, it can be said that the maritime trade of India was, to a large extent, influenced by the involvement of the Fuggers who emerged as very powerful capitalists of the century.

NOTES AND REFERENCES

1. Martim Behaim was born in 1460 in a family that migrated from Bohemia to Nürnberg probably in the 11th century A.D. He began his career as a businessman in Flanders in 1476. He must have heard about the Portuguese enterprises during his contacts with Flanders. He moved definitively to Lisbon in 1484 and married Joana de Macedo, daughter of the Flemish Jobst Hurter (Jos d'Utra). He is known as the disciple of the famous astronomer Joan de Monte Regio. It is reported that he was invited by the

king John II of Portugal several times to discuss the details of the astronomy of navigation. Back in Nürnberg in 1491 he started the construction of his famous globe which is now preserved in the National German Museum in Nürnberg. He died in Lisbon in 1507 and was buried in the church of St. Dominic. Wolfgang, one of his brothers, came to Lisbon in 1503 as the representative of Hirschvogel of Germany. He too died in Lisbon in the same year and was buried in the church of Our Lady of Conception (*nossa Senhora de Conceição*) next to the sepulcher of Ulrich Imhof (*Imcuria*). Ref. Marion Erhardt, A *Alemanha e os Descobrimentos Portugueses*, Lisboa, 1989, pp. 21- 24; Barros, *Da Asia*, Decada I, Livro 4, cap. 2; Hermann Kellenbenz, "Die Beziehungen Nürnbergs zur Iberischen Halbinsel, besonders im 15 und in der ersten Hälfte des 16 Jahrhunderts" in *Beiträge* zur *Wirtschaftsgeschichte Nürnbergs*, Vol. 1, Nürnberg, 1967, pp. 472 ff.

2. Karl H. Panhorst, *Deutschland und America: Rückblick auf das Zeitalter der Entdeckungen und die ersten deutsch-amerikanischen Verbindungen unter besonderer Beachtung der Unternehmungen der Fugger und Welser,* München, 1928, pp. 38-41.
3. E. A. Strassen, A. Gandara, *op. cit.,* pp. 111-117; Venacio Deslandes, *Documentos para a historia da typographia Portugueza nos seculos XVI e XVII*, Lisboa, 1888, p. 2.
4. Antonio Baião, *O Manuscrito Valentin Fernandes*, Academia Portuguesa da Historia, Lisboa, 1940.
5. Hedwig Kömmerling-Fitzler, "Der Nürnberger Kaufmann. . . ", *op. cit.,* pp. 140-141.
6. Peter Krendly, "Ein neuer Brief zur ersten Indienfahrt Vasco da Gamas", *Mitteilungen des Österreichischen Staatsarchivs* 33 (1980) pp. 1-21.
7. Marino Sanuto, *op. cit.,* tom. IV, cols. 66-67.
8. ANTT. C. C., Part I, maço 3, doc. 20.
9. "Neue Quellen zur zweiten Indienfahrt Vasco da Gamas" in *Quellen und Forschungen zur Geschichte der Geographie und Völkerkunde*, Vol. 3, Leipzig, 1939, pp. 8-51. Based on the style of the language and on account of the fact that there were regular correspondences between the Moravian printer Valentin Fernandes who was in Lisbon and Konrad Peutinger related to Anton Welser, Hermann Kellenbenz underlines the important role of Valentin Fernandes in the composition of these reports.
10. Miloslav Krasa *et al., op. cit.*
11. Karl Otto Müller, "Welthandelesbräuche" in *Deutsche Handelsakten des Mittelalters und der Neuzeit*, Vol. IX, Stuttgart, 1934, quoted in Hermann Kellenbenz "Neues zum oberdeutschen Ostindienhandel. . . ", *op. cit.,* pp. 82-96; The first account of the voyage of Vasco da Gama appeared in the printed form under the title *Calcoen* in 1504 in Antwerp. This was authored by an anonymous Flemish sailor who travelled on the ship *Leitoa* which left Lisbon on 10 February 1502. Only two copies of this old print

are reported to be extant. One in the British Museum and the other in the Queen's College in Birmingham. The copy in the British Museum was translated and published under the title: *Calcoen: A Dutch Narrative of the Second Voyage of Vasco da Gama to Calicut Printed at Antwerp circa 1504* with introduction and translation by J. Ph. Berjeau, London, 1874. The introduction of the same was published in Portuguese by A. C. Teixeira de Aragão in his work "Vasco da Gama e da Vidugeira, estudo historico" in *Boletim da Sociedade* de *Geografia de Lisboa, Lisboa*, VI series, 1886, pp. 585 ff. The first Portuguese translation by Oliveira Martins was published in *Sociedade de Geografia de Com. do Porto*, no. 3,1, series, 1881, pp. 110-117. The copy of Queen's college was translated into German by H. C. G. Stier and published as *Vlämisches Tagebuch über Vasco da Gamas zweite Reise 1502-1503*, Braunschweig, 1880. Another contemporary report of the second voyage of Vasco da Gama in Portuguese written by an anonymous author was found in the collection of Philippine Welser kept in the Ambras castle near Innsbruck (Austria). This was transferred to the Imperial Library in Vienna in 1665 and was entered in the printed catalogue of manuscripts as *Diarium itieneris ex Ulissipone Lusitaniae urbe in Indiam Occidentalem [sic] suscepti anno 1502 die Februarii duce Vasco da Gama....* Christine von Rohr made a study of this in 1929 ref. "Neue Quellen zu den Entdeckungsfahrten der Portugiesen im Indischen Ozean" in Mzik, H., ed., *Beiträge zur historischen Geographie, Kulturgeographie, Ethnographie und Kartographie, vornehmlich des Orients*, Leipzig und Wien, 1929, pp. 77-83; Christine von Rohr, "Neue Quellen zur zweiten Indienfahrt Vasco da Gamas" in *Quellen und Forschungen zur Geschichte der Geographie und Völkerkunde,* edited by A. Hermann, Leipzig, 1939.

12. The Order of the king was written in Latin language on parchment sealed with pendent seal of lead. The Portuguese translation made by Jorge Francisco (?) on 18 March 1511 is available in handwriting of a subsequent period. Another Portuguese version of the privilege in the printed version is furnished by J. A. Pinto Ferreira in *Boletim Cultural da Camara Municipal do Porto*, Vol. xxxii, Março-Junho (1969) Fasc. 1-2, pp. 352-359. Ferreira has brought out a number of other privileges granted by the Portuguese kings to the German merchants which are preserved in the Gabinete de Historia da Cidade do Porto and published in the same bulletin, pp. 339-396; For further details, refer also, J. P. Cassel, *op. cit.* ; J. Denuce, *op. cit.*, Vol. vii, 1909, pp. 381-383. Refer appendix I.
13. Konrad Häbler, *Die überseeischen Unternehmungen. . . ., op. cit.,* pp. 15, 19.
14. ANTT. Chancellaria de D. Manuel, liv. 35, folio. 53; Documentos para a historia da typographia Portugueza nos seculos xvi xvii, part II, Lisboa, Imprensa Nacional, 1882, appendice. Refer appendix II.
15. Theodor Gustav Werner, "Repräsentanten der Augsburger Fugger und

Nürnberger Imhoff als Urheber der wichtigsten Handschriften des Paumgartner-Archivs über Welthandelsbräuche im Spätmittelalter und am Beginn der Neuzeit", Hermann Aubin, ed., *Vierteljahrschrift für Sozial- und Wirtrschaftsgeschichte*, 52 Band, April 1965, p. 19; Pölnitz, *Jakob Fugger: Kaiser, Kirche und Kapital in der oberdeutschen Renaissance*, Vol. I, Tübingen, 1949, p. 147, Vol. II, p. 133; Konrad Häbler, *Die Geschichte der Fugger'schen Handlung in Spanien*, Weimar, 1897, pp. 20-41.

16. J. A. Perrera Pinto, *op. cit.*, p. 359; Hermann Kellenbenz, *Die Fugger in Spanien. . ., op. cit.*, Band 1, pp. 50-52. Refer appendix III.
17. E. A. Strassen/Alfredo Gandara, *op. cit.*, p. 138.
18. The report of Hans Mayr in Portuguese is available in the famous codex of Valentim Fernandes, published by Antonio Baião, *op. cit.* Baltazar Sprenger narrated the voyage to India which is reproduced in *Die Merfart unn erfarung nüwer Schiffung und Wege zû viln onerkanten Inseln und Künigreichen. . . ., wie ich Balthasar Sprenger sollichs: in kurzverschynen zeiten gesehen unn erfaren habe, gedruckt anno MDIX*; Kunstmann, *op. cit.* ; F. Hümmerich, *Quellen und Untersuchungen zur Fahrt der ersten Deutschen nach dem portugiesischen Indien 1505/06*, München, 1918. According to the details of the settlement of accounts with Bartholomeu Marchioni, the Florentine merchant, the consortium of Italian and German merchants purchased the three ships namely, *S. Jeronymo, S. Rafael* and *Lyonarda* from the Portuguese for a sum of 5,938,998 *reis.* The price fixed for pepper per quintal was 22 *crusados* in 1505. Refer ANTT. *Chancellaria de D. Manuel*, liv. 46, fl. 130v; *Archivo Historico Portuguez*, Vol. I, pp. 360-361.
19. Kunstmann, *op. cit.*, p. 6; Häbler, *Die Geschichte der Fugger'schen Handlung*, *op. cit.*, p. 24 f.
20. Konrad Häbler, *Die überseeischen Unternehmungen. . ., op. cit.*, S. 15ff, 19; Theodor Gustav Werner, "Repräsentanten der Augsburger Fugger. . .", *op. cit.*, p. 19.
21. Hermann Kellenbenz, "Briefe über Pfeffer und Kupfer" in Eric Hassinger, J. Heinz Müller und Hugo Ott", Geschichte *Wirtschaft Gesellschaft*, Berlin, 1974, p. 208.
22. Hermann Kellenbenz, *Die Fugger in Spanien. . ., op. cit.*, Band I, p. 53.
23. ANTT. CC. part 1, maço 17 document 126; Max Jansen, *Jakob Fugger der Reiche: Studien und Quellen I,* Leipzig, 1910, pp. 227.
24. ANTT. C. C., Part I, maço. 21, doc. 26.
25. ANTT. C. C., Part I, maço. 26, doc. 122. Refer appendix IV.
26. ANTT. C. C., Part I, maço. 25, doc. 76.
27. ANTT. C. C., Part I, maço. 27, doc. 3.
28. Häbler, *Die Geschichte der Fuggerschen. . ., op. cit.*, p. 30; Pölnitz, *Jakob Fugger*, *op. cit.*, Band II, p. 467.
29. Kellenbenz, *Fugger in Spanien*, *op. cit.*, Band I, p. 60.

30. Konrad Häbler, *Die Geschichte der Fuggers'chen. . .*, *op. cit.*, p. 31.
31. *Cartas*, Tomo I, p. 413.
32. Thomé Lopez, *op. cit.*, Tomo II, nos. 1 & 2, p. 200. *Cartas*, Tomo III, pp. 202, 298, *Documentação Ultramarina Portuguesa*, Tomo III, Lisboa, 1963, p. 373.
33. *Cartas*, Tomo I, pp. 168, 248; Tomo II, p. 111.
34. *Cartas*, Tomo I, pp. 197, 265, 424; Tomo IV, p. 78; Tomo VII, pp. 41-42, 132.
35. *Cartas*, Tomo III, p. 396.
36. *Cartas*, Tomo I, Lisboa, 1884, p. 240.
37. ANTT. C. C. I-19-111; I-22-25; I-27-3.
38. ANTT. Nucleo Antigo No. 804, fl. 10^{v} ff.
39. ANTT. *Ibid.*, fl. 11^{r}-11^{v}.
40. *Cartas*, Tomo I, p. 41.
41. V. M. Godinho, *Os Descobrimentos e a Economia Mundial*, Vol. II, Lisboa, 1971, pp. 31-70.
42. Fugger Archives, 2. 5. 12. Refer also Hermann Kellenbenz, *Die Fugger in Spanien. . . op. cit.*, Band I, pp. 363-65.
43. Bibliotheca Nacional de Lisboa MSS. Fundo Geral Codex No. 801, fls. 148-172.
44. Reinhard Hildebrandt, *op. cit.*, p. 145.
45. MSS. National Library of Vienna, Cos. 8953, fol. 23-28; Victor von Klarwill (1924), *op. cit.*, pp. 38-46.
46. Klarwill (1926) *op. cit.*, p. 45.
47. K. Häbler, "Konrad Roth und die thüringische Gesellschaft", *Neues Archiv für schwäbische Geschichte und Alterthumskunde*, Vol. XV (1895), pp. 179-181.
48. Klarwill (1924), *op. cit.*, p. 73.
49. Sasseti wrote a large number of letters from India regarding various aspects of India during his life here. Ref. *Lettere di Filippo Sassetti*; *Opra I suoi Viaggi nelle Indie Orientali dal 1578 al 1588*, Reggio, 1844. This has been later re-edited by Vanni Bramanti as *Lettere da Vari Paesi 1570-1588*, Milano, 1970.
50. Mss. Fugger Archives, codex no. 46, 1, fls. 33-38; Reinhard Hildebrandt, *op. cit.*, pp. 191-196; K. S. Mathew, "India Contract of the Indo-Portuguese Trade in the Last Quarter of the Sixteenth Century" in V. K. Chavda, ed., *Studies in Trade and Urbanisation in Western India*, Baroda, 1985, pp. 165-171. Refer appendix V.
51. M. A. Hedwig Fitzler-Berlin, "Der Anteil. . . ", *op. cit.*, p. 8. The details of the money brought to India according to the terms of the contract and the instruction to keep this money in the coffers of the Franciscans at Cochin are found in a document brought out by J.H. da Cunha Rivara, *Archivo Portuguez Oriental*, vo Fasciculo 3, Nova Goa, 1861, pp. 52-54, 68-69.

The manuscripts kept in the Historical Archives of Goa too refer to the contract and the terms thereof. Ref. Goa Historical Archives, *Livro das Monções*. No. 1 document nos, 4 and 5. Livro 2 A document no. 10.

52. Friedrich Dobel, "Ueber einen Pfefferhandel der Fugger und Welser 1586-91", *Zeitschrift des Historischen Vereins für Schwaben und Neuburg: Dreizehnter Jahrgang*, Augsburg, 1886, pp. 125 ff.

53. Mss. Fugger Archives 46. 1. The Latin version of the Spanish text is given in this codex. The same is reproduced by Hildebrandt, *op. cit.*, pp. 196-201. This is dated 9 May 1587; Hermann Kellenbenz, "Le Commerce du Poivre des Fugger et le March International du Poivre", *Annales - Économies-Sociétés-Civilisations*, 11° année, Janvier-Mars 1956, No. 1, pp. 1-28. Refer appendix VI.

54. There are a lot of reports sent by the agents in India about the problems they faced. Ferdinand Cron, the chief agent of the Fuggers, could be considered the most important person who gave detailed narrative about the milieu in which he worked for a long time. His missive dated 31 December 1587 written from Cochin and Goa sent to Augsburg runs into several folios in the manuscript form. Ref. Fugger Archives Codex No. 46. 1 fols. 39-82. This unpublished letter contains not only detailed information about political and economic conditions, but also very clear ideas about the entire Portuguese colonial regime in the East Indies. It constitutes an important source for the study of the Western coast of India; Ref. also Victor Klarwill, ed., *Fugger zeitungen: Ungedruckte Briefe an das Haus Fugger aus den Jahren 1568-1605*, Leipzig, 1923, letter dated 15 December 1588, p. 126; letter dated 13 January 1589, p. 138; National Bibli, Vienna, cod. 8953 fols. 23-28 for the letter dated 10 January 1580 at Cochin; Code. 8961, fol. 891 ff. from Goa without date; dated 15 December 1588 at Cochin; codex 8963, fols. 40-42 dated 13 January 1590. Refer appendix VII.

55. Hermann Kellenbenz, "Der Pfeffermarkt um 1600 und die Hansestädte", *Hansische Geschichtsblätter*, 74 Jahrgang, Böhlau, 1956, pp. 28-49.

56. Mss. Fugger Archives 46. 1. fl. 13.

57. Friedrich Dobel, *op. cit.*, pp. 128-131; Reinhard Hildebrandt, *op. cit.*, p. 158; Mss. Fugger Archives, 2. 1. 30d fols. 1-2 to Kron/Schneeberger dated 4 January 1588.

58. Mss. Fugger Archives 46. 1. fol. 2.

59. Mss. Fugger Archives 46. 1. folio 2v.

60. Hildebrandt, *op. cit.*, p. 159. The names of the ships as well as the cargo taken from India to Portugal from 1586-1598 are provided by Luiz de Figueiredo, Falcão. ref. *Livro em que se Contem Toda a Fazenda e Real Patrimonio dos Reinos de Portugal, India e Illhas Adjacentes e Outras Particularidades*, Lisboa, 1859, pp. 6 ff.

61. Mss. Fugger Archives 2. 1. 3le fol. 3, to Kron/Schneeberger dated 5 January 1591.

62. Klarwill (1926), *op. cit.*, pp. 242-243.

63. *Ibid.*, p. 221.

64. *Ibid.*, p. 240.
65. *Ibid.*
66. *Ibid.*
67. *Ibid.*, p. 241.
68. *Ibid.*
69. *Ibid.*, p. 244.
70. *Ibid.*, pp. 239-240.
71. Mss. Fugger Archives 2. 1. 31d fol. 54/61/146 to Hartlieb 26. 9., 24 October 1592 and 23 October 1593; Hildebrandt, *op. cit.*, p. 162.
72. Mss. Bibliotheca Nacional de Lisboa, "Colecção Pombalina", fls. 210-219.
73. Anthony Disney, "The Portuguese Overland Courier Service between Europe and India in the Sixteenth and Seventeenth Centuries", pp. 51-61.
74. For details on Ferdinand Cron ref. Mss. Biblioteca Nacional de Lisboa, "Colecção Pombalina", no. 647, fls. 210- 219; C. R. Boxer, "Uma raridade bibliografica. . . " *op. cit.*, pp. 323-364; Sanjay Subrahmanyam, "An Augsburger in Asia Portuguesa: Further Light on the Commercial World of Ferdinand Cron, 1587-1624" in Roderich Ptak and Dietmar Rothermund, eds., *Emporia, Commodities and Entrepreneurs in Asian Maritime Trade. C. 1400-1750*, Stuttgart,1991, pp. 4001-422; Hermann Kellenbenz, "Le front hispano-Portugais contre l'Inde et le rôle d'une agence de renseignements au service de marchands allemands et flamands", *Studia*, 11 January 1963, pp. 263-298; K. S. Mathew, "German Merchant Financiers in Goa during the 16th and 17th Centuries" in P. P. Shirodkar, ed., *Goa's External Relations*, Panaji, 1992, pp. 32-56; Anthony Disney, "The Portuguese and Foreign European Overland Merchants trading between the Eastern Mediterranean and South and Southwest Asia c. 1515-1645", *Vice-Almirante A. Teixeira da Mota in Memoriam*, Vol. II, Lisboa, 1989, pp. 169-181; Hermann Kellenbenz, "Ferdinand Cron" in Wolfgang Zorn, *Lebensbilder aus dem Bayerischen Schwaben,* München, 1966, pp. 194-210.
75. Mss. *Arhivio General de Simancas, Secret. Prov. 1571*, fol. 13; *Documentação Ultramarina Portuguesa op. cit.*, Vol. III, p. 314.
76. Reinhard Hildebrandt, *op. cit.*, p. 167.
77. Hermann Kellenbenz, "Der Pfeffermarkt um 1600 und die Hansestädte", *Hansische Geschichtsblätter*, 74 Jahrgang, Böhlau, 1956, pp. 31-33; Reinhard Hildebrandt, *op. cit.*, pp. 165-171.
78. Hermann Kellenbenz, "Der Pfeffermarkt. . . " *op. cit.*, pp. 31-33.

CHAPTER 6

ANIMAL TRADE BETWEEN INDIA AND WESTERN EURASIA IN THE SIXTEENTH CENTURY— THE ROLE OF THE FUGGERS IN ANIMAL TRADING

Michael Gorgas

Even centuries before the development of the sea route from Western Europe to India, which resulted from Vasco da Gama's landing on the reef of Kappad, north of Calicut, on 20 May 1498, people of the Occident were fascinated by the variety of the Indian subcontinent's fauna; this applied to domestic animals as well. As far back as the twelfth century B.C. the Aryans from Iran and Armenia flocked to North-West India accompanied by domestic animals like horses, cattle, goats and sheep which became more and more established in their new habitat. The ruler of the Pharaohs, Hatshepsut (1490-1470 B.C.), imported wild animals like elephants and leopards from India and kept them in her "Garden of Amun" in Thebes, Northern Egypt. King Salomon (965-926 B.C.) also received ivory, monkeys and peacocks from South India. Alexander the Great (356-333 B.C.) captured 200 Indian elephants from King Porus and used them for fighting on his way to the east, from where he sent live peacocks and parakeets to his European home. The Romans used vast numbers of Indian animals for the fights in their arenas.

Increasingly more exotic animals from India came to Western Europe. It was a real sensation when, on 20 July 802, Emperor

Charlemagne (742-814) got the Indian elephant "Abul Abaz" with the help of the Caliph of Baghdad, Harun al Rashid, in his residence in Aachen. In 1517 Emperor Maximilian moved from the Iberian Peninsula to Vienna together with an Indian Elephant who, however, died there one year later.

In 1490, when the Mughals came to the height of their power, the Indian subcontinent was populated by between 100 and 140 million men. The exchange and trade in animals between India and Europe was especially intensive and successful in the sixteenth century owing to the increased use of ocean-going ships. Numerous species of the fauna of South-East Asia and the island world north of Australia were brought by sea via the Middle East to Western Europe and from there to all the European states. Various transportation routes can be identified, namely, intra-Asian and Euro-Asian. A host of aspects in the movement of animals could be studied. The mode of transportation, the number of animals transported from one place to another, their source, the biological factors that should be attended to in their transportation, the means of obtaining them, the price of the animals, the victuals needed during the course of transportation, the possibility of acclimatising to the varying climates en route, adjusting to the different environments, the people and the type of vessels used in their transport, the reaction of the people in Europe, etc. But we shall only focus our attention on one important aspect, namely, the trade in the animal species that developed with the aid of improved transportation ships and which was important for the economy and for representative purposes. In this context we shall try to highlight the usefulness of these animals and their upkeep beginning with the horses.

(A) Horses

In spite of the import of these solidungulates through the Indo-Aryans from as early as 1200 B.C. they did not become completely indigenous, they had to be imported again into the country as they were necessary for the battles there. Marco Polo, for example, reported on this in detail. The import of milk-white Persian horses by the sea-route via the western coast of India to the ports of Southeast India is mentioned in the poems of the Sangam period.[1] Some of them mention various breeds of horses known by the name of their country of origin. Among them are Vanayuja (from Arabia), Parasika (from Persia) and Kambhoja in the sixth century. In fact, the import of horses has been continuously carried on in subsequent periods.

The most important animals that were transported in the Indian Ocean regions were horses in the intra-Asian trade.

The political conditions of the Deccan, especially since the establishment of the Vijayanagar empire around 1336 and of the kingdom of the Bahmanis about 1347, required a large number of horses for the innumerable wars of conquest. The system of *nayaks* and the duty imposed on them by the Vijayanagar emperor to assist him in the battles of expansion increased the demand for horses. The eagerness to acquire more horses is clearly expressed in the instructions given by the emperor of Vijayanagar who asked the officials to pay the full price for a horse even if a dealer, whose horse died on the way, only brought the horse's tail as reported by Fernão Nuniz. The rulers of the Saluva dynasty in Vijayanagar beginning with Saluva Narasimha (1486-1505) made arrangements for the import of horses from Ormuz and Aden into their kingdom. The merchants who dealt in horses reaped great profit since horses were purchased at the rate dictated by them. Approximately 1,000 *pardaos* were paid for three horses whether dead or alive.[2] The ruler of Vijayanagar owned more than 20,000 horses according to an estimate made by a Portuguese observer in the first quarter of the sixteenth century. Each horse cost between four and six hundred *cruzados*. The emperor sometimes paid 800 to 1,000 *cruzados* if they were of good quality.[3] He distributed the horses thus purchased to the great lords who were supposed to look after them and give detailed accounts from time to time to the emperor. He gave each nobleman one horse for his own riding purposes together with a groom and a slave-girl to look after it and besides this a monthly allowance of four or five *pardaos*. Daily supplies for the horse and the groom were made available by the ruler in the great kitchens financed by the king to feed his elephants and horses. Food for horses and elephants was cooked in large copper cauldrons in big houses under the supervision of several officials in the kingdom. Usually rice boiled with chick-peas and other pulses were given as food. Everybody who had a horse or an elephant from the ruler was allowed to collect the ration from such houses. The ruler saw to it that horses and elephants given to his lords and nobles were looked after well. If they did not thrive well, they were taken away from the grantees and given to someone else. Most of the horses in Vijayanagar were brought from Ormuz or from Gujarat.[4]

Zafar Khan alias Hasan Bahman Shah alias Hasan Gangu (1347-1358), the Turkish governor of the Deccan under the Delhi sultanate, laid the foundations of the Bahmani kingdom with Gulbarga as its capital. As horses were required in large numbers for the kingdom, his successors developed better contacts with the regions of the Red Sea and the Persian Gulf. Goa was a great centre for the import of horses from Arabia and the Gulf regions. In 1510 Affonso de Albuquerque reported from Cannanore to his king that Goa had big reserves of hay for feeding the horses. Firuz Shah Bahmani (1397-1422) developed Chaul and Dabhol as centres of trade with the above-mentioned regions west of the subcontinent of India. Later Harihara II (1377-1406) wrested Belgaum and Goa from the Bahmanis with a view to conducting active trade with West Asia, chiefly in horses. Aware of the importance of Goa and Belgaum in the matter of horse trading, Khwaja Mahmud Gawan, the capable minister of the Bahmanis, captured the former in 1472 and the latter in 1473 from the Vijayanagar rulers. Afterwards, Goa and Belgaum fell into the hands of Adil Shah of Bijapur who, according to calculations made by the Portuguese writers, collected about 100,000 *pardaos* per year just from the city of Goa. This amount was chiefly derived from the import of horses from Ormuz and Persia.[5] Forty-two *pardaos* per horse were collected in customs duties. The richness of Goa was chiefly attributed to the income from trade in horses that were brought from Ormuz by sea and taken to various parts of the hinterland where they were sold at very high prices. A lot of horses and other commodities were sent from Goa to various parts of the Vijayanagar empire and the entire Deccan.[6] The horses brought to Goa from different parts of Arabia and Persia were not sent to other areas of India. The merchants themselves were supposed to come and purchase them from Goa which made the city develop economically.[7]

The Indian rulers, particularly the kings of Vijayanagar, were in need of horses. The import of horses from the Persian Gulf regions and Arabia was directed to the ports of Goa and Cannanore. The king of Cannanore reported about how all the horses from Ormuz and Arabia were brought to Cannanore and how the kings of Cannanore used to derive large revenues by way of taxes. The merchants at this port traded in horses and elephants and made large profits. The king lamented the fact that since the Portuguese conquered Goa and diverted the import of horses to that port he was deprived of a large amount of revenue that he could have otherwise obtained from the trade in horses at the port of Cannanore. The Portuguese governors gave the kings of Cannanore permission to send four ships every year with the local merchants to bring horses and other merchandise from Ormuz.[8] It was from these chief export centres that horses were sent to Vijayanagar. The port of Cannanore had been under the strict vigilance of the Portuguese since the beginning of the sixteenth century, especially after the construction of the fort St. Angelo in 1505.

A number of horses were brought to Goa from where, after paying taxes, they were taken to various parts of India during the period before its conquest.[9] The horses from Ormuz were brought in large numbers to Cambay as well as Goa and were sold throughout the western coastal regions.[10]

Similarly, when Goa was conquered by the Portuguese in 1510 both these centres for the import of horses came under the sway of the Portuguese. Hence the rulers of Vijayanagar approached the Portuguese governor Affonso de Albuquerque to gain the monopoly on the import of horses from West Asian regions. A special messenger was sent to the Portuguese officials in Goa in 1510 to request them not to prevent the horses from being taken to Bhatkal. This request was made especially in the light of the obligation imposed on the merchants to take all the horses from Ormuz directly to Goa.[11] The Portuguese asserted their monopoly right for horse trading and captured the ships that carried horses from West Asia without their permission. In 1514 the ruler of Vijayanagar once again sent an ambassador to the governor at Goa to discuss the details of the import of horses and the dire necessity felt in the empire for horses. It was reported that a large number of horses arriving in Goa were taken by the merchants from Balghat to the region under the rule of Bijapur. The ambassador was received very solemnly by the governor. He had brought along with him a lot of presents from the king to Affonso de Albuquerque and handed over a letter written on golden leaf asking for permission to send the horses to the territory of Vijayanagar. The ruler of Bijapur got to know of the attempts made by the emperor of Vijayanagar to be on more friendly terms with the Portuguese than before and his intention of importing horses directly to his country. The Adil Shah became aware of the danger that could transpire from such a situation. He sent his ambassador to the Portuguese governor to avoid any such steps being taken. The governor sent his envoy to the ruler of Vijayanagar informing him of the fact that the Adil Shah sent his man to Goa to see that the horses were not sent to Vijayanagar. This demonstrates the fight among the Indian rulers for the horses to be obtained from Goa where all those imported from Ormuz and Arabia were taken.[12] Krsna Deva Raya of Vijayanagar purchased 600 horses from the Portuguese at a price of 1,000 *pardaos* when he was confronted with Adil Shah of Bijapur for Rachol in Goa. The man in charge of the Portuguese horse trading with the kingdom of Vijayanagar in the first half of the sixteenth century wrote that the ruler bought 13,000 horses every year from Ormuz and from locally bred horses of which he chose the best for his own stables and the rest were given to his captains. Large profits were made through horse trading. He sold five locally bred horses for 1,000 *pardaos*. The price of the horses sold thus was to be paid within the month of September. The money he obtained from such sales was re-invested in the purchase of horses imported by the Portuguese from Arabia. He employed 1,600 grooms to look after the horses in his stables, and gave away horses to 6,000 horsemen which were marked with the king's emblem. The king paid 1,000 *pardaos* for 12 or 15 locally bred horses.[13] In 1546 a ship belonging to Khwaja Sofar of Gujarat was pursued by the Portuguese because it was transporting horses.[14]

Horses were profusely used by the rulers of Vijayanagar in warfare. The cavalry were mounted on horses in full caparison. Plates of silver or gilded with fringes of multi-coloured twisted silk and reins were fixed on the foreheads of the horses used in warfare. Some of the horses had trappings of velvet from Mecca and others had silk such as satins and damask or brocade from China and Persia on their foreheads. Sometimes the gilded plates on the horses were studded with precious stones. Small stones were placed on the borders of the lace-work. Heads of serpents and various other large animals were placed on the foreheads of these horses in order to create an appearance of magnificence. The horsemen were dressed in quilted tunics made out of brocade and velvet as well as of various varieties of silk. The tunics were made of layers of very strong raw leather furnished with iron plates. The headdress of the horsemen was like a helmet with borders covering the neck. It had a special device to protect the face. They wore gilded gorgets on the neck. Gorgets made of silk with plates of gold, silver or steel were also worn. Swords and small battleaxes were kept at the waist while javelins with shafts covered in gold and silver were brandished in their hands. Ornamental umbrellas with embroidered velvet and damask were also used on the horses. A beautifully decorated horse was used by the king when he went out. Two state umbrellas belonging to the king were placed on one of the horses that led the procession.[15]

The Portuguese officials at Ormuz collected horses from various parts of the region and sent them to India. But, according to the Portuguese official at Ormuz, a certain Xatamaz (Shah Tamas) sometimes got in the way of the Portuguese getting a sufficient number of horses at Ormuz. He collected excessive taxes which exceeded the price of the horses. Bassorah and Lara together with the surrounding regions used to supply a large number of horses that were taken by the Portuguese to India.[16] The flow of horses from Lara to Aden began to run more smoothly after it was captured from the Turks around 1547.[17] Sometimes four to five ships at a time were prepared for sailing with horses from Ormuz intended for import into India. The ruler of Ormuz occasionally obtained permission from the Portuguese authorities at Ormuz to send horses to private merchants at Gujarat.[18] Sometimes a horse fetched 200 *pardaos*. Luis Falcão, who had been the captain of Ormuz since 1544, purchased one for this price in 1547. Horses of a more inferior quality were sold for 150 *pardaos*.[19]

Goa turned out to be a great centre for horse trading during the sixteenth century. Arab merchants brought large numbers of horses from their regions to Goa.[20] Several ships loaded with horses at the port of Ormuz left for Goa. Sometimes ships to the tune of twenty were found leaving Ormuz carrying horses.[21] Since horses were needed by the various rulers of the subcontinent of India and the Portuguese tried to insist on the import of them directly to Goa, the local rulers were faced with a lot of problems. Some of them concluded treaties with the Portuguese in which special mention was made of the number of horses they were allowed to import without any taxes being imposed in certain cases. In fact Adil Shah of Bijapur was successful in making the Portuguese sign a contract in 1546 permitting him to import twelve horses from Arabia every year without any taxes being levied.[22] Through another agreement dated 22 August 1548 he was able to increase the number of horses from twelve to fifteen. Furthermore the Portuguese agreed not to prevent the horse dealers from going over to the kingdom of Adil Shah.[23]

The Portuguese administration at Goa reaped a handsome profit from the taxes on horses. It was agreed that an amount of forty two *pardaos* of gold should be paid per horse as exise duty.[24] All the merchants who brought horses to India were bound to come to Goa where they were obliged to pay the stipulated customs duties. Only after the payment of the duties were the horses allowed to be taken to places like Bhatkal, Chaul and Dabhol with *cartazes* and security.[25] Sometimes more than ten ships loaded with horses from

Ormuz were found in Goa. These horses were taken to Gujarat after the payment of the taxes was made.[26]

The interest in horses made the ruler of Vijayanagar remain on friendly terms with the Portuguese even after Goa passed into the hands of the Portuguese. Affonso de Albuqerque sent Gaspar Chanoca to the king of Vijayanagar to establish a Portuguese trading post at Bhatkal from where the horses could be purchased by the ruler of Vijayanagar. With a view to acquiring more horses for his country, Krsna Deva Raya of Vijayanagar permitted the Portuguese to establish a trading house in his territory at Bhatkal around 1510. After the final break up of the Bahmani kingdom and the rise of the kingdoms of Golconda, Ahmadnagar and Bijapur, the ports like Dabhol, Chaul, Goa and Bhatkal still occupied an important position with regard to the import of horses. Rama Raya of Vijayanagar acting in the name of Sadasiva Raya (1542-1567) entered into a treaty with the Portuguese in 1547 whereby the supply of horses to Bijapur was stopped. Rama Raya exercised power in the name of Sadasiva Raya from 1542 onwards and the details of horse trading with Vijayanagar at Goa were finalised.[27]

Large numbers of horses were bought by the ruler of Vijayanagar, each one costing four hundred to six hundred *cruzados*. It was calculated that the emperor of Vijayanagar had more than 20,000 horses.[28] Sizeable amounts of income were collected by way of taxes on horses sold in the country of Vijayanagar. It was reported that the sale of horses to Vijayanagar for two years amounted to 60,000 *fanoes* in 1546 as customs duties appropriated by the Zamorin of Calicut.[29] Some of them were purchased at Cannanore for the emperor who paid twenty-five ducats per horse.[30]

The Nizam Shah of Ahmadnagar used to purchase horses at the port of Chaul where the Portuguese set up a trading post in the first decade of the sixteenth century and later a fortress. In a treaty dated 22 April 1539 the Nizam Shah of Ahmadnagar agreed that all the horses originating from Ormuz should be taken to Goa and not to any other place. But he was allowed to send people to Ormuz to buy 100 horses for him every year which could be brought directly to Chaul where the customs duties were paid to the king of Portugal.[31]

The Portuguese governor, Vasco da Gama, further agreed, on 30 March 1542, to issue passes to the Nizam Shah of Ahmadnagar every year authorising the import of horses. He made provisions so that the Portuguese officials from Goa might be sent to collect the taxes on the horses at the appointed time and to issue receipts.[32] It was reported that the Nizam-ul-Mulk (Zamaluquo) owed a certain amount to the Portuguese for the horses he purchased from them. João de Castro (1545-48), the governor of Portuguese India, issued an order favouring Pedro Alvares de Mesquita on 10 November 1545 which mentions the indebtedness of the ruler of Ahmadnagar to the Portuguese.[33]

Portuguese merchants accumulated large amounts of money through horse trading. On his death Rui Fernandes, the factor of Chaul, is reported to have left an amount of 4,000 *pardaos* from the horse business which was transferred to Diu in 1546.[34] A horse fetched 325 to 400 *pardaos* in the first half of the sixteenth century.[35] The horses imported into Chaul were sent to Cochin and sometimes to Cape Comorin for resale.[36] Horses from Ormuz were transported to Chaul as well as Bengal. During the rule of Martim Afonso de Sousa (1542-45) the Portugese governor of India, the captain at Ormuz, had been instructed to despatch forty horses every year to Chaul and twenty to Bengal.[37]

Bhatkal was an important port through which horses from Ormuz were brought into the kingdom of Vijayanagar. This was the case until the Portuguese established their sway over Goa and diverted the horses from Bhatkal.[38] A host of merchants were engaged in trade in this port in the first decade of the sixteenth century.[39]

The Portuguese, who insisted on having the monopoly on horse trading, took the animals to various parts of the western coast of India for trading. Horses brought by the Portuguese to Cochin were purchased by some merchants and taken to Cape Comorin for further sale. It was reported in 1546 that forty horses were sold in Cochin for resale at Cape Comorin.[40] The married settlers at Cochin made a considerable profit from the trade in horses with Cape Comorin.[41] As mentioned above, horses imported into Chaul were taken to Cochin as well as Cape Comorin. Some Portuguese merchants like Pedro Alvarez de Mesquita and Diogo de Lisboa, who specialised in horse trading, stayed at Cape Comorin. They used to take the ships to the ports on the Coromandel Coast. They collected information about the arrival of horses from Arabia at Cannanore and Chaul.[42] Some married settlers at Cochin used to take the horses to the Coromandel Coast to make money.[43] The Nayak of Thanjavur used to collect horses from the Portuguese at Nagappattinam. These horses were brought from West Asia to this port to be sold to the Nayak. The Portuguese *casado*, Marcus by name, was appointed by the Portuguese captain of the Coromandel to treat the sick horses brought to the Coromandel Coast.[44] Antonio Fernandes, a native of the Malabar Coast, had his horse trading establishment at Cape Comorin. It seems that there was a brisk trade in horses at Cape Comorin and the horses were taken to Cape Comorin by the residents at Cochin.[45] Ruy Conçalves de Caminha, who was appointed controller of finances in 1547, was a horse dealer before he took up his position as financial controller.[46]

The Portuguese, who continued to have a monopolistic hold on the movement of horses in Asia, insisted in the treaty made with the ruler of Gujarat that all the horses from Arabia should go to the port of Bassein. Taxes had to be paid to the Portuguese for the first three years after the construction of the fortress at Bassein from where they could be sent to the vassals of the king for sale. This was agreed upon in the contract of 1534.[47] Later, when the Portuguese obtained a place for a fortress in Diu, it was stipulated in the treaty with the sultan of Gujarat that all the horses from Ormuz and Arabia should be taken to Diu instead of Bassein so that the customs duties could be paid there.[48]

Several brokers had been appointed by the Portuguese in the ports mainly for the sale of horses. The chief horse-broker, mentioned in the Portuguese sources, had been stationed at Goa—he was a Brahmin whose name was Krisna.[49]

To conclude we may say that Goa had emerged as the chief centre of horse trading ever since the Portuguese shifted their capital from Cochin to Goa during 1530. It derived a large revenue from the import of horses and the trade declined when the Vijayanagar forces were defeated at the battle of Talikota in 1565.

(B) Elephants

Although there were a lot of wild elephants on the Malabar Coast—tamed ones were available above all in Ceylon during the sixteenth century—they were much sought-after by the kings of Vijayanagar. These elephants were imported and presented as gifts to the rulers.[50] The king of Vijayanagar had 3,000 men to look after the elephants in the stables.[51] Great kitchens were run by the king for feeding the elephants. Several officials supervised the upkeep of the elephants. Food comprising boiled rice, chick-peas and other pulses was prepared in great copper cauldrons. If the elephants given over to the care of some lords in the kingdom were not properly looked after, they were taken away from them and handed over to others. The price of elephants in the first quarter of the sixteenth century varied from 1,500 to 2,000 *cruzados* in Vijayanagar.[52] Large numbers of elephants were used for warfare in the kingdom. They were covered with a caparison of fringed velvet and gold, and rich multi-coloured cloths and with bells which caused the earth to vibrate. Faces of giants and other kinds of beasts were painted on the heads of the elephants employed in warfare. Domingos Pães described how three or four men dressed in quilted tunics and armed with shields and javelins were seated on the back of the elephants. Whenever the king went out, a lot of nobles accompanied him. Many elephants with their coverings and ornaments went in front to add grandeur to the procession and to declare to the people through their cries that some important person was on the move.[53]

Elephants from Ceylon and later on from the Malabar Coast were taken by the merchants to the kingdom of Gujarat and were employed in battles. The sultan purchased large numbers of elephants which were brought to his shores. An elephant cost 1,500 *cruzados* in the first quarter of the sixteenth century according to the records of contemporary Portuguese writers. Seats like wooden castles were fitted onto the back of the elephant and accommodated three to four armed men in battle. Those who were seated on such elephants had bows, arrows, arquebuses and other weapons with them to fight against the enemy. They were given excellent training so that they were able to strike both horses and warriors with their tusks. If the elephant was wounded in action, it ran and trampled down others. It was reported that the sultan of Gujarat kept four to five hundred trained elephants.[54]

Even in the seventeenth century, elephants continued to be bestowed upon rulers: three elephants were presented to the Nayak of Thanjavur and two elephants to the Nayak of Madurai.[55] The Portuguese, in some instances, adopted an enterprising policy to supply elephants in return for the help rendered by the rulers against their commercial rivals. They offered six elephants to the king of Vijayanagar to drive the Dutch away from the port of Pulicat in the seventeenth century.[56] Elephants from Ceylon had been generally imported to the port of Nagapattinam on the Coromandel Coast. The Portuguese viceroy of India sent Sebastião Rodrigues Pessanha, the judge of Nagapattinam, to the town of Madurai to negotiate a trade agreement with the Nayak. They arranged to exchange saltpeter for the elephants from Ceylon. The ambassador was welcomed and an agreement was concluded on 12 November 1633.[57] According to the agreement, the Nayak was obliged to sell all the saltpeter available in the kingdom exclusively to the Portuguese in exchange for elephants delivered to the port of Tuticorin, each at the price of 662 *xerafins*.[58] The Portuguese captain, Diogo de Mello de Castro, disliked this agreement; he raised the objection that the price fixed for the elephants was below the market-rate.[59] However, a compromise was reached, the elephants were sent to Madurai where they were exchanged for saltpeter in 1633.[60] During the following year the viceroy of Goa concluded an agreement with the Nayak of Madurai to exchange elephants from Ceylon for saltpeter.[61] Once again the Portuguese captain felt this to be disadvantageous and he prevented the despatch of elephants to Madurai. He made an excuse, saying that the transport of the elephants was risky and difficult because of the draught that prevailed in 1634.[62] According to the contract, the Portuguese had promised to supply elephants to the

Nayak of Madurai at Tuticorin by November or December 1633.[63] No elephants had been delivered even by the month of January 1635 and the contract became null and void. The Nayak preferred to exchange the tusked elephants in 1638 and the Portuguese captain, Diogo Mendez de Brito, was instructed by the Portuguese viceroy to make all possible efforts in Ceylon to arrange for elephant hunting and to send elephants to Tuticorin in 1639.[64]

Elephants attracted the attention of the Europeans for various reasons but mainly because of their size and usefulness. The kingdom of Cambay had a large number of elephants. The king himself reared 300 elephants of which 100 were used in battle.[65] Adil Shah of Bijapur kept a considerable number of elephants.[66] The ruler of Vijayanagar owned 500 elephants of which 200 were employed in battles.[67] The king of Ceylon, who was a vassal of the ruler of Quilon, used to present the latter with forty elephants every year.[68] In fact Ceylon conducted a flourishing trade in elephants. A Portuguese writer in the first quarter of the sixteenth century reported that they were sold by the cubit and were measured from the tip of the forefoot to the top of the shoulder. Ceylon sold an enormous amount of ivory.[69]

The king of Orissa was also in possession of a great many elephants. The king of Pegu boasted of approximately six to seven hundred elephants in the first quarter of the sixteenth century.[70] Similarly the ruler of Burma owned a large number of elephants.[71]

Elephants were used in India for pulling and loading heavy items onto ships. In fact, at some of the Portuguese trading posts like the one in Cochin, elephants were kept and special allowances were paid by the Portuguese to the elephant keeper. Some of the Indian rulers sometimes kept the elephants under their control and permitted the subjects to hire the services of the elephants for labour against fixed charges. Jan Huyghen van Linschoten described graphically the way in which the elephant keeper got on its neck and made it lift heavy weights. Just like the cranes in the modern period the elephants used to pull the boats towards the coast and loaded heavy items onto the boat by lifting them from the land. Big cannons and shots were pulled by the elephants. Similarly they were used in hauling pinnace (*fusta*), small gallies, caravels and big boats from the water onto the land. Linschoten narrates an incident which he witnessed in Goa. A great pinnace was to be drawn from the water by an elephant. Since it was beyond the capacity of the elephant engaged in pulling the pinnace another elephant was brought in by the men in charge. But the first elephant, though desperate, did not accept the help extended to it and pushed away the newcomer as if it felt that it was being humiliated. The same elephant struggled to pull in the vessel. As it was totally beyond its powers it broke down and died on the spot in the process of pulling the pinnace out of the sea.

The service rendered by an elephant at Cochin is vividly described by the same author. The rudder of the ship carrying Linschoten, which was leaving Cochin for Portugal, was not working properly on account of which it had to be brought to land for the necessary repairs. The young elephant tried its level best to bring the vessel closer to the shore. As it was unable to complete the work it fell on its forelegs and wept, shedding tears from its eyes. The elephant keeper chided it because of the fact that he was put to shame in the presence of the onlookers. Finally another elephant was brought to render assistance. Both of them pulled the vessel half way out of the water. At this stage the first elephant pushed the second one aside and drew the ship out by himself as if it wanted to get the entire credit for itself.

The sixteenth-century writers often described the way in which elephants displayed their sense of gratitude. The elephant keepers used to collect gifts on New Year's Day from the viceroy, the archbishop of Goa, governors and noblemen. The elephants accompanying the keepers used to incline their heads and kneel displaying gratitude for the gifts received by their masters. Some of the elephants were trained to bow their heads in front of the church, the crosses and the gates of certain important personalities. Similarly when the elephants passed through market places and were given leafy vegetables they thanked the generous people who did them a favour.[72]

The elephant tusks or ivory were used a lot in the kingdom of

Gujarat in the sixteenth century. Many curious items like bangles and bracelets were made out of ivory for women. Gujarat got a lot of ivory from Ethiopia and Moçambique for the artisans who did carvings for women. Elephants were used in warfare in Ceylon and Pegu as well as in India. Linschoten describes the wooden castles fitted on the back of elephants to seat five or six men during battles.

Elephants were also used for adding solemnity to processions in the sixteenth-century Goa. Big elephants accompanied the young ones on such occasions. The Portuguese cross and pictures of saints were painted on the elephants that participated in the procession. Five or six trumpet players sat on the back of the animals engaged in the ceremony.

As in former centuries elephants were taken to Europe. Besides monkeys and parrots Manuel I of Portugal received six elephants from India for his animal park in Lisbon in 1503. With the latter he formed processions for his subjects: three of his elephants which led the procession were decorated with precious carpets and accompanied by mahouts. More exotic animals followed, an Indian cheetah and its entourage including monkeys, the other three big elephants brought the procession to a close. They were not makchnas, i.e. toothless animals but representative male tusk bearers. An elephant from Cannanore was exported to Portugal in 1510.[73] It seems that special care was taken to look after the elephant during the voyage from India for fear that it should fall sick en route. A receipt issued by Garcia de Souza on 31 December 1510 makes mention of six *cotonias* that he received for the elephant shipped to Portugal.[74] In 1512 two elephants from Cochin were conveyed to Portugal.[75] Another elephant was transported to Portugal in 1513. As the elephant was kept in the trading house at Cochin, 100 *paras* of jaggery and twenty-five *paras* of rice were provided for its upkeep for twenty-five days at Cochin.[76] The same year Pope Leo X (1475-1521) established a menagerie in the Vatican and in 1514 Manuel I presented him with the Indian elephant "Hanno" as a sign of his friendship.[77] Three elephants were delivered to Portugal in 1515. A sum of 3,200 *fanões* was sanctioned by the governor, Affonso de Albuquerque, to cover the freight charges for these elephants from

Cochin to Goa.[78] Some of the *marakkayars* used to transport the elephants from the Malabar Coast to Goa from where they were taken to Europe. Thus, Chilay Marakkar provided his ship for carrying elephants to Goa in 1514.[79] This was an extremely large elephant intended for the king of Portugal as mentioned in the document quoted. It was reported by the Portuguese themselves that some of the ships belonging to the Indian merchants in the early part of the sixteenth century were loaded with up to seven elephants besides 300 people.[80] Most of the *marakkayars* who were involved in trade and commerce in Cochin were originally from the ports of Kunimedu and Nagore on the eastern coast of India. They were closely associated with the Portuguese right from the beginning of the sixteenth century. They were held in high esteem by both the Portuguese and the local ruler of Cochin. Cherianina *marakkayars* and Mamale *marakkayars* were the most important *marakkayar* merchants based in Cochin. They used to visit the Portuguese viceroy at Cochin along with the local king.[81] Their role was of great importance to the Portuguese trade and it prompted Affonso de Albuquerque to write to the king of Portugal requesting him to grant some special privileges to these *marakkayars*.[82] They had large estates on the eastern coast of India. Nino *marakkayar*, who was a merchant of great wealth in Cochin, provided 1,500 fighting men to defend Portuguese interests on the eastern coast of India in 1505. Nino Marakkar's brother had a large estate there.[83]

The rulers of Ceylon used to supply elephants to the Portuguese as part of the arrangement. This was done in the light of the contract concluded with the Portuguese king.[84]

(c) Great Indian Rhinoceroses and Other Hoofed Animals

Unlike horses and elephants, Great Indian rhinoceroses with their relatively small distribution area in North-West India were not a target for tactical or practical warfare but were taken to fight for the entertainment of the subcontinent's rulers in their residences. In the arenas the public were amused by the tame handraised animals, which can gain a body weight of 1.5 tons when they reach maturity. They fought in a similar way with the bulls in Spain. This is shown in a historical illustration in the Padorado museum in Cochin. These rare solidungulates were, however, of more importance because of their big horns which consist of keratin, a substance which was used as pseudomedicine by the superstitious people of China and Europe in the Middle Ages. It was misjudged in its effect but some people paid three-fold its weight in gold as it was said to increase potency. The Europeans thought cups made of rhino horn would burst or their content begin to foam if a highly dangerous poison was put in them.[85] As a result of this not only the few Great Indian rhinoceroses but also those from Sumatra and Java were continuously decimated and their horns brought to Europe, a very lucrative business.

The Europeans had relatively few opportunities to see live Great Indian rhinoceroses as they were very unruly during transportation by land or by sea. Manuel I of Portugal wanted to present such a mighty specimen to the Pope for his animal park in Rome. The sultan of Gujarat sent him a tame rhino together with experienced keepers on a caravel from Khambat to Europe. On 20 May 1513 it arrived in the harbour of Lisbon and people marvelled at its sight. During the ensuing voyage to Italy the ship entered into a storm near Genoa and foundered irretrievably in the sea with its rare freight destined to the Pope.[86] But in Lisbon several sketches of the exotic animal had been made. In 1515, Valentin Fernandes, the Moravian printer who acted as the intermediary between the king of Portugal and the German trading financiers in the first decade of the sixteenth century, sent a graphical description of this zoological treasure to his friends in Nürnberg. It reached the Franconian trading centre via the Augsburg merchant Bartholomew Welser.[87] The popular German graphic artist and painter Albrecht Dürer who resided there painted the rhinoceros without having ever set eyes on it by using the material he received along with the following text:

Em I de Maio do ano de 1513 (sic) depois do nascimento de Cristo trouxeram ao poderosissimo rei de Portugal Manuel em Lisboa vindo da

India um animal vivo como este, a quem chamam rinoceronte. Aqui se encontra desenhada toda a sua figura. Tem a cor de tartaruga salpicada e muito maciamente coberto por cascos espessos e tão grande como o elefante mas com pernas mais baixas e muito capaz de se defender. Na ponta do nariz tem um corno agudo e forte que começa a afiar logo que se encontra junto de pedras. O impassivel animal inimigo mortal do elefante que lhe tem um medo muito grande porque, quando dele se aproxima, o animal corre, metendo-lhe a cabeça entre as patas dianteiras, abrindo-lhe a barriga por baixo e da cabo dele, o que ele não pode evitar. Porque o animal esta tão armado que o elefante nada lhe pode fazer. Dizem também que o rinoceronte é rapido, veemente e manhoso.

The fact that they were small in number and that they were hunted for their horns meant that live rhinos very seldom came to Europe after the first attempt of transportation. It was not until 1748 that a live 8-year-old female Great Indian rhinoceros was shown in Augsburg. Here, the artists Johann Elias Riedinger and Georg Philipp Rugendas got the opportunity to portray the animal, which was transported in a cage caravan, in a more true-to-life fashion.[88]

In its homeland the long-horned Indian water buffalo was of great economic importance as it is said to have been domesticated there 5000 years ago; the animal was able to pull ploughs in marshy areas and tread down seeds.[89] A greenish white butter is made from its milk. In the Middle Ages, especially, it was exported via Iran and the Balkans to Italy and the southern coasts of the Mediterranean because of its varied uses. In comparison, the biggest wild cattle in India, the Gaur, from the hilly forest regions of the south, were only of economic importance as hunting prey.

Of all the antelopes, the Blackbuck was regarded by the Hindus as being holy, they believed it was related to the moon, and therefore worthy of protection. However the Mughal rulers hunted them with their cheetahs. The extermination process continued and of the estimated 4 million blackbucks in the sixteenth century there only remain about 40,000 Blackbucks today.[90] Particularly at the end of the century many of them were imported into Europe. The same fate did not befall the Nilgais and the Four-horned antelopes to the same degree. The latter, also known as Chousinghas, are very shy animals and only grow to a height of between 60 and 65 cm. The fact that the first pair of horns only reach a length of about 3 cm meant that their economic or pseudo-medicinal use was negligible. Another kind of hoofed animal, the Khurs or Gorkhars, were almost extinct. Herodot reported on how, in the past, Indian people used to harness these Indian wild asses to their chariots but this custom ceased because of the reduction in the animal population in the Middle Ages.

(D) MONKEYS

On the Indian subcontinent young monkeys of various species were taken out of the forest and were tamed by their owners. After the arrival of European conquerors and merchants in India, different species of monkeys were exported, whether they be Rhesus macaques, Entellus langurs, Bonnet monkeys or other breeds. As a result of an improvement in the sea route to Europe they were exported and sold to noblemen and wealthier citizens, they acted as fellow lodgers, or were used for public entertainment at local fairs. Many of them wore precious Indian collars.[91] John's langurs were of even greater value; the Indian people were so superstitious that they believed that the monkey's flesh, blood and organs possessed healing powers against different diseases, this resulted in their almost complete decimation. Hundreds of these monkeys were transported by ship to Western Europe or they were exported directly via the silk route and by ships belonging to Arabian merchants to Alexandria.

(E) PREDATORS

The Indian pantherini and their skins were in just as much demand in sixteenth-century Europe as they had been in the times of the animal fights in the Roman arenas. In the Middle Ages, the distribution area of lions ranged from the whole of North West India to the regions of the Narmada river and the Satpura mountains in the south, the Indian tigers were also distributed over a large area.[92] Whole shipments of these animal skins, excellently preserved by skilled tanners, often filled up the holds of the *Naos* and galleons destined for the west, they were then treated and made into splendid garments for the royal houses and rich citizens.

In the sixteenth-century, too, kings and popes kept Indian tigers in their animal parks to the delight of the illustrious visitors. Travelling menageries journeyed with them across Europe together with Indian leopards and black panthers.

The cheetahs which move as quickly as lightning were also easy to tame and export. The Mughal ruler Akbar alone is said to have kept 1,000 of these wild cats which have now become so rare in the Asia of today.[93] The excretions of the perineum glands of the Large Indian civets were especially in demand during the plague epidemics in the Middle Ages. In a much diluted form, the perfume industry was able to develop pleasant scents from them. On the other hand people mistakenly thought, after the shock of the plague epidemic in the Europe of 1347, that one could avoid the terrible epidemic by wearing plague or smelling balls which were filled with the above-mentioned excretions of the civet mixed together with the content of the Musk glands of little Indian and Far Eastern deer, the musk deer, and ambergris, a waxlike odoriferous substance found in the intestines of Sperm Whales. The European demand for civet became so great that finally live Large Indian civets together with African ones were brought to Portugal which had a monopolistic hold on the keeping of these animals. Later the little predatories reached other European states as well. Musk was mainly transported in lead tins so that the fragrance and colour did not disappear on the journey.

Another important product for export was castoreum.[94] At that time, in contrast to today, beavers were still to be found in Northern India.

(F) BIRDS

The avifauna of the Indian subcontinent with its different climatic zones is extremely attractive and varied with more than 1,200 species and was therefore of great interest to the Eurpean importers. Despite the fact that Alexander the Great, fascinated by the splendour of their upper tail covers, had 200 Indian peafowls brought to Greece and that the beauty of the Indian national bird also caused a sensation amongst the Romans, the feathers of the breeding birds exported to Europe in the sixteenth century were not sufficent, as they were used as decoration for knights' helmets, as material for noble ladies' fans and for decorating their hair. It was not usually necessary to kill these shy birds in India because the males loose their splendid upper tail covers anyway when they are moulting and they then have only to be collected by the locals and prepared for export.

Indian parrots ranging from Rose-ringed parakeets, Alexandrine parakeets, Plum-headed parakeets to Vernal hanging parrots and other species were shipped alive; they had already been tamed when they were introduced into European households. Aristotles had already reported that Indian parrots find it easy to imitate human voices, especially the Indian Hill-*mynas* linguistically-talented relatives of the starlings, are able to do so very realistically. Therefore one could always see long rows of cages ready for export on the ships from India which sailed around the Cape of Good Hope in the sixteenth century. It was rare that Sarus and Demoiselle cranes and White, Dalmatian and Spotbilled pelicans reached the harbours of Venice, Lisbon and Antwerp.

For a long time it was unknown where the skins of the Birds of Paradise, which came via Southwest Indian harbours to Europe, originated from. When, on 6 September 1522, the *Santa Victoria* the only remaining ship of Ferdinand Magellan's fleet which set sail on 19 September 1519 for the Pacific, arrived in the Spanish home one could read in the records of Antonic Pigafetta that they came from the Moluccas. The much sought-after birds of the gods of Malay, also used for decorating ladies' hats, were said to always live in the air and to only come down to earth before they died without their feet and wings. It was not until 1594 that Carolus Clusius, a natural scientist at the court of the Habsburger Rudolf II, discovered that clever taxidermists on the Moluccas expertly skinned this rare feathered species after their death and then stitched and smoked them prior to their exportation.

(G) Reptiles

Lots of tales, especially about Indian reptiles, were recounted to Europe as early as Roman times. After Plinius, for example, Megasthenes wrote that snakes in India reached a size which enabled them to devour whole oxen. Furthermore, a description was given about how the shell of a single sea turtle was large enough to be able to cover a residential building. At that time crocodiles were ruthlessly hunted and their skins tanned and sent to Europe, too. In the eighteenth century the Franciscan Udorico still wrote that the backwaters of Cochin, for example, were teeming with crocodiles. Today, one does not even get the chance to see any of the big lizards there. In the Middle Ages they were taken out of their natural habitat, nowadays they are almost exclusively bred on crocodile farms. The horn plates of the Hawksbills from the Indian Ocean were also of great importance for the export to Europe. If they are warmed up their solid body covers can be formed in any way that is wished for; hence their extensive transport to Europe where they were used to make combs, fans, inlays and jewellery boxes. The latter were often combined with ivory inlaid-work.[95]

(H) Invertebrates

The following original animal species became especially important as trade products in the sixteenth century trade relations: the Pearly nautilus known as pearl boats, murex with their purple colour produced by a body gland as well as pearl oysters and corals were all important for making jewellery.

The relationship between the Ship worm, a member of the snail family, and the flotillas of the Iberian Peninsula was more negative. Although they are related to the snail—they derived their name from their disposition and their size of up to 1 m in length—they often acted so aggressively in the wooden constructions of the trading ships that they sometimes collapsed beyond repair before returning home. Rigorous inspections were therefore necessary prior to setting sail for India in order to avoid the loss of the entire flotilla.

The name of the nautilus is also deceptive. They are tetrabranchiata which are related to the sepia which were either washed ashore after heavy storms or picked up by deep-sea divers with creels. After their export to Europe craftsmen fixed them onto bases and decorated them with gold and silver ornaments. Several European trading centres ran workshops which made such treasures. The pearls from the pearl oysters were especially sought after as jewellery to wear in church and at secular celebrations. India played a special role in their import—the pearls from the Coromandel Coast in the south near to Tuticorin were said to be the best. At the end of April or at the beginning of May, the ruler of this region, the Naik, opened the pearl fishing season which lasted for two weeks. In the sixteenth century 500 and sometimes as many as 1,000 divers picked up the oysters in creels and threw them onto the beach to die. The sale of the pearls which took place from June to September had such a long tradition that even the Roman historian Perikles had already reported on it. The pea- to walnut-sized pieces of jewellery were sorted and, according to their quality, passed on to the European dealers. Especially in the Middle Ages, they were of great economic importance as they were regarded in Europe as a symbol of God's love and used for decorating crucifixes as well as clerical robes.

We herewith conclude this short survey about Indian species and animal products which were of especial economic importance to the European merchants in the sixteenth century.

(I) The Role of the Fuggers in the Animal Trade with India in the Sixteenth Century

In the introduction to this chapter it is mentioned that for centuries live Indian animals and animal products had reached Europe through the trading houses in Venice with Arabian ships via Alexandria and through transport on the silk road to Constantinople. Initially this was very difficult after the development of the sea route around Africa to Portugal. We only need to think about the first return journey of Vasco da Gama in 1499 where the crew even fought against each other to decide who could eat the leather rigging. However, the conditions of transportation continued to improve and soon it was no longer thought to be unusual for live Asiatic animals and their products to be brought to Europe on the direct ship route around the Cape of Good Hope in Africa.

The Fuggers became interested in trading and keeping animals in captivity. In Europe they ran a successful business with cattle skins as early as the beginning of the sixteenth century. In some years together with the Welsers they earned 12,000 Augsburg Kurant from this business alone.[96] In 1508 Jakob Fugger rented a lark hunting ground near to Oberhausen. Cages with larks and nightingales were hung up in the Augsburg trading offices in order to entertain the employees whilst they worked. After the Fuggers' participation in the expedition to East India under the viceroy Francisco de Almeida in 1505 where of course on the return journey the transport of spices was all-important, Jakob Fugger the Rich also realised the significance of the import of Indian animals and their products. In 1523 the Welsers, too, purchased Indian animals from Dom Manuel's animal park and brought them to Augsburg. During the reign of Manuel I up until 1521 live animals like monkeys, big cats, parrots, peafowl etc. reached Augsburg merchants' clients via the Fuggers' trading post in Lisbon which was managed by Markus Zimmermann, Hans von Schüren and Georg Herwart. Despite the fact that they were imported over the centuries, peacocks were the most expensive birds in Europe up to the beginning of the sixteenth century, which only rulers and noblemen could afford to keep. Even in 1546 the Fuggers still bred them on a large scale at a place nearby Neusohl in order to obtain the attractive upper tail covers. Especially at that time the Fuggers' business with parrots, monkeys, big cats, animal skins and birds' feathers from India flourished. Their office books contain voluminous correspondence to this effect.

In 1526 Anton Fugger took over the management of the company after the death of Jakob Fugger the Rich in 1525. As early as 1508 Jakob Fugger had purchased Rechterghens house in Antwerp and set up a trading post for pepper and other exotic products.[97]

Lisbon was no longer so important to the merchant family because the traders who worked for the Portuguese king were very experienced and worked, to a large extent, independently. Between 1520 and 1530 the Fugger representatives in Antwerp moved into excellently equipped business premises with a large garden next to which there were big cages to transport animals. Many of the above-mentioned animals from India were temporarily kept here and then sold to rulers, princes and rich citizens in Europe. This trading post expanded to such an extent that the factors in Antwerp complained to the Augsburg head office about the large amount of work involved with "Meerkätzlein", i.e. monkeys from India, Africa and South America.[98] But the head office ignored their plea because the business with live animals and their products was gaining more and more economic importance. On 20 January 1548, the Fuggers' Augsburg office in Antwerp made an agreement to deliver 6,750 hundredweight of brass rings to Benin in Africa. In return they received ivory from which the Augsburg craftsmen produced rings, pearls and other works of art. The demand for elephant tusks was so great that the Indian trading posts were asked to supply them as well.

After Venice and Lisbon it was Antwerp which became the import metropolis for the Fuggers. Especially the cheap water route presented by the Rhine with connections to many parts of Europe was increasingly important for further transportation. The 1550s were very successful with regard to imports from India in cooperation with different shipping lines. The Fuggers' Antwerp office relied totally on animal imports which arrived on these ships. Anton Fugger died on 14 September 1560 and was buried in the Babenhausen chapel. His son, Hans Fugger, became interested in the animal trade and animal keeping, he inherited the gardens "auf der Walk" and in front of the "Neidbadtörlein" in Augsburg in 1560. Hans supported the import of animals as he was very concerned about horticulture and the keeping of indigenous and exotic animals in captivity. From 1566 onwards, the Italian gardener Peter Passalaqua landscaped the so-called "Welsche Garden" in the "Jakobervorstadt" in a renaissance style with ornamental plants including orange and almond trees, rosemary bushes and flowers from all over the world.[99] In 1570, Hans Fugger, whose residence was decorated with leopard skins, enlarged his aviaries and animal enclosures so that exotic animals from Africa, Central America and of course from India, too, could be exhibited to the public. Different species of parrots and gallinaceans and mammals including several species of monkeys and predators could be admired[100,101,102]. Emperor Maximilian II was highly impressed, when, in 1575, he visited this park as he also owned a menagerie with numerous exotic animals in Ebersdorf, south-east of Vienna, and later a second one was set up at Neugebäu. Inspite of the fact that Hans Fugger had the old castle Kirchheim on the Mindel extended into a castle of immense proportions in 1578, the Fuggers' Zoo didn't suffer as in 1580 the French traveller and animal psychologist Michel de Montaigne was most impressed by the animal stock during his visit to Augsburg.

In 1578 the company "Georg Fuggersche Erben" was founded which also established important relations with India almost 10 years later. George Fugger's sons, Oktavian Secundus Fugger and Philipp Eduard Fugger who were from a different branch of the family from Hans, sent the factor Ferdinand Cron to Goa with the "San Antonio" which arrived there on 2 October 1587. This capable merchant was quick to become acquainted with his new field of interest and was soon the leading factor there. He was responsible for the execution of the so-called contracts for Asia and Europe, which the Fuggers, Welsers and other merchants had agreed upon with King Philipp II. Cron devoted all his time to the fauna and flora of his new homeland India. He acquired camphor from Borneo, visited Macao, which even today is Chinese territory under Portuguese rule, and visited Nagasaki in Japan for two weeks. Cron was assisted by Gabriel Holzschuher of Nürnberg and other Germans like Sebastian Zangenmeister. Christian Schneeberger, a former employee of Philipp Eduard Fugger, was his reliable administrator. Cron also got permission to enter into relations with the Arab traders in the eastern Mediterranean. In addition to the main merchandise of pepper and other spices Ferdinand Cron also transported animal products like pearls sold in Tuticorin from June to September, big quantities of indigo, the product taken from muricids for splendid garments in Europe, as well as live animals for menageries and private parks in Europe. This task was made all the more easier as Akbar, the Great Mughal, had established animal parks in several towns in the north of the subcontinent in the sixteenth century where merchants like Cron could purchase animals.

The last year of the Fuggers' running contract with Asia ended in a catastrophe. Of the five ships put to sea from Lisbon on 3 April 1590, which were to return transporting partly animals and a heavy load ranging from indigo down to pepper, none arrived back in Portugal. Consequently, the official relations of the Fuggers with the trade in India came to an end. Their employee Ferdinand Cron, however, continued the trade relations as a private merchant for many years so that Indian exotic animals continued to reach Europe.

NOTES AND REFERENCES

1. N. Uppal, *Maritime Trade of South India, 400-200 B.C. and 320-550 A.D.*, Ph.D. dissertation, University of Bombay, 1990, p. 117; Chelliah, *Perumparanathupadai: Six Long Poems from Sangam Tamil*, n.d. p. 78; Ranabir Chakravarthi, "Overseas Trade in Horses in Early Medieval India: Shipping and Piracy", *Prachi Prabha; Perspectives in Indology: Essays in honour of Professor B.N. Mukherjee*, New Delhi, 1989, p. 348.
2. Vasundhara Filliozat, ed., *The Vijayanagara Empire as seen by Domingos Paes and Fernão Nuniz*, New Delhi, NBT, 1977, pp. 87-88.
3. Duarte Barbosa worked in the Portuguese factory at Cannanore and so his calculations could be taken at their face value. Fernão Nuniz who reports about the price of horses in Vijayanagar could be taken seriously since he was in charge of the Portuguese horse trade with Vijayanagar.
4. Duarte Barbosa, *Book of Duarte Barbosa*, Vol. 1, New Delhi, AES reprint, 1989, p. 210.
5. Ref. João de Barros, *op. cit.*, Decada II, part 1, Lisboa 1777, pp. 442-458.
6. Gaspar Correa, *op. cit.*, tomo II, Coimbra 1923, pp. 55-56.
7. *Ibid.*, p. 66.
8. Armando Cortesão e Luis de Albuquerque, eds. *Obras Completas de D. João de Castro*, Vol. III, Coimbra, 1976, pp. 109-110.
9. Correa, *op. cit.*, tomo 2, pp. 65-66.
10. *Ibid.*, p. 74
11. Correa, *op. cit.*, tomo. II. p. 172.

12. *Ibid.*, pp. 377-381.
13. Vasundhara Filliozat, *op. cit.,* pp. 140, 158.
14. Armando Cortesão e Luis de Albuquerque, eds., *op. cit.*, Vol. III, p. 165.
15. Vasundhara Filliozat, *op. cit.,* pp. 51, 55.
16. *Ibid.*, Vol. III. pp. 254, 271, 454.
17. *Ibid.*, p. 452.
18. *Ibid.*, pp. 259-260.
19. A. Silva Reg, ed., *Colecção de São Lourenço,* Vol. 2, Lisboa1975, pp. 75, 81.
20. Armando Cortesão, *Obras. III*, p. 343.
21. *Ibid.*, p. 424.
22. Simão Botelho, "Tombo do Estado da India..... pp. 39-41.
23. *Ibid.*, pp. 43-44.
24. *Ibid.*, p. 55.
25. Correa, *op.cit.*, tomo II, pp. 335-336.
26. *Ibid.*, pp. 401-402.
27. Simão Botelho, *op. cit.*, pp. 255-257.
28. Barros, *ibid.*, p. 210; Ludvico di Varthema, *Travels of Ludovico di Varthema in Egypt, Syria, Arabia Deserta, and Arabia Felix, in Persia, and Ethiopia A.D. 1503-1508,* translated from the original Italian edition of 1510, London 1863, p. 51.
29. Armando Cortesão e Luis de Albuquerque, *op. cit.*, Vol. III, Coimbra 1976, p. 217.
30. Varthema, *op. cit.,* p. 50.
31. *Tombo.*, pp. 115-117.
32. *Ibid.*, tombo., pp. 117-120.
33. Armando Cortesão e Luis de Albuquerque, eds., *op. cit.*, Vol. III, Coimbra 1976, p. 100.
34. *Ibid.*, p. 230.
35. *Ibid.*, p. 537.
36. *Ibid.*, p. 393.
37. Antonio da Silva Rego, ed., *Colecção de S. Lourenço,* Vol. II. p. 120.
38. Duarte Barbosa, *op. cit.*, p. 18; Tomé Pires, *op. cit.*, pp. 61-62.
39. Ludovico di Varthema, *op. cit.*, p. 49.
40. Armando Cortesão e Luis de Albuquerque, *op. cit.*, p. 215.
41. *Ibid.*, p. 438.
42. Armando Cortesão, *op. cit.,* Vol. III., p. 100; Vol. IV, p. 50.
43. *Colecção de S. Lourenço*, Vol. II., p. 335, 364, 372.
44. ANTT. C.C. part II-A, Maco 117, document 156.
45. *Collecção de S. Lourenço*, Vol. II, pp. 300, 335, 368.
46. *Ibid.*, p. 85.
47. Simão Botelho, *Tombo.*, p. 136.
48. *Ibid.*, pp. 221, 225, 226, 231.
49. ANTT, Chancelleria de D. Manuel I., Livro 18, fl. 62v.

50. Duarte Barbosa, *op. cit.,* Vol. II, p. 113.
51. Vasundhara Filliozat, *op. cit.,* p. 158.
52. Barbosa, *op. cit.,* Vol. 1, pp. 210-211.
53. Vasundhara Filliozat, *op. cit.,* pp. 56, 57.
54. Duarte Barbosa, *op. cit.*, pp. 118-119.
55. A.H.U. Assentos do Conselho da Fazenda, codex 116, p. 9.
56. *Indian Antiquary*, November 1916, p. 182.
57. ANTT, D.R.I. Liv. 30, fl. 59; Liv. 31, fl. 207.
58. D.R.I. Liv. 36, fl. 17.
59. A.H.U. Assentos do Conselho da Fazenda, codice 1164, p. 116v.
60. A.H.U. India, Caixa 11, Doc. 44.
61. D.R.I. Liv. 36, fl. 415-415v.
62. D.R.I. Liv. 36, fl. 16; Liv. 31, fl. 227.
63. B.N.L. *Diario de 3 de Conde de Linhares*, Vicerei da India, fl. 260.
64. Historical Archives of Goa, codex 1419, fl. 79; codex 1420, fl. 54a and 183.
65. Tomé Pires, *op. cit.,* Vol. 1, pp. 33, 40-41.
66. *Ibid.*, p. 52.
67. *Ibid.*, p. 64.
68. *Ibid.*, pp. 80, 87.
69. *Ibid.*, p. 86.
70. *Ibid.*, p. 102.
71. *Ibid.*, p. 111.
72. John Huyghen van Linschoten, *op. cit.*, Vol. 2, New Delhi (reprint), 1988, pp. 6-8.
73. *Cartas.,* tomo. vi, p. 412.
74. *Cartas.,* tomo. vi, p. 412.
75. *Cartas.,* tomo. vii, p. 12.
76. *Ibid.*, p. 104.
77. Hermann Dembeck, *Mit Tieren leben,* Düsseldorf, Wien, 1961.
78. *Ibid.*, tomo. vi, p. 206.
79. *Ibid.*, tomo. vi, p. 31.
80. Gaspar Correa, *op. cit.,* tom. I, part 1, p. 226.
81. *Cartas.*, tomo II, pp. 361, 368.
82. A.B. de Bragança Pereira, *Arquivo Portuguese Oriental*, tomo IV, Vol. 1, part 1, p. 681, *cartas* tomo. III, p. 401.
83. *Cartas*, tomo. ii, pp. 377-78.
84. Simão Botelho, *op. cit.*, p. 240.
85. Fred Kurt, *Die Gärtner von Eden,* Hamburg, 1991.
86. Hermann Dembeck, *op. cit.*
87. A. Fontora da Costa, *Deambulações da Ganda de Modafar, Rei de Cambaia de 1514 a 1516*, Lisboa 1937, pp. 29 ff.
88. Michael Gorgas, *Tiere - Kaiser - Anekdoten, Von Fuggers Menagerie zum Großstadtzoo,* Gersthofen, 1986.
89. Frederick E. Zeuner, *A History of Domesticated Animals,* London 1963.

90. E. P. Gee, *Indiens Tierwelt in Gefahr*, Zürich, Stuttgart, Wien, 1967.
91. Hermann Kellenbenz, *Die Fugger in Spanien und Portugal 1560*, München, 1990.
92. E. P. Gee, *op. cit.*, 1967.
93. Rudolf Arnold, *Das Tier in der Weltgeschichte,* Frankfurt am Main, 1939.
94. Karl Otto Müller, *Welthandelsbräuche (1480-1540),* Stuttgart und Berlin, 1934, pp. 111-299.
95. Karl Heinz Reger, *Pfeffer aus Fernost, Das abenteuerliche Leben eines Augsburger Kaufmanns,* Pfaffenhofen, 1986.
96. Hermann Dembeck, *op. cit.*, 1961.
97. Hermann Kellenbenz, *Die Fugger in Spanien und Portugal 1560,* München, 1990.
98. Fuggerarchiv Dillingen.
99. Sylvia Specker, *Untersuchung typischer Gestaltungsmerkmale der Gärten des Spätmittelalters und der Renaissance in Süddeutschland in Bezug auf die Gärten der Fugger*, Diplomarbeit Fachhochschule Weihenstephan, 1983, pp. 64-113.
100. Hermann Dembeck, *op. cit.*, 1961.
101. Michael Gorgas, *op. cit.*
102. Wilhelm Liebhart und Josef Mancal, *Augsburger Stadtlexikon,* Augsburg, 1985.

CHAPTER 7

CONCLUSION

Spices and other exotic items of the Orient reached various parts of Europe chiefly through the regions of Red Sea and Persian Gulf till the opening of the direct sea-route connecting India with Europe towards the end of the fifteenth century. The Muslims, chiefly the Al-Karim merchants specialising in spice trade, held a sort of monopoly over the supply of these items to the centres of trade like Cairo, Alexandria, Aleppo, Beirut and Damascus. Pepper, ginger, saffron and other products of the subcontinent of India taken to the Mediterranean ports were made available at Venice from where merchants took them to the various parts of Europe. In other words, Indian commodities found their way to the far-flung regions of Europe via the Mediterranean.

The native merchants too took active part in sending the Indian commodities to the East African coast as well as the centres of the trade in the Red Sea and Persian Gulf regions. Merchants from Gujarat and the Malabar coast were found on the East African coast busying themselves with trade in oriental goods when Vasco da Gama reached there. This confirms the view that India had a long-distance trade with the West and that too in bulk goods.

The same may be said of India's relations with Southeast Asia especially Malacca which was located at the limit of the monsoons. Thousands of Indian merchants used to stay there and visit the centre for trade and commerce every year. In fact Malacca provided a very congenial atmosphere for exchanging commodities from China for those of India. Indian textiles in large quantities were taken by the merchants for purchasing the commodities available in Malacca. Long-distance trade of this nature cannot be categorised as a phase of peddling trade because it involved bulk goods and places lying in far away regions. Moreover, such a pattern of trade necessarily involved substantial capital and many of the factors characteristic of capitalist economy. Braudel speaking of the Indian merchants in the sixteenth century and thereafter affirms ". . . it is easier to understand . . . the role of the merchants of India—certainly not peddlers in this case—who can be found from the sixteenth to the eighteenth century settled in Persia, Istanbul, Astrakhan or Moscow". He adds "Since the fourteenth century, India had possessed a monetary economy of some vitality, which was soon on the way towards a certain capitalism—but one that would not encompass the entire society."[1] Speaking about the Indian bankers in general and about Virji Vohra and others of the seventeenth century Braudel writes that like the European "banker", the Indian money changer was often a merchant who invested large amounts and handled transport too. He makes mention of the fabulous wealth of Virji Vohra and Abd-ul Ghafur. Therefore, it is reasonably concluded that even before the arrival of the Portuguese, India's trade formed part of the capitalist economy.

The subcontinent of India, which is now placed among the countries of the "third world" as a result of the "development of under development" sedulously followed up by the colonial powers for the last four centuries and a half, was the target of the Europeans in the second half of the fifteenth century. The powers of the present "first world" were driven from pillar to post to get their claim over India established. Some of them giving weightage to religious authorities approached the popes to get bulls issued lest contesting powers should encroach upon the areas they claimed. In this process they formulated theories buttressing their claims. Apart from intellectual clashes the frictions taking shape in Europe found their expression in the Indian Ocean regions. As a result, international mercantile battles were waged for getting a foothold on the coastal regions of India and to accumulate capital through maritime trade with them. The Portuguese for quite some time managed to guard their possessions jealously under the protection extended by the popes. But on the wake of the Lutheran reformation, the papal authority was challenged and the Portuguese possessions began to be attacked by peoples embracing Protestant religion. Thus, on account of the economic importance of India the Indian Ocean regions turned out to be an arena of international rivalries.

Though the Portuguese strained every nerve to divert the flow of pepper and other spices from the routes leading to the Mediterranean and to keep Italian as well as the German merchants away from the scene and send the commodities to Lisbon via the Cape of Good Hope their attempts did not meet with lasting success. As Kulischer, a German historian, surmises Germany continued to get spices and pepper from Venice in the sixteenth century with a short-lived setback in the early decades.[2] It is evident that the Portuguese success in establishing direct trade with India gave a serious shock to the Venetians who asserted that the loss of spice trade "would be like the loss of milk to a new born babe".

The spices brought by the Portuguese to Europe were made available in the Netherlands by 1501 and in England by 1504. The German firms of Anton Welser and Conrad Vöhlim decided to purchase pepper from Lisbon and sent their messengers in 1503. There was considerable slump in the price of pepper in the international market after king Dom Manuel of Portugal fixed its price in Lisbon in 1504. The *Magna Societas* of Ravensburg resolved in 1507 to purchase spices and pepper from the Portuguese factor at Antwerp. The Viennese merchants requested the emperor to permit foreign merchants to supply spices from Antwerp, Frankfurt or Nürnberg since the supply from Venice was inadequate in 1512-1513.[3] Pepper brought by the Portuguese from India was sold in 1524 in western France, Castile and Medina del Campo. Doubtless this pepper penetrated the Mediterranean, especially Genoa, through the Portuguese merchants since 1503. On account of the eagerness to get spices at Venice, the Venetian Senate waived customs duties on vessels bringing pepper. Desperate as she was, Signoria sent vessels to Lisbon for taking stock of pepper and furnishing her stores in 1515. In fact, by 1527 she went so far as to suggest to Dom John III, the Portuguese king, that the sales contracts for pepper imported into Lisbon be farmed out to Venice excluding the domestic consumption in Portugal.[4] This shows that in the first quarter of the sixteenth century Venice was deprived of the usual supply of pepper and other spices from the east through the Red Sea as well as the Persian Gulf.

The ephemeral success of the Portuguese to arrest the flow of spices to Europe through the Mediterranean did not deal a fatal blow to the prosperity of the spice trade of the ports on the Mediterranean for a long time. As Fernand Braudel holds, though it is hard to pinpoint the exact time the tide turned in favour of the Mediterranean, the movement of prices after the 1540s disturbed the prosperity of trade in Lisbon. There was, besides, a rumour spread in Venice and Spain that the spices brought by the Portuguese lost their aroma on account of the long sea voyages. Moreover, the Portuguese could not get the better quality of spices from India since they were insisting on the prices fixed at the dawn of the sixteenth century. On the contrary, the Arab merchants who purchased spices at the prevailing market rates in India obtained better quality of spices and furnished the Mediterranean ports with them. The routes connecting India with the Mediterranean were shorter and less risky compared to the one followed by the Portuguese. Moreover, the merchants of the route leading to the Mediterranean were able to supply gold from Egypt and silver from the West for spices and pepper from India. Coral and saffron from the Mediterranean, opium from Egypt, woollen cloth from the West, quick silver and madder from the Red Sea were in great demand in India and the Southeast Asian countries. All these factors worked in conjunction for the revival of the Mediterranean trade in spices and pepper towards the second half of the sixteenth century.[5]

Pepper received from the East through the Mediterranean began to appear in Antwerp regularly in the second half of the sixteenth century and the Mediterranean pepper began to influence the price of pepper in the Scheldt market. It was recorded at Marseilles that pepper was sent to Lyon and Toulouse in 1543 despite the pepper blockade operated by the Iberians against the French. Consequently a large number of ships with money and commodities of exchange frequented Alexandria and Syria so much so that the Portuguese Ambassador at Rome became greatly nervous about the damage it could cause to the direct Portuguese trade with India.[6] The Fuggers themselves dispatched a factor to Alexandria and organised the transportation of spices from there via Fiume and Ragusa after 1559.[7] The Turks seized about 20,000 quintals of Portuguese pepper on the Indian Ocean and sent them to Alexandria in 1561.[8]

It is calculated that the Venetian merchants purchased annually 12,000 quintals of spices from Cairo as gleaned from the consular documents between 1560 and 1564. The Portuguese ambassador at Rome estimated that the total amount of Alexandrian spice trade was 40,000 quintals. A Portuguese spy reported in 1564 that Alexandria trade consisted in 30,000 quintals of spices out of which pepper alone constituted 25,000 quintals. The Venetian consul at Jeddah informed that 20,000 quintals of pepper were brought to Jeddah in 1565. This was besides the cargo of twenty-three ships that came from Gujarat and Calicut with spices to Jeddah. Thus the volume of spice trade in the route via Egypt besides the one through Syria rose approximately to 30,000 to 40,000 quintals.[9] In fact F.C. Lane is of the opinion that the volume of spices imported into Lisbon was less than this. Rouen and Toulouse received pepper in 1565 and it competed with the one brought from Lisbon and purchased at Bordeaux. Realising the impossibility to maintain a strict monopoly over spice trade, the Portuguese King Dom Sebastian relaxed it and opened the trade in pepper and spices to all on certain conditions in 1570.[10]

King Philip II of Spain, who was dreaming of a Hispano-Portuguese salt and spice trade, was encouraged by two Germans, Roth and Nathaniel Jung, who were making their plans to apply for the Portuguese spice contract in 1575. The dream of the King became a reality when he managed to annex Portugal in 1580 and became the King of Portugal as well. He wanted to block the flourishing trade of the Mediterranean in spices and pepper from the East. He suggested in 1581 to the Venetians to take up a contract for the sale of Portuguese pepper. Despite the reports presented by the experts the Venetians, who weighed the pros and cons of the suggested deal, did not take it up.[11] Milan, Genoa and Florence were also approached by the Portuguese King for taking up the contract offered to the Venetians. But all of them turned down the request. Italian capitalism frowned on the scheme. In fact the offer made by the Portuguese was only for the disposal of the commodities brought from the east to Lisbon, in other words, the Europa Contract. The Asia Contract on the other hand was taken up by the consortium consisting of Giraldo Paris, a German who got the collaboration of capitalists like the Welsers and Fuggers who brought pepper from the east and sold to the king at Lisbon for sixteen *cruzados* per quintal and resold by the king at thirty-seven *cruzados.*[12] The Fuggers were dragged also into the Europa Contract by 1591.

It was reported by a Spanish merchant in 1591 that *naos de Yndias* did not come to Lisbon and so the prices of spices had gone up. He added that the price of pepper alone remained the same since large supplies had arrived at Venice from the Levant. The revival of the Mediterranean trade in spices and pepper enhanced the prosperity of the two cities looking on to the Mediterranean, namely, Aleppo and the active quays of Tripoli in the north and, Cairo and its port, Alexandria in the south. Merchants of Venice, to a large extent and those of Marseilles and Ragusa to a lesser degree, profited from the revival of this trade.

With the discovery of the rich resources of the countries in the western hemisphere and of the direct maritime route from Europe to the east, especially India, avenue was opened up for accumulation of capital for entrepreneurs. Capitalist enterprise began to take deeper roots in world economy. Metals like copper, silver and gold played an important role in the international trade and commerce. Business men motivated by large profit that could be reaped from the exchange of metals entered into the industry of mining. Those who had accumulated capital through small-scale industries like weaving and short-haul trade invested profusely in large-scale industry like copper mining. Rulers who became preys to the financiers leased out the copper mines to such industrialists. The demands of trade with India provided a golden opportunity for these industrialists to find markets for the outputs of their mines. Hence, those who had hold on copper and other metals received better chances to enhance their capital.

The growth of international trade covering far-flung regions of Europe, America and Asia gave rise to the development of financial arrangements through banking and issue of bills of exchange. Large scale merchants and industrialists, besides rulers, required loans galore. A milieu of this nature provided ample opportunity for financiers interested in making capital out of the demands of international relations.

It may be thus said that the sixteenth and seventeenth centuries furnished suitable chances for the development of capitalistic undertakings. The Fuggers, who had already reaped large profits out of weaving and small-scale trade, were looking for a chance to enhance the capital. They advanced large amounts to the rulers like the emperor of Holy Roman Empire and the kings of Spain, Denmark, Hungary, the Netherlands and even to the English rulers. They obtained unlimited rights over the mines from where they could furnish required copper and silver for the trade with the east. Their establishment in Flanders enabled them to be closer to the Portuguese activities there. They went on opening factories in various parts of Europe for developing international trade. As they were looking for further chances to enhance their capital, they accepted very gratefully the invitation extended by the king of Portugal to participate in their trade with India.

One of the hurdles faced by a Catholic capitalist during the sixteenth century was the problem of taking interest. The Catholic church prevented the true faithful from collecting interest on loans advanced to others. They approached the theologians to find a way out for them in this regard and finally in 1514 one of the experts came to their rescue and resolved that a moderate interest of 5 per cent could be levied on loans. Though this was accepted by a couple of universities, some theologians refused to endorse the decision. At last with the help of the emperor of the Holy Roman Empire who was in dire need of loans from the Fuggers the solution given by the theologian of the University of Ingolstadt was ratified and the Fuggers were left free to develop the capital also by giving loans.

The firm of the Fuggers under Jakob the Rich became one of the greatest capitalist institutions of Europe in the sixteenth century. It reached its zenith under Anton Fugger having branches in almost all the important centres of trade and contacts with various rulers of Europe. Therefore, it may be concluded that the Fuggers developed their capitalistic endeavours in the wake of the commercial revolution inaugurated with the discovery of Americas and the sea-route to India.

The Portuguese king who could not find sufficient funds as well as commodities for trade with India had to depend on merchant-financiers who could provide the requirements. The Fuggers who had already developed necessary capital input were the most suitable persons to take up the work. They obtained special privileges like the other German firms and established their agencies in Lisbon and Flanders to be in touch with the Portuguese. In fact, they were financially powerful enough to monopolise the entire trade with India. But the Portuguese king interested in keeping his monopoly did not yield to the pressures on the side of the Fuggers. He entered on commercial contracts with the Fuggers and took the required volume of copper to be despatched to India and made them purchase spices at the *Casa da India* in Lisbon at the mutually agreed price. They advanced money, silver and gold besides copper. Though they were frustrated in their attempt to get monopoly over direct trade in spices with India, they entered into trade in other items like precious stones, diamonds and pearls from India with the approval of the Portuguese.

Under Philip II of Spain, the Portuguese trade with India took on a different turn. The Fuggers and other German and Italian financiers who had been craving for direct trade in spices with India managed to get an Asia Contract from the Portuguese king. They opened a number of factories on the coastal regions of India and sent their agents to look after their interest. Thus, the capitalistic endeavours of the Fuggers were extended to the subcontinent of India. On the expiry of the term of the Asia Contract they were asked to be a party to the Europa Contract along with other merchant financiers. Besides conducting trade and commerce, the Fuggers ran a newsletter service through their agents in various parts of the world. This was chiefly meant to keep them abreast with the movements in international markets. In fact, this can find a parallel among the modern capitalists running newspaper services. It may thus be concluded that the involvement of the Fuggers in the Portuguese trade with India in the sixteenth century formed part of the various ramifications of their capitalist enterprise.

Paradoxically enough Roman Emperors were instrumental in the rise and fall of the financial empire of the Fuggers. The Emperor came forward to insist that the theologians and the church at large should accept the principle that it was lawful to take a reasonable interest on loans. Had this been not recognised by the Church, the Fuggers, who were staunch Catholics, would not have had the opportunity to enhance the capital during the period of the commercial revolution when the Portuguese king needed money and material for his overseas enterprise. Maximilian I and Charles V themselves would have been rendered helpless if the Fuggers were not permitted to advance loans on interest. The same was the case with a number of other potentates of Europe who depended largely on the loans from the Fuggers. When the pope himself was trying to alienate the large sum clandestinely invested by one of the princes of the church as noted elsewhere in this work, the Emperor came to the defense of the Fuggers forbidding the transfer of money to the Vatican. If the Emperor, a Catholic subjected to the papal authority, had given in to the pope, the Fuggers would have collapsed in the second decade of the sixteenth century.

Similarly, by contrast, the financial weakness of the Archduke and the Emperors like Maximilian I and Charles V paved the way for the surrender of a number of areas rich in copper, silver and mercury to the Fuggers in the absence of which they could not have developed such an enormous capital in the sixteenth century especially in the context of the need for copper and other metals in the international trade. Overseas enterprise of the Portuguese demanded more metals especially copper. The copper mines of the emperor and other kings of Europe pledged to the Fuggers against loans advanced by them helped the latter to develop their capital.

The emperors themselves on the other hand accelerated the decline of the Fuggers. They were appointed as the direct financiers of the Emperor of the Holy Roman Empire. Time and again the emperor facing financial crises in his empire approached the Fuggers for loans. Though the other financiers turned a deaf ear to the requests made by him, the Fuggers, despite initial reluctance, extended a helping hand to him. They were fully aware of the insolvency of the spend-thrift emperor. But they could not but advance loans. This was indeed the weakness of the Fuggers before the Emperor and enormous amounts remained unpaid to them. Anton Fugger himself, who took loans from others and helped the Emperor several times, decided not to advance any more loan to him. But a personal call from the Emperor made him change his decision.

As noted elsewhere in this work, the princes of the Catholic church who amassed money in dubious ways did not want to disclose their assets to the church at large for fear of losing them to the church. They preferred to deposit their funds with the Fuggers who were devout Catholics and kept confidentiality about the investments. As these princes did not have any legitimate successors, their size of their investment was not known to anybody and it was possible that the same could be added to the funds of the Fuggers. The Fugger bank in Rome was profusely used by the ecclesiastical princes. The association of the Fuggers with the church helped them in ways more than one to enhance their capital. They were closely connected with the sale of indulgences and the transfer of money from various parts of Europe to Rome, the headquarters of the Pope.

The close relations between the Fuggers and the Catholic church in some sense paved the way for the decline of the financial position of the Fuggers. Large sums were invested for the maintenance of the church, patronising the religious activities.

The involvement in the fight against the Lutherans in the wake of the Protestant Reformation drained a lot of finance from the Fuggers' capital. Large sums were advanced to the Emperor to defend the Catholic faith against the heresy.

The unification of the Spanish and Portuguese crowns since 1580 and the constant fight between the English and the Spaniards disturbed the movement of ships in the Indian Ocean regions and especially from the ports of the subcontinent of India. Consequently the trade with India in the fourth quarter of the sixteenth century, which was open to the merchant-financiers of Europe, did not bring the expected profit. The Fuggers, who were actively involved in the Asia and Europa contracts, could thrive well. Despite the attempts made by them, the ships that were captured by the English were not returned as discussed above. Thus the disturbance caused to the overseas trade had some impact on the financial position of the Fuggers.

Side by side with the movement of pepper and other spices from the east to the west, there was the export of exotic animals from India to Europe. Some of them were sent from Lisbon to other part of continental Europe. The interest shown by the Fuggers in developing a zoo in Augsburg made them look for the Indian species through Lisbon.

In conclusion it may be said that the Fuggers played an important role in the Indo-Portuguese trade of the sixteenth century. Their participation in the Portuguese overseas trade was of great importance for the Portuguese crown since commodities and money needed for the trade were not readily available in Portugal. Decline of the merchant capital of the Fuggers paved the way for the emergence of another economic formation. As the theoreticians hold, the emergence of industrial capitalism required the gradual disappearance of merchant capitalism. The phase of the economic growth of the sixteenth century and that of the Fuggers in the period of commercial revolution could be considered a transitional one leading to the industrial capitalist form of economy. The role played by the Fuggers in the overseas trade of Portugal has to be considered in the wider framework of economic activity.

NOTES AND REFERENCES

1. Fernand Braudel, *The Wheels of Commerce*, London, 1985, p. 124.
2. Josef Kulischer, *Allgemeine Wirtschaftgeschichte des Mittelalters und der Neuzeit,* Munich, 1928-1929, 2 vols., reprint, 1958, Vol. II, p. 235.

3. Kulischer, *op. cit.*, Vol. II, p. 234.)
4. Visconde de Soveral, *Apontamentos sobre as antigas relações politicas e comerciães de Portugal com a Republica de Veneza*, Lisboa, 1893, pp. 6-7.
5. Fernand Braudel, *The Mediterranean and the Mediterranean World in the Age of Philip II,* Vol. 1, London, Collins, 1972, p. 545; Frederick C. Lane, *Venice and History*, Baltimore, 1966, p. 33.
6. Communication of 23 January1552: *Corpo diplomatico port*, VII, p. 108.
7. F. C. Lane, *op. cit.*, p. 588.
8. Jean Nicot, *Sa Correspondence Diplomatique*, publ. by Ed. Falgairoelle, 1897, 12 April 1561, p. 127.
9. Braudel, *The Mediterranean. . . op. cit.,* Vol. I, p. 551.
10. Bibliotheca Nacional de Lisboa, Fundo Geral, codex no. 801, fl. 148-172; J. H. da Cunha Rivara, ed., *Archivo Portuguez Oriental*, Fasciculo v. part 2, New Delhi (AES Reprint), pp. 715-726.
11. For details ref. *Informazione sul commercio dei Veneziani in Portogallo e sui mezzi di ristorarlo, 1584,* published by B. Cecchetti, *Nozze Thiene da Sachio*, 1869, A. Bragadino and J. Foscarini, *Parere intorno al trattato fra Venezia e Spagna sul traffico del pepe e delle spezierie delle Indie Orientali, 1585*, published by Fr. Stefani, Nozze Correr-Fornasari, 1870.
12. F. Dobel, "Ueber einen Pfefferhandel der Fugger und Welser, 1586-1591" in *Zeitschrift des hist. Vereins f. Schawben u. Neubrug,* XIII, pp. 125-38.
13. Baltasar Suarez to Simon Ruiz, Archivo Ruiz, Valladolid, 29 November 1951, quoted by Braudel, *The Mediterranean . . . , op. cit.,* p. 548.

APPENDIX I

PRIVILEGES GRANTED TO THE GERMAN MERCHANT FINANCIERS IN 1503

J. Denuce in *Archivo Histórico Portuguez*, Lisboa, 1909, Vol. VII, pp. 381-83; J.A. Pinto Ferreira, "Privilégios Concedidos pelos Reis de Portugal aos Alemães nos Séculos XV e XVI" (Documentos Arquivados no Gabinete de historia da Cidade), *Boletim Cultural da Câmara Municipal do Porto,* Vol. XXXII, Março-Junho, 1969, Fasc. 1-2, pp. 352-359; J.P. Cassel, *Previlegia und Handelungfreiheiten Welche die Könige von Portugal ehedem den deutschen Kaufleuten zu Lissabon ertheilt haben*, Part I, No. 1, Bremen, 1771. The original document written in Latin on parchament is not found in the respective collection of ducuments in the Archivo Nacional da Torre do Tombo in Lisbon. The Portuguese version of the same document in the eighteenth century manuscript form is found in the Bibliotheca de História de Cidade do Porto - B. 2, Registo Geral. Another copy of the same is found in the Fundo Geral, No. 2771 of the Bibliotheca Nacional de Lisboa.

Dom Manuel I, king of Portugal in view of the representation made by Simon Seitz on the part of the German financiers granted special privileges to them on 13 February 1503. Having great regard to the company of the noble merchants of the emperial city of Augsburg and other towns of Germany and also to Maximilian I, the emperor of Holy Roman Empire, the nephew of the king of Portugal, Dom Manuel permitted the German merchants to conduct trade freely in the Portuguese kingdom and the territories. They were allowed to conduct business through their factors or employees. The privilege was initially for a period of fifteen years. They were exempted from all taxes except the five per cent while others were paying more. They were expected to choose their agent (*Corretor*) or middlemen to stand between the officials of the king and themselves. The king has clearly indicated that a privilege of this sort was never given to anyone so far. He added that though this was given to the company of merchants represented by Simon Seitz any other German merchants individually or collectively could come and settle down in the city of Lisbon for conducting trade and commerce and enjoy the same privileges.

Dom Manoel por graça de Deos Rey de Portugal, e dos Algarues, daquem e dalem mar. em Africa Senhor de guine, e da conquista, nauegação, commercio de Ethiopia, Arabia, Persia e da India etc.ª A todos que estas nossas Letras virem, muita saude e dezejo de amor. por quanto de boa vontade acustumamos a honrrar aos que são dignos de Honrra, e com Liberal benefficio os proseguir, chegando a nos o aprouado varão Simão Seyes com a custumada humanidade o Ouuimos, e liberalmente o despachamos segundo em estas Letras se mostra, elle veyo a nos em nome dos respeitaueis varoes Antonio de Belzer, e Conrrado filim em nome seu, e da sua Companhia dos nobres mercadores do Imperial Cidade Augusta, e doutras villas de Alemanha Significando nos que elles querião em esta nossa cidade de Lixboa asentar sua casa de sua companhia pera negocear, e tratar mercadorias em nossos Reinos se a nos approuesse outorgandolhe algũas graças, e Liberadades que nos pedião segundo em outras terras lhe erão dadas, e nos entendendo em seu requerimento, e considerando quanta honrra, e Humanidade a taes varões seia diuida assi pollas suas proprias pessoas dignas de todo fauor como pello seu commẽdavel trato que segundo nos pareçe aos nossos aproueitara como tambem por serem Cidadões imperiaes do muito Augusto Maximiliano emperador dos Romanos nosso muito amado sobrinho pollo qual com boa vontade demos consentimento a sua petição outorgandolhe as Liberdades, e priuilegios que pedião os quaes a nenhuũs outros nem aos nossos subditos ainda forão conçedidos segundo todos em estas Letras Largamente será conteudo.

Item Primeiramente outorgamos aos ditos nobres mercadores que possão Liuremente negocear, e tratar, e comprar, e vender por todos os nossos Reynos, e senhorios por suas pessoas ou por seus feitores, e seruidores.

Item queremos que toda a prata que por mar ou terra a nossos Reinos, e senhorios trouxerem não seião obrigados pagar portagem nem disima nem outro algum direito ou tributo, e que a tal prata que assi trouxerem possão vender a quem lhe aprouuer, e a que não venderem possão Livremente tornar a Leuar fora de nossos Reinos sem impedimento algum.

Item queremos tambem, e outorgamos aos ditos mercadores, e companhia que das mercadorias a baixo nomeadas que a nossos Reinos, e senhorios trouxerem. S. Latão, Cobre por Laurar, vermelham, azougue, Mastos de Naos antenas, Pez, Alcatrã, e Pilitaria não paguem elles nem aquelles que dos ditos Mercadores as comprarem outro direito ou tributo senão dez por sento assi pagos possão Leuar, essas mercadorias sem mais paguarem alguma siza ou portagem ou outro algum direito ou tributo, e se por uentura os ditos mercadores não venderem as ditas mercadorias queremos que as possão Liuremente tornar a leuar fora de nossos Reinos. e senhorios sem lhe cousa alguma embargar, e porem nas outras mercadorias que afora as em sima declaradas os ditos mercadores trouxerem sera guardado no pagamento do direito ou tributo dellas o Vzo, e custume de nossos Reinos, e senhorios.

Item Nos praz, e conçedemos que se os ditos mercadores comprarem em pequena ou grande quantidade Especiarias ou brazil ou outras quaes quer mercadorias trazidas da India ou de terras nouas proximamente achadas não seião obrigados por tal compra pagar siza nem outro algum direito ou tributo Leuando as ditas mercadorias fora de nossos Reinos, e Senhorios tirando aquellas mercadorias que comprarem da frota e Naos que o anno passado o nosso Almirante Leuou a India nem tambem na tornada das Naos das duas frotas que ora temos prestes pera a India das quaes mercadorias em as ditas Naos quando as comprarem pagarão os ditos mercadores de sisa somente sinquo por sento, e pello semelhante pagarão outro tanto das mercadorias que comprarem das Naos de fernão de Noronha nosso subdito durando o seu contrato que por nos com elle he firmado das terras nouas o qual trato se acabara no anno de quinhentos, e sinquo, e por compra das mercadorias das outras Naos que daqui em diante da India vierem e tambem das terras nouas depois do tempo do dito fernão de Noronha não pagarão os ditos mercadores cousa algũa de dereito ou tributo dahy auante.

Item queremos tambem que toda a moeda douro, e prata que aos ditos mercadores sobejar, e remaneçer daquellas que a nossos Reinos, e senhorios trouxerem a propia moeda a quizerem Leuar fora de nossos Reinos, e Senhorios que o possão fazer liurementte, e se por uentura algũa prata uenderem dequella que a nossos Reinos trouxerem a nos praz que o ouro que por tal venda receberem possão semelhantemente leuar fora de nossos Reinos, e senhorios posto que seia em moeda deste Reino, e quando quer que as taes moedas quizerem Leuar aueram nossas cartas para os officiaes dos passos, e portos dos nossos Reinos, e senhorios com as quaes Liuremente possão passar com o ouro que consigo Leuarem o qula ouro sera posto em boetas ou borjoletas suas serradas, e uistas primeiro por nosso official que nesta cidade de Lixboa pera ello ordenamos o qual as assinara as fechaduras das boetas ou borjoletas com o sello tambem para ello ordenado de giza que dada assi tal ordem, e modo mediante nossas cartas possam os dittos mercadores Liuremente passar, e sair de nossos Reinos sem mais impedimento algum ou manifestação ou inquiricão das pessoas, e couzas suas que se soem de fazer segundo as Leys, e o custume do Reino a qual cousa nos assi pareçeo por ben dos ditos Mercadores para de todo, euitar toda a occaziam de damno que doutra maneira facilmente poderia acõteçer, e assim a cauza delles nos seria muito molesta.

Item Outorgamos aos ditos mercadores que se por ventura em nossos Reinos, e Senhorios fizerem algũas Naos de qual quer grandura que sejão possam com ellas gosar, e gosem dos priuilegios, e Liberdades que tem nossos subditos em todas nossas partes, e costas do mar assi esses nauios como as mercadorias que trouxerem não somente aos nossos Reinos, e senhorios mas a quaes quer outros com tanto que pera gosarem dos dittos priuilegios, e Liberdades os ditos seus nauios sejão ministrados, e gouernados por marinheiros, e mestres naturaes de nossos Reinos tirando que esta immunidade não aja Lugar nas nossas Ilhas da madeira como em todalas outras por que lhe são dados tães priuilegios contra que se não pode hir.

Item Nos praz que se os ditos mercadores Edificarem algua caza em qual quer Lugar desta cidade dentro, ou fora dos muros não lhe seja dado varejo em suas mercadorias que tiuerem em sua caza assi por elles edifficada no chão que por elles for comprado pello modo que aos flamengos que vierem a nossos Reinos por nos he outorgado.

Item Conçedemos aos ditos mercadores que sejão Liures e não sejão obrigados a colaçoes ou pagamentos de peitas ou pedidos que pellos Reinos ou prouincias se custumão muitas uezes pedir, e poer.

E se o que Deos tolha emtre os nossos Reinos, e as gentes, e terras dos ditos mercadores nasçer guerra ou outro algum Principe ou Rey de que se sigua alguma toruação a estada delles em nossos Reinos a nos apraz, e outorgamos que as pessoas dos ditos mercadores, e de seus feitores, e seruidores, e tambem as mercadorias, e todos os seus bens. não reçebão ditrimento a algum nem posão. em elles ser feitos embargos nem Reprezarias por nenhum pacto por nos ou por nossos subditos mas em verdade se quisermos, e mãdarmos que os ditos mercadores se uão de nossos Reinos, e Senhorios queremos, e outorgamos lhe de graça special que alem do termo publicamente devulgado tenhão ainda espaço alongado de hum inteiro anno, e dia para estarem em nossos Reinos em que mais conuenientemente possão suas cousas dispoer, e tirar fora de nossos Reinos para onde quizerem.

E tambem Nos praz Conçeder aos ditos mercadores faculdade de escolherem hum so Corretor que segundo parese pode abastar para tratar suas mercadorias porem com tal Limitação que este corretor que assi escolherem seia obrigado nas compras, e uedas das mercadorias ajuntar consigo outros corretores desta cidade, e sobsinar com elles nos seus Liuros, e tambem, commonicar com elles o proueito, e ganho de seu officio igualmente.

Item Conçedemos aos ditos mercadores que quando suas mercadorias vierem a nossas Alfandegas seião dizimadas, e despachadas primeiro que todas as outras que ahy estiuerem, e mandamos aos officiaes dellas que com diligencia o cumprão e não fação o contrario.

E tambem Mandamos aos officiaes da nossa moeda que quando quer que os ditos mercadores lhe derem algua prata pera laurar em moeda que seia primeiro Laurada que qual quer outra que ahe este.

Item Estes Priuilegios, e immunidades Conçedemos aos ditos mercadores por tempo de quinze annos da Dada destas nossas Letras em diante.

E Mais porque o dito Simão Seyẽs não somente procurou estas immunidades, e priuilegios pera a dita sua Companhia mas tambem pera qual quer outra companhia de Alemães que em a nossa cidade de Lisboa quizer assentar caza pera a dytta nossa negoceação de trato nos apras por estas letras conçeder a qual quer outra companhia de mercadores Alemães estes nossos priuilegios, e immunidades que aqui são conteudos, e tambem singularmente a qual quer Alemão mercador que pera Sy so aqui quizer tratar comtanto que a faculdade de seu trato possa valler somma de dez mil cruzados tirando que na compra das mercadorias das naos que com o nosso Almirante vão, e tambem daquellas duas frottas que ora estão prestes pera irem, e tãobem das naos de fernão de Noronha durando o tempo de seu trato das terras nouas assi como asima he declarado, e expresso de que a companhia do dito Simão Syẽs não he obrigado pagar mais que sinquo por sento, os outros mercadores pagem dez por sento de siza mas das mercadorias que despois vierem em outras naos sejão Liures, e não sejão obrigados pagar cousa alguma assi como a companhia do dito Simão Syes por beneficio do dito priuilegio, e em fé, e em testemunho desta conçeção, e tambem por segurança dos ditos mercadores mandamos fazer estas Letras por nossa propria mão assinadas, e do nosso çello de chumbo pendente selladas. Dada em a Cidade de Lixboa a treze de feuereiro do anno de mil, e quinhentos, e tres. —El Rey.

APPENDIX II

VALENTIM FERNANDES

As indicated in the grant of privileges to the German financiers they were supposed to suggest a name of a qualified person who could act as the middleman in the contacts with the Portuguese king and his officials. He should be a person knowing Portuguese and familiar with the life in Portugal. Valentim Fernandes of Moravia in Germany was acquainted with the printing introduced by Gutenberg. He had been in Lisbon closely attached to the royal family discharging several duties for long time. Therefore, it was quite natural that his name was easily accepted by the king of Portugal as the middleman in the transactions between the German financiers and the Portuguese. He was appointed as one among the collectors in Lisbon. The German merchants were allowed to establish their own house in Lisbon and conduct trade through the mediation of the Moravian printer Valentim Fernandes. He was supposed to prepare the drafts of the contracts and translate the important documents for the king and his officials. Through the letter issued by Dom Manuel on 21 February 1503 he was appointed to the post. This document is reproduced in *Documentos para a historia da typographia Portugueza nos seculos xvi e xvii*, Part II, Lisboa, Imprensa Nacional, 1882.

El-rei D. Manuel, por carta de 21 de fevereiro de 1503, nomeia corretor da praça de Lisboa a Valentim Fernandes, alemão, escudeiro da casa da rainha sua senhora e irmã, para o ser em todas as transacções que, sobre especiarias, se realisassem entre allemães e portuguezes, por n'elle haver as circumstancias necessarias para bem e fielmente servir esse officio, e em attenção, a lh'o assim pedir Simão Zayz, gerente da companhia allemã, com quem fizera contrato para estabelecer casa e negocio em a cidade de Lisboa. No mesmo diploma é tambem Valentim Fernandes nomeado tabellião, para fazer as escripturas, contratos e quaesquer outras cousas que os mercadores allemães entre si uns com os outras tratassem e quizessem põr em sua linguagem, e para tirar em portuguez ou latim as publicas formas d'estes documentos, que, firmadas e rubricadas por elle, deviam ter sé com se o fossem por tabellião publico, para o que devia de receber do chanceller mór seu regimento e registrar seu signal na chancellaria.

Dom Manuel, etc. Aquamtos esta nosa carta virem fazemos saber que, avemdo nos Respeyto ao gramde negocio que com ajuda de noso Senhor esperamos que aja nesta cidade de Lixboa, por causa de muitas mercadorias e mercadores estrangeiros que a ella am de vir, pera nella trautarem e asemtarem casas pera o trauto da especiaria, pera omde nos parece necesario acrecemtarmos mais huum coretor alem dos doze que ora ha na dita cidade; avemdo iso mesmo respeyto a Valemtym Fernamdez, escudeiro da casa da Rainha mynha Senhora e Irmaã, ser pesoa que neste negocio por causa de sua linguagem e descryçom nos sabera bem e fiellmente seruir; e como yso mesmo Symam Zayz mercador alemaão, que ora com nosco em nome de sua companhya asemtou e fez comcerto pera vir asemtar casa e trautar nesta cidade, nos pedio que o dito Valemtym Fernamdez ouuesemos por bem ser coretor e terceiro amtre elles e nosos naturaes; e por lhe fazermos graça e mercee: temos por bem e nos praz lhe fazermos mercee do dito oficio de coretor, que ora asy nouamemte acrecemtamos pera serem treze na dita cidade, o quall seruyra asy e na maneira que ho seruem nos doze que ora som, avemdo todos iguallmente o proueito dos ditos oficios como amtre elles he ordenado. E queremos que, alem do dito Valemtym Fernamdez asy ser coretor, elle posa fazer e faça pubrico aquellas sprituras, contrautos e quaesquer outras cousas que hos ditos mercadores alemães antre sy huuns com os outros fezerem, e asy treladara seus contratos e obrigaçõees e quaesquer outras sprituras, que em sua lymgoagem tyuerem e quyserem tirar em latyam ou em limgoagem portugues, asynamdoas elle dito Valemtym Fernamdez do seu pubrico synall queremos que valham e sejam asy verdadeiras como se fosem feitas e asynadas por tabeliam pubrico. E esto nom avera lugar nem se emtemdera naquelles comtratos obrigaçõees que se fizerem antre alemãees e protuguezes, porque estes se faram per os tabelliãees pubricos segundo nosa ordenamça. E porem mamdamos ao noso chamceler moor que lhe mamde dar pera iso seu Rigymemto, e seu pubrico synall faça Regystar nos liuros da nosa chamcelaria. E asy mamdamos aos vereadores e oficiaees que ora sam e ao diamte forem na dita cidade que leyxem servyr o dito Valemtym Fernamdez o dito oficio e aver iguallmemte com os outros seu solairo proees e percalços que lhe direitamente pertemcerem sem duuida alguũa, porque asy he nosa mercee. Dada em a nosa cidade de Lixboa aos xxj de feuereiro, Vicemte Carneiro a fez, anno de noso Senhor Jezu Christo de mil e b^c iij. E esta merce que lhe asy fazemos he por quamto nós podemos acrecemtar mais coretores, alem dos doze ordenados, crecemdo o trauto e maneo delle, como louuores a noso Senhor crece: e quamdo capitolar estes alemãees com nosco da companhia do dito Symom ho outorgamos por ser o dito Valemtym de sua lingoagem e mylhor se emtemder com elles. E ele seruira o dito oficio em quamto a companhia dos ditos alemãees esteuerem nestes Regnos.

APPENDIX III

PRIVILEGES GIVEN TO THE FUGGERS

J.A. Pinto Ferreira, "Privilégios Concedidos pelos Reis de Portugal aos Alemães nos Séculos XV e XVI" (Documentos Arquivados no Gabinete de historia da Cidade), *Boletim Cultural da Câmara, Municipal do Porto*, Vol. XXXII, Março-Junho, 1969, Fasc. 1-2, pp. 359-369; A certain "Marco Alemão", otherwise Markus Zimmermann who was the representative of the firm of Fuggers who were also in Lisbon approached the king of Portugal and showed two orders issued in favour of the Germans. Ref. Hermann Kellenbenz, *Die Fugger in Spanien und Portugal bis 1560*, Band I, München, 1990, p. 52. One was dated 3rd October 1504 and the other was of 3rd August 1509. Both are transcribed below.

(a) Dom Manoel per graça de Deus Rey de Portugal e dos Algarves da quem e da lem mar em Africa senhor de Guine e da conquista navegação comercio de Ethiopia Arabia Persia e da India etc. A quantos esta nossa carta testemunhavel virem fazemos saber que perante nos pareceo Marco Alemão em nome das companhias dos Alemães que estão na Cidade de Lixboa e nos apresentou dous alvaras nossos dos quaes ho teor delles de verbo a verbo são estes que se seguem.

Nos El Rey fazemos saber a vos Regedor da nossa casa da suplicação e ao governador da casa do civel e a todolos corregedores da cidade e a todos os alcaides e meirinhos e a todas outras justiças officiaes a que este alvara for mostrado e ho conhecimento delle pertencer que ha nos apraz por alguns respeitos que nos a ello moverão e por fazermos mais favor has companhias dos Alemães que nesta cidade estão que nenhuuns dos ditos Alemães das ditas Companhias não seja preso nem reteudo nem lhe seja seja feito constrangimento alguum por caso que seja de crime ou que de cousa crime dependa salvo de João Cotrim Corregedor dos feitos civeis em ha nossa corte ou por seu mandado e não for nenhuum outro Corregedor e Juiz nem justiça. Outro sy nos praz que não entre outra nenhuma justiça em suas casas quando convier por bem de justiça salvo ho dito Corregedor ou aquellas pessoas que por elle forem mandadas e não outras algumas posto que pera cousa de justiça seja; porque por ambos estes casos queremos que abaste ho dito João Cotrim e porem solo notificamos assi e vos mandamos que asy ho cumpraes e guardeis asy nos praz feito em Lixboa a tres doutubro, Antonio Carneiro o fez de mil e quinhentos e quatro anos.

(b) Dom Manoel per graças de Deus Rey de Portugal e dos Algarves dequem e dalem mar em Africa senhor de Guine e da conquista navegação comercio de Ethiopia Arabia Persia e da India etc. a quantos esta nossa carta virem fazemos saber que por folguarmos de os mercadores Alemães estantes em ha nossa cidade de Lixboa serem bem tratados e favorecidos em nossos Reynos asy em suas pessoas e de seus feitores e criados como em suas mercadorias e pera que com mães rezão possão e devão em elles tratar e negocear e quarendo lhes fazer graça e merce temos por bema lhe outorgamos has graças previlegios e liberdades adiante declaradas e esto por tempo de xb. annos que se começarão da feitura desta nossa carta em diante.

Item primeiramente queremos e mandamos que quaesquer que suas mercacdorias vierem em alguma nao ou navio davante ho porto da dita cidade ao tempo que se ouverem de descarregar nossos officiaes da descargua lho farão saber da descargua primeiro que venhão estar a ella se quiserem e traguão barcas em que has descarreguem e despois de passarem tres horas pouco maes ou menos não vindo elles ou mandando então hos ditos officiaes has poderão descarregar sem elles e esto estando elles em ha cidade.

Item mandamos que tanto que suas mercadorias forem na alfandega paguem logo a dizima e sisa tirando hos panos de laam dos quaes pagarão a sisa ao bispo que venderem segundos se ora faz e em nossos artiguos he conteudo. A qual sisa paguarão aos officiaes das casas a quem perteneerem e se assentara em seus livros como ha pagarão pera ho diante não poder hi aver maes duvida e tanto que pagarem os ditos direitos e lhe forem entreges has ditas mercadorias has leverão pera onde quiserem por todos os nossos Reynos e senhorios sem serem obriguados fazer saber as mudanças e vendas que dellas fizerem saber a casa alguma de nossos direitos nem descaminharão por ello nem cairão em pena alguma por não fazerem has dellingencias que são ordenados segundo forma de nossos foraes artigos e ordenações e isto daquellas mercadorias, de que tiverem pagos nossos direitos e lhe forem despachados de que averão certidão dos nossos officiaes pera por ella livremente as poderem levar e vender por nossos Reynos sem maes pagar cousa alguma tendosse com elles a maneira que se tem com os flamengos e em seus previlegios he conteudo.

Item nos praz que possão carregar todas suas mercadorias em quaes quer navios e naos que quiserem asy de naturaes como de estrangeiros e pera onde quiserem tirando hos açucares que se carregarão em naos e navios de nossos naturaes como se ora faz.

Item queremos e mandamos que nenhum Official nem Rendeiro de nossos direitos nem outra alguma pessoa entre em suas casas a lhe dar varejo nem lhe fazer oppressão alguma salvo por mandado do nosso contador mor avendo primeiro enformação por pessoa ou pessoas sem sospeita como tem alguma mercadoria sonegada a nossa alfandega. E quando ha ouver de enviar ira a isso huum escrivão della com hum rendeiro quando ho ahy ouver a sem o dito escrivã não poderão ir a suas casas buscar tal mercadoria sonegada.

Item queremos que não paguem direito alguum dos mantimentos e alfaias que pera suas casas e usos dellas lhe vierem en menos lhe pagarão direito a alguum dos panos de laã que vierem pera vestido de cada feitor e dos servidores dando lhe por ano dous vestidos a cada pessoa nem menos de canhamo e sarapilheiras destopa pera sacas e cascos de pipas pera suas mercadorias jurando elles que vem tudo pera isso e não pera vender por que sendo pera vender pagarão hos direitos ordenados.

Item poderão comprar e render todalas mercadorias que quiserem e pello preço que quiserem caro ou barato a sua avença e das partes tirando ha pimenta em que esta preço ordenado e achandosse qualquer rico em has cousas que venderem não lhas poderão os ditos compradores tomar nem lhe conhecerão de debate alguum salvo dentro em tres dias despois que hos compradores forem entregues das taes cousas.

Item tanto que lhe for entregue qualquer especearia ha poderão livremente levar pera suas casas a carregala como e quando quiserem sem lhe ser posto impedimento alguum sem embargo de teremos ordenado e mandado que se não entreque a especearia has partes salvo ao tempo que se ouver de descarregar nas naos e navios em que ouver de ir.

Item tanto que alguum contrato for celebrado antre hos ditos Alemães e ho nosso feitor da casa da India o fara logo asentar no livro dos contratos por huum escrivão antes que dali partão ho qual escrivão e feitor deixarão todolos outros negoceos ate se acabar de asentar e assinar e não sendo assentado não valha cousa alguma nem serão has partes obrigadas estar por elle nem ho dito feitor e officiaes serão obrigados a comprir em quanto não for asentado.

Item todo o ouro ou prata que trouxerem ha estes Reynos se levara a alfandega como has outras mercadorias e ali secretamente no tempo que elles quiserem com dous officiaes da dita alfandega sera despachada e atirarão e levarão das vasilhas em que ha trouxerem livramente per as suas casas ou casa da moeda sem lhe ser posto impedimento alguum e estando seu ouro ou prata na casa da moeda ha entregarão ao nosso thesoureiro della e elle lhe dara seu conhecimento segundo forma de nosso Regimento e com elle poderão fazer qualque pagamento que quiserem na dita casa da India dequalquer especearia ou mercadoria outra que nella comprarem e mandamos ao nosso feitor thesoureiro que lho recebão e por elle arrecadem o pagamento na dita moeda do que lhe asy venderem como se ora faz.

Item queremos e nos praz que tenhão e ajam todolos previlegios e liberdades franquezas e isenções que por nos são dadas e outorgadas aos nossos naturaes tirando somente os direitos de nossas ilhas de que não usarão nem isso mesmo se entendera que ajam de tratar na India em caso que alguma ordenação façamos ao diante per que mandemos que não ajam de tratar nellas senão naturaes do Reyno.

Item nos praz que posão ter pesos e balanças em suas casas pera justificarem suas mercadorias e não pera venderem sem embarguo de qualquer mandado que em contrairo ahi aja.

Item nos praz por milhor e maes brevemente poderem aver despacho de suas contendas e demandas e de si por que esta maneira o direito das outras partes lhe ficara guardado que ho nosso Corregedor da dita cidade de Lixboa seja seu Juiz em todolos feitos asi crimes como civeis que nella e seu termo ate seis legoas tiverem ora sejão autores ora reos não se entenda isto contra pessoas previligiadas que tenhão Juiz por seu previlegio por que acerca das taes se gardara ha disposição do direito comum. O qual Corregedor queremos que tenha alçada ate contia de dez mil reis sem delle aver appellação nem agravo e dahi pera cima elle fara ho feito concluso sem das interlucutorias dar agravo alguum e sendo concluso pera final vira despachar a nossa casa do civel com dous letrados que ho governador lhe dara pera isso diga dara hos quaes poderão prover com ho dito Corregedor de qualquer agravo que nas interlucutorias acharem que seja feito por elle e despacharão todo finalmente como acharem que he direito sem delle aver appelação nem agravo de qualquer contia que seja e se a contia por tamanha que pareça ao dito governador que são necessarios maes Letrados dar lheão hos que bem parecerem ate quatro e bem asy queremos e mandamos que ho dito Corregedor seja execujtor das sentenças que dante elle e hos ditos desembargadores sairem em caso que ho conhecimento disso podesse pertencer a outras justiças e o faça com toda diligencia e brevidade que com direito poder.

Item quremos e mandamos que em has ditas suas casas não entrem nem possão entrar officiaes alguuns de nossas justiças salvo ho dito corregedor ou quem elle mandar e não outrem sob pena de xx cruzados pera elles salvo indo a Justiça apos algum mao feitor em fragante delito achado por que em tal caso podera entrar.

Item nos praz que asy elles como seus servidores hate seis de sua companhia que elles tenhão de suas portas adentro possão trazer armas de noite e de dia por todos nossos Reinos e senhorios asi antes do sino de correr como despois e asi com lume como sem elle não fazendo porem com ellas ho que não devem e esto sem embarguo de nossas ordenações e defesas em contrairo os quaes servidores não serão espanhoes pera gozarem da dita liberdade.

Item queremos que acontecendo caso que em esta terra alguum dos feitors faleça não ficando sota feitor daquella companhia quem em recado ponha a fazenda de que tiver carrego ho dito corregedor va a casa do defunto com huum escrivão e fseus feitores das outras companhias que lhe bem parecesem que ao tal tempo aqui estiverem e fara presente todos inventario de tudo o que hy ouver e entregara todo aos ditos dous feitores e os constrangera que o recebão e darão conta a seu tempo quando vier pessoa a que se deva de entregar a tal fazenda ao qual Corregedor mandamos que asy ho cumpra.

Item nos praz que passão andar em mullas e . . . sem embrago de nossas ordenacões e asi lhe sejam dadas pousadas e camas e mantimentos por seus direitos asy em nossa Corte como em todolos lugares ha onde estiverem e forem tirando Lixboa.

Item o que toca nestes previlegios a quinta de nossos direitos entender se ha que usem delles acabado ho arrendamento dos rendeiros que ora são da hi em diante.

Item nos parz e queremos que outro previlegio geral que de nos tem lhe sera largado como de feito por esta alargamos concedemos e outor gamos pello dito tempo de quinze annos que se começarão daqui em diante asi como este que de novo lhe asi damos em caso que delles seia ja passado alguma parte do tempo que nelle lhe declaramos que vallesse porem mandamos ha todos nossos Corregedores Juizes e Justiças officiaes e pessoas ha que esta nossa carta for mostrada e ho conhecimento della pertencer que a cumprão e guardem e fação muy inteiramente comprir e guardar como em ella faz menção sem lhe nosso porem duvida nem embargua alguum porque asy he nossa merce a por certidão e firmesa dello lhe mandamos dar esta nossa carta asindada por nos e sellada por nosso sello pendente dada em Sintra aos XXX do mes de agosto Ano do nascimento de Nosso Senhor Jesus Cristo de mil e quinhentos e nove annos. —El Rey.

APPENDIX IV

JAKOB FUGGER AND THE SUPPLY OF COPPER

Rui Fernandes, the writer of the Portuguese Factory at Antwerp wrote to Dom Manuel, king of Portugal on 4 February 1521 regarding the political importance and assests of the Fuggers of Augsburg. He affirms that Jakob Fugger was the most powerful men in Germany who had influences over all the princes and kings and that no prince would be able to live without having Jakob Fugger as his friend. He added that without the help of Fugger, Charles V would not have been elected emperor of Holy Roman Empire who took charge on the 28 June 1519 setting aside the claims of the king of France. Therefore, he recommended that even if the copper supplied by the Fuggers was still expensive, the king of Portugal should not take any decision against the proposed contract. This document preserved in the National Archieves of Lisbon is also reproduced in the *Archivo Historico Portugues*, p. 379.

"De Osburguo (*Augusbergo*) escrevi a V.A. em 10 de janeiro, como recebera sua arta de 9 de dezembro per que havia por bem que alargasse o Focoro (*Fugger*) da palavra que me tinha dado; ao qual fui logo falar e lhe disse, o milhor que pude e soube, de como V.A. o avia assi por seu serviço. Elle, ao que mostrou, folgou muito e passãmos muitas praticas como amigos . . . O dia antes que me partisse lhe fui falar; ao despedir pediu-me, que escrevesse a V.A. sua recomendação e quanto elle era seu servidor, e assi o tinha mandado aos seus feitores per todas partes, que comprazessem em tudo aos criados de V.A. . . . Elle, senhor, é o mor homem de Alemanha e que governa todos os principes e reis; e é de maneira, que nenhum principe vive sem elle e folga de o ter por amigo; e o que elle quer acaba-o. Tem-se que se elle não fõra, depois de Deus, que el Rei não fõra emlejido (*Carlos I de Espanha eleito imperador em 28 de junho de 1519*), porque el Rei de França lhe dava vinte por cento de ganho por todo seu dinheiro e credito, e que respondesse e fizesse porelle; e elle não quis, tendo boa seguridade, sõmente servir a el Rey; e prometeu assãs a todos os emleitores e escreveu; e é de maneira, que tem tamanho cedito com elles e com todos os principes, que fazem o que elle quer; e tambem elle é justo e quer a rezão; porem, com quanta amizade ha, elle nom ousa de sair de Osburgo mais que duas ou tres legoas e a bom recado. El Rei lhe escreve muitas vezes e o correia, porque mais lhe vale ter a elle, que a quatro outros principes, pera o que lhe compre; porque nem um Alemão nom faz nada sem dinheiro; e creia V.A., que quem ha de negociar alguma cousa em Alemanha, que lhe é bom tẽ-lo por sua parte. É tal, que os duques e principes emleitores, quando em Aosburgo, vam a sua casa vẽ-lo e a jogar com a molher, per o honrar, porque elle quer muito esta honra. Tem nas milhores casas de toda a terra, em demasia boas.

A' minha partida tive muitas praticas com elle, e como amigos elle me disse, antre outras cousas, como estava determinado de alevantar o cobre, porque lhe custa muito mais que os tempos passados . . . Elle fica grande servidor de V.A., e tenho, que se elle viver, que ha de governar el Rei milhor que o Imperador (*Maximiliano, avo de Carlos V, falecido em 12 de janeiro de 1519*), ainda que estã velho e quebrado todo, que dizem nom viver muito; tem uma perna aberta; faz muito trabalho, porque tudo passa por sua mão; é de mais de sessenta annos..."

APPENDIX V

ASIA CONTRACT OF 1585

Fugger Archives Mss. 46. 1 fls. 33-38; ref also K.S. Mathew, "Indian Contract", in V.K. Chavda, ed. *Studies in Trade and Urbanisation in Western India*, Baroda, 1984, pp. 165-171; Hildebrandt, *Die Georg Fuggerischen Erben . . .*, *op. cit.*, pp. 191-196; The conditions stipulated in the contract concluded on 29 November 1585 and accepted by the king on 1 December 1585 and ratified on 5 December of the same year are found in Spanish language in the Fugger Archives. Giraldo Paris in the name of Juan Baptista Rovelasca was instrumental in finalising the terms of the contract. The merchant financiers who concluded the contract obliged themselves for a period of six years to send 170,000 *crusados* to India and Malacca for the purchase of 30,000 quintals of pepper and for the expenses related to the same. Moreover, they were bound to send 24,000 *crusados* each for the repair of five ships. The king of Portugal took upon himself the responsibility to send six ships every year to India, out of which one was to be directed to Malacca. The price of pepper at which it should be delivered in the India House in Lisbon and the freight charges are also discussed in detail in the treaty.

Estas condiçiones que siguen son los que Giraldo paris En nombre de Juan baptista Rovelasca y en el suyo por seruir al Rey nuestro, señor se han contendado de contratar la pimienta de yndia, para traerla al Reyno por hazienda de su magd.-

1. Que se obligaran por tiempo de seys años a embiar en yndia y malaca çiento y setenta mill cruçados de diez reales por cruçado, para la compra de treynta mill quintales de pimienta y gastos que on ella han de hazer, hasta ser metidos de baxo de cubierta o tela y qué entregandola en la casa de la yndia esta quantia cada año diez dias antes dela partida delos naos, no sean mas obligados, para effeto de traer la dha. pimienta.-

2. Y que embiaran mas beynte y qantro mill cruçados de diez reales cada Uno que En la India hazen triynta mill, para el conçierto delas çinco naos, que aella han de yr, a Razon de seys mill cruçados pro cada nao, los quales seran a quenta de los fleytes los quales entregaran Juntamente con los ciento y setenta mill Cruçados dela compra dela pimienta delos quales trienta mill Cruçados de moneda de India se han de pagar por descuento delos fleytes, en si mismos, y esto al respeto de como se les pagauan en el contrato que se acaba agora.-

3. Con condiçion que su mag. mandera armar cada año seys naos, para lleuar este dinero, y traer la carga dello es a sauer çinco para la India Y Una para malaca y que se procurara que las de India partan alos diez de março y la de malaca Un mes antes.-

4. Con condiçion que la pimienta no pueda subir del preçio en que agora esta por el contracto que corre.-

5. Y que su mag. mandara por sus prouisiones que no se cargue la pimienta para el Reyno si no fuere enxuta y la mejor condiçionada que ser pudiere, y en caso que Venga pimienta uerde, al peso se comprara y benefiçiara para cargarse quando estuuiere en estado para ello o en el año siguiente haziendose las taxas que huuiere de pimienta verde, por la mesma forma, y orden que se tiene en los contratos, passados, alo qual asistiran los hazedores delos contratadores, Juntamente con los offiçiales de su magd.-

6. Y que En la entrega del dinero en la casa de India en lisboa y alla en la yndia en la guarda y distribuiçon dello se tenga la horden que se contiene en el contrato que agora corre, con declaraçion que en llegando alguno, los dhos. contratadores le reçiban como cosa suy que es, sin que sean obligados a embiar le en el año ni años siguientes mas quantia que la obligaçion de cada Un año.-

7. Y que en la yndia ni tampoco en el Reyno no se puede tomar el caudal o prinçipal ni parte alguna del, para ningun otro efecto, si no fuere para la compra de la dha. primienta, y con consentimiento delos agentes delos tractantes.-

8. Que podran emuiar ala India sus haçedores de qualquier naçion que quisieren no siendo hombres de mar, ni françeses ni Ingleses, y que alas naos se les de sus albaranes y Regla ala

yda y ala Veniada a cada Una nao en que fueren.-

9. Con condiçion que toda la pimienta que truxeren se pasara en la balança de puente o almazen y los mesmos contractatores se entregaran della como de hazienda de su magd. por ante dos esçriuanos dela casa dela India, o por ante otro esçriuano y otro official, o persona que ue su magd. ordenare y se le hara cargo y recibo dello y ellos los ternan y guardaran en Almazenes apartados dentro la casa dela India, que su magd. para ello les mandara dar de que los dhos. contratadores solamente ternan las llaues para poder abrir, y cercar sus Almazenes, cada y quando les paresciere exepto las llaues delas puertas de fuera, que agora tiene el proveedor dela casa, las quales terna el, como agora las tiene, y los dhos. contratadores ternan las de la pimienta todas como dho. es.-

10. Que en llegando las naos a Cascays y a otra qualqier parte de Espa. los dhos. contratadores pongan Iluego por su parte las guardas que quisieren, y se tenga en el descargar dellas la mesma orden que se tuuo en es descargar que hizieron las que Vinieron en el año passado de ochenta y çinoc. -

11. Con condiçion que sean obligados a comprar en la India y malaca todos los dhos. treynta mill quintales de pimienta Viniendo al peso o toda la que mas se pudiere hauer, por el preçio deste contracto, como queda dho. y daran para ello el dinero neçesario en caso que el caudal no baste, y por parte de su mag. se le recebira y pagara en la manera que a baxo se declarara y su mag. dara naos en que se cargue no bastando las de la armada.-

12. Que por cada quintal de pimienta, que Entregaren y les fuere reçebida en quenta hauran los contratadores doçe Cruçados de quatroçientos reys por Cruçado para si, del Valor que agora corre, y quatro cruçados para pagar los fleytes y esto del primer dinero que se huuiere por Venta dela pimienta, de que hauran los contratadores las tres partes, y los fleytes la quarta parte, que es al Respecto delo que cada Uno ha de auer, por cada quintal, y esto assi de las naos del Reyno como de las naos de malaca, los quales pagamentos se haran por rata hasta que sean acabaods, de pagar descontando y pagandose en si mismos delo que anis huuieren dado a quenta delos dhos. fleytes.-

13. La qual pimienta los dhos. Contratadores Venderan y administraran por quenta dela hazienda de su magd. en lisboa por el precio y horden que su magd. les dara ala Venida de cada armada, la qual orden y preçion su magd. podra alterar o mudar cada Vez que fuere servido, y ellos recaudaran y recibiran todo el dinero, o qualiqier otra cosa que se hiziere por Venta dela dha. pimienta, o trueco della, sin que en esto haya mudanca, ni alteracion, ninguna durante el contracto, y ternan su peso apartado, para pesar la dha. pimienta, quando la huuieren de Vender y el escriuano dela casa dela India, que hiziere el reçibo hara tambien la del gasto delo que se fuere Vendiendo, para loqual haura Un libro en los dhos. almazenes, loqual el dho. escriuano hara cada vez fuen requerido por ellos, y quando estuuiere ocupado llamaran a otro qualqier dela dha. casa, y queriendo tomar Un pesador que no sea dela casa, lo podran hazer pagando lo de su dinero.-

14. Y todo el dinero que quedare delo proçedido dela pimienta despues de pagados los contratadores delo que huuieren de hauer del perçio dela pimienta y delos fleytes lo entregaran ala persona o personas que su magd. mandare por prouisiones firmadas de su mano, y no de otra manera.-

15. Con condicion que el executor dela casa dela India Executara quales quier personas que el deuieren, el dinero de la compra dela dha pimienta quando ellos lo pidieren y no lo haziendo el proueedor de la dha. çasa le apreminera a ello.-

16. Y por quanto dhos. contratadores antes de reçebir minguna pimienta han de proueer de su hazienda dos caudales o prinçipales que ymporta con el dinero para el conçierto de las naos tresçientos y ochenta y ocho mill Cruçados, y despues de Venida la primera armada a seys meses poco mas o menos, han de proueer el terçer caudal, que son çiento y nouenta y quatro mill Cruçados, sera su magd. obligado ale mandar dar orden para las Ventas dela pimienta a tiempo conueniente, para poderse Valer delo, que pudieren, por Venta della, para el dho. terçero caudal, de menera que por Impedimento de su magd. no reçiban daño alguno, y En caso que su magd. haga contracto de Venta desta pimienta, o parte della sera con expressa condiçion, que antes de sacar la pimienta de mano

delos dhos. contractadores los compradores seran obligados a les pagar todo lo que huuieren de auer, sobre la dha. pimienta, assi del preçio della como delos fleytes.-

17. Con condiçion que despues de partida de India y de malaca la armada de cada año se haga luego quenta del dinero que sobrare de caudal, y dexando, lo que paresçiere necesario para emplearse en pimienta en el Inuierno para el año siguiente lo demas se entregara a sus hazedores, para poder le emplear como cosa suya, en lo que quisieren, quedando por obligado a comprar y pagar toda la pimienta que se pudiere hauer para el dho. año siguiente, puesto que sea mas quantidad delo que se montare el dinero, que para ello quedare reseruado, y en el Ult°. año deste contracto despues de hecha la carga delos naos todo el dinero que sobrare se entregara libremente alos contratadores, y si ellos le quisieren traer en pimienta se le pagara como por este contracto.-

18. Y quendando en la mano del Rey do Cochin, o de otras personas algunas por fin del contracto algun dinero que le fusse dado en quenta dela pimenta que su magd. o los contratadores nuebos sean obligados a los pagar en portugal cruçado por cruçado, monstrando certificaçion de como se le deue, y que lo dieron, por la orden que se acostumbra dar para el effecto de la compra dela pimienta, o no hauiendo contratadores ellos se pagaran en si mismos del dinero que se hiziere o proçediere dela pimienta cuya administration ha de ser por la manera declarada arriba, y que con effecto seran pagados de todo loque se le deuiere, por Razon deste contracto.-

19. Con condiçion que su magd. les hara mrd. cada año del arbitrio del Clauo todo que se dio alos contratadores Conrado Rotte y parcioneros en el contrato passado y que lo puedan traer de India o malaca y lo que no truxeren en Unos años los puedan traer en los siguientes de manera que el dho. arbitrio, haya cumplido effecto y la parte que no truxeren en Clauos, podran traer en otras espeçerias o drogas, que no sean defendidas, o contratadas haziendo Justa computation delos derechos de los Unos y los otros, de manera que todo Venga a Una quenta.-

20. Con condiçion que todas las costas que se hizieren con la

dha. pimienta en la India y en el Viage y en el descargar y quiebra que en ella huuiere, que se pese en el peso dela puente o Almazenes sera a costa delos contratadores y por toda la que pesaren y reçibieren y se les reçibiere hauran los dhos. doçe Cruçados por quintal, horros para si, de quales quier otros derechos costas y gastos que se hayan de hazer excepto los arriba declarados.-.

21. Con condiçion que toda la pimienta que entregaren en el peso les ha deser pagada a doçe Cruçados y quatro de fleyte por quintal como a tras queda declarada, en el Capitulo doçe y despues que la reçebieren por quenta de hazienda de su magd. para la Vender y benefiçiar por quenta della, como atras queda declarado se les tomaran en quenta a dos y medio porçiento de quiebra, los quales, sele descontaran luego al tiempo que se hiziere el reçibo, y de todo lo de mas descontada la dha. quiebra han de dar quenta por entero puesto que la quiebra sea mas, o menos porque si fuere mas sera a su costa y si fuere menos sera a su prouecho.-

22. Con condiçion que durante el tiempo deste contracto no se haga concierto con otra persona o personas algunas, para traer pimienta dela India, o malaca, o otras partes, de solo à portugal ni a otra parte alguna, ni se hara ninguna innouaccion en prejuyçio dello, excepto que para hauer la quantidad pimienta que se pretende, se podra en la India hazer partidos con las personas que paresçiere que den pimienta, para este contracto, y cargarse en la India, o malaca en las naos de Viage y esto por el preçio a respeto delos çiento y setenta mill Cruçados por trienta mill quintales, y con ynteruençion delos hazedores delos contratadores, y de manera que sea en beneficio deste contracto, y no en su prejuyçio, y que toda la pimienta que estuuiere hecha en la India y malaca, por quenta dela hazienda de su magd. se le de por lo que huuiere costado y se pagara del caudal qu se embiare el segundo año.-

23. Con condiçion que se les de todas las prouisiones necessaries y que en la India y malaca se les de Un escriuano qual ellos nombraren, que les haga sus papelles y otorgue sus Instrumentos y certificaçiones, quando los pidieren, y les haga sus protestos quando le requieren, so pena de perder sus offiçios.-

24. Con condiçion que teniendo Informaçion que algunas

personas tratan en pimienta o que se lleua en algunos naos o nauios, lo haran saber al Vissorrey o al capitan o Justitias del lugar, donde acontesçiere, y esto en secreto o en puplico como mas quisieren, y en Viniendo a noticia de qualquier dellos sobre dhos., haran todas las diligençias neçesarias, y haran buscar qualesquier naos y nauios, que les fuere requerido o y hallando algunos culpados proçederan contra ellos confrome a las leyes y regimientos que sobre allo ay.-

25. Con condiçion que en la India no pagaran derechos ningunos de pimienta mas delos que agora se pagan por el contracto que corre aunque la pimienta Venga de Cunda o de qualquier otra parte.-

26. Con condiçion que la pimenta mojada se enxugara benefiçiara y acomodara a costa delos contratadores, y despues de enxuta y acriuelada se pesara y hauran por ella el mesmo preçio de doçe cruçados, como han de auer por la otra y se les dara para enxugar la los Instrumentos en que agora se acostumbra hazer.-

27. Con condiçion que la pimienta que huuiere en la casa al tiempo que llegare la primera nao de su contracto se le entregue para benefiçiar la por guenta dela hazienda de su magd. misticamente como las otras.-

28. Con condiçion que su magd. les mandera dar çinco quentos de Juro de resguardo en la casa del Alfandiga de lisboa o en otras consignaçiones, de que sean contentos a Razon de diez y seis mill reis, el millar sobre que mandara despachar luego priuilegios, alos dhos. contratadores, y alas personas que ellos nombraran y les mandara pagar cada año los reditos en las hojas delos assientos, como es costumbre, y los dhos. contratadores del preçio que huuieren de auer, por la pimienta que entregaren pagaran los mesmos çinco quentos al thesorero dela dha. Alfandiga, para quedar enterado delos reditos del Juro que se huuiere de pagar a para con ellos hazer pagamento alas partes si aun no fueren pagados y acabado el contracto despues que los dhos. contratadores seran enteramente pagados desempenaran los dhos. Çinço quentos, o otros en las mesmas cosas, donde las tuuieren, y del mesmo precio, para quedar libre la hazienda de su magd de manera que ni en lo principal ni en los reditos la hazienda de su magd. no reçiba daño ni Interes alguno el qual Juro hade començar a correr desde Enero de

año que Viene de quinientos y ochenta seis, y esta condiçion no sera declarada en el contracto y se hara en aluaran de fuera que e registrara en los libros de la casa de la yndia, donde se registrara el contracto

29. Con condiçion que en caso que se haga ley de Vedamento para no lleuar dinero, plata, o oro ȩn la India, no se entienda con los contratadores hasta la quantia que por su contracto se ofresçiere embiar, y fuere neçesario para bien del contracto, y compra dela pimienta, y carga con della, y para el arbitrio que han de hauuer por este contracto.-

30. Con condiçion qué su magd. mandera açeptar este contracto antes de su partida de Monçon, y en caso que su magd. sea seruido de mandar le comunicar y abrir lançe a otras personas lo podra hazer con declaraçion que Viniendo a contracto con otras personas, los dhos. contratadores hayan para si el albitrio delos clauos en todos seys años teniendo se respecto al seruiçio que hazen a su magd. en este modo de contracto, y esto de manera que el lançe no este abierto mas que por tiempo de Un mes, y que dentro del, se concluya el contracto, atento la breuedad del tiempo, en que se han de proueer para el buen effecto dello.-

31. Y con todas las de mas condiçiones y declaraçiones en fauor de los contratadores, contenidas en el contrato passado que no fueren contrarias a las condiçiones arriba declaradas, y de todo lo en ellos contenido.-

32. Y con condiçion que la condiçion quarta deste contracto que dice, que la pimienta no subiera en la India de perçio que costo en el contracto passado, se ha de entender durante al tiempo deste contracto, no podia subir a mas preçio Una por otra que a razon delos çiento y setenta mill Cruzados, de diez Reales, por los treynta mill quintales, y costas, hasta estar embarcados, y quando llegaren al dho. preçio o se comprare por menos hautan por cada quintal doçe cruçados, de quatro çientos reis, por la manera declarada en el capitulo duodeçimo deste contracto, pero si en algun año o años, deste contracto su magd fuere seruido y tuuiere por bien que la pimienta suba, del dho. preçio todo lo que subiere dos xerafines o menos, dellos sera la mitad a costa de su magd. y la otra mitad a costa

delos dhos. contratadores, y subiendo mas delos dhos. dos xerafines sera todo lo que subiere allende dellos a costa dela hazienda de su magd. in solidum y los dhos. contratadores daran en la India el dinero neçesario para los dhos. cresçimientos a lende delos çiento y setenta mill Cruçados, y loque tocare ala parte de su magd. se pagaran dela manera que han de pagar los doçe Cruçados por quintal, a razon de tresçientos Reys por xerafin en la Venida de cada armada, y esta condiçion toda se ha de meter En prouision fuera de contracto por no entenderse en India que ay algun Intento de subir la pimienta, En Monçon a Veynte y nuebe de nouiembre, de mill y quinientos y ochenta y çinco años. —Giraldo paris.

El Rey n' ro. señor açepta estos apuntamientos de Geraldo paris en nombre de Juan batt[a]. Rouelasca, y en el suyo, con todas las condiciones en ellos declaradas, y ha por bien que el lançe este abierto todo este mes de deçiembre, para concluyrse el contracto hasta en fin del, y hauiendo quien al dho. contracto haga major lançe, de que su magd. sea seruido y contento de açeptar que de alos dhos. Geraldo paris y Juan bastista Rovelasca el arbitrio del clauo, en todos seys años conforme al capitulo 30 puesto que el contracto que de en otras personas y por auer lo ansi por bien su magd. mandado al señor Don xpoual de mora, gentil hombre de su camera del consejo de estado y Veedor de su hazienda hazer este assiento, El qual firmo fecho por mi Nuño Aluarez pereyra escriuano dela hazienda, En Monçon a primero de deçiembre de mill y guinientos y ochenta y çinco años. —Don xpoual de Mora.-

Conçertado por mi con el original que queda en mi poder, En monçon a çinco de deçiembre de mill y quinientos y ochenta y çinco años. —Nuño aluarez pereyra. -

(CONTRACT OF 1586)

[The contract concluded by Mark and Mathäus Welser and company in connection with the trade in pepper is found in Spanish language. A copy of the same is preserved in the Fugger Archives 46. 1 folio 17. The agreement was between the Welsers and Giraldo Paris. This was signed on 29 March 1586.]

Declaro por la presente que por quanto los señores Marco y matheo Welzares y-compa. treirien y participan en el contrato de la pimienta que agora se ha hecho por mi y giraldo Paris los çinco dozanos dello como consta y porque se avia de dar orden en la India para fatorizar la dha. parte e aviendo yo alla mis fatores nos avemos concertado con el sor. Juan Xpoval manlich, en nombre de los sobredhos. senhores que se fatorizasse toda Junta la dha. su parte con lamsia por, manos de mis fatores por la qual fatoria me haran buenos a racion de tres porçiento delo que en cada año montare su porçion é yo porla presente me obligo por los dihos mis fatores de buena administration y que de toda daran quenta con pago delo que por cuenta delos dhos ss les yra en manos y donde algo faltasse, me obligo de satisfarlo, demi propria hazienda.-

Digo que a mas delo que toca al contrato dela pimienta que debaxo dela misma obligaçion sera lo que embiare por otraquenta y uno y otro hasta tanto que a los ss. Welzares les stuviere bien, y que se les stubiere bien de embiar persona o fator suyo particular que lo puedam haçer, e yo no que de obligado a mas delo que Siviere, entrado, en su poder delos sobre dhos y lo mismo que quando y o no quisiere estar mas obligado que con avisar les aqui en Portugal primero que suseiren de em viar candalo, o tra cosa, se entiende que en tal caso y o quedo libre y por que ansi lo cumplire hize el presente scrito firmada e mi nombre, en Lisbona a veinte y nueve de março de 1586.

Por la carta del contrato que en çinco de Abril les escriuimos, pensan do que alos seis del dho partiessen, las çinco ñaos para India que por e contrario tiempo basta o y se de tuvieron, auan vs. ms. por extenso entendido como se hieo nueuo contrato de pimirenta y que en el tienen los ss. Juan Batt. Roue lasca y giraldo Paris, los 7/12 y mis ss. Marco e Mathco Welzarie Coms. los rehtantes s delos qua les y o tengo aguir la administration y por el los me a conae conel. s. Juan Batt. Roue lasco que redrèsse alla en la India, a vs. ms. assi que para la de todo el contrato passamo avs. ms. poaer Juntos, que con las dhos naos' les embia mos, yen ellas repartido mandamos en el nombre de Dios. 194,000 *crusados* es a saber los 170,000 *crusados* para compra dela pimienta, y los 24, 000 *crusados* para el adresso delas naos, como por los con o scinirentos enten deran , delo que delhos recebieren, mandaran vs. ms. en sus libros, alos ahos dhos mis ss. ponsus $^{5}/_{22}$ partes con crescimiento y sana faige, dan credito y con el emplio dellos y com pra dela pimienta tiendran la orden que en la general scdechara, y a su tiempo seran servico os, de los avirsar y mandar quenta de todo, y ques en la dha carta general se a scriue avs. ms. sobre este particular y todo lo que para la compra dela pim. ta assi en la India como malaqua enteridemos ser neçesario no me alargare en esta mas, -.

Y lo quo agora se offresçe que decir os que a fuera delos 80,000 & 33 $^{1}/_{3}$ *crusados* que mont las $^{5}/_{12}$ partes demis ss. del caudal, dela pimienta emhis a vs. ms. por su quenta dellos en estas cinco naos otros, cinco mill cruzado's en cada nao mill cruçados, en los saquos; canuazo-de 500,000 *crusados* cada vno, lacra dos condoze sellos y marquados con marca de fuera, los quales entregaran avs. ms. los maestires de cada nao, como por los con o scinvientos que con esta van veran, y del fleite dellos estan agui pagados, y san registrado recibien do les sacaran certihumbre y lo embiaran con los naos para que sebuelua arisgar el registro, y por quanto para el gasto del contra to a fuera el que se haçe con la pimienta, abrain menester algunos dineros, nos con çertamos e laseñor quan Batt. y, yo, que de dhos 5000,000 *crusados* que embio tomassen vs. ms. 2000 *crusados* para los dhos gastos, y otros que podran sacer, y el resto de dhos çinco mill cruzados empleanar por quenta del, me nos preçio delo que digo, que sera tanto me yor; y sobre todo tiendran cuidado que el que enbiaren se a limpio de fusti y madre, por quanto sa a dezir muchoen esto y en caso que no se halle dans hue no y limipio amen os de. ho barda os y de a y ençima empleanan vs. ms. no mas que lamita d del linero que les am bis en dano y esto en qual guirer preçio que valiere -.

Y por que esteañio se hizo agui mas prouechio en la canella que en todas otras drogas hallandose en el preçro del año passado delos. 40. hasta. 50 gardaos, canella, fresca bien colorada y cumplida de seilon emplearan la otra mitah delos 3,000 *crusados* en el, y nosles embiaran aun que pro que entiendo que todas las caitas pidiran canèlla, reçelo que este preçio notenga lugar, y que los muchos compradores le suban mas alto , no veniends mucha quantidad y no mas que a treçientas quintales por nao se podran alargar hasta se senta y canco bardaos, por que, el qual preçio por mingun caso sc podra passar ni Clegara e sino auiendo poca en la India, por quanto veniendo quantidad, nose mantiendra agui en los preçios que agora vale que son 53,000 6 el quintal.-.-

Las nuels valen agui agora 40,000 6. que causara que much os las pidran de alla pero como suelen venir carga das de cal. horada das y que brada y es espeçie que no se dexa quardar mucho ni tampoco no avy que pensar que este preçio dure no nos embiaran dellas mingunas, por masbarato que alla valgan.-

Nitampoeo dela maca por quan to de alla nunca suele venir tan limpia qruessa y bien colorada, como de malaca, y con todo lotienen en muiy altos preçios y agui esta muiy abatida y sin despae ho letienen en sol el quinital, que al respeto delos 80 baradao que alla valia y muchos dered que agui paga es harta baxo preçio.-

Del Anil por que entiendo que no valdra allamas banato que el año, passado saluo auirendo mucha quantidad, del no embiaran vs. ms. por quentade mis scñores minquno por que in de una ni de otra manera les esta na bien agui vale el de cer que ja 60,000 y. y de Albeus, 56,000 y. el fardo.-

Aluitre enlas mercaderias que adelante les dire, y les embiaran a la buelta, con estao naos que en buen ora van declarando y registranco en el quaterno que se embia alos offiçiales dela casa de India, que essas mercadunias van por quenita delas $^{5}/_{12}$ part es del dho aluitre, del claus de mis ss. Marco y Matheo Welzari, e comp. de manera que a qua no nos haqan los dhos offiçiales difficultad en el despaçho, y los fardos y ran marquados con la marca de arriba, a entregar aqui also ya nombrados ss. Marco y Matheo Welzari, o quiren por elhos, que venqar los dhos fardos en buen os a casalhados y a cargo dehombres conoscidos ya vs. ms. entiende quanto vaen ello de manera que no tengo que airsarles desto.-

Como por el contrato veran tenemos Abertad de traer, este aluitre delos 400 quintales de clauo en clayo o otra gualguier suerte de espeçcria, baciendo agir valencia delos drechos, de suerte que no se nos Lescuente mas, que lo que montan los dhos: 400 las de clauo, por tanto bolgara que seaçcrtassen de Emplear estos 3v que para este e feto lesembio, en la suerte que meyor a ca respondiesse y como para, tanta distançia, de lugar y tiempo no se puede dar comision, Gimitada, por quanto no se pue de saber lka mudanca que abran sec so las especenias, declarare a vs. m. mi paresçcr lo que se deue de bu zer. al qua lauiendo lugar seran servidos de seguir y en caso que no se pue da bazer mc sumeto al del senor felipe sasseti el qual en tien do sera el mas acertado, tcniendo auiso que por quanto es la intençion delos dhos mis scnones que estos 3v *crusados* se emplean por quenta del aluitre, que no compran pon elles ropa denimiguanasuerte rvi seda, pedrina, almiscar, niamoar, sl no dno maço, gengibre, Canclla, Anil , y de todas estas tengo mas afficion a Clauo que a, ninguna otra por tanto ballandose ala llegada destas naos clauo Limpio sin fusti y madre, en el priero basta de 50 bardaos, 5 masomenos empleran Vs. Ms. todos los 3V *crusados* enclauo, y por que entiendo que no abro guien de agir Copida por se aver sallado, los años passados malconel, espero que le podran al cançar aun a El gengibre siendo fresco y sano no deyara de dar muy buen prouecho, pero como tiene libertad de swyo y se hallara a comp rar Cas guintaladas delos marineros, poronde no se paga mas de 1500y^{6} de drecso, pagan do sinellas 5v^{6}. no nose stabien descontarse el aluitra en el por entiro y como en el discontar de las guintala das avy no esaçertado comprarlas, assique nosoy de parescen que nos embien Vs.Ms. del, vale agir por el presente 12^{6}y con la nueua dela tomada de santo Domingo delos Ingleses subira mas y el de conerua 140^{6} - la6.-.-

Los precios delas piedras, ropas, seda, almiscar, y ambar entenderan Vs. Ms. de otras que como de todas essa suertes demis senõres no tiendran que embiar, no tratave dellas, y bueluo a con firman a Vs. Ms. que procuren en todo caso de les embiar elre tono delos 3V *crusados* que a fuera delos 2V *crusados* apra gastos les embio, empleado en clauo o Canella, en la manera que anba les declaro, y para que queriendo assegurar dela buelta los dhos mis SS. Copueden baher tiendran Vs. Ms. encargar los dbos mis, ss. lo pueden baher tiendvan Vs. Ms. encargar las dhos mercadenias la orden que agir les significo, asaber cargando en las dos naos del ney no destostras, mill cruçados tuwie ren que cargar, y en las otras dos que despues delas primeras partienen en cada Vn la mitad del $^1/_3$ que queda , y en la vltima awiendo çinco naos no carganan nada, y en caso que en la India sc baga nao nucua y se embie para aca no cargaran por quenta delhos tres mill dricados tam poconada en ella, y por quanto sobre esta se bara quenta no saladran sin neçesidad desta orden.-.-

Antes que cemasse esta me auem con el s. on Juan Bat[a]. que delo que delos 5V *crusados* que lesembio empleassen contassen. 3 porc[o]. de responsion y por quanto el escriuira a. Vs. Ms. Comismo lo baran. Vs. Ms. assi, y no se offresçiendo obo que de Zir bago fin enesta con espenanca que maniana muy temprano salgan Casçinco naos que dios quiere quardar y el estado delas Illy es. personas de Vs.Ms. prospere y augmente, como desean, y xpo con todos. En Lisbona a 11. de Abril de 1586.-.

APPENDIX VI

ASIA CONTRACT

The Fugger brothers concluded a contract with the Welsers and accepted a few shares in the Asia Contract. The way in which the Welsers purchased the shares is described first and later the details of selling the shares to the Fuggers brothers are described in this contract written in Latin.

This is a document preserved in the Fugger Arcives under no. 46.1. The contract was between the firm of "Georg Fuggerischen Erben" and Markus, Matthäus Welser and Company. This document is reproduced by Hildebrandt in his work *Fuggerischen Erben...*, pp. 196-201.

IN NOMINE DOMINI, AMEN:

Universis et singulis praesentis publici Instrumenti Cessionis et declarationis, omniumque in eo contentorum seriem inspecturis, lecturis, pariter et audituris pateat evidenter et sit notum: Quod Anno Nativitatis Eiusdem Millesimo, quingentesimo octogesimo septimo: Indictione decima quinta Regnante-Serenissimo et Potentissimo Principe ac Domino, Domino Rudolpho, hujus nominis secundo Romanorum Imperatore semper Augusto, Germaniae, Hungariae, Bohemiae Rege, Archeduce Austriae, Domino nostro Clementissimo, Anno Regni Majestatis Eius Romani duodecimo: Die decima septima mensis Aprilis, circiter horam nonam ante meridiem, in inclita urbe Imperiali Germaniae Augusta Vindelycorum, ibidemque in aedibus Illustris Domini Philippi Eduardi Fuggeri, Domini in Kirchberg et Weissenhorn, in hypocausta Eiusdem consueto: In mei Notarii publici, testimoniumque infra scriptorum adhaec specialiter vocatorum et rogatorum prasentia personaliter Constituti Nobiles et Magnifici viri, Marcus senior et Matthaeus Welseri suo et sociorum suorum nomine, mihi infra scripto Notario cogniti, ex eorum et cujuslibet eorum certa scientia et spontanea voluntate exposuerunt dicentes, quod cum Gerardus Parisius Germanus, tam suo, quam nomine et pro parte Joannis Baptistae Rovelasca Mediolanensis, virtute Instrumenti procuratorij, sibi desuper facti conventionem fecit, et ut vulgo dicitur fecit et accepit assentum cum Don Christophero de Mora, nobili domus Philippi Hispaniarum Regis, Et de eius consilio status, eiusque partimonij virore, quod quidem assentum sine (sive?) conventionem dictus Gerardus Parisius suo et nomine praedicto accepit in civitate Valentia, ubi tunc reperiebatur Catholica Majestas, cum sua Curia, die decima quinta Mensis Februarij praeteriti Anni Millesimi, quingentesimi octuagesimi sexti; de et super contractu piperic Indiarum Orientalium et emptione trigenta Milliam Centipondiorum piperis in quolibet annorum sex, incipiendorum a mense Januarij praedicti Anni Millesimi quingentesimi octuagesimi sexti in antea. Quod quidem Instrumentum sive contractum approbatum et ratificatum fuit per eandem Catholicam Majestatem Hispaniarum Regis in dicta Ciuitate Valentia Die decima septima praecalendati mensis Februarij prout apparere, asseruerunt per eandem ratificationem per eundem Regem subscriptam et per praefatum Don Christophorum coram Nunno Aluarez Pereira ejusdem Catholicae Majestatis Secretario, in quo quidem Instrumento reperitur quoddam capitulum literatura et Idiomate Lusitano, quod versum seu traductum in sermonem Hispanum seu Castellanum.

Et de dicto Hispano sermone versum seu traductum in Idioma latinum est tenoris sequentis.

Cum pacto et conditione, quod contrahentes possint nominare apud provisorem et officiales Domus Indiarum partionem, quam quilibet ipsorum in hoc contractu tenere seu habere debet, et quod pro eo possint nominare socios, quos voluerint, dum modo quod sint tales, de quibus sua Majestas contenta sit: remanentibus tamen dictis contrahentibus obligatis proportione in qua nominaverint socios, qui etiam remanebunt obligati proportione in qua nominati remanserint, de quo in libris dictae domus in pede registri hujusmodi contractus fient assenti seu conventiones necessariae subscriptae per portes et per illius provisorem.

Virtute cuius quidem capituli: Idem Gerardus Parisius utendo facultate sibi dictoque Joanni Baptae. Rouelasca data et concessa suo et nomine dicti Joannis Baptistae declaravit et nominavit praefatos Nobiles et Magnificos Viros Welseros pro quinque ex duodecim partibus in participantes et socios in dicto contractu piperis pro tempore et cum conditionibus, declarationibus, limitationibus, prouentibus, praeminentijs et praerogativis, ac cum omnibus alijs in dicto assentu contentis et declaratis absque aliqua exceptione nec reservatione, quam quidem nominationem et declarationem, dictus Gerardus Parisius suo et nomine dicti Joannis Baptistae Rouelasca fecit in Personam dictorum Dominorum Welserorum pro quinq. ex duodecim partibus dicti contractus piperis seque suo et dicto nomine obligauit, quod infra menses duos a die factae dictae declarationis et nominationis iuxta dictam conditionem sine capitulum vigesimum octauum praeinsertum faceret et curaret quod describeretur prout desuper continetur in pede Registri dicti contractus piperis saptu et stipulatum cum dicta Catholica Maiestate Regis Philippi dictis respectiue diebus decima quinta et decima septima mansis februarii, Et in libris patrimonij Regni Portugaliae et in omnibus officiis, libris et partibus, ubi opus fuerit pro validitate et securitate praefatorum Dominorum Welserorum praesentium et stipulantium.

Ita quod dicta nominatio, societas et participatio suum sortiretur effectum, et hac de causa expediret, seu expediri faceret, et consignaret procuratori eorundem Dominorum Welserorum sociorum stipulantium provisiones, Cedulas et expeditiones Regias desuper necessarias et opportunas, informa debita, iuxta stilum, usum et consuetudinem dicti Regni Portugalliae eo modo et forma quod infra dictos duos menses, praefati Domini Welseri stipulantes admisci fuissent per eundem Catholicum Regem omnesque suos ministros dicti Regnii Portugalliae in tales participantes et socios dictorum Joannis Bap^{tae}. Rouelasca et Gerardi Parisij in dicto contractu piperis pro dictis quinque ex duodecim partibus iuxta praeinsertum capitulum vigesimum octauum. Ita quod nihil eis ex so deficeret, nec eorum conditio, nomen, reputatio et prouentus in dicta quantitate dictarum quinque ex duodecim partibus, non fuisset, minoris momenti, quam ipsorum in reliquis septem ex duodecim partibus—Hac tamen conditione et declaratione, quod praefati Domini Welseri obligati fuissent ac se obligarent in dictis libris patrimonij Portugalliae adimplere soluere et manutenere dictum assentum, in omnibus et per omnia pro dictis quinq. ex duodecim partibus. Nec non contribuere omnibus sumtibus et expensis factis vel faciendis pro beneficio dicti contractus et assenti piperis facti cum dicta Catholica Maiestate Regis Hispaniarum pro dictis quinque ex duodecim partibus—Et dictus Gerardus Parisius obligavit dictam Joannem Baptista Rouelasca approbaturum et ratificaturum fore dicta scripturam seu Instrumentum declarationis, nominationis et participationis, quodque etiam dicta ratificatio et approbatio fieri deberet per procuratorem dictorum Dominorum Welserorum, prout haec omnia et alia latius continentur in dicta scriptura seu Instrumento declarationis et nominationis desuper facto et stipulato per dictum Gerardum Parisium in oppido Madritti, Die decima septima menis Wartii Anni Millesimi quingentesimi Octuagesimi sexti, in actis Casconi de Galuez Pu.[ci] scribae Regii.

Et deinde idem Catholicus Hispaniarum Rex per suam Cedulam propria manu subscriptam et referendatam per petrum de Pinto et per dictum Nunno Aluarez Pereyra datam in Aranzuez die decima Octaua dicti Mensis Martij praecalendati Anni Millesimi quingentesimi Octuagesimi sexti contentus fuit et consensit, quod praefati Joannes Baptista Rouelasca et Gerardus Parisius potuissent nominare praefactos Dominos Welseros in socios dicti contractus piperis, pro dictis quinque ex duodecim partibus iussit que provisori et officialibus Domous Indiarum ut acceptarent et admitterent dictum societatem et de praemissis facerent assentum siue descriptionem in calce Registri dicti contractus et quod ibi se subscriberent dicti Joannes Baptista et Gerardus Parisius ac persona habens potestatem siue procuram praefatorum Dominorum Welserorum. Nec non et dicti prouisor et officiales dictae Domus Indiarum—Et deinde die vigesima secunda mensis Aprilis Anni praeteriti millesimi quingentesimi Octuagesimi sexti coram prouisore et officialibus dictae domus Indiarum dictus Jo. Baptista Rouelasca tã proprio nomine quam procuratorio nomine dicti Gerardi Parisij virtute Instrumenti Procuratorij sibi desuper dati nominauit praefatos Dominos Welseros in socios dicti contractus piperis pro dictis quinque ex duodecim partibus—Et Joannes Chiristophorus Manlique procurator et procuratorio nomine dictorum Dominorum Welserorum virtute Instrumenti procuratorij generalis sibi dati per eosdem Dominios supra dictos Welseros. Its acceptauit ac eos obligauit pro adimplemento dicti contractus pro dictis quinq. ex duodecim partibus, que quidem nominatio et acceptatio facta fuit in pede Registri dicti Contractus subscriptaq. fuit per eundem Joannem Baptistam Rouelasca suo et nomine dicit Gerardi Parisij, et per dictos prouisorem et officiales, ac per eundem Joannem Christophorum Manlique eorum procuratorem procuratio nomine—

Et quoniam iuxta superius dicta et relata praefati domini Welseri et socij sunt Domini dictarum quinque ex duodecim partibus dicti assenti et contractus piperis. Ideo omni meliori modo, via, iure et forma, quibus possunt, et de iure debent, fatentur ac palam et publive declarant, quod de dictis quinque ex duodecim partibus, illarum tres sunt, spectant et pertinent, a Illustres viros Dominum Phillippum Eduardum et Octauianum secundum fratres Fuggeros Dominos in Kirchberg et Weissenhorn, suo et curatorio noie: ipsorum fratris Domini Raymundi Fuggeri qui succedere et habere debent prouentus et luera dante Doie: proveniendas ex dicto contractu pro dictis tribus ex duodecim partibus, pro quibus etiam contribuere et participare debent pro amissione et damno forte (quod absit) in dicto contractu habendo et patiendo, participareque debent in dicto contractu piperis pro dictis eorum tribus ex duodecim partibus, pro tempore et cum conditionibus, limitationibus lucris, praeminentijs et praerogativis, omnibusque alijs in dicto contractu et assentu piperis contentis et declaratis, absque aliqua execeptione seu reseruatione — Hac tamen conditione et declaratione, quod sint et esse debeant seu debent remanere obligati adimplere soluere et manutenere dictum assentum in omnibus et per omnia pro dictis eorum tribus ex duodecim partibus.

Nec non contribuere in omnibus sumptibus et expensis factis et faciendis pro beneficio dicti assenti et contractus piperis, quarum quidem expensarum liquidatio et declaratio remanere debet et remaneat in computo et ratione danda seu redenda ex libris communibus dicti contractus, remanendo tamẽ, prout remanere debet et remaneat Administratio omnium dictarum quinq. ex duodecim partibus in eisdem Dominis Welseris et in dictum eorum procuratorem de praesenti Constitutum, vel in antea constituendum, durante tempore dictorum sex Annorum dicti contractus in quibus praefati Domini Fuggeri suo et Curatorio nomine (ut supra) contribuere debent pro dictis eorum tribus ex duodecim partibus cum omnibus pecuniis necessariis, pro capitali sumptibus et expensis, factis et faciendis in dicto contractu et assentu. Et in fine dictorum sex Annorum dicti contractus fieri et finire debet computa et rationes de omnibus praedictis inter praefatos Dominos Welseros, et supradictos Dominos Fuggeros pro dictis eorum tribus ex duodecim partibus dicti contractus iuxta computum desuper dandum ex libris dicti contractus, Pro quo praefatorum welserorum procurator nunc constitutus et in antea constituendus cum ipsorum Welserorum consensu et bona voluntate nunquam ab ipsis reuocanda vel mutanda se obligabit dare et reddere verum, certum et legale computum et rationem cum solutione et restitutione reliquorum absque alique fraude, dolo, cautela vel collusione.

Nec non cum declaratione, quod quotiescumque placuerit dictis Dominis Fuggeris seu ipsorum haeredibus in tempore dictorum sex Annorum praefatorum Welserorum procurator teneatur, non solum menstruas rationum Cedulas, uti vocant, singulis mensibus offerre, sed etiam semel et pluries et quoties requisitum fuerit reddere computum et rationem de statu et conditione dicti contractus, Et de pecunijs erogatis in provisione capitalis, eiusq. sumtuum et expensarum desuper factarum usque ad diem redditionis dicti computi quod quidem computum praefati Welseri promiserunt se mandaturos reddi per procuratorẽ ipsorum verum, certum bonum et legale particulariter et generaliter eo modo et forma, prout dicti Domini Fuggeri, siue eorum haeredes, vel eorum legitimus procurator petierint.

Haec diserta pactione adiuncta, quod Domini Welseri praefati atq. ipsorum gentes siue Administratores aut factores, et illi personae, quam praefati Domini Fuggeri huius negociationis causa adiuncturi sunt, id quod in ipsorum potestate et libera facultate situm est, omnia totius illius negociationis secreta scripturas et libros, bona et integra fide pandere et communicare, et plane nihil ipsum adiunctum selare sed inspiciendi libros, rationes et secreta illius, negociationis aditum et potestatem eidem concedere, adde etiam eundem adjunctum apud Domum Indiae et omnibus aliis in locis, quibus ista negociatio geritus aut geretur, fideliter docere et instruere de omnibus teneantur atque debeant, ut viros bonos facere decet.

Ac etiam cum conditione et declaratione, quod ei dicti Domini Fuggeri vel eorum haeredes voluerint, vel eis placuerit Administrare dictas eorum tres ex duodecim partibus, hoc ipsum facere possint per se ipsos vel eorum procuratorem in quouis tempore eis beneuiso durante tempore dictorum sex Annorum dicti contractus, et in tali casu praefati Domini Welseri et socij siue ipsorum haeredes teneantur in tempore, quo dicti domini Fuggeri aut eorum haeredes voluerint in se accipere dictam Administrationem liquidare et finire omnia & singula computa et rationes inter dictos Dominos Welseros et socios et praefatos dominos Fuggeros capiendo dicti Domini Welseri et socij competentem ratam pro eorum duabus ex duodecim partibus, dicti que vero Domini Fuggeri pro dictis reliquis eorum tribus ex duodecim partibus prouent us et lucrum vel damnum et amissionem, quod seu quam reperiri contigerit, usque ad dictum diem. Et diende in antea praefati Domini Welseri et socij seu ipsorum haeredes teneantur, prout solemniter se obligauerunt et obligant cedere, renunciare et transferre eisdem Dominis Fuggeris sive ipsorum haeredibus ius et actionem dictarum earum trium ex duodecim partibus in eo statu, quo reperiri contigerit ac eos constituere procuratores in rem propriam nec non dare reliqua recapita necessaria, quae praefati Domini Welseri et socij aut ipsorum haeredes dare pocerunt seu debebunt, et si opus fuerit consensum hujus Administrationis a Catholica Majestate promouere, ut deinde in antea dicti Domini Fuggeri, ve ipsorum haeredes vel eorum procurator possint sine (sive?) poscit gubernare et Administrare dictas eorum tres ex duodecim partibus, et de eis disponere ad eorum libitum et voluntatem. Pro quibus omnibus et singulis sic adimplendis firmiterque obseruandis praefati Domini Welseri suo et sociorum suorũ nomine obligauerunt se ipsos eorumque haeredes successores et bona quaecumq. mobilia et stabilia, praesentia et futura. Nec non ibique praesentes coram nobis praefati Illustres Domini Fuggeri fratres, tam suo, quã Curatorio nomine Domini Raymundi Fuggeri ipsorum fratris interveniendes stipulationi et declarationi praesentis contractus omniumq. et singulorum in eo contentorum appositorum et declaratorum, dictoque contractu omniaque et singula in eo contenta, per eos bene incellecta praesentem contractum, omniaque et singula in eo contenta acceptauerunt et acceptant eo modo et forma, ac cum conditionibus et declarationibus in eo contentis et declaratis, seque solenniter obligauerunt et obligant pro adimplemento et obseruatione ac solutione praesentis contractus eo modo et forma, prout in eo continetur et declaratur, praedictaque omnia rata et firma habere, absque aliqua exceptione nec reseruatione.

Pro quibus omnibus et singulis sic adimplendis et obseruandis obligauerunt se ipsos eorumque haeredes successores et bona quaecunq. mobii ia et stabilia praesentia et futura ubicunq. existentia et milius apparentia. Nec non omnes supra dicta partes et personae in praesenti contractu nominate pro executione et adimplemento presentis contractus omniumque et singulorum in eo contentorum se submiserunt Jurisdictioni quorumcumq. Judiciorum etiam incompetentium, ut toto iustitiae vigore de huius modi causis et executione presentis contractus, etiam via executiva cognoscant et procedant, omnesque supradictos et eorum singules compellat, pro adimplemento dicti contractus et solutione contentorum in eo tanq. per sententiam diffinitivam, per iudicem competentem contra eos & eorum quemlibet latam et pronunciatam et transactam in rem iudicatam.

Renunciantes ad inuicem omnibus et quibuscumque Juribus et legibus in eorum fauorem quo modocumque dictantibus, etiam in corpore utriusque iuris clausis priuilegio fori et legi si convenerit de Jurisdictione omnium Judicum et specialiter legi dicenti generalem renunicationem non valere nihi praecesserit specialis.

Et quia tam praefati Welseri cedentes Dominis Fuggeris saepe dictas tres ex duodecim partibus cum omnibus praeminentijs et praerogativis, guam ipsi Domini Fuggeri easdem acceptantes et se obligantes ad omnia onera, quae ratione dictarum trium partium ad ipsos spectare possunt, futuris temporibus istius inter ipsos celebratae Cessionis, acceptationis, conuentionis et obligationis respectiue publicum et fide dignum Instrumentum utrinq. sibi opus esse duxerunt a me Notario infrascripto petierunt sibi duo pro nunc et alias quot opus fuerit, desuper confici Instrumenta, quibus utrauis partes pro quacumque occasione seu necessitatc sua uti et qaudere possint. Acta fuerunt haec omnia sub anno Indictione Imperio, Merse, die, hora et loco quibus supra: praesentibus Magnificis et Honestis viris, Domino Joanne Bechler Consule, praedictae Civitatis Augustae, Daniele Krel & Ruberto Hillmair, Ciuibus et irocolis Augustanis, qui dictos Dominos Comparentes una mecum Notario probe norunt, testibus ad praemissa specialiter vocatis & rogatis.

Et quoniam Ego Joannes Spreng Ciuis Augustanus s. Imperiali Authoritate publicus approbatus & spirae in inclyto Camerae Imperialis Judicio Immatriculatus Notarius praemissis omnibus et singulis, dum sicuti praemittitur fierent et agerentur una cum praefatis testibus praesenes interfui eademq. omnia et singula sic fieri vidi et audivi: Quocirca praesens hos publicum instrumentum desuper confeci, manu propria subscripsi, signoq. meo Notariatus consueto, nomine et cognomine pariter signavi et publicavi, in fidem ac testimonium praemissorum, ex officio adhaec specialiter vocatus, rogatus et reguisitus. Nos Praefecti, Consules et Senatores Imperialius Civitatis Augustae Vindelicorum his Literis publice fatemur honestum ciuem nostrum Joannem Spreng, qui praesens, instrumentum confecit, apud nos, et in regionibus nostris, fuisse & adhuc esse Imperiali auctoritate Notarium publicum bonae existimationis et famae, proq. tali vulgo ab omnibus reputari et haberi cuius instrumentis et scriptis, in publicam formam redactis tam in Jidiciis, quam extra Jidicia, plena fides adhibetur. In testimonium hujus rei euidens, has Litteras sigillo ciuitatis nostrae appenso communiri fecimus, nona die mensis May, anno Doj., millesimo quingentesimo, octogesimo septimo.

APPENDIX VII

The Portuguese ships plying in the Indian Ocean regions were put to a lot of difficulties in the fourth quarter of the sixteenth century. There were a lot of pirates from the African coast to Malacca. The English and French were enemies of the Portuguese and used to fight and capture the ships with the cargo. The German agents give details about the troubles faced by them in the Indian ocean region. Two letters written by them are included in this appendix. Victor Klarwill, *Fugger-Zeitungen: Ungedrukte Briefe an das haus Fugger aus den Jahren 1568-1605,* Wien, 1923, p. 126. A letter from India was received on the 15 December 1588 in Augsburg.

LETTER FROM EAST INDIES

Brief aus ben Orientalischen Indien, der am 15. December 1588 in Augsburg empfangen wurde.

Im vergangenen Monat Ianuar haben die Portugiesen eine Armada nach der Küste von Melindo gesandt, weil dort vor einem Iahr die Türken großen Schaden getan haben. Man hat sie auch dieseß Iahr erwartet. Sie sind aber nicht gekommen, Weil nun dort etliche. Schlösser den Türken Gunst gegeben haben, hat die Armada deren drei in den Ground abgebrannt und alles Bolt (?), was über fünf Iahre alt war, getötet. Einem König hat man den Kopf abgeschlagen und denselben icher (?) gesandt. Andere Schlösser haben Gnade begehrt und ich mit den Capitän erglichen (?). Als nun dies alles fur Ruhe gebracht worben war, ist die Armada vor zwei Monaten nieder hicher gekommen. Nach Malacca ift in April auch eine Armada abgegangen. Dort hat der Köng von Gior die Stadt belagert, die in großer Gefahr gestanden ist. In einem Monat sollen die

Schiffe wieder zurückkommen. An dieser Stadt ist viel gelegen wegen der Schiffahrt nach China, Japan und den Moluccen, weil dort die Schiffe in den Hafen alufen müssen. Da die Moluccen sich in Revolte befinden, sind von dort im vergangenen Iahr zwei Galleonen mit nur wenig Gewürznägeln gekommen. Es wird ziemlich viel Kriegsvolk dahingesandt, aber neistenteils (?) dort begraben, weil die Mohren sie mit Gift töten. Ceylon ist acht Monate lang von dem König Raq zue Wasser und zu Land belagert gewesen. Dorthin hat man im September großen Succurs gesandt, der aber bisher wenig ausgerichtet hat. Es steht in großer Gefahr, und es soll täglich eine Armada von Goa hingesandt werden. Gott verleihe gutes Berrichten, da an dieser Festung dem hiesigen Land am meisten gelegen ist, weil es die reichste Insel auf dieser Küste ist, und weil alle Schiffe, die von China, Malacca, den Moluccen, Bengalen hieherkommen, dort einlaufen müssen. Man will ausgeben, daß in der straße von Moqua zwölf oder mehr Gateeren mit Türken sein sollen, wohin sie wollen, weiß man noch nicht. Es ist aber die Bermutung, daß sie nach der Küste von Melindo wollen, wohin im Iänner wieder iene Armada gehen soll. Hier an der Küste von Dug bis zum Cap von Camerin gibt es viele Seeräuber, die großen Schaden tun, Schiffe nehmen und viele Portugiesen töten. Man kann ihnen aber wegen der vielen anderen Geschäfte nicht mehren.

Letter from India

Zeitung, die mic Briefen vom 13. Januar 1590
aus den Orientalischen Indien eingelaufen ist

Nach Abfahrt der lesten Schiffe in Jahre 1589 hat sich im Kriegswesen folgendes verlaufen: Die Armada, die Manuel Coutinho und sein Bruder Thomas de Sansa am 10. Jänner 1589 nach der Küste von Melindo gesandt haben, zählte fünf Galeeren und fünfzehn andere Schiffe. Darauf waren zwölfhundert Portugiesen. Wie sie nun nach großen Stüren gegen Estrecho de Moqua kamen, merkten sie, daß vier türkische Galeeren an die Küste von Melindo bei einem Orte namens Mombassa gelandet waren. Auf dieser Insel haben sie zu ihrem Schutz eine Feste gebaut und waren der Hinkunft der Portugieser nicht gewärtig. Sie sind ans Land gegangen, und de hat sich das wilde Volk, bei dreimalhunderttausend Mann stark, zusammengetan, um bei seichtem Wasser aus die Insel zu kommen und das dort wohnende Volk auszufressen, was sie auf dem Lande hin und wieder auch getan hatten. Deshalb hatten die Türken zu ihrer Verteidigung das Geschütz aus den Galeeren genommen und von der Wasserseite keinen Feind gefürchtet. Die portugiesische Armada ist aber hinzugekommen und hat die türkischen Galeeren ohne Widerstand genommen, worauf die Portugiesen aus Land seßten. Als die Türken dies sahen, haben sie sics auf das Festland retten wollen, wo sie aber von dem wolden Volk ibel zugerichtet und aufgefressen worden sind. Ein Teil der Türken ist den Portugiesen zugelaufen, da sie lieber gefangen als aufgefressen werden wollten. Es haben denn auch die Portugiesen etliche Türken und arabische Mohren gefangen genommen.

Der portugiesische General hat dem König von Mombassa, der dem König von Portugal unterthan ist, den Kopf abschlagen lassen, weil er den Türken Zuflucht gewährt hat. Die von den Türken erbaute Feste wurde zerstört und die Insel geplündert. Dann haben die Portugiesen den Simbas das Feld geräumt, die im Angesicht der Armada die Leute umgebracht und alsbald aufgefressen haben, so caß nach fünf Tagen keine Creatur mehr vorhanden gewesen ist. Als sie alles aufgeräumt und nichts mehr zu Essen hatten, sind sie wieder aufs Feltland gegangen. Dann nahmen sie ihren Weg gegen Norden, in das Land des Priesters Johannes. Die auf der Armada erzählen, daß sie mit scharfen Pfeilen wohl bewaffnet sind und alle Menschen fressen, die sie bekommen können. Deren Weiber führen sie lebendig hinweg. Sie leiden aber keinen Kraken unter sich. Sobald sich einer übel befindet, richten sie ihn hin und fressen ihn auf. Die Portugiesen sagen, daß die Wilden bei ihrem Auszug sechsmal-hunderttaufend Mann stark gewesen sind. Wenn sie an einen Ort Kommen, gehen sie so lange nicht weg, als sie noch einen Menschen zum Treffen finden, dann ziehen sie wieder fort. Der sieg unserer Armada kommt daher, daß die Simbas den Türken viel zu schaffen gaben, weshalb die Galeeren leicht zu nehmen gewesen sind, die am 16. März zu Goa eingebracht worden sind.

Mit dem Schiff Santa Cruz ist im vergangenen Jänner nach Portugal geschrieben worden, daß zwei unserer Galeeren und zwölf Galeotten sich bei Goa mit schwarzen Mohren tapser geschlagen haben. Die Galeotten haben sich in einen Hafen zwölf Meilen von Goa zurückgezogen, wohin der Gouverneur eine Flotte sandte. Die hat die Küste erobert, und das Volk ist ins Land hineingelaufen.

Die von unserer Armada in Lande von Malacca zerstörte Feste ist von dem dortigen Volk neu ausgebaut worden. Der Gouverneur hat aber mit dreihundert Portugiesen das Volk nochmals vertrieben und das Gebäuda zerstöre. Alle Orte von Malacca sind sehr wichtig, weil dort alle Schiffe hinkommen, um Pfeffer, Droguen und andere Sachen zu laden. Es wäre gut, die Insel Sumatra zu erobern. Wenn man vier bis sechstausend Portugiesen hätte, könnte man die ganze Schiffahrt nach Moqua verhindern. Es fehlt aber an Geld. Im vergangene Jahr ist ein englisches Schiff in die Sunda gekommen und hat allda eine Ladung Pfeffer genommen. Der Capitän hatte einen Brief und ein Praesent für den daselbst mohnenden Bischof, der aber weder das eine nocha das andere angenommen hat. Als der Engländer um das Cap der Guten Hoffnung nah England zu fuhr, ist er mit noch zwei Schiffen ausgelaufen und hat seinen Weg durch die Estrecho de Moqua genommen, wo ein Schiff zugrunde ging. Mit den zwei anderen fuhr er nach Neu-Spanien und Mexiko, und dort hat er geplündert und genommen, was ihm in die Hand fiel. Von dort ist er nach den Philippinen gefahren, wo er allerlei Sachen aus China geladen hat. Dann ist er mit dem einen Schiff nach Hause gefahren, das andere ist, um Pfeffer zu laden, nach der Sunda gesegelt. Die Schiffahrt von Neu-Spanien nach China ist ganz gewöhnlich geworden. Es kommen täglich Schiffe dahin. Im vergangenen Jahr ist Don Johann de Gona in einem Schiff nach Mexiko gesegelt. Als dies der hiesige Gouverneur vernahm, hat er ihm eine Galeotte entgegengeschickt, denn es wäre as Verderben Indiens, wenn man ihm dies erlauben wollte. Denn es gibt zwischen dem König von Portugal und den König von Spanien Capitulationen, daß die Spanier nicht nach den Philippinen fahren dürfen. Dies hat der

König, unser Herr, zu halten gelobt, als er Portugal eingenommen hat.

Die Herren Jesuiten convertieren in Japan alle Tage Leute zum christlichen Glauben. Die beherrshen diese Insel ganz und gar.

Die Mohren von Ceylon haben einen Christen zum König genommen. Erist der Vetter des vorigen König. Er begehrt zweihundert Mönche, um seine Unterthanen zu taufen.

SELECT BIBLIOGRAPHY

Abraham, Meera, *Two Medieval Merchant Guilds of South India,* New Delhi, 1988.

Abu-l-Fazl, *Akbar Nama,* Vol. III, New Delhi, 1977.

Alberi, Eugenio, *Relazioni degli Ambasciatori Veneti al Senato*, Firenze, 1839-63, 15 vols.

Albuquerque Afonso de, *Cartas de Afonso de Albuquerque,* edited by Raymundo Antonio de Bulhão Pato, Lisboa, 1884-1935, 7 vols.

Alexandrowicz, C.H., *An Introduction to the History of the Law of Nations in the East Indies: 16th, 17th and 18th Centuries,* Oxford, 1967.

———, *Alguns Documentos de Archivo Nacional da Torre do Tombo,* Lisboa, 1892.

Amaral, Maria Valentina Cotta do, *Privilégios de Mercadores Estrangeiros no Reinado de D.João* III, Lisboa, 1965.

Aragão, Texeira de, "Vasco da Gama e de Vidugueira: estudo historico", *Boletim da Sociedade da Gerografia de Lisboa,* vi series, 1886.

Ashtor, Eliyashu, "The Karimi Merchants", *Journal of the Royal Asiatic Society of Great Britain and Ireland,* London, 1956.

Ashtor, Eliyashu, "The Venetian Supremacy in Levantine Trade: Monopoly or Pre-colonialism", *The Journal of European Economic History,* Vol. 3, no.1, Rome, 1974.

Aubin, Jean, "Le Orçamento do Estado da India de Antonio de Abreu", *Studia,* Vol. 4, Lisboa, 1959.

Baião, Antonio, *O Manuscrito Valentim Fernandez,* Academia Portuguesa da Historia, Lisboa, 1940.

Barbosa, Duarte, *The Book of Duarte Barbosa: An Account of the Countries Bordering on the Indian Ocean and their Inhabitants, Written by Duarte Barbosa and Completed about the Year 1518 A.D.,* Delhi, 1989 (reprint).

Barros, João de, *Da Asia*, Decadas I-IV, Lisboa, 1778.

Begley, Vimala and Puma, Richard Daniel de, eds., *Rome and India: The Ancient Sea Trade*, Wisconsin, 1991.

Begley, Vimala, "New Investigations at the Port of Arikamedu", *Journal of Roman Archaeology*, Vol. 6, 1993, pp. 93-108.

Berchet, G., *Del Comercio dei Veneti nell'Asia -Memoria letta all' Ateneo Veneto II,* Venezia, 1864.

Berjeau, J.Ph. (transl.), *Calcoen: A Dutch Narrative of the Second Voyage of Vasco da Gama to Calicut printed at Atwerp circa 1504,* London, 1874.

Biker, Julio Firmino Judice, ed., *Collecção de Tratados e Concertos de Pazes que o Estado da India, Portugueza fez com os Reis e Senhores com que teve Relações nas partes da Asia e Africa Oriental desde o principio da conquista até ao fim do seculo XVIII, tomo.* I, Lisboa, 1881.

Borsa, Giorgio, ed., *Trade and Politics in the Indian Ocean: Historical and Contemporary Perspectives,* New Delhi, 1990.

Bouchon, Geneviève, *Navires et cargaisons retour de l'Inde en 1518,* Paris, 1977.

————, *Regent of the Sea: Cannanore's Response to Portuguese Expansion, 1507-1528,* Delhi, 1988.

Boxer, C.R., *The Portuguese Seaborne Empire, 1415-1825,* London, 1969.

————, "Uma raridade bibliografica sobre Fernão Cron" *Bibliofilia : De Bibligrafia Luso-Brasileira*, Vol XII, Numero 1, Janeiro-Março, 1971, pp. 323-344.

Bramanti, Vanni, *Lettere da Vari Paesi 1570- 1588*, Milano, 1970.

Brasio, Antonio, *Uma Carta inedita de Velentim Fernandes,* Coimbra, 1959.

Braudel, Fernand, *The Mediterranean and the Mediterranean World in the Age of Philip II*, Vol. 2, London, 1972.

————, *The Wheels of Commerce: Civilization & Capitalism, 15th-18th Centuries,* London, 1979.

Bulhão Pato, Raymundo Antonio de, ed., *Cartas de Affonso de Albuquerque*, tomos 1-7, Lisboa, 1884-1915.

Ca'Masser, Leonardo da, "Relazioni di Leonardo da Ca'Masser alla Serenissima Republica di Venezia sopra il Commercio dei Portoghesi nell'India dopo la scoperta del Capo Buona Speranza, 1497-1506", *Archivio Storico Italiano*, Appendice tomo iii, Firenze, 1845, pp. 8-51.

Carevallense, Archangelo (transl.), *Itinerariu Portugallensiu e Lusitania in India et inde in Occidentem et demum ad Aquilonem,* Milano, 1508.

Cassel, Johann Philipp, *Privilegia und Handelungfreiheiten, welche die Könige von Portugal ehedem den deutschen Kaufleuten zu Lissabon ertheilet haben,* Bremen, 1771.

Castanheda, Fernão Lopes de, *História do Descobrimento & Conquista da India pelos Portugueses*, livros 1-9, Coimbra, 1924-1933.

Chakrabarti, Dilip K., *The External Trade of the Indus Civilization,* Delhi, 1990.

Chaudhuri, K.N., *Asia before Europe: Economy and Civilisation of the Indian Ocean from the Rise of Islam to 1750,* Cambridge, 1990.

———, *Trade and Civilisation in the Indian Ocean: An Economic History from the Rise of Islam to 1750*, Delhi, 1985.

Chavda, V.K., ed., *Studies in Trade and Urbanisation in Western India*, Baroda, 1985.

Correa, Gaspar, *Lendas da India*, tomos 1-4, Lisboa, 1864-1967.

Cortesão, Armando e Luis de Albuquerque, eds., *Obras Completas de D. João de Castro,* Vol. II, Coimbra, 1976.

Cortesão, Jaime, *A Expedição de Pedro Alvares Cabral e o Descobrimento do Brasil,* Lisboa, 1967.

Costa Lobo, F.M. da, *A Acção diplomatica dos Portugueses nos seculos XV e XVI destinada a relaização de descobertas e conquistas*, Lisboa, 1937.

Costa, A. Fontoura da, ed., *Roteiro da Primeira Viagem de Vasco da Gama, 1497-1499*, Lisboa, 1969.

Couto, Diogo de, *Da Asia,* Decadas IV-XII, Lisboa, 1778.

———, *Cronical do Descobrimento e Conquista da India pelos Portugueses,* codice anonymo, Museu Britanico, Egerton 20901, Coimbra, 1974.

Deininger, Heinz Friedrich, *Das Reiche Augsburg:* Ausgewählte Aufsätze Jakob Strieders zur Augsburger und süddeutschen Wirtschaftsgeschichte des 15. und 16. Jahrhunderts, München, 1938.

Denuce, J., *Inventaire des Affaitadi Banquiers Italiens à Anvers de l'Année 1568*, Antwerp, 1934.

———, "Privileges commerciaux accordes par les Rois de Portugal aux Flamands et aux Allemands, XVe, et XVIe Siècles", *Arquivo Historico Portuguez,* Vol.VII, Lisboa, 1909.

Deslandes, Venacio, *Documentos para a historia da typographia portugesa nos seculos xvi e xvii part II*, Lisboa, Imprensa Nacional, 1888.

Disney, Anthony, "The Portuguese Overland Courier Service between Europe and India in the Sixteenth and Seventeenth Centuries", pp. 51-63.

Dobel, Friedrich, "Ueber einen Pfefferhandel der Fugger und Welser 1586-91" in *Zeitschrift des Historischen Vereins für Schwaben und Neuburg*, Dreizehnter Jahrgang, Augsburg, 1886, pp. 125-138.

Eden, Richard, *The First Three English Books on America 1511-1555*, Birmingham, 1885.

Ehrenberg, Richard, *Das Zeitalter der Fugger: Geldkapital und Creditverkehr im 16 Jahrhundert,* Vols. 2, Jena, 1922.

————, *Capital and Finance in the Age of the Renaissance: A Study of the Fuggers and their Connections*, translated by H.M. Lucas, New York, 1963.

Ehrhardt, Marion, *A Alemanha e os Descobrimentos Portugueses,* Lisboa, 1989.

————"Ein Gutachten Conrad Peutingers in Sachen der Handelsgesellschaften, Ende 1522", *Zeitschrift des Historischen Vereins für Schwaben und Neuburg*, Zweiter Jahrgang, Zweites Heft, Augsburg, 1875, pp. 189-215.

Emmer, Piet C. *et. al.*, *Wirtschaft und Handel der Kolonialreiche*, München, 1988.

Empoli, Giovanni da, "Viagem as Indian Orientães por João de Empoli, Feitor de huma Nao Portugeza, armada por conta dos Marchiones de Lisboa traduzida do Italiano", *Collecção de noticias para a Historia e Geografia das nações Ultramarinas que vivem nos dominios portugueses ou lhes são vizinhas,* tomo 2, no.7, Lisboa, 1813, pp. 219-229.

Falcão, Luiz de Figueiredo, *Livro em que se contem toda a Fazenda e real patrimonio dos Reinos de Portugal, India e ilhas adjacentes e outras particularidades*, Lisboa, 1859.

Ferishta, *History of the Rise of the Mohammedan Power in India,* Vol. 1, Delhi, 1981.

Fernandes, Valentim, *O Livro de Marco Polo; O Livro de Nicolão Veneto; Carta de Jeronimo de Santo Estevam*, Lisboa, 1502, edited with facsimile by Francisco Maria Esteves Pereira, Lisboa, Biblioteca Nacional, 1922.

Ferreira, J.A. Pinto, "Privilegios concedidos pelos reis de Portugal aos alemães nos seculos xv e xvi" *Boletim Cultural da Camara Municipal do Porto*, Vol. XXXII, fascs.1-2, Porto, 1969, pp. 339-396.

Ficalho, Conde de, *Viagens de Pedro da Covilham*, Lisboa, 1898.

Filliozat, Vasundhara, *The Vijayanagar Empire as seen by Domingos Pães and Fernão Nuniz*, New Delhi, 1977.

Fischel, Walter J., "The Spice Trade in Mamluk Egypt—A Contribution to the Economic History of Medieval Islam", *Journal of the Economic and Social History of the Orient,* Vol. 1, Leiden, 1958, pp. 157-74.

———, "Über die Gruppe der Karimi-Kauflaute: ein Beitrag zur Geschichte des Orienthandeles Ägyptens unter den Mamelukken", *Analexta Orientalia*, No.14, Studia Arabica, Roma, 1937, pp. 67-82.

Fitzler, M.A. Hedwig, "Der Anteil der Deutschen an der Kolonial-politik Philipps II. von Spanien in Asien" *Vierteljahreschr.f. Sozial-und Wirtschaftsgeschichte*, 28, 1935, pp. 1-39.

———, "Die Entstehung der sogenannten Fuggerzeitungen in der Wiener Nationalbibliothek", Josef Kallbrunner, ed., *Veröffentlichungen des Wiener Hofkammerarchivs*, Wien, 1937.

Freitas, Frei Serafim de, *Do Justo Império Asi tico dos Portugueses*, Vol. 2, Lisboa, 1983.

Fulin, Rinaldo, ed., *Archivio Veneto*, Vol. XXI, Part I, Venezia, 1881.

Ghillany, F.W., *Geschichte des Seefahrers Ritter Martin Behaim nach den ältesten vorhandenen Urkunden beareitet,* Nürnberg, 1853.

———, "Der Fuggerzug geht über Land: vom Bauernweber, in Augsburg 1367-1408", *Hei grüss di Gott, Ländle*", Augsburg, 1961.

Godinho, Vitorino Magalhães *Os Descobrimentos e a Economia Mundial,* 2 Vols., Lisboa, 1963.

Gois, Damião de, *Cronica do Felicissimo Rei D. Manuel I*, Part II, Coimbra, 1953.

Goitein, S.D., "New Light on the Beginnings of the Karim Merchants", *Journal of the Economic and Social History of the Orient,* Vol. 1, Leiden, 1958, pp. 175-84.

Gomçallves, Nycolão, *Livro que trata das cousas da India e do Japão,* edited by Andelino de Almeida Calado, Coimbra, 1957.

Gopal, Surendra, *Commerce and Crafts in Gujarat: 16th and 17th Centuries,* Delhi, 1975.

Goris, A., *Les Colonies Marchandes Meridionales (Portugais, Espagnols, Italiens) à Anvers de 1488 à 1567*, Louvain, 1925.

Gracias, Amancio, "Alemais na India nos seculos XV a XVIII", *Boletim do Instituto Vasco da Gama,* no. 50, Goa, 1941, pp. 1-95.

Greenlee, William Brooks, *The Voyage of Pedro Alvares Cabral to Brazil and India,* London, 1938.

Greiff, B., ed., *Tagebuch des Lucas Rem aus den Jahren 1494- 1541:* Ein Beitrag zur Handelsgeschichte der Stadt Augsburg, Augsburg, 1861.

Grotius, Hugo, *The Freedom of the Seas or the Right which belongs to the Dutch to take part in the East Indian Trade,* transl. by Ralph Van Deman Magoffin, London, 1916.

Häbler, Konrad, *Die Überseeischen Unternehmungen der Welser und ihrer Gesellschafter,* Leipzig, 1903.

————, "Die Fugger und der spanische Gewürzhandel", *Zeitschrift des Historischen Vereins für Schwaben und Neuburg*, Zweiter Jahrgang, Erstes Heft, Augsburg, 1875, pp. 25-44.

————, *Die Geschichte der Fugger'schen Handlung in Spanien*, Weimar, 1897.

————, "Konrad Rott und die thüringische Gesellschaft", *Neues Archiv für schwäbische Geschichte und Alterthumskunde,* Vol. XV, 1895, pp. 179-81.

Herre, Franz, *The Age of the Fuggers,* Augsburg, 1985.

————, *Hei Grüss di Gott, Ländle: Der Fuggerzug geht über Land vom Bauernweber zum Handelsherren*, Kempten (Allgäu), 1961.

Hildebrandt, Reinhard, *Die "Georg Fugger'schen Erben":* Kaufmännische Tätigkeit und Sozialer Status 1555-1600, Berlin, 1966.

Hinsch, J.D., "Bertholomäus-Brüderschaft der Deutschen in Lissabon" in *Hansische Geschichtsblätter*, 1888, Leipzig, 1890, pp. 3-27.

Hornell, James, "The Sailing Craft of Western India", *Mariners' Mirror,* Vol. 32, Cambridge, 1946, pp. 195-216.

Hümmerich, Franz, *Die Erste Deutsche Handelsfahrt nach Indien 1505/05,* München, 1922.

————, *Vasco da Gama und die Entdeckung des Seewegs nach Ostindien,* München, 1898.

————, *Quellen und Untersuchungen zur Fahrt der ersten Deutschen nach dem portugiesischen Indien 1505/06*, München, 1918.

Imhof, Christoph von, "Nürnberger Indienpioniere, Reiseberichte von der ersten oberdeutschen Handelsfahrt nach Indien (1505/06)" in *Reiseberichte der Frühen Neuzeit: Wirtshafts-und kulturhistorische Quellen, Pirkheimer Jahrbuch,* 1986, Bd.2, München, 1987.

Iyas, Ibn, *Journal d'un Bourgeois du Cairo*, transl. by Gaston Wiet, Paris, 1955.

Jansen, Max, *Jakob Fugger. Der Reiche* - Studien und Quellen I, Leipzig, 1910.

————, *Anfänge der Fugger* (Bis 1494), Leipzig, 1907.

Jordão, Levy Maria, *Bullarium Patronatus Portugalliac Regum in Ecclesiis Africae, Asiae, atque Oceaniae*, tomus 1, Olisipone, 1868.

Kasinathan, Natana, ed., *Seminar on Marine Archaeology,* Madras, 1992.

Kellenbenz, Hermann, *Die Fugger in Spanien und Portugal bis 1560*, 3 vols, München, 1990.

————, "Briefe über Pfeffer und Kupfer" in Eric Hassinger, J. Heinz

Müller und Hugo Ott, *Geschichte Wirtschaft Gesellschaft,* Berlin, Duncker & Humboldt, 1974, pp. 205-227.

———, "Die Beziehungen Nürnbergs zur Iberischen Halbinsel, besonders im 15.und in der ersten Hälfte des 16.Jahrhunderts", *Beiträge zur Wirtschaftsgeschichte Nürnbergs*, Band 1, Nürnberg, 1967, pp. 456-557.

———, "Neues zum oberdeutschen Ostindienhandel, insbesondere der Herwarts in der ersten Hälfte des 16. Jahrhunderts", *Forschungen zur schwäbischen Geschichte,* Sigmaringen, 1991, pp. 80-96.

———, "Der Pfeffermarkt um 1600 und die Hansestädte", *Hansische Geschichtsblätter,* Köln, 1956, pp. 28-49.

———, "Le Commerce du Poivre des Fugger et le Marché International du Poivre", *Annales: Économies-Sociétés- Civilisations,* 11e Année, Janvier-Mars, 1956, No 1.

———, "The Portuguese Discoveries and the Italian and German Initiatives in the Indian Trade in the first Two Decades of the 16th Century", *Congresso Internacional: Bartolomeu Dias e a sua Época: Actas,* Vol. III, Porto, 1989, pp. 609-623.

———, *Dynamik in einer Quasi-Statischen Welt:* Kleine Schriften II, Stuttgart, 1991.

———, "Jakob Fugger der Reiche", Wolfgang Zorn, ed., *Lebensbilder aus dem Bayerischen Schwaben*, Band 10, Augsburg, 1973, pp. 35-76.

———, "Anton Fugger", in Adolf Layer, ed., *Lebensbilder aus dem Bayerischen Schwaben*, Band 11, Augsburg, 1976, pp. 46-124.

———, "Hans Jakob Fugger", Adolf Layer (ed.), *Lebensbilder aus dem Bayerischen Schwaben,* Band 12, Augsburg, 1980, pp. 48-104.

———, *Fremde Kaufleute auf der Iberischen Halbinsel*, Köln, 1970 (Sonderdruck).

———, "Ferdinand Cron", Wolfgang Zorn, ed., *Lebensbilder aus dem Bayerischen Schwaben*, Band 9, München, 1966, pp. 194-210.

———, "Océan Indien et Méditerranée, Travaux du Sixième Colloque International d'Histoire Maritime et du Deuxième Congrès de l'Association Historique Internationale de l'Océan Indien (Session de Lourenço Marques: 13-18 août, 1962)" in *Hansische Geschichtsblätter* (85. Jahrgang), Köln, 1967, pp. 166-167.

———, *Os Mercadores Alemães de Lisboa por volta de 1530*, Coimbra, 1961.

———, "Schwäbische Kaufherren im Tiroler Bergbau (1400-1650)", *Beiträge: Schwaben Tirol*, Rosenheimer, 1989, pp. 208-218.

————, *Schwerpunkte der Kupferproduktion und des Kupferhandels in Europa 1500-1650,* Köln, Bohlau Verlag, 1977.

————, "Le front hispano-portugais contre l'Inde et le rôle d'une agence de renseignements au service de marchands allemands et flamands", *Studia*, No.11, Lisboa, 1963, pp. 263-290.

————, "From Melchior Manlich to Ferdinand Cron: German Levantine and Oriental Trade Relations: Second half of the Sixteenth and Beginning of the Seventeenth century", unpublished paper presented at the seminar at Pondicherry in 1990, pp. 6-7.

Kempter, Kaspar, *Die wirtschaftliche Berichterstattung in den sogenannten Fuggerzeitungen*, München, 1936.

Klarwill, Victor von, ed., *Fugger-Zeitungen: Ungedruckte Briefe an das Haus Fugger aus den Jahren 1568-1605,* Leipzig, 1923.

————, *The Fugger News-letters being a Selection of Unpublished Letters from the Correspondents of the House of Fugger during the years 1568-1605* (translated by H. Gordon Selfridge), London, 1924.

————, *The Fugger News-letters (Second series) being a Selection of Unpublished Letters from the Correspondents of the House of Fugger during the years 1568-1605* (translated by L.S.R. Byrne), London, 1926.

Knabe, Wolfgang, "Kartographische Anmerkungen zur Zielregion des oberdeutschen Indienhandels" in Pankraz Fried, *Forschungen zur schäbischen Geschichte*, Sigmaringen, Jan Thorbecke Verlag, 1991, pp. 98-101.

————, *Auf den Spuren der ersten deutschen Kaufleute in Indien,* Anhausen, 1993.

Kömmerling-Fitzler, Hedwig, "Der Nürnberger Kaufmann Georg Pock (+ 1528/9) in Portugiesisch-Indien und im Edelsteinland Vijayanagara, *Mitteilungen des Vereins für Geschichte der Stadt Nürnberg* (55. Band, 1967-68), Nürnberg, 1968, pp. 137-138.

Krása, Miloslav *et al.*, *European Expansion, 1494-1519: The Voyages of Discovery in the Bratislava Manuscript Lyc.515/8 (Codex Bratislavensis),* Prague, 1986.

Krendly, Peter, "Ein neuer Brief zur ersten Indienfahrt Vasco da Gamas", *Mitteilungen des Österreichischen Staatsarchivs*, 33, (1980), pp. 1-21

Kroell, Anne., "Le voyage de Lazarus Nürnberger en Inde 1517-1518", *Bulletin des Etudes Portugaises,* Paris, 1980, pp. 59-87.

Kuhn, Ernst, *Quellen und Untersuchungen zur Fahrt der ersten Deutschen nach dem portugiesischen Indien 1505/06 von Franz Hümmerich*, München, 1918.

Kulischer, Josef, *Allgemeine Wirtschaftsgeschichte des Mittelalters und der Neuzeit*, Münich, 2 Vols., 1928-29, reprint 1958.

Kunstmann, Friedrich, *Die Merfart unn erfarung nüwer Schiffung und Wege zû viln onerkanten Inseln und Künigreichen..., wie ich Balthasar Sprenger sollichs: in kurzverschynen zeiten gesehen unn erfaren habe, gedruckt anno MDIX - Die Fahrt der ersten Deutschen nach dem portgiesischen Indien*, München, 1861.

Lane, Frederick C., *Venice and History*, Baltimore, 1966, p. 33.

Leur, J.C. Van, *Indonesian Trade and Society—Essays in Asian Social and Economic History*, The Hague, 1955.

Lima Felner, Rodrigo José de, ed., *Subsidios para a Historia da India Portugueza*, Lisboa, 1868.

Linschoten, John Huyghen van, *The Voyage of John Huyghen van Linschoten to the East Indies*, Vol. 2, Delhi, 1988 (reprint).

Lopes, Thomé, "Navegação as Indias Orientães escrita em Portugues por Thomé Lopes", *Collecção de Noticias para a Historia e Geografia das Nações Ultramarinas que vivem nos dominios portugueses ou lhes são vizinhas*, tomo II, Nos.1 & 2, Lisboa, 1812.

Lopes, David, ed., *Historio dos Portugueses no Malabar por Zinadím*, Lisboa, 1898.

Lutz, Elmar, *Die rechtliche Struktur süddeutscher Handelsgesellschaften in der Zeit der Fugger:* Urkunden, Tübingen, 1976.

Lutz, Heinrich, *Conrad Peutinger*: Beiträge zu einer Politischen Biographie, Augsburg, 1958.

Luz, Francisco Mendes da, "Regimento da caza da India: Manuscrito do seculo XVII existente no Arquivo Geral de Simancas" in *Anais de Junta de Investigações do Ultramar*, Vol. XI, tom. II, Lisboa, 1951.

Lyber, A.H. "The Ottoman Turks and the Routes of the Oriental Trade", *The English Historical Review*, No. CXX, October 1915, pp. 577-588.

Major, R.H., ed., *India in the Fifteenth Century*, London, 1857.

Marques, Antonio Henrique de Oliveira, "Relações entre Portugal e a Alemanha no seculo XVI", *Revista da Faculdade de Letras de Lisboa*, III, serie no. 4, 1960, pp. 36-55.

Mathew, K.S., "Khwaja Shams-ud-din Giloni: A Sixteenth Century Entrepreneur in Portuguese India", Roderich Ptak and Dietmar Rothermund, eds., *Emporia, Commodities and Entrepreneurs in Asian Maritime Trade, c.1400-1750*, Stuttgart, 1991, pp. 363-371.

————, "German Merchant-Financiers in Goa during the 16th and 17th Centuries" in P. P. Shirodkar, ed., *Goa's External Relations,* Goa, 1992, pp. 32-56.

————, *Portuguese and the Sultanate of Gujarat,* Delhi , 1976.

————, "Trade Economy of Coastal Gujarat in the Sixteenth Century", *Journal of the Oriental Institute*, Vol. XXXIV, nos.3-4, Baroda, 1985, pp. 201-215.

————, "Khwaja Safar, the Merchant Governor of Surat and the Portuguese Trade in the Early Sixteenth Century", *Proceedings of the Indian History Congress,* Kurukshetra Session, 1982.

————, "India Contract of the Indo-Portuguese Trade in the Last Quarter of the Sixteenth Century" in V.K. Chavda, ed., *Studies in Trade and Urbanisation in Western India*, Baroda, 1985, pp. 165-171.

Montalbodo, Francanzano, *Paesi nuovamente retrovati & nivo Mondo da Aberico Vesputio Florentino Intitulato*, Venezia, 1597 Facsimile, London, 1916.

Müller, Karl Otto, *Quellen zur Handelsgeschichte der Paumgartner von Augsburg* (1480-1570), Wiesbaden, 1955.

Müller, Karl Otto, *Welthandelsbräuche : Deutsche Handelsakten des Mittelalters und der Neuzeit IX*, Stuttgart, 1934.

Müller, Peter, "Alemais na terra portuguesa" in *Publicação comemorativa do decimo aniversario do Instituto Alemão*, suplemento ao Vol. V do *Boletim do Instituto Alemão*, Coimbra, 26-x-1935, pp. 29-37.

————, "Neue Quellen zur zweiten Indienfahrt Vasco da Gamas" in *Quellen und Forschungen zur Geschichte der Geographie und Völkerkunde*, Vol. 3, Leipzig, 1939, pp. 8-51.

Noonan, Laurence A., *John of Empoli and his Relations with Afonso de Albuquerque,* Lisboa, 1989.

Ogger, Günter, *Kauf Dir einen Kaiser: Die Geschichte der Fugger,* München, Droemersche Verlagsanstalt, 1978.

Orta, Garcia da, *Coloquios dos Simples e Drogas da India*, Vol. I, Lisboa, 1891.

Otte, Enrique, "Jacob und Hans Cromberger und Lazarus Nürnberger, die Begründer des Deutschen Amerikahandels", *Mitteilungen des Vereins für Geschichte der Stadt Nürnberg*, Zweiundfünfzigster Band, Nürnberg, 1963-64.

Pães, Domingos and Nuniz Fernão, *The Vijayanagar Empire*, edited by Vasundhra Filliozat, New Delhi, 1977.

Panhorst, Karl. H., *Deutschland und Amerika*: Ein Rückblick auf das Zeitalter der Entdeckungen und die ersten deutschamerikanischen

Verbindungen unter besonderer Beachtung der Unternehmungen der Fugger und Welser, München, 1928.

Pearson, M.N., *Before Colonialism: Theories on Asian-European Relations, 1500-1750*, Delhi, 1988.

————, *Merchants and Rulers in Gujarat: The Response to the Portuguese in the Sixteenth Century*, New Delhi, 1976.

————, *Coastal Western India: Studies from the Portuguese Records*, New Delhi, 1981.

Peragallo, Prospero, ed., "Cartas de Alberto e de Pietro Pascaligo", *Centenario do Descobrimento de America*, Lisboa, 1892, pp. 99-104.

————, *Viaggio di Matteo Bergamo in India sulla flota di Vasco da Gama* (1502-1503), Roma, 1902.

Peres, Damião, *Regemento das Cazas das Indias e Mina*, Coimbra, 1947.

————, ed., *Dià rio da Viagem de Vasco da Gama: Fac Simile do Codice Original*, 2 Vols., Porto, 1945.

Perlin, Frank, "Proto-Industrialisation and Pre-colonial South Asia", *Past and Present*, No. 98, 1983.

Pinto, Fernão Mendes, *Peregrinação*, Vol. I, Lisboa, 1957.

Pires, Tomé, *The Suma Oriental of Tomé Pires*, Vols. I-II, Delhi, 1990 (reprint).

Pissurlencar, Panduronga S.S., *Regimentos das Fortalezas da India*, Bastora, 1951.

Pölnitz, Götz Freiherr von, *Fugger und Hanse: Ein Hundertjahriges Ringen um Ostsee und Nordsee*, Tübingen, 1953.

————, *Die Fugger in Nürnberg*, Nürnberg, 1967 (Sonderdruck aus *Beiträge zur Wirtschaftsgeschichte Nürnbergs*, Band 1).

————, *Jakob Fugger: Kaiser, Kirche und Kapital in der oberdeutschen Renaissance*, Vol. 1, Tübingen, 1949.

————, *Jakob Fugger: Quellen und Erläuterungen*, Vol. II, Tübingen, 1951.

Priuli, Girolamo, *I Diarii di Girolamo Priuli 1494-1512*, Vol. I, Citta di Castello, 1921, Vols. II to IV, Bologna, 1933-46.

Ptak, Roderich and Dietmar Rothermund, *Emporia, Commodities and Entrepreneurs in Asian Maritime Trade c. 1400-1750*, Stuttgart, 1991.

Ramusio, Giovanni Battista, *Delle Navigationi et Viaggi*, Vol. I, second edition, Venezia, 1554.

Ratkos, Peter *et al.*, eds. *The Voyages of Discovery in the Bratislava Manuscript Lyc.515/8*, Prague, 1986.

Rau, Virginia, "Um grande Mercador-Banqueiro Italiano em Portugal:

Lucas Giraldi", separata de *Estudos Italianos em Portugal,* No. 24, Lisboa, 1965.

Ravenstein, E.G., *A Journal of the First Voyage of Vasco da Gama (1497-1499)*, London, 1848.

Ray, Haraprasad, "An Inquiry into the Presence of the Chinese in South and Southeast Asia after the Voyages of Zheng He in Early Fifteenth Century" in K.S. Mathew, *Mariners, Merchants and Oceans,* New Delhi, 1995.

Reger, Karl Heinz, *Pfeffer aus Fernost:* Das abenteuerliche Leben eines Augsburger Kaufmanns, München, 1986.

Rivara, J.H. da Cunha, ed., *Archivo Portuguez Oriental*, 6 fasciculos em 10 partes, New Delhi, 1992.

Rockhill, W.W., "Notes on the Relations and Trade of China with the Eastern Archipelago and the Coast of the Indian Ocean during the Fourteenth Century", *T'oung Pao*, Vol. XV, Leiden, 1914.

Rohr, Christine von, "Neue Quellen zur zweiten Indienfahrt Vasco da Gamas", *Quellen und Forschungen zur Geschichte der Geographie und Völkerkunde*, Band 3, Leipzig, 1939, pp. 8- 51.

————, "Neue Quellen zu den Entdeckungsfahrten der Portugiesen im Indischen Ozean" in Mzik, H., ed., *Beiträge zur historischen Geographie, Kulturgeographie, Ethnographie und Kartographie, vornehmlich des Orients,* Leipzig und Wien, 1929, pp. 77-83.

Ross, Denison, "The Portuguese in India and Arabia between 1507 and 1517", *The Journal of the Royal Asiatic Society of Great Britain and Ireland*, London, 1921.

Rothermund, Dietmar, *Asian Trade and European Expansion in the Age of Mercantilism*, New Delhi, 1981.

Salentiny, Ferdinand, *Die Gewürzroute*: Die Entdeckung des Seewegs nach Asien, Köln, 1991.

Samhaber, Ernst, *Merchants Make History*, London, 1963.

Sanuto, Marino, *I Diarii de Marino Sanuto: 1496-1533*, edited by G. Berchet, R. Fulin *et al.* Venezia, 1897-1903, 58 vols.

Sassetti, Filippo, *Lettere da vari paesi, 1570-1588: a cura di V. Bramanti,* Vol.10, Milano, 1970.

Schaper, Christa, "Die Hirschvogel von Nürnberg und ihr Handelshaus", *Nürnberger Forschungen* 18, Nürnberg, 1973.

Schmeller, Johann Andreas, *Ueber Valent Fernandez Alemã und seine Sammlung von Nachrichten über die Entdeckungen und Besitzungen der Portugiesen in Afrika und Asien bis zum Jahre 1508 enthalten in einer portugiesischen Handschrift der königl. Hof- und Staats-Bibliothek zu München*, München, 1847.

Schoff, Wilfred H., ed., *The Periplus of the Erythraean Sea: Travel and Trade in the Indian Ocean by a Merchant of the First Century,* Delhi, Second edition, 1974.

Schulze, Franz, *Balthasar Sprengers Indienfahrt 1505/06: Wissenschaftliche Würdigung der Reiseberichte Sprengers zur Einführung in den Neudruck Seiner "Merfart" vom Jahre* 1509, Strassburg, 1902.

————, *Die wissenschaftliche Bedeutung der Reiseberichte Balthasar Springers,* Strassburg, 1902.

Serjeant, R.B., *The Portuguese off the South Arabian Coast: Hadrami Chronicles,* Oxford, 1963.

Shayk Zaynud din, *Tuhfat-al- Mujahidin,* translated by David Lopes as *Historia dos Portugueses no Malabar*, Lisboa, 1898.

Sleen, W.G.N. Van der, "Ancient Glass Beads with Special Reference to the Beads of East and Central Africa and the Indian Ocean", *Journal of the Royal Anthropological Institute of Great Britain and Ireland,* Vol. 88, Part II, July-December 1958, pp. 203-217.

Smith, Bishop R., *Lazarus Nürnberger, being a Photograph of the Manuscript Account of his Voyage to India in 1517 and 1518 preserved in the Central Library of the Slovakian Academy of Sciences in Bratislava, Czechoslovakia*, Lisboa, 1974.

Sousa, Frei Luis de, *Anais de D. João III,* Lisboa, 1951-54, 2 vols.

Souveral, Visconde, *Apontamentos sobre as antigas relações politicas e commerciães de Portugal com a Republica de Venezia,* Lisboa, 1893.

Steensgaard, Niels, *The Asian Trade Revolution of the Seventeenth Century: The East India Companies and the Decline of the Caravan Trade*, Chicago, 1974.

Stetten, *Jahrbuch MDCCCCLV*, II Band, München.

Stier, H.C.G., (transl), *Vlämisches Tagebuch über Vasco da Gamas zweite Reise 1502-1503,* Braunschweig, 1880.

Strassen, E.A. e Alfredo Gandara, *Oito seculos de historia lusoalemão*, Berlin, 1944.

Strieder, Jakob, *Jacob Fugger der Reiche*, Leipzig, n.d.

————, "Deutscher Metallwarenexport nach Westafrika im 16. Jahrhundert", pp. 179-185.

————, *Zur Genesis des modernen Kapitalismus:* Forschungen zur Entstehung der großen bürgerlichen Kapitalvermögen am Ausgange des Mittelalters und zu Beginn der Neuzeit, zunächst in Augsburg, München, 1935.

————, *Deutsche Handelsakten Des Mittelalters Und Der Neuzeit:* Quellen aus Antwerpener Notariatsarchiven, Wiesbaden, 1962.

———, *Studien zur Geschichte Kapitalistischer Organisationsformen*: Monopole, Kartelle und Aktiengesellschaften im Mittelalter und zu Beginn der Neuzeit, München, 1914.

———, *Aus Antwerpener Notariatsarchiven: Quellen zur Deutschen Wirtschaftsgeschichte des 16 Jahrhunderts,* Wiesbaden, 1962.

Subrahmanyam, Sanjay, *The Political Economy of Commerce: Southern India, 1500-1650,* Cambridge, 1990.

———, ed., *Merchants, Markets and the State in Early Modern India,* Oxford University Press, Delhi, 1990.

———, *Improvising Empire: Portuguese Trade and Settlement in the Bay of Bengal, 1500-1700*, Oxford University Press, Delhi, 1990.

———, *The Portuguese Empire in Asia 1500-1700: A Political Economic History,* Longman, New York, 1993.

———, "An Augsburger in Asia Portuguesa: Further Light on the Commercial World of Ferdinand Cron, 1587-1624", Roderich Ptak and Dietmar Rothermund, eds., *Emporia, Commodities and Entrepreneurs in Asian Maritime Trade, c.1400-1750,* Stuttgart, 1991, pp. 401-425.

Thapar, Romila, *A History of India*, Vol. 1, Penguin, 1972.

Vallavanthara, Antony, *India in 1500 A.D.: The Narratives of Joseph the Indian,* Mannanam, 1984.

Varthema, di Ludovico, *The Itinerary of Ludovico di Varthema of Bologna from 1502 to 1508,* London, 1928.

Vasconcellos, Joaquim de, *Albrecht Dürer e a sua Influência na Península: Renascença Portuguesa Estudos sobre as Relações Artísticas de Portugal nos séculos XV et XVI*, second edition, Coimbra, 1929.

Velho, Alvaro, *Roteiro da primeira Viagem de Vasco da Gama,* edited by Fontoura da Costa, Lisboa, 1969.

———, "Valentim Fernandes", Documentos para a historia da typographia Portuguesa nos seculos XVI e XVII, Part II, Lisboa, Imprensa Nacional, 1882.

———, *Vice-Almirante A. Teixeira da Mota in Memoriam*, Vol. II, Lisboa, 1989.

Viterbo, Sousa, "Bartholameu Florentym: Antigas Relações Commerciaes e Maritimas de Portugal com a Italia- Um grande Negociante Florentino em Lisboa nos Principios do Seculo XVI", *Economista,* Outubro 24, 1884, No.1951, pp. 1-2.

Wallerstein, Immanuel, *The Modern World System*, New York, 1974.

Wee, Herman van der, *The Growth of the Antwerp Market and the European Economy,* The Hague, 1963, 2 vols.

Weinstein, Donald, *Ambassador from Venice Pietro Pasqualigo in Lisbon 1501,* Minneapolis, 1960.

Werner, Theodor Gustav, "Repräsentanten der Augsburger Fugger und Nürnberger Imhoff als Urheber der wichtigsten Handschriften des Paumgartner-Archivs über Welthandelsbräuche im Spätmittelalter und am Beginn der Neuzeit", in Hermann Aubin, ed., *Vierteljahrschrift für Sozial-und Wirtschaftsgeschichte*, Band 52, Wiesbaden, 1965, pp. 1- 41.

Wheeler, R.E.M. *et al.*, "Arikamedu: An Indo-Roman Trading-station on the East Coast of India", *Ancient India: Bulletin of the Archaeological Survey of India*, No. 2, 1946, pp. 17-124.

Wicki, Josef, "Duas relações sobre a situação da India Portuguesa nos anos 1568 e 1569", *Studia*, No. 8, Lisboa, 1961.

Wiet, Gaston, "Les Marchands D'Epices sous les Sultans Mamlouks", *Cahiers D'Histoire Egyptienne,* Serie VII, Fasc. 1, Cairo, 1955, pp. 81-135.

————, "Ein Gutachten Conrad Peutingers in Sachen der Handelsgesellschaften. Ende 1522", Zeitschrift des Historischen Vereins für Schwaben und Neuburg, Zweiter Jahrgang, Zweites Heft, Augsburg, 1875, pp. 188-215.

INDEX